The Peoples of Ireland

In memory of Hilary and David

The Peoples of Ireland

From prehistory to modern times

Liam de Paor

Lecturer in Modern History, University College, Dublin

Hutchinson

London Melbourne Sydney Auckland Johannesburg

University of Notre Dame Press
Notre Dame, Indiana

Hutchinson & Co. (Publishers) Ltd

An imprint of the Hutchinson Publishing Group

62–65 Chandos Place, London WC2N 4NW

Hutchinson Publishing Group (Australia) Pty Ltd
16–22 Church Street, Hawthorn, Melbourne, Victoria 3122

Hutchinson Group (NZ) Ltd
32–34 View Road, PO Box 40–086, Glenfield, Auckland 10

Hutchinson Group (SA) (Pty) Ltd
PO Box 337, Bergvlei 2012, South Africa

First published 1986

US edition 1986 by
University of Notre Dame Press
Notre Dame, Indiana 46556

© Liam de Paor 1986

Set in Garamond

Printed and bound in Great Britain by
Anchor Brendon Ltd, Tiptree, Essex

British Library Cataloguing in Publication Data

De Paor, Liam
    The peoples of Ireland: from prehistory to modern times
    1. Ireland—History
    I. Title
    941.5   DA910

ISBN (UK) 0 09 156140 X cased
ISBN (UK) 0 09 156141 8 paper
ISBN (US) 0-268-01562-7

Library of Congress Catalog Card Number
85-52221

Contents

Figures, maps and plates

Figures

Maps

Plates

Acknowledgments

I wish to thank the library staffs of University College, Dublin, the Hillman Library of the University of Pittsburgh, and the library system of the University of Toronto (in particular the librarian of the Pontifical Institute of Medieval Studies) for the courtesy and help they showed me when I was working on this book. The librarians of the Royal Irish Academy have been particularly helpful. I should also like to thank Mark Cohen, Sarah Conibear and Joan Lovell, of Hutchinson Education, for their patient co-operation.

The author and publishers would like to thank the copyright holders below for their kind permission to reproduce the following material.

Plate 7, copyright Armagh Museum, Plate 8 reproduced by permission of the British Library, Commissioners of Public Works, Ireland for Plate 3, the *Illustrated London News* for Figures 16 and 17, the National Gallery of Ireland for Plates 9 and 10, the National Library of Ireland for Figure 11, Map 16 reproduced by permission of the Director General of the Ordnance Survey Office, Dublin, *Punch* for Figure 18, Royal Irish Academy for Figure 2, Trinity College, Dublin for Figure 7, The Ulster Museum for Plates 11, 12, 13, 14 and 15, and Thomas Kinsella and the Dolman Press.

Introduction

To survey any sequence of human activities from the beginning of record to the present day is to try to do several things at once. It is, for example, to make a decision and to define the unit of study: the study of *what*?, or of *whom*? It is to select a point of view and a depth of focus; then to delineate those elements in the history that will give an outline of some perceived order in the chaos of events and the randomness of information.

In this case the chosen unit is the island of Ireland. The title indicates the focus. The book looks at the many varied groups of people who have, through many centuries, acted or settled in Ireland. Its chief interest is in the interaction of one group with another, and this shapes the narrative and the exposition. Ireland is a mother country. If there has been much immigration there has also, from time to time, been much emigration, and there are many millions of people around the world who reckon themselves to be of Irish origin. And Ireland has given the world, among other things, two literatures, one – spanning more than 1000 years – in Irish, the other in English, in modern times. Only for brief periods can Irish history be treated as a wholly autonomous unit of study. Mostly, the story is one of interactions between the inhabitants of the island and a wider world.

The Peoples of Ireland is a personal view, but it aims at being sufficiently comprehensive to serve the needs of those, for example, who study European or British history and need a summary account dealing with Ireland. In other words, it intends to help the reader who wishes to know something about Ireland's history, and it attempts therefore at least to touch on most of the major episodes and developments of the country's past. But it is also an interpretative essay, addressed to those who already know the country.

In the past half century or so there has been something of a revolution in Irish historiography, in terms of the informing ideology and prejudice, and the methods of investigation used. And a great deal of information has been made available through specialized studies. We are informed, as never before, about ether-drinking in nineteenth-century County Derry, about the genealogies of minor eighth-century dynasts, about the sub-infeudation of thirteenth-century Meath, about seasonal migration as a prelude to permanent emigration, and about a thousand other topics.

This, in the end, is all grist to a generalizing mill. Because of the work of many scholars pursuing the kind of detail which is at once both arcane and commonplace (like the minutiae that provided Sherlock Holmes with his eurekas), new attempts at synthesis are possible. For some decades academically acceptable 'short histories' of Ireland have been forthcoming. Some are listed in the short select bibliography.

Obviously those who undertake such summaries must depend heavily on the detailed work of others, all the more so since there is so much of it. I certainly do so here.

In this account, I have brought the narrative down more or less to the present, but have given no special emphasis to very recent events. Present discontents in Ireland are important and interesting, obscured though they may be by half a dozen contending propaganda smoke-screens in current reporting. But in a survey of this kind it is appropriate that they should fall into the perspective of the centuries. Perhaps that perspective in itself helps our understanding of what has just been happening.

But nobody lived, loved or died in the tenth century to prove a point about the twentieth. I have tried to bear that in mind.

Part One

Early and Medieval Ireland

1 *Before history*

About 10,000 years ago, western Europe began to assume something like its present physical shape. For thousands of years, enormous masses of ice had been withdrawing slowly northwards, as, century after century, the climate improved. Then the warming of the earth became more rapid. Melt-water began to flood the north-westerly extremities of Europe with shallow seas. The ocean encroached on great expanses of land which now form the submarine 'continental shelf'. Flooding created, in stages, the archipelago which is usually known as the 'British Isles'. Ireland became an island at about this time, separated from the British peninsula (as it still was) by the North Channel. The width of this channel fluctuated in the complicated adjustments between a steadily augmented (and therefore rising) sea, and the elastic rebound of land released from the downward pressure of a mass of billions of tons of ice. Some thousands of years later the larger island, Great Britain, was created when the incoming waters flowed across the most westerly extension of the North European Plain to form the Straits of Dover.

These changes affected living populations. Tundra gave way to forest – first cold birch and pine forest, then growths of warmer temperate species like oak, ash and hazel. Animal and plant species migrated northwards, continuing to colonize Britain after that land had already been cut off by sea from Ireland. As a result, Great Britain has more indigenous species than has Ireland – about half as many again. Western Ireland, however, has a tiny scattering of species of flora, and even fauna, which are absent from Britain – refugees from a land which once extended where the Atlantic now rolls. Bog formation began, greatly to influence and modify the environment in areas exposed to Atlantic moisture and to the mild temperatures fostered by warm oceanic currents.

The North European Plain continues into south-eastern England, interrupted only superficially by the Dover Straits. On a line very roughly from the Bristol Channel to Teesmouth, the plain meets ancient, and different, formations. This line, marking the transition from the 'lowland zone' to the 'highland zone' of Britain, has always been a cultural divide

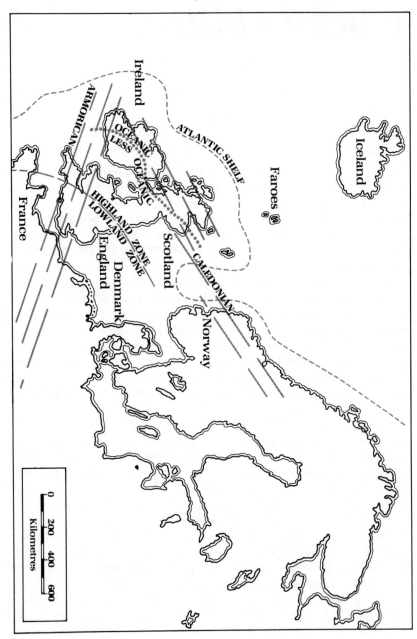

Map 1   Ireland's spatial relations

of some significance. In 1932 Sir Cyril Fox, following Mackinder, pointed out that the lowland zone was open to incoming cultures, which tended to displace their predecessors. Cultures were absorbed only slowly and with difficulty into the highland zone; but there elements of them might survive long after they had been extirpated in the south-east. [1]*

The ancient rock-formations of the highland zone include Ireland in their scope, but Ireland is further separated by the formidable divide of the 'inland sea of Britain', the Irish Sea. There are east–west folds which run from central Germany to terminate in the long fingers of the Kerry peninsulas in south-west Ireland. There are very ancient (Caledonian) formations which run north-east to south-west, from Scotland through Donegal, with parallel ranges in Galway, Wicklow and the south midlands. These give Ireland its distinctive form, for within the island the highlands lie mainly round the perimeter, and between them the centre of the island is relatively low-lying. Much of the drainage is therefore initially towards the interior, which is full of winding streams, spreading lakes and bogs. A most important feature is the deposit of sediments – drifts and moraines – left by the retreating ice over a great part of the country. Through immense periods of geological time, long before the ice ages, Ireland has had its Atlantic climates, with relatively rapid erosion. Its landscapes are fragmented and variegated: a country difficult to grasp.

If Ireland is part of the same structural system as highland Britain, it is also subject to some of the important qualifications by which Fox modified his basic formula of highland and lowland zones. It is, largely, a country of the Atlantic. The Viking route, from the fjords of Bergen and Stavanger to Shetland, the Hebrides, the islands of Donegal, the headlands of Kerry, the capes of Brittany, the Biscay coast, the mouths of Minho, Tagus and Guadalquivir and the slopes of the Atlas, followed a corridor along which those perceptive seafarers would have observed many similarities of landform, local climate and way of life. The corridor has its importance in what might be called a secondary orientation of Ireland, more or less independent of lowland Britain.

At intervals in the recurrent ice ages human hunters occupied lowland Britain, but we have no certain evidence of human activity in Ireland until after the withdrawal of the ice. By then the hunting and gathering population of western Europe had adapted to the forest. It was a major adaptation. On the whole they pursued smaller game than the palaeolithic people, who had hunted mammoth or reindeer, but, more importantly,

*Superior figures refer to the Notes, beginning on p. 316.

they hunted the game in very different conditions. Their prey included red and roe deer and many smaller species. The forest would have supplied an increasing abundance of vegetable food, at least in season, including berries, nuts and many varieties of edible seeds. Long pursuits of big game over open country were no longer so much in question, and many mesolithic populations could have subsisted on the food available within a much shorter range of winter and summer camps.

The mesolithic people who lived in Ireland in the millennia after the retreat of the ice are known mainly from the remains of their more durable implements, those of flint or stone. It is a meagre record, from which little can be reconstructed except some information on their basic economy. They derived at least some of their food supply from what was available on the shores of sea, river and lake – and it seems likely that there was an abundance. There are, in their surviving equipment and traces, some affinities with material from western Scotland, and more generalized affinities with mesolithic material from Atlantic Europe. We may envisage small bands, in the centuries after the withdrawal of the ice, following the shores and waterways into the Irish interior and adjusting, generation after generation, to the local conditions of different parts of Ireland. The valley of the Bann, close to good supplies of flint, seems to have offered them particularly favourable conditions.

Early hunting populations were small, but the post-glacial environment provided sustenance for increasing numbers. It is probable that in some Irish locations conditions were sufficiently favourable – in terms of the variety of available food – to make possible some control of, as distinct from dependence on, the environment. This is the 'pre-adaptation' which is the first stage in the long-drawn-out processes of the transition to food production. The island has an area of just under 33,000 square miles (85,000 square kilometres) and we may guess that its population rose in mesolithic times from a few thousand to some tens of thousands. Although we know very little about the mesolithic people, it is proper to begin with them. It is highly probable that they form the basic genetic stock of 'the Irish people'. It is also probable that the origins of the first immigrant bands were diverse. If we think of prehistory – as was once usual – in terms of a sequence of 'invasions', by mesolithic hunter-gatherers, neolithic farmers, megalith-builders, 'Beaker Folk', and so on, it is difficult to avoid a narrative model in which one population after another replaces its predecessor. The accumulating evidence suggests that cultural change came about differently. Intrusions there certainly were. New groups of people arrived from time to time, with new ideas, languages, equipment. But if we compare the population to a stock-pot, which is topped up as it is drawn off and to which new ingredients are added from day to day, we probably have a more useful model of the process. We have to deal with both change and continuity.

Intrusions of some sort were necessary to introduce full neolithic economies to Ireland, round about the fifth and fourth millennia BC. Domesticated plants and animals, not indigenous in the island, were brought in. The slow but steady spread of food-producing cultures across continental Europe (by the colonization of new land at the contact zone where cultivating communities, with expanding population, intruded on the long established mesolithic communities) has been studied by central European scholars. They have found an interesting regularity in the pace of the progression from the original centres of European farming in the south Balkans, at a fairly steady rate of 0.72 km a year – or, say, about 45 miles a century. However, the coastwise spread of new techniques, seed, stock and equipment was somewhat less regular and more rapid – involving leapfrogging journeys, such as were not possible in the interior, past arid or unsuitable stretches of land.

Elements of an Atlantic, or western, neolithic appear to have reached Ireland, as well as some influences from the main continental development. It seems that the already well established mesolithic people adopted neolithic techniques and customs, producing a mixed economy and a variety of cultural traditions within the island. The forest remained, and was long to remain, important, but food production could maintain a larger total population than hunting–gathering. On the other hand, the clearance of forest for tillage by slash-and-burn and other techniques had unexpected and unintended effects. It is possible that the rapid spread of some types of bog – with peat growing over early tillage areas – may be due in part to the intervention of the people who disturbed the natural vegetation at this time.[2] But the population rose. By the close of the neolithic period it may have numbered 100,000 or 200,000 people.

The cultivators used hoes on plots that were more like garden beds than the fields of later times. It is more than possible that the initiators of tillage were women. Only a shallow light soil was suitable. In the prospecting of grazing lands too, light soils which did not support a heavy forest growth would have been preferred. Half a century's research on the neolithic settlement of Ireland has shed much light, but a great deal remains to be discovered or understood. However, it seems probable that settlement was mainly on drift-free soils, commonly on high ground above the densely wooded valleys. But the neolithic people had implements well suited to working wood, including the polished stone axes which are found on their settlements everywhere in Europe. At least some of the communities built long rectangular houses of wooden post construction, supporting rafters and thatch, broadly in the tradition which is known from many European sites. Variants of this house-type were to continue into modern times in many places, a reminder that in Ireland as elsewhere, up to 100 or 200 years ago, large numbers of people lived working lives not very different from those of their distant neolithic ancestors. Many were to live at a lower level of comfort – and in early Victorian Ireland hundreds of thousands of people were worse off than their forebears of 5000 years ago.

The Irish evidence is so far quite insufficient for confident generalization, but there are no indications of social differentiation on the early neolithic settlements. If the continental evidence may be called upon it is possible that there were villages of six to a dozen houses, each village perhaps inhabited by a few extended families who farmed and herded in common. If this pattern indeed existed, it was to be a very durable one. There is evidence, from the refuse on habitation sites, of the importance of cattle in the economy, an importance which they have not lost through changing times and cultures.

Some of the neolithic communities built great and imposing monuments, which raise numerous questions about social organization and religious belief and motivation. There are two groups, or families, of megalithic chambered tombs, built in neolithic times. In one of the groups a round mound was heaped over the inner structure of very large stones. In the other, the mound was long, often rectangular. The two groups are at least in part contemporary, but the difference in general design is reflected in some differences in the style of the objects and materials found deposited with the dead.

In a very general way it may be said that the round mounds reflect an Atlantic tradition, with analogues in the Iberian and Breton peninsulas and in western and northern Britain. The general shape of the long cairns, which have quite close relations in western and southern Britain, may derive from the style of central and northern European mound-building, but the grave-goods are usually western in character.

In the large form, the long barrows (up to 60 m, in mound-length) have open courts or fore-courts, from which covered galleries, constructed of massive stones, may be entered. The galleries are stone-roofed and covered by mound material, and within them the bones of the dead, sometimes cremated, were deposited. Large numbers of tombs of this type (with variants) survive in a fairly dense band running across Ireland from Killala Bay and Donegal Bay to Carlingford Lough and, beyond the Channel, to the Firth of Clyde. There are many other examples, less densely distributed, in the northern half of Ireland, but only one or two stray

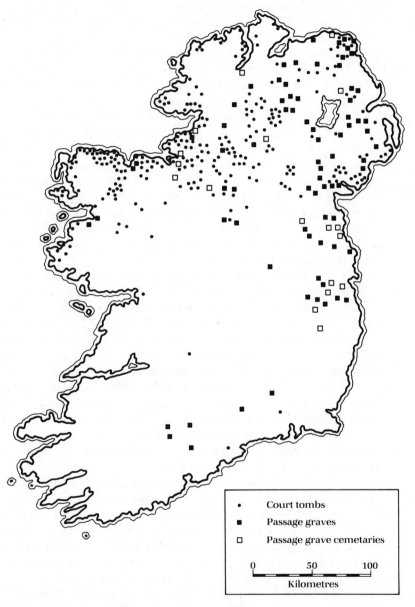

Map 2 Distribution of court cairns and passage graves
After M. Herity and G. Eogan, *Ireland in Prehistory*, London, 1977, with some
additional material.

below the line Dublin–Galway. There are smaller megalithic chambered tombs, apparently quite closely related to this large type but probably continuing to be built after the large form had gone out of fashion. These are usually seen denuded of their mounds, exhibiting therefore what is often the stark grandeur of their megalithic structure. They are known as 'portal graves' or 'portal dolmens'. They extend much farther south than the large types, but only in certain areas, being by no means uniformly distributed over the country as a whole. On present evidence, it seems possible that the people who built these monuments may have settled initially in northerly parts, clustering more densely in coastal areas, in Mayo, Sligo and Donegal, and around the North Channel and its estuaries and inlets. Later generations migrated (or perhaps transmitted their customs) southwards, chiefly along the west and east coastal regions, at a time when the building of very large mounds had given way to the custom of making smaller monuments – but still with a very impressive megalithic structure. The court cairns, although some of them are very large, could have been family burial places.

The round mounds are interestingly different. Their builders often arranged them in hilltop cemeteries, in each of which there are usually mounds of widely varying size clustered closely together. Some are huge, a single mound covering more than half a hectare, and such an immense mound is commonly the centre of a cluster of much smaller satellites. The mound is revetted by a ring of massive stones, set on edge and end to end. It covers a passage, formed of great standing stones, close-set and spanned by lintel-stones, which leads into a burial chamber, also formed of great stones and sometimes roofed by a false dome (a corbelled vault). There are usually smaller chambers opening off the main vault. The chamber falls short of the centre of the mound, so that it is possible to have another passage and chamber entering from the opposite direction along the same diameter, as at Knowth in the Boyne valley.[3]

Passage-grave cemeteries have a somewhat scattered and discontinuous distribution, but again the principal examples lie mainly in the northern half of the island. By far the most remarkable cemetery is that whose focus is along a short stretch of the river Boyne, where the stream bends in a loop, about 20 km upstream from the river mouth. There are numerous outliers of this central Boyne group, some in the surrounding hills, others just across the Irish Sea in north Wales. The Boyne tombs are on comparatively low-lying eminences, just above the valley bottom. Some distance inland, a large cemetery crowns the ragged hills of Lough Crew, which, although not of any great elevation, command extensive and impressive views over the countryside. Beyond the central lowlands to the

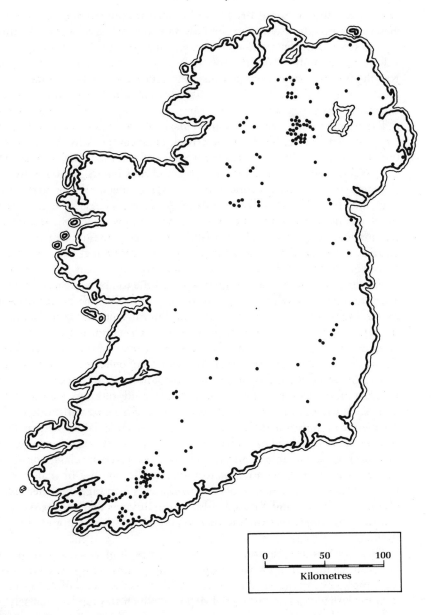

Map 3   Distribution of stone circles
After Aubrey Burl, *The Stone Circles of the British Isles*, New Haven and London,
1976, with modifications.

north-west, in Co. Sligo, Bricklieve Mountain, again commanding wide views over Lough Arrow and the hills and lakes which characterize this region, has another large cemetery strung out along its ridges. Farther west still, on the bluffs fronting the Atlantic, the high bare summit of Knocknarea is conspicuous because of a huge mound (surrounded by much smaller satellites) which is visible for many miles around. Smaller and more scattered tombs are numerous.

The passage-grave cemeteries are remarkable enough in their scale and size and in the basic, but far from trivial, engineering skills that went to their construction. But some of them, especially in the Boyne group, are most elaborately carved with a complex and mysterious iconography of abstract symbols – spirals, concentric circles, meanders, zig-zag, lozenges, branching linear forms and many others. And the evidence for their burial ritual reveals elaboration. They are collective tombs, in which, as well as inhumations, deposits of clean washed cremated bone (of many, many individuals) were deposited, after previous processes had dealt with the bodies of the dead, including probably decay or semi-decay in temporary burials or mortuary houses. Construction of the tombs was carefully and accurately planned, with due regard to orientation. In the great tomb of Newgrange, in the Boyne valley, the sun, just after it rises at midwinter, shines through a specially made aperture over the entrance and along the 20 metre passage to illuminate the stone at the rear of the end chamber. Clearly we are dealing here with an elaboration of belief, ritual, ceremony and oganization which demands some explanation.

The tombs cannot be regarded, like the pyramids of Egypt (which were built somewhat later) as sepulchres of great and powerful individuals. They are communal, and the evidence so far available would suggest that the amount of cremated bone deposited in them is sufficient to account for the dead of a sizeable community, or of a sizeable class within a community. And if we attempt to calculate the number of man-hours required for the construction of such works as Newgrange, or other great tumuli like Dowth and Knowth, also in the Boyne valley, we arrive at a similar conclusion: that the monuments are the work of a population of some size.

There are further questions. Were these tombs primarily monuments of the dead, as the pyramids were? Or were they rather temples, centres of a complex cult, to which the remains of the dead came as offerings to a divinity rather than as the sacred deposits which the tombs themselves were intended to honour? Perhaps not quite either. But they must represent a communal effort comparable to that involved in the erection of Chartres and Rheims in the extraordinary age of cathedral building. This

Figure 1   Spirals from a carved stone at Newgrange, County Meath

implies complexity of social organization. There must have been experts of various kinds – priests, engineers, gangers, carvers. There must have been, or so it would seem, an organization of society more open and complex than that of extended families communally farming. And, about the passage-type megalithic tombs in particular, there are features which, oddly, suggest almost an urban background (the formal monumentality, the grouping of the tombs, the specialization implied, the underlying questions about food supply and direction of labour).

There is a small version of these tombs just as there is of the court tombs, but in the case of the passage graves there is some reason to believe that the series may have begun with the smaller types. These are best known from a large and concentrated cemetery which occupied the site of the present town of Sligo and extended to the west of it through the townland of Carrowmore. Work here has suggested that in this coastal area a mesolithic population adopted both agriculture and the custom of tomb-building. Such dating evidence as is available, however, suggests that the megalithic chambered tombs belong in the main not only to the more northerly parts of the island but to the later phases of purely neolithic culture, from about 3500 BC onward. The larger and more elaborate of them are probably associated with the development of less egalitarian societies, probably marking a shift from the tribe to the chiefdom in certain communities within the island. But, as yet, we are left with more questions than answers.

About 2000 BC it seems that metallic ores were being exploited in Ireland. Metal industries had long been established in both south-eastern and south-western Europe, and in a period of expanding populations, and perhaps of tribal migrations, were introducing to the comparatively static world of isolated neolithic communities the dynamic of long-distance trade and communications. In some parts of the neolithic world, specialized industries – flint-mining, axe-manufacture – had already developed trade to quite distant markets (as in the case of axes from Tievebulliagh in Antrim in Ireland), and luxury items like special kinds of sea-shells had long been widely distributed. But once people learned how to extract metals from their ores the impulse to trade became greater, and larger distances were involved.

Ireland was fairly rich in suitable copper ores. The best known early system of mine-workings is on Mount Gabriel in western Co. Cork, where copper was extracted, but there may have been others of importance. Native gold was to be found in the streams of Co. Wicklow, and perhaps elsewhere. Ireland became one of the early metal-producing centres of western Europe. The metal-workers produced flat axes in simple open moulds, and in due course a decorated form was traded across Ireland and into Britain. The ornament reflected some of the patterns of the carvings on neolithic passage graves. Gold-workers made decorated and decorative personal ornaments, notably a type of neck-pendant known (from its crescentic form) as a lunula, and these too were traded, through Cornwall, to northern France.

There were many other cultural innovations at about this time. For a couple of centuries after about 2000 BC it seems that metal-using people in Ireland were making insular variants of the distinctive pottery type known as Beaker – found across Europe from the lower Danube to the Atlantic – and were taking over many of the old neolithic sites, including some of the now ruined megalithic round cairns. They, and others, continued the megalithic tradition, building monuments which are impressive enough although they do not approach the grand scale of the great passage-grave tumuli. The new type is known, from its ground-plan, as a 'wedge-shaped grave'. It is a distinctively Irish type, although there are some similarities to tombs in the Seine–Oise–Marne region of France. The tombs are found very widely throughout the island. In some areas (such as north Co. Clare) where they are densely concentrated, it is clear that their builders were primarily cattlemen.

The herding economies spread widely, following the winding moraines and eskers and other glacial deposits of boulder clay and sand which provided islands or raised trackways among the forests and bogs. There was a great development of new religious monuments, in which Ireland appears to share with Great Britain and western France. These include various kinds of large sacred circles of ritual purpose, including circles of standing stones. Along the Boyne in this period the megalithic tombs of neolithic origin, already ancient, continued to be treated as religious centres. A ring of standing stones was erected around the great mound at Newgrange, for example. Again we find that the distribution of such monuments is patchy and uneven, but now there were many more centres in the south. There are local and regional differences and distinctions. The peoples of the second millennium BC were not subject to any great centralized control or impulse, but developed their local cultural styles. Certain culture-traits (such as the types of pot known in archaeological jargon as 'Food Vessels', which also extend across northern Britain) did become very widespread indeed. But even the Food Vessels did not penetrate to every corner of the island, and the extreme south-west remained outside their influence.

Pastoralism and trade suggest much more mobile communities, perhaps practising transhumance and possibly including travelling smiths and other specialists. This would tend to diffuse ideas, customs and fashions. If there were periodic tribal or inter-tribal assemblies (and the religious monuments suggest the possibility) these again would greatly facilitate the exchange of ideas and fashions as well as commodities. But we know nothing about some important elements of the cultures of the time, about language, for example (there may well have been dozens of local languages), and next to nothing about social organization. Even the material evidence for settlement, as distinct from burial and ritual, is extremely sparse for this long period. Irish developments were probably parallel to those on the continent, perhaps with some time-lag. There, important and enduring social and political changes had been taking place. Although new knowledge and new interpretations have upset much of Gordon Childe's masterly exposition of the course of European prehistory, his words on this period in his last book are still worth quoting:

In temperate Europe by 1500 BC had been established a distinctive politico-economic structure such as had existed a thousand years earlier in the Aegean, but nowhere else in the Bronze Age world. An international commercial system linked up a turbulent multitude of tiny political units. All these, whether city-states or tribes, while jealously guarding their autonomy, and at the same time seeking to subjugate one another, had nonetheless surrendered their economic independence by adopting for essential equipment materials that had to be imported. As an additional return for this sacrifice they also benefited from a free circulation of ideas and their exponents, while new opportunities for a livelihood were opened up to farmers' younger sons.[4]

Generally all this can be discerned only dimly in the Irish evidence so far available but there are occasional illuminating glimpses. A burial, of the Food Vessel phase, at Tara illustrates the 'international' commercial system. This was a crouched single burial, one of many inserted by Bronze Age people into a mound which covered a neolithic passage grave. It was of a youth, whose body had been buried wearing a necklace of beads of different materials. There was copper, probably Irish, jet from Yorkshire, amber from Jutland or the Baltic, and faience – a glassy substance of Egyptian inspiration, but possibly of British origin. The boy was the possessor of a kind of wealth which was not simply produced on the family farm, and his wealth was displayed in a way to indicate that he was a person of importance. Another of the single burials (they were mostly cremated) in the same secondary use of the 'Mound of the Hostages' at Tara had a ceremonial stone battle-axe – a symbol of authority.[5] Aristocratic societies clearly were emerging, in which some were rich, some poor, some gave orders, others obeyed them. When people buried the *important* dead, they were giving them, presumably for use in another world, weapons rather than tools or other everyday possessions.

Towards the end of the second millennium BC we can discern further changes in Ireland, although, again, the evidence so far is so sketchy that our interpretation must be largely speculative. This was, however, a time when in Europe – about 1200 BC – social, cultural and economic change became rapid and turbulent. In Ireland the traditions of megalithic burial and early Bronze Age pottery types fade away: an indication of transformations in more significant matters. It is clear that there were at least pockets of quite considerable wealth. Metalworkers acquired new skills and techniques, and there were many splendid and luxurious articles (mostly personal ornaments) of gold, made with dazzling expertise.

Another period of rapid and important change is observable about 500 or 600 years later, about the seventh century BC. By this date peoples who spoke languages of the Indo-European group had imposed themselves almost all over Europe. Central and western Europe was dominated by warrior chieftains belonging to one of the western branches of the Indo-Europeans – the Celts. We can infer, from several kinds of evidence, that Celtic-speaking peoples were well established by this date in France and Britain and that Celtic-speakers were already settled, or at least settling in Ireland.

Some climatic deterioration may have set in about then, with wetter seasons and a rising water table. But, initially, at any rate, our evidence (still very sketchy) suggests a further increase in prosperity, as well as more innovations. Frank Mitchell suggests that there was an important change in agricultural methods:

It is very probable that this expansion is due to the introduction of some form of plough. At this time ox-drawn ard-ploughs were being used in Scandinavia, and finds of amber beads in Ireland prove that there must have been trading connections with the north. Similar ards found in Danish bogs range in radiocarbon age from 900 to 350 BC, and an ard in Scotland was dated to 400 BC. If the ard-plough was being used in Scotland at this time it will certainly have been in use in Ireland also.[6]

The ard was the simplest type of plough – a piece of tackle designed to draw a pointed oak stick, point forward, across the ground, pushing a shallow groove through the soil. It brought into play for the growth of crops nutrients from a layer immediately below that which could be reached by the earlier digging-sticks and spades. It had disadvantages too. The wear on the ard was very great and it had to be replaced frequently; it could not push through the matted roots of grassland until digging had first been done, and stony soil had to be cleared by hand before the ard could be employed.

Mitchell points out a longer-term disadvantage:

It may well be that the ard, which in the short term appeared to be such a boon, turned out in the long run to be a disaster. In the beginning the ard did bring new nutrient material to the surface, but only from the still very limited depth to which it could reach; it probably created a good 'tilth' more easily than the spade, and for a time all went well. But the more finely divided the tilth became, the more easily nutrient could be lost from it by leaching, and a very acid surface layer created. If the climate did deteriorate around 600 BC, leaching may have become still more severe.[7]

In the initial prosperity of this phase (the 'Dowris period' in current archaeological terminology) we can again distinguish some quite local and regional manifestations, showing that there was far from being a unified culture throughout the country. For example, there is a group of heavy gold collars or breast ornaments, richly decorated in a baroque repoussé ornament and seemingly designed for aristocratic display. These are conventionally known as 'gorgets'. They are found only in the area around the Shannon estuary, suggesting perhaps a local overlordship by warrior chiefs who controlled considerable sources of wealth.

Hilltop enclosures were occupied or used, presumably by such groups, throughout most of the last millennium BC. Sometimes these were defensive in character, with a rampart and an external fosse forming the enclosure; sometimes they seemed to carry on the early Bronze Age tradition of the sacred or ritual enclosure, having the fosse on the *inside* of the encircling rampart. Within some of these enclosures there were circles and other arrangements of timber posts and stockades, which have been interpreted as ceremonial centres of some kind. All this is broadly within the pattern of developments in Europe, and we can reasonably interpret the hilltop sites as centres of tribal chiefdoms. Not all of them were permanently occupied: they seem to have been used primarily for periodic ceremonies or assemblies. Most often they were sites marked by sacred monuments of much earlier times, such as neolithic tombs.

Some of the evidence we have for the last 500 years BC comes from *crannogs* – artificial islands formed by laying layers of brushwood and stones in the shallow waters of lakes. Well-to-do, perhaps ruling, families lived on these islands, and the material found suggests an increasing uniformity of culture throughout Ireland at the time. Then, one by one, the crannog dwellings were overwhelmed by the rising waters of their lakes. Bog growth was rapid, and the peats and mosses were choking and damming streams, causing them to pond, so that lakes increased in both number and extent. The climate was also, probably, somewhat wetter. And the soil cultivable by the ard became impoverished, as Mitchell suggests.

At any rate the palaeobotanical evidence (mainly from counts of fossil pollen) shows a regression of forest and scrub and a great diminution of cultivation. We may infer a falling population. The trade contacts which had operated through so many phases of the Bronze Age ended. Ireland entered a kind of dark age, which we may date from round about 200 BC to round about AD 300. It is within this period that the technology of iron was established in the country. The Romans, after unsuccessful attempts under Julius Caesar in the first century BC, occupied Britain 100 years later and extended their empire to the shores of the Irish Sea. Late in the first century AD, when Agricola was governor of Britain, they contemplated the subjection of Ireland and carried out reconnaissance. But, although they calculated that the island could be taken with one legion and some auxiliaries, they decided that it was not worth the effort. So, as we begin to obtain our first descriptions and accounts of Ireland by literate observers, we must record as a matter of primary importance for the island's history something that didn't happen. The Romans never came.

2 Celtic Ireland

Of the ancient languages of prehistoric western Europe only one fragment survives, the Basque language of the Pyrenean region of Spain. Languages of the Indo-European family have replaced them everywhere else. The homeland of the Indo-European languages appears to lie somewhere in the west Asian steppe, from which the pastoral nomads of original 'Indo-European' speech expanded westward into Europe, south-westward into the Near East, southward into Iran, and south-eastward into India. Different dialects became distinct languages, developing in their own ways. It seems probable that a language ancestral to Greek was being spoken in south-eastern Europe soon after 2000 BC – certainly well before 1000 BC. About the same time an early version of another Indo-European tongue, Hittite, was spoken in Asia Minor. It can be inferred, although without direct evidence, that the main European groups of Indo-European, including the Germanic group in the north, the Italic group in the south, and the Celtic group in the centre and west, had already become differentiated in the same period. Each group in turn, in the course of time, formed distinct dialects which ultimately gave rise to mutually incomprehensible languages.

In the course of the first millennium BC, as Greek became firmly established in the south-east, and Italic languages steadily displaced the pre-Indo-European Etruscan (and perhaps other tongues) in the Italian peninsula, we learn that much of central and western Europe was dominated by people whom the Greeks called *Keltoi* – the Celts. The geographic ranges attributed to them by the ancient ethnographers and historians match very well with the material evidence available to archaeologists. For example, the very large body of material, with broad distinctive characteristics, given the material-culture label 'Hallstatt' extended, in the period from about 1200 to about 600 BC, over the areas which we can infer from the documentary evidence to have been dominated by 'Celts' and 'Illyrians' (speakers of dialects ancestral to the Slav languages). And the later grouping of distinctive materials, labelled

'La Tène', matches very well in its extent the known territories of the later
Celts, including Bohemia, Hungary, parts of Germany, France, parts of
the Iberian peninsula, and Britain.

Apart from these good correlations between the territorial extents of the
'Celts' indicated by written sources on the one hand and by archaeological
material on the other, the material evidence in general tends to bear out
what we are told by the writers about the character of Celtic society. Some
caution is necessary here, however, for the social systems of all the early
Indo-European groups were similar in many respects. Much of what
Tacitus tells us about the ancient Germans would apply also to the Celts.
It is difficult, in some 'La Tène' material, to distinguish between Celtic
work and Illyrian. There are reminiscences in the earliest Irish literature of
strange and interesting passages in the most ancient literature of India.

What characterizes the Indo-Europeans in general is their background
in pastoral nomadism, which left many traces even after cultural and
economic patterns had changed. They seem to have achieved their
comparatively rapid expansion over large parts of the ancient world by
acquiring techniques and equipment – including iron metallurgy, horses
and wheeled vehicles – which enabled them to develop an essentially
parasitic military economy by seizing the wealth produced by more settled
– even civilized and organized – communities and establishing themselves
as exploiters. This pattern of explosive expansion out of the central Asian
steppe was to be recurrent, and may be observed in later history in the
conquests of Mongols, Turks and other groups. The great period of
turmoil in the thirteenth and twelfth centuries BC, which brought about
the 'Dark Age of the Aegean', the temporary collapse of Egypt, and other
less easily traceable events, appears to mark a crucial point in the Indo-
European expansion into Europe, which had perhaps been proceeding in
less dramatic form for the previous 1000 years.

The descriptions of the Celts given from about 600 BC onwards picture
a 'heroic' society of quarrelsome, boastful barbarian chiefs who were
formidable in war, who drank copiously, who were head-hunters, who
feared nothing except 'that the sky might fall'. The writers also describe
them as tall, blond and blue-eyed. But this is a conventional description of
barbarians from beyond the Alps, since the existence of people of such
appearance in the more northerly parts of Europe was a matter of interest
to the peoples of the Mediterranean. There are various other problems in
the interpretation of ancient ethnographical writings, largely arising from
the retailing of stereotypes. 'Celtic' societies in Europe were probably
formed by the intrusion of Celtic-speaking war-bands, or perhaps
migrating tribes, into the more numerous indigenous or longer-settled

populations of the different regions in a vast and extensive territory – some of whom may well have been blond and blue-eyed. There was no Celtic race.

Migration on a fairly large scale brought large numbers southward across the Alps, from the Celtic zone and under Celtic leadership, about 400 BC. The event figures as a major catastrophe in the legendary phase of Roman history, for it appears that they occupied the little city briefly. More importantly, they established a province of their own south of the Alps which the Romans knew as *Gallia Cisalpina*. More than a century later Celtic migrations are reported into Greece and Asia Minor, and before the end of the second century BC the Romans had annexed not only *Gallia Cisalpina* but also the Celtic territory in the south of France. By the time Caesar came to conduct his campaigns in the remainder of *Gallia* – France and Belgium – in the first century BC the Celts (Gauls) of that region were already in process of making the change from chiefdom to state in their social and political organization.

Caesar's two expeditions across the Channel to Britain were to a country which was also largely under Celtic domination, although it is possible that non-Celtic languages were still spoken in the far north. By the time Roman generals, under the emperor Claudius, returned to subdue the country systematically a century later, there was a marked contrast between the societies of the lowland and highland zones, although both were 'Celtic'. The Britons' style of warfare, with impetuous massed chariot-charges, was not effective against the military techniques of the Romans, and by the end of the first century AD the island had been subdued, although its more northerly parts were left outside the Roman province.

The Celtic impact on Ireland was probably less than that on Gaul and Britain, but by the time the Romans were on the Irish Sea the place-names and tribal names reported from Ireland were all Celtic in form. The Irish section of Ptolemy's description of the world, which he compiled in the second century, is now thought to have been based on intelligence gathered for Agricola in the late first century, when he contemplated the conquest of the island. Tacitus, in recounting this episode, tells us that coastal Ireland was well known through the reports of merchants, but that the interior parts were less well known. The map which can be constructed on the basis of Ptolemy's account shows that the coasts were known, after a fashion, from the Shannon estuary round by the south, east and north seaboards to Donegal Bay, but that the coast of Connacht appears to have been unknown. This western gap is reflected in some maps of Ireland down to the sixteenth century.

Ptolemy's description is the oldest which gives us any detailed

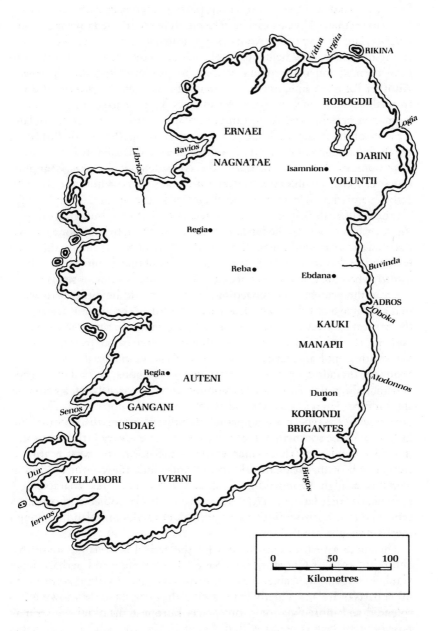

Map 4 Early Ireland, after Ptolemy. The locations are mostly speculative

information about Ireland. However, passing references to the island were made more than 600 years earlier. The oldest name attested for the country is *Ierne*, later *Ivernia*. The Romans appear to have assimilated these forms to the notion, widely held, that Ireland was a country so far north as to have been a land of perpetual winter, to produce the name *Hibernia*. Another Roman name, perhaps somewhat commoner, is *Scottia*, derived from the *Scotti* – the dominant inhabitants of all or part of the island in Roman imperial times. According to the most ancient references Ireland was one of the Pretanic isles, but in later sources the *Pritani*, or *Brittones*, are the inhabitants of the larger island, which we still call Great Britain. In Irish sources the word *Cruthin*, the equivalent of *Pritani*, is applied however to the inhabitants of *northern* Britain, those whom the Romans called 'painted people' (*Picti*) as well as to people in north-eastern Ireland. To the early Irish Britain as a whole was *Albu* (Albion) but, confusingly, this term came to be applied in later times to northern Britain alone, so that the modern Irish word for Scotland is *Alba*. Equally confusingly, the name Scotland itself is derived from the colonization of that country by the Irish (*Scotti*) when the Roman province gave way to small successor states.

From the evidence of archaeology alone it would be difficult to guess that a language of Celtic form had been established throughout Ireland by the first century AD. There is 'La Tène' material, from a period beginning perhaps in the third century BC, but it is somewhat puzzling in its distribution and incidence. There is a body of material west of the Shannon, including bronze horse-trappings, weapons, and other objects, and including also carved stone monuments, apparently of a religious significance. There is another body of material in the north-east. There are burials with 'La Tène' material, which slightly extend this distribution, but in general in the southern half of the country there is very little undoubted 'La Tène' evidence. That which exists in the north and west is thin in comparison with the material from Britain and the continent, but it contains a high proportion of objects of a luxurious character. A particularly rich late 'La Tène' art-style, in display objects in metal, is centred on the Irish Sea with a scattering of examples in Ireland, although the main weight is in Britain.

This gives a picture consistent with the arrival in Ireland, somewhat before the time of Christ, of war-bands, from Britain and perhaps from Gaul, who established chiefdoms for themselves in parts of the country. In other parts of Ireland, chiefly in the south, the material so far known is less splendid and more everyday, but it has European affinities which may possibly represent contacts with different Celtic groups. Celtic languages may have been introduced over quite a long period.

By the time we have direct internal evidence – the sixth century AD – one language was dominant throughout Ireland – Irish. There are a few references which indicate that some other languages or 'difficult' dialects survived into this period. The Irish language itself is of the Celtic group, but with many features which distinguish it from British and continental Celtic. David Greene, acknowledging its mixed character, preferred to define it simply as the 'language of the people of Ireland'.[1] Heinrich Wagner, studying the traces of other languages picked up by Irish, finds the closest affinities for these in North African languages, and traces parallels in Berber and ancient Egyptian.[2] This may mean no more than that some of the pre-Indo-European languages of western Europe shared these affinities. It is not necessary to assume that Celtic-speakers entered Ireland in very large numbers to displace the earlier dialects of the country. They may simply have achieved dominance through military superiority or by securing through some other means a special prestige for their language.

At about AD 300 there is both archaeological and palaeobotanical evidence for new developments in the country. The pollen and radiocarbon records show a dramatic expansion in agriculture at about this date, and the change has been attributed to the introduction of the coulter-plough. The *coulter*, a vertical iron knife, was fitted to the frame of the plough so that it could cut through matted roots, allowing the *share*, also now shod with iron, to break through the soil. There was as yet no *mouldboard*, to turn over the clods as the ground was broken, and in order to break down the soil enough for the growing of crops, cross-ploughing was necessary – the technique which produced the characteristic squarish 'Celtic fields'. These are well known in Britain, where the coulter-plough had long been established. It was most probably from Roman Britain that the coulter-plough was introduced to Ireland, becoming sufficiently widespread in its use by the end of the third century to produce the marked change in the pollen-diagrams, indicating the colonization of new land by farmers. The final establishment of the technology of iron throughout the island and its general use for everyday implements such as knives, axes and saws, must also have contributed greatly to the breakthrough into a new economy.

The archaeological record shows another, and probably closely related, change at about the same time. This is a sharp increase in the amount of Roman influence observable in the evidence. The amount of material actually originating in the Roman provinces which has been found in Ireland is small – as compared, for example, with the amount from parts of the Germanic world that lay far beyond the imperial frontiers.[3] But from the first century onwards, there is sufficient material to show continuity of contacts, by trade or otherwise. There is some slight evidence for an early Roman presence (presumably for reconnaissance) on the east coast (e.g., at Loughshinny, Co. Dublin). Roman pilgrim–tourists apparently visited Newgrange in the Boyne valley, where they deposited votive offerings – just as their counterparts did at the Pyramids. A scattering of coins indicates contacts which most likely concerned trade across the Irish Sea.

But it seems that, from about the end of the third century, fashions from the Roman world began to flood into Ireland. It may be that this concerned only the dominant or ruling groups. Personal equipment and ornaments, such as pins for fastening the clothes, began to be modelled on those common in the frontier, or military, provinces of the empire. It is likely that it was about this time that the élite groups who dominated the Irish chiefdoms abandoned the style of clothing (including breeches) of their prehistoric forebears, and adapted a style more closely resembling Mediterranean and Roman military dress: a linen tunic with an outer woollen cloak, worn by men and women alike. All the changes, although recognizably of Roman inspiration, were rapidly absorbed into Irish technology and culture and were modified in significantly distinctive ways. They suggest imitation at a distance, or intermittent rather than close and continuous contacts. They may involve a compound of trade, occasional raids (with the introduction perhaps of Roman slaves into Ireland), perhaps the occasional service of Irish war-bands as Roman mercenaries or auxiliaries, possibly the transmission of influences indirectly through contacts between the Irish and half-Romanized auxiliaries such as the southern Picts. The meagre written record is not sufficient to explain the material evidence.

A glance at contemporary happenings in the Roman world, however, may help to put the Irish evidence in perspective. The empire, for all its magnificent organizational achievements, retained at its heart the parasitic economy of barbarians. The Age of the Antonines was financed by the loot of conquest; the empire failed to devise a machinery for replenishing the sources of its supply of wealth, and when it attempted to lift itself by its own bootstraps, falling back on the familiarly futile devices of inflation, over-taxation and fiscal controls, it began to collapse. The western provinces in particular suffered disaster in the second half of the third century. A cycle of military *coups d'états* exposed the true nature of imperial politics; Britain became a usurpers' base, at times separated from the other provinces, at times used as a springboard in bids for power; Germanic barbarians, including the Franks, now first heard of, overran the western continental provinces for the space of a whole generation.

It is within this context that we receive our first written accounts of Irish events – as distinct from descriptive references to the country. The precarious order restored in the Roman west by the end of the third century began to break down again late in the fourth. Among the other troubles of the empire were raids on Roman Britain by the Picts from the north and by fleets of Irish *curraghs* (timber-framed ships with a covering of hides). In 367, according to Ammianus Marcellinus, a 'barbarian conspiracy' brought a combined attack not only of Irish and Picts but also of Saxons from across the North Sea. This was devastating, but the Roman commanders responded with furious improvizations, setting up new frontier and coastal defence systems. Magnus Maximus, the governor who was proclaimed emperor in Britain in 383 and promptly crossed with his army to Gaul to pursue his ambitions, is said to have defeated the Picts and Scots. But the raids continued, or were renewed. A quarter of a century later, Britain ceased to be effectively governed from Rome. Its defence was left to the Romanized Britons, under their provincial officials and leaders. The Saxon threat, as well as the Pictish and Irish, continued, and it seems that some of the Britons tried to secure the services of these Germans against the attacks from Scotland and Ireland. But in the course of the fifth century there was Germanic migration to eastern Britain on a large scale, and ultimately the Britons were unable to prevent the settlement of Angles, Saxons and Jutes from extending over a large part of the island.

We may surmise that these events had considerable internal repercussions in Ireland. The oldest recorded legends and pseudo-historical traditions reflect, consistently, a period of upheaval which is linked, at least in part, to raiding and campaigning overseas.

In these traditions there is an assumption of an 'original' or 'natural' fivefold division of Ireland, although this is not depicted as a functioning political apportionment at any stage in the stories. The division, however, conforms to the world-view of early Irish literature, in which Ireland itself is treated as a cosmos. The country's name was *Ériu* (*Éire* in modern Irish) and the concept of Ireland as an entity is very clear from the earliest written records. Indeed, all lands outside Ireland, although their real existence was of course acknowledged, could be treated according to the requirements of the storytellers, under their proper names but as parts of a mythological Otherworld. Nine waves out from the coast was the magical boundary of Ireland, which could be, in some sense, the boundary between the real world and the world of spirits and mythical beings. This concept, this clear and sharp division between the 'inside' and the 'outside', was for the Irish as powerful as the concept of Hellas for the Greeks, and it was to have long-continuing importance.

The cosmos was, as it were, a *mandala*, with a fivefold division – the centre, and the four cardinal directions. Each direction was given colour, attributes and qualities, and a special meaning was given to the omphalic middle. A place called Uisnech, a hill in Co. Westmeath, was said in the traditions to be the centre.[4]

The fivefold division, however, also conformed to the natural regional geography of the island, which because of its general shape, and its structure, with a hilly perimeter and a low-lying interior, fits the concept quite well. The northern part of the island forms in itself almost a miniature of the whole, having a rim of hills round lowlands through which the Bann flows north like a smaller Shannon. The northern province is separated from the rest of the island by a broad zone of drumlins – small whale-backed glacial hills – and by the endless meandering lakelets and myriad islands of the river Erne. The far west was characterized by systems of bleak hills and exposed coasts on the Atlantic, and, at this date, by great expanses of bog. Apart from some districts in the northern part of the region, it was thinly inhabited. The east, or rather south-east, a region shielded by ranges of difficult hills south of where Dublin now is, was bounded on the west by the steep-sided valley of the Barrow – not a formidable obstacle. The southern third of the island, characterized by the very strongly marked east–west folding which shows most clearly in the Cork and Kerry peninsulas, had range after range of hills and broad rich valleys, with endless remote defiles and corners. In between them all rolled the broad midlands, reaching the sea along a 50-mile gap between the hills, where the coast faced across to north Wales; otherwise poorly defined and fading into the surrounding highland regions, traversed by winding streams and most notably by the Shannon, with its broad flood-plains and its spreading lakes.

This geography is stamped on the island's history. The modern tradition of the 'four provinces' of Ireland reflects the cardinal divisions – Ulster in the north, Leinster in the east, Munster in the south, Connacht in the west. The centre, marked for a time by a political division known as *Mide* ('the middle') has faded from the picture, although the modern Irish word for a province (*cúige*) derives from a word meaning 'fifth'.

The ancient sagas and tales, written down and modified from miscellaneous oral traditions, suggest to us that at the end of the prehistoric period in Ireland, the island was dominated by a number of groups who were recognized as having distinct origins. Some of the groups appear to have organized themselves in complex chiefdoms and to have formed extensive tribal federations with paramount chiefs. Notable among these tribal nations were the *Lagin*, based on the south-east and apparently controlling a large part of the midlands, and the *Ulaid*, dominating the

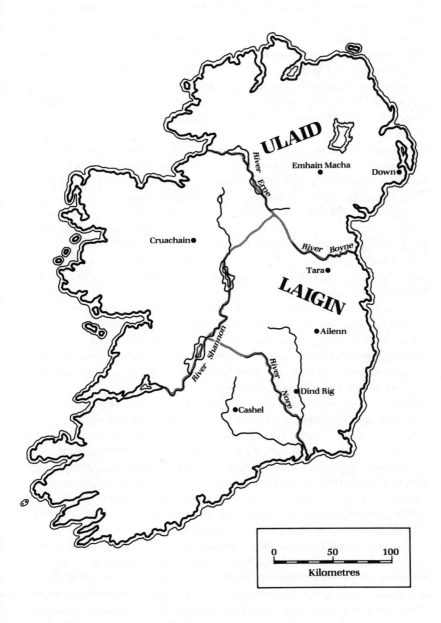

Map 5   Royal sites and ancient nations

country north of Boyne and Erne. Less clearly defined in the traditions were the *Érainn*, of the south. These dominant groups appear to have found it necessary or important to control certain hilltop sites, of ancient sacral significance, situated mainly around the rim of the central lowlands and commanding wide views over the countryside. Most of them were marked both by hilltop enclosures and by burial mounds. Most also figure as the setting of all kinds of mythical or legendary events in the storytelling – in which they are occupied by 'royal palaces' – but there is little evidence that they were permanently occupied in this sense at the times most likely to be in question.

Emhain Macha, in Co. Armagh, is the scene of many episodes in one of the main cycles of epic and heroic tales, the cycle which includes Ireland's *Iliad*, the epic known as *Táin Bó Cuailgne* ('the cattle-raid of Cuailgne'). The core of this story is mythological – a battle between divine bulls – but it is given an elaborate pseudo-historical setting which depicts warfare between the *Connachta* and their allies on the one hand, and on the other the *Ulaid*. The *Connachta* were led by their queen, Medb, whose 'palace' was at Cruachain in Co. Roscommon. Medb herself was a goddess of sovereignty, whose embraces conferred kingship, but in the tales she was treated as an historical person.

Some reality almost certainly lies behind the heroic narratives. But by the time contemporary accounts of secular events begin to become available to us – in practice not much earlier than the end of the seventh century – information about the fifth, sixth and seventh centuries has been so rearranged for current dynastic and political purposes that it is quite difficult to reconstruct that reality.

However, it does seem that (beginning possibly early in the fifth century) the northern federation of the *Ulaid* was broken up, in a prolonged series of skirmishes and realignments, and replaced by a new alliance which became dominant over much of its former territory. The new alliance appears to have expanded from the general neighbourhood of Cruachain, north-westward into the Sligo–Mayo region, northward into Donegal, and eastward and south-eastward into the lowland territories formerly dominated by the *Lagin*. By the eighth century the 'fifth' of the *Ulaid* had been reduced to territories east of the Bann.

The new alliance which, in one form or another, was to dominate the northern half of Ireland for centuries, was led by chiefs who, in their different chiefdoms, came to claim a common descent from a king sufficiently remote in prehistoric time, one Conn 'of the hundred battles'. They could all therefore be called *Connachta* – 'descendants of Conn' – but in practice, in the historic period, this term was reserved for the chiefdoms west of the Shannon, at Cruachain and beyond.[5] Those in the north and in the midlands found it convenient to trace their common origin to an alleged descendant of Conn – Niall 'of the nine hostages'. They are known in the texts as the *uí Néill* – the 'descendants of Niall'. (The personal name Niall continued to be favoured among them, and a later ruler, Niall Glúndubh, killed in 919, was the ancestor of a sub-group of 'descendants of Niall' – the O'Neills of Tyrone.) In the origin-legends of both the *Connachta* and the *uí Néill*, their heroic ancestors are associated with the raids and campaigns which marked the end of the Roman empire in the west.

They marked their new dominance by seizure of the great sacral site of Tara, in the area known as *Brega* (Tara is in Co. Meath). Here a solemn ceremony at irregular intervals – the *féis* – conferred on the paramount chief of the time a special recognition as priest-king, husband of the sovereignty-goddess, guardian of the people against the Otherworld. The ceremony lapsed in Christian times, but the possession of Tara continued to be a matter of great prestige.

The Irish word for a chief was *rí* (cf. Latin *rex*, Gaulish *-rix*). The word for a chiefdom was *tuath* (from Celtic **teuto-*, **touto* – 'a people'). These are commonly translated as 'king' and 'tribe'. Eligibility for election to the office of *rí* depended on membership of the dominant kin-group of the chiefdom, and in practice also partly depended on the command of sufficient wealth to retain the loyalty of a reasonably large following of clients. The *rí* was the representative of his *tuath* in dealings with the outer world as well as with the Otherworld. He could accept the primacy of another chief, or be accepted in primacy. Such relationships were signified by the exchange of hostages and formal gifts, and there were various mitigations to safeguard honour and pride. The socio-political unit was the *tuath* (of which there were perhaps about 150 in early historic Ireland) and there was really no mechanism for the functioning of larger units: alliances and federations of chiefdoms depended on highly volatile relationships between potential equals. But it seems that the prestige peculiar to certain ancient and sacred places and ceremonies could give additional charisma to some rulers.

In the southern half of Ireland, the pseudo-historical traditions are a little less clear. They seem to suggest, however, that there too, probably in the fifth century, there came into being a new alliance of chiefdoms which was to dominate Munster for some hundreds of years. In the process the *Lagin* of the south-east may again have lost some territory formerly under their dominance. Otherwise, the drift of the tradition would seem to suggest that the new order was brought about largely through the

Map 6   The conversion of Ireland: bishops, presbyters and holy women in fifth-century Ireland, according to seventh-century writers

activities of large bodies of auxiliaries or mercenaries, analogous to the *Laeti* and other such groups employed by the Romans on their frontiers. A persistent tradition brings the main group of these southward from the midlands to conquer lands for the emerging overlords and to be granted lands of their own along the south coast. The word for these mercenary groups is *Dési*, and the main section of the *Dési* occupied what is now Co. Waterford. A smaller group of *Dési* is said to have settled along the lower Shannon from which they later crossed to win a new territory for their overlords in what is now eastern Co. Clare.

The new configuration in Munster, like that farther north, was associated with the decline of Roman power in the west. The *Dési* of the southern coast colonized the nearer parts of Roman Britain and settled fairly densely in what was until recently Pembrokeshire, as well as making small intrusions elsewhere. In their territory, numerous epigraphs cut on standing stones employ a curious form of rune-like inscription – *ogam* – which is based on the Roman alphabet. These occur in south-west Wales, with bilingual inscriptions in Irish and Latin, until the eighth century.

The new alliance in the south established its ceremonial centre on the rock of Cashel, in Co. Tipperary; an acropolis which, unlike Tara or Cruachain or Emhain, appears to have had no ancient sacred significance. The very name, *Caisel*, is a borrowing from the Latin (*castellum*) and it is probable that it was Christian from its very origin. The heads of the significant chiefdoms in Munster, like their counterparts in the north, agreed that they were descended from a common ancestor, Mug Nuadat, otherwise known as Eógan. They were termed the *Eóganachta*, 'descendants of Eógan'.

At a somewhat later date in the historical period a basic twofold division of Ireland was recognized. The line of division was marked by a glacial esker ridge which snakes across the countryside from Dublin bay to Galway bay, almost exactly bisecting the island. It was known as *Eiscir Riada*. South of this was 'the half of Mug'. North of it was 'the half of Conn'. During a long period of comparative stability which lasted until the late eighth century, the confederations in the two halves seem to have got along with comparatively little contact or friction. Friction, on the other hand, regularly occurred between the *Lagin*, who retained the country east of the Barrow, and the *uí Neill*, who had usurped their control of the midlands. In both halves great prestige and significance were attached to control of the chief 'royal site' – Tara on the one hand, Cashel on the other – and inevitably the time came, with the emergence of primitive statehood, when rivalry arose between the two, perhaps giving rise to the stylized bipartite concept.

The society which we first begin to discern through texts of the sixth, seventh and eighth centuries, was one in the process of being profoundly modified by external influences, mainly Roman or sub-Roman, including Christianity and literacy.

It was a rural society which was intricately stratified in patterns which are in part analogous to caste. At the head of each *tuath* (chiefdom) was the *rí*. He was, in early times at least, bound by taboos as well as by the customary traditions of the *tuath*. He was, as D. A. Binchy put it, 'originally a sacred personage tracing his descent from one or other of the ancestral deities and mystically invested with sovereignty by means of immemorial inauguration rites'. He was responsible in a magical way for the welfare of the *tuath*:[6] he had to be free from physical blemish, had to adhere to *fír flatha* (the 'lord's truth', which included just judgement), and he had to lead in war and preside in peace over the *oenach* (tribal assembly) of the *tuath*. A king who gave false judgement or who failed in other ways brought disaster to the *tuath*.

The *rí* was singled out by his office, but he came from the class (itself subdivided into seven grades according to some texts) of the *flaithi* (which we might translate as 'lords', or 'nobles'), free property-holders who belonged to the dominant families. Beneath them were two main grades of clients of the *flaithi* – ordinary freemen who cultivated the land and paid food-rent, and 'base' clients – freemen of lower grade – over whom the lord had greater rights. Clientship was based on the granting of a 'permanent loan' (*rath*) of cattle, in return for which the lord received rents and service. There was an unfree class (*cumal* was the word for a bondswoman, and a *cumal* was a standard of value; *mug* was the word for a male slave). This was probably declining in numbers and importance, although the taking of slaves had played a large part in the 'heroic age' of raids on the declining Roman empire.

There was a class whose role was of great importance in creating a unity of culture throughout the island. This was the *oes dána* ('class of learning'), which included poets, judges, doctors, and practitioners of certain skilled crafts such as joinery and metalworking. These, especially the poets, enjoyed privileges which among other things, entitled them to protection even outside their own *tuath* and beyond the reach of their kinsmen's entitlement to recompense for an injury done to them.

Dumézil has discerned the basic threefold division (warrior, husbandman, priest – or *equites*, *plebs*, *druides*, as Caesar names them among the Gauls) throughout Indo-European societies.[7] The position of the poet (*fili*) is worth special note. There were various grades of poet, of which the highest was the *ollamh*, who in legal status was equal to a *rí*. In pagan times the poet was a seer and magician, and belief in the mystical powers of poets continued (and was fostered by the poets) down to modern times. There was a long and intensive training for the office, including committing to memory many thousands of lines of verse. The poet's function was to praise his patron, preserve his genealogy, remember the history, not only of the *tuath*, but of Ireland, know the lore of the gods, transmit the wisdom of the ages. Poets were arrogant, often demanding great rewards. They were feared: a poet's satire could cause physical blemish and suffering.

It was a society with an intensified sense of place. F. J. Byrne emphasizes this in contrasting the comparative freedom of manoeuvre of the Germanic king (essentially the leader of a war-band) with the more restricted powers of the *rí*.

. . . but in Ireland – at least in the law-tracts which describe the society of the seventh and eighth centuries – the war-band as such is not obtrusive: the picture given is rather that of a simple farming economy in which even the nobleman is only on occasion a warrior. . . . In Germanic society the bond between lord and retainer seems to overshadow the ties of kindred. . . . But the Irish kings and the people they ruled were rooted in the soil. They were strengthened by all the forces of a powerful and ancient tradition. They were also hamstrung: it was not only divinity which hedged them round. Tribal law and custom was no vague body of lore dependent on the memory of the oldest men. It was jealously preserved in druidical schools by a professional class who quickly profited by the new learning of the monasteries to become literate in their own language and commit the tradition to writing. The king was never to become the fountain of justice. . . .[8]

Indeed, the impression left by the evidence is that although conquering war-bands may from time to time in the late prehistoric past have intruded into Irish society, and even placed themselves and their kin in its upper layers, they were also absorbed into it quite rapidly. If they took over ancient hallowed places like Tara or Emhain, they were also taken over by them, by their spirits and their gods and goddesses. The landscape itself was steeped in story and was peopled with earth-goddesses, water-spirits, hero-gods, shape-changing creatures and the glamour of an unseen but ever-present Otherworld. It was also the scene of ancestral deeds tenaciously remembered. A whole class of literature was devoted to the 'storytelling of places'.

The society was also a good deal more complex than the simple outline of the stratification of a regular chiefdom, or *tuath*, would suggest. The people who formed the upper layers of these *tuatha*, who possessed the wealth in cattle and land, and who chose from their favoured kin-groups the *rí* of each *tuath*; these called themselves *Féni*, at least in the territories dominated by *uí Néill* and Connachta. But there were lots of other population groups recognized, who were not *Féni*, who belonged to unfree *tuatha* or tribute-paying *tuatha* or base *tuatha* of other kinds. These cannot have been normal chiefdoms, but tribal groups standing in some kind of client relationship to the lords of the regular chiefdoms. Some of them were specialized in certain crafts. Others appear to have been representatives of ancient population groups displaced and reduced in status in the distant past. Often the same archaic tribal group-name will be found widely scattered in several different parts of the island – a survival distribution on the periphery of lands long sequestered by intruders, sometimes successive intruders. The archaic names, the ancient relationships, the original ownership, were all carefully and tenaciously remembered and passed from generation to generation. At least three 'layers' of populations can be discerned. These depressed tribes are by no means always contiguous with the dominant chiefdoms: they may overlap from one to another; some, especially of the craft-specialized tribes, may have been semi-nomadic, like tinkers or gypsies today. There were also groups of travelling players or buffoons, who seem to have been almost in the position of outcasts. Workers in iron, feared and apart, were, probably, quite often travellers who followed a round from farm to farm, supplying the knives and axes. And there were outlaws and forest-dwellers on the edge of settled society. The large village community in modern India, with its complex caste-differentiation and craft-specialization provides some analogies for the Irish *tuath*.

The dominant class, the *flaithi*, have left an enduring mark on the countryside in the form of a type of earthwork, of which about 50,000 are known to have survived until recently. These, variously termed 'rath', 'liss', 'ring-fort' or simply 'fort', consist in their weathered-down form of a roughly round space, either level with the surrounding ground or raised above it, delimited by a bank of earth, or earth-and-stones, with a gap at the entrance, surrounded by an outer fosse, also interrupted, by a causeway, at the entrance. Many of them were enclosed farmsteads, usually with a timber wall reinforcing or surmounting the embankment, and when excavated are found to have traces of timber buildings within the enclosure. Others on excavation are found not to have had habitation structures – they may have been cattle-pens. A small proportion have more than one surrounding bank and ditch. In some areas – chiefly in the stony and treeless west – there is what seems to be an equivalent type of monument – round enclosures built of stone without mortar, without an external fosse.

Since these raths are frequently mentioned in the early texts, we know that they were the dwellings or possessions of the upper orders of society, that prestige was attached to them, and that special prestige was attached to the multi-vallate types. From the evidence so far available it would seem that the great majority date from within the span between the fourth century AD and the eleventh. While houses in round enclosures are found in many places and times, the rath has some distinctive features. It is found elsewhere only in the Irish-colonized areas in Wales (and not, interestingly, in the Irish-colonized areas in western Scotland).

The raths are the monuments of the cow-lords. Their distribution avoids both valley bottoms and high ground but is quite widespread throughout Ireland. The other grades of society have left no such monuments, and their dwellings are much more difficult to locate. But there is some evidence to suggest that the *clachan* type of cluster village, with infield–outfield cultivation, may have been occupied by at least some parts of the population.[9]

3 Church and state

The most important of the Romanizing influences that began to transform aspects of life in Ireland after about AD 300 was the Christian religion.

This, of course, had begun as an unorthodox variety of Judaism, spreading rapidly in the first century through the Jewish communities of the Diaspora, who formed up to a tenth of the population of the cities of the eastern Roman empire. By the end of the first century Christianity was a distinct religion, hostile to Judaism. Although in general tolerant of creeds and cults, the Romans found the clannish exclusiveness of the Christians troublesome, and they made repeated attempts to stamp out the religion.

Like other cults, that of the Christians was brought from its East Mediterranean source by soldiers and merchants travelling to remote parts of the empire. It was well established in Gaul by the second century, and infant British churches grew under Gaulish auspices. Under the Emperor Constantine, at the beginning of the fourth century, Christianity was granted official toleration and shortly afterwards became the state religion. Its ideology and organization then underwent rapid and turbulent transformation, in a period of ferocious debates about fine points of belief. There were persecutions and counter-persecutions. Christian practices became diversified and included, in the East especially, movements of withdrawal from the world – either by retreating to practise extravagant mortification of the flesh in remote and barren desert places, or by following a celibate regime of prayer and discipline in seclusion in a well-to-do household. In fourth-century Italy and Gaul, the bishops Ambrose, Jerome and Martin were sponsors of such movements.

Martin (of Tours) was also one of those who initiated attempts to bring the urban religion of Christianity to the *pagani* – the country people. While he was orthodox, others with missionary impulses carried beyond the imperial frontiers teachings which had been suppressed within the empire. Nestorianism travelled eastward, Arianism northward to the Germanic barbarians.

By the end of the fourth century the empire was becoming increasingly bogged-down in inextricable difficulties. The conquests of the central-Asian Huns had set in train great westward migrations from the steppe, and barbarian peoples were clamouring for admission to the empire and for official employment and the grant of lands. The imperial system, gravely weakened by what might be termed the economic hopelessness that had demoralized its ruling classes, collapsed in western Europe. The new vigorous organization of the Christian churches survived. When the unthinkable happened and the imperial city fell to the Goths in 410, it was the bishop of Rome who came to the fore: Leo used his prestige to defend the city, successfully against Attila and the Huns in 451, unsuccessfully against Genseric in 455. And the patrician Roman bishops took over the direction of affairs, not only ecclesiastical, in the successor-states which began to form in western Europe.

By the time the legions abandoned Britain, Christianity was firmly established there. The church was organized, as elsewhere, on the basis of the Roman *civitates* (cities with their administrative districts) under a number of bishops. These in turn still functioned under the tutelage of the Gaulish metropolitans, and the Gauls reported to Rome. In the early fifth century an unorthodox interpretation of Christianity was being preached in North Africa, where it was countered by the disputatious apologetics of the bishop of Hippo, St Augustine. Its originator was apparently a Briton, one Pelagius – described by St Jerome, in a phrase characteristic of the ecclesiastical debate of the time, as being 'stuffed with Irish porridge' – and 'pelagianism', as the heresy was known, was reported to be firmly rooted in Britain. It had apparently been extirpated, when it revived again in a slightly different form.

At this stage, one of the leading Gaulish bishops, Germanus of Auxerre, appears to have sent a deacon of his church, Palladius, to report on the matter to Rome. The bishop of the time was Pope Celestine, strongly opposed to pelagianism (and also unenthusiastic about the growing monastic movement). Celestine sent Germanus himself to Britain to supervise a pelagian purge. He consecrated Palladius and sent him in 431 to be the 'first bishop of the Irish Christians'.[1] .

This is the earliest extant reference to Christians in Ireland. It is, however, not at all surprising that the religion should have been established there by the beginning of the fifth century, since there had been continuous intercourse, in several ways, with Roman Gaul and Britain. The general practice of the time, reaffirmed by several papal rulings, was that bishops were appointed only to established Christian communities, and only on request from them. It seems likely that the pelagian problem was seen as

CENÉL
Derry † CENÉL
RIATA
DÁL
† Coleraine

CENÉL
CONAILL
Ailech • EOGAIN

Connor
†
DÁL
ARAIDE
†Raphoe

NORTHERN UÍ NÉILL

Bangor
†
Clogher
†

Armagh
†
Downpatrick †

UÍ BRIÚIN
BRÉIFNE
AIRGIALLA
Killala †
Drumcliff
UÍ FIACHRACH UÍ AILELLO
†|Clones

BRÉIFNE
†|Kilmore

CONNACHTA Cruachain TETHBAE
Knowth
•

†|Mayo UÍ BRIÚIN
AÍ
SOUTHERN
UÍ NÉILL
BREGA
•Tara

† Cong
Ardagh
MIDE
Uisnech

† Tuam
†|Durrow

UÍ MAINE †Clonmacnoise
Clonfert †
UÍ FAILGE
Kildare †
Nás
•

UÍ MÁIL
•Ailenn

† Birr
CORCO
MRUAD † Kilmacduagh
MÚSCRAIGE
TÍRE
Aghaboe
Glendalough

Mag Adair
LAIGIN
CORCO
BAISCINN † Killaloe
•Dind Ríg

Ferns
†
CIARRAIGE
LUACHRA
Cashel
Emly †
† St Mullins

EÓGANACHT
CHAISIL
UÍ CENNSALAIGH

MUMA
DÉSI
MUMAN
EÓGANACHT
LOCHA LÉIN Lismore †

Cork †

CORCO
LOÍGDE

•   Secular sites

†   Church sites

0   50   100
Kilometres ◆

Map 7   Early historic Ireland

requiring reorganization in the whole area of Gaulish influence, which included Britain and, by extension, Ireland. Moving the regular organization of the church outside the imperial frontiers, however, created problems, since the organization itself was based and modelled on the administrative structures and divisions of the empire.

What became of Palladius, Ireland's first bishop, is unknown. Irish scholars in later centuries, when they became aware of the entry in the *Chronicle* of Prosper of Acquitaine which is the evidence for the appointment, produced some vague and contradictory stories, none of which carries any conviction (the writers were embarrassed because by then the cult of St Patrick had reached its full development and his primacy might not be questioned).

About the same time, some of the British churches, as the Roman system broke down and communications failed, were apparently attempting to organize their own efforts across the frontier. Charles Thomas has assembled various kinds of evidence – archaeological, epigraphic, onomastic, linguistic and historical – to suggest persuasively that Carlisle, at the western end of Hadrian's Wall, which, though not a *civitas*, had a bishop in the fifth century, was active in this way. He suggests that the Christians of Carlisle supported the somewhat mysterious St Nynia in his foundation of a church at Candida Casa (Whithorn) in Galloway – opposite the Co. Down coast.[2] Nynia was a bishop – which presupposes a Christian community in Galloway (outside the frontier) by the early fifth century. As the zone just beyond the Wall was well Romanized, this is not unlikely. From Candida Casa, the southern Picts are said to have been evangelized in the fifth and sixth centuries.

On present evidence, Carlisle also appears to be the most likely base of support for the episcopate of St Patrick, although almost everything concerning Patrick is problematic. Two of his writings, however, have been preserved. One is fairly short: a letter of protest and excommunication directed to the soldiers of a British chief named Coroticus (probably Ceredig Gwledig, ruler of Strathclyde) who in a raid on Ireland had taken some of Patrick's newly baptized Christians as slaves. The other somewhat longer document is later – written it would seem in Patrick's old age – and is also a letter of sorts, addressed to those in Britain who supported Patrick's episcopate in Ireland. He calls it (perhaps emulating St Augustine) his *Confessio* – a word which in this context means something between 'declaration' and 'explanation'. This is a defence of his ministry apparently in reply to criticism of some kind. It tells us a good deal about Patrick's character and spirituality (both of which were plainly formidable) but little about his circumstances. However, he tells us something about his background.

He was a Roman Briton, son of a landowner – a Roman official who was also in minor ecclesiastical orders (possibly to evade the crippling taxes). Patrick's education was interrupted in his adolescence, when he, along with 'thousands' of others, was carried off as a captive in an Irish raid. He spent six years in servitude as a herd, and then escaped from his master and from Ireland. During his captivity he underwent a classic 'conversion' and determined to devote his life to God. He was a visionary, directed in his actions by vivid dreams, which he attributed to the immediate action of God on his spirit. He became convinced that he was called to return to those among whom he had been a captive, and he overcame many obstacles (among which he emphasizes his inadequate education) to be consecrated bishop and provided with the call and the means to return to Ireland. What he stresses throughout his protest is that what he has done has not been of his volition; however unworthy, he is the instrument of God. He says he has gone into regions where no one before him had come to baptize and ordain, and that he has baptized many thousands. He plainly regards his life as a penitential one, spent among barbarians in God's cause.

Patrick's visionary call was to 'the wood of Foclut by the western sea', where those among whom he had laboured lived. There is no other Irish placename in his *Confessio*. Fortunately, one of the earlier writers about Patrick (in the late seventh century) was a man from what is now Co. Mayo – Bishop Tírechán – and we learn from him that the wood of Foclut (which was then still there) was in his native region. Patrick, however, is also inextricably connected with east Ulster – with Armagh, whose claim to be his chief church was unchallenged, with Downpatrick, the chief centre of the *Ulaid* in their reduced overlordship after they had lost Emhain Macha, with Slemish in Co. Antrim, which in the later legends was said to have been his place of captivity, and with other places in Antrim and Down.

It is possible that he had two careers. It is more than probable that there were Christian communities by the end of the fourth century on the Irish coasts facing Britain across the narrow North Channel. Patrick most likely was sent as bishop to minister to them. But he informs us himself, more than once, that his call from God was to return to the very remote people among whom he had spent his captivity. It may be that, having successfully seen a church flourishing among the *Ulaid*, he 'deserted' his ministry and went to the far west, not to a Christian community but to the heathen whose appeal had come to him in dreams. This is consistent both with his protestations in the *Confessio* and with the sense of mission he reveals in it.

He was obviously an extremely successful missionary. He also left writings, which were preserved in Armagh and elsewhere. When, in the sixth and seventh centuries, the Roman church organization that had been implanted in fifth-century Ireland came under great pressure from new ecclesiastical movements, its heirs fell back on all the arguments they could muster, including the prestige and the unique documents of Patrick – and successfully established the all-Ireland primacy of Patrick's church of Armagh, although in the process they found it necessary to reorganize themselves according to the monastic model of their innovating opponents.

The *Letter against the soldiers of Coroticus* and the *Confessio* are our only fifth-century documents from Ireland (indeed they are virtually unique for fifth-century Britain too) and it is understandable that this light in a great darkness should have shown up the figure of Patrick in such sharp relief. He was one of many bishops who worked in Ireland in that century, but most of the others are no more to us than names – where we possess even that much. There was great and early activity in the midlands, where, among others, the bishops Lommanus, Secundinus, Iserninus and Auxilius worked. There were early Christian bishops in the south, too, but such stories as survived of their doings have been so assimilated into old mythological tales as to obscure reality. But in many parts of Munster the early-medieval claims of Armagh on Patrick's behalf were resisted to the extent that, although the primacy of Armagh among Irish churches was finally acknowledged, it was yet held that there had been 'pre-Patrician' bishops in the south. Those chiefly remembered were Ibarus of Begerin (in Wexford harbour, in the extreme south of the territory of the *Lagin*), Declan of Ardmore, patron of the *Desi* of Waterford, Ailbhe of *Imblech Iubhair*, the chief evangelist of Munster, and Ciaran of *Saighir*. If Palladius, the first bishop of the Irish, came to the country from Gaul, it is most probable that the Christians to whom he ministered were somewhere along the south coast, and he may be concealed behind the identity of one of these 'pre-Patrician' saints. But Ailbhe shares a name and many attributes with a divine hound, and his church has a distinctly unchristian name – *Imblech Iubhair* – 'yew-centre'; Ibarus appears to be himself a yew-tree; Ciaran, according to his legend, had as his first 'monks' animals of the forest. Like water running into sand, Christianity ran into the absorptive capacities of a powerful pre-Christian tradition, and the saints were soon lost in the shadow of the gods.

One of the most interesting examples of this process is that of St Brigid of Kildare. Brigid was one of the high goddesses worshipped throughout the Celtic world, commonly in triple form. Her name means something like 'the high one' and is found in many Celtic name-formations (for example, the several tribes, in Gaul, Britain and elsewhere, known as

Brigantes). She was patron of poetry, music, learning, healing, and above all of fertility. One of the very early churches of the east midlands, originally known as *Civitas Brigidae*, was founded in Co. Kildare, probably as early as the fifth century. Its foundress is said to have been a bondswoman, Brigid, whose attributes are those of the great goddess. Her festival was on 1 February, the old Celtic quarterly feast of *Imbolc* the name may refer to 'belly' or 'bag', the feast marked, according to an early text, 'the beginning of the lactation of the ewes'[3] – corresponding to the Roman *Lupercalia*, the Hindu *Holi*. *Civitas Brigidae* may have been presided over by a female bishop, who gave way in due course to an abbess with a male bishop as her coadjutor. The oldest surviving *Life* of an Irish saint is that written about the middle of the seventh century by Cogitosus of Kildare, giving an account of Brigid. The *Life* is chiefly made up of reports of miracles, largely concerned with such matters as butter-making, but it also includes an account of Brigid's city (Kildare, as it was later known), a place of good order and safe-keeping. The great wooden church, adorned with carvings, paintings and hangings, was divided along its length, for men on one side, women on the other, and there were shrines for the bones of Brigid and her reputed coadjutor Bishop Conlaed. Many centuries later, just before 1200, Gerald the Welshman visited Kildare and observed the nuns of the double monastery tending a perpetual fire. He also gives a vivid description of a marvellously illuminated Gospel-book kept in the church.[4]

The process by which Christianity accommodated itself to Irish society and Irish society adopted Christianity can be traced only sketchily. Not only was the translation of Roman organization into a society of rural chiefdoms difficult in itself; it also occurred just as Roman order in the west fell apart. By the late fifth century the newly implanted church in Ireland was left to thrive or wither on its own.

What was Roman had prestige, and the rulers appear to have made no determined attempt to suppress the new religion by force. But there was plainly a period of very uneasy relations. The early bishops challenged, not the right to rule, but the divinity which the paramount rulers acquired through the ritual nuptials with goddesses of the land, consummated in ceremonies on the sacred high places. The churches challenged the holy hills. Patrick placed his on *Ard Macha*, the hill that is the twin of *Emhain Macha*: Sacellus founded *Basilica Sanctorum* on the very slope of *Cruachain*; Mel built his church of Ardagh on the counterslope of *Brí Léith*; Secundinus built Dunshaughlin (*Domhnach Shechnaill*, from *Dominica Secundini*) in full view of Tara; Iserninus founded his church on the hill at Kilcullen to look across at the ramparts of *Ailenn*, the great sacred site of the *Lagin*. Triumphalist poems were to celebrate the victory of the churches:

> *The great settlement of Tara has died with the loss of its princes;*
> *great Armagh lives on with its choirs of scholars . . .*
> *. . . The fortress of Cruachain has vanished with Ailill, victory's child;*
> *a fair dignity greater than kingdoms is in the city of Clonmacnois . . .*
> *. . . The proud settlement of Aillin has died with its boasting hosts;*
> *great is victorious Brigit and lovely her thronged sanctuary.*
> *The fort of Emain Machae has melted away, all but its stones;*
> *thronged Glendalough is the sanctuary of the western world . . .*[5]

The victory was by no means complete. The old gods and goddesses lived on. The Celtic quarterly festivals, a Christian interpretation hardly veiling their meaning, have continued to be observed right down to the present – *Imbolc* (celebrated as St Brigid's Day on the 1 February, with blessing of cattle and sheep, and charms nailed up in the house and byre to bring fertility), *Beltaine* (the beginning of summer on the 1 May, the celebration of which continued until recently), *Lugnasad* (the end of summer, marked on the last Sunday of July by hilltop gatherings to collect and eat berries), and *Samain* (the festival of the dead at the beginning of winter on the 1 November, marked by the rituals and divinations of Hallowe'en). Caesar tells us that the god most worshipped by the Celts was Mercury – supplying here for his readers the nearest Roman equivalent. The proper name is *Lug*, which appears in the common Celtic placename *Lugdunum* – giving *Laon, Lyon, Leiden*. Máire MacNeill has shown how widely, down to recent times, the festival of Lúg continued to be celebrated in immemorial ways, and how he appears in different guises – as the hero *Finn mac Cumaill*; often as St Patrick.[6] One of his enduring transformations in the folk tradition was as *Lug-chorpán* ('*Lug*-little body'), corrupted as *Luparchán* to provide Walt Disney and St Patrick's Day in New York with the familiar Leprechaun. The other gods and goddesses of the old pantheon were envisaged as living in the neolithic burial mounds – *Medb* in the great cairn that crowns Knocknarea over Sligo Bay, where Yeats was to celebrate her, *Aonghus* of the *Brugh* in the tumuli of the Boyne – and the goddesses of place, especially in Munster – *Áine, Danu, Aoibhell* and many others – continued to preside over their hilltops.

The few texts left us by the early Christian communities show that in the beginning they found it necessary to live a life apart from the pagan society around them, taking pains to avoid the various abominations – from their new point of view – which could casually occur in ordinary day-to-day life. They distinguished themselves in their dress, and even in the way they wore their hair. They had put off barbarian ways and become Romans. One of their concerns, it seems, was to collect the means by which they might redeem those of their number who were in slavery.

The early bishops attempted to transfer the Roman organization of the church to Ireland. As there were no cities, they took the *tuath* as the equivalent of the *civitas*, to form the base for a bishopric. The bishop's church then had to provide the nucleus for the new Christian *civitas*, and difficulties arose. Alienation of land was difficult within the Irish legal system where rights of private property were limited by the reversionary rights of the extended kin-group (the *fine*). There was strong pressure of custom towards regarding the ultimate holder of property as a *family*, backed by an elaborate system of sanctions and distraint which placed the enforcement of legal dues and obligations on the shoulders of guarantors and kin-groups.

Many churches, and later monasteries, were founded on waste, border, or marginal land. Otherwise there was considerable pressure to keep church property within the control of the kin-group from which the initial 'grant' had been made. There was also the problem of fitting the church into the social hierarchy. The clerics were fitted in by being rated as the equivalents in status of members of the *oes dána*: the honour-price of a bishop, like that of the highest grade of poet, made him the equal of a *rí*. As John Kelleher has pointed out, however, Christianity undoubtedly had a liberating effect within this archaic and conservative society by giving opportunities to people of low degree to break through some of the tyrannous restrictions of custom.[7] But, once the difficulties of accommodation had been overcome, it also provided advantages for the upper orders.

The church brought the Latin language, Latin letters and Roman law. Its clerics were, *ex officio* and of necessity, a learned class, literate, and transmitters of a tradition. They were the counterparts of the poets and historians and genealogists of the Irish *oes dána*. The *oes dána* could regard the clerics as interlopers and rivals, and for a time they did. There was some conflict between the two groups, but there is little evidence to show that this was either great or extensive. In the long run the *oes dána* accepted Christianity and took it over as their own preserve. In the process they altered it profoundly.

It may be that they were able to do this with relative ease because many of the missionary churches founded in the fifth century suffered a sharp decline. Events overseas must have weakened them considerably, by cutting off finances, in particular. (Patrick, in his *Confessio*, reckons that he has spent the price of *'fifteen men'* – much of it apparently in the form of what would nowadays be called 'protection money': he was compelled to hire the sons of chiefs to travel with him and provide safe conduct.) On the other hand, there must have been some reinforcement of personnel, but by people with a different disposition from that of the pioneering bishops. We have some evidence that numbers of Gauls and Britons, escaping the troubles of their own lands, were finding some peace, if not comfort, in Ireland in the late fifth and early sixth centuries. But in the 540s the churches were severely affected by a plague, often known as 'Justinian's plague', which spread across Europe from the east, and swept through the churches of Gaul, being carried to Ireland perhaps by some of these very refugees. At any rate, many churchmen in Ireland died, and the decline of the ecclesiastical organization implanted in Ireland was accentuated.

Then the religious fervour of renunciation of the world, which had happened so dramatically in Egypt and Syria two or three centuries earlier, swept through Ireland. Such renunciations had occurred from time to time in the past, among peoples of different cultures. The revulsion of fanatical believers at the luxury and corruption of Alexandria and Damascus may explain the origins of Christian monasticism, at least in part. The movement had reached Italy and Gaul by the fourth century, being sponsored by, among others, Martin, bishop of Tours. It may have reached Britain and Ireland by the end of the fifth century; but it is round about the time of Justinian's plague that it made its great impact.

Monasticism reached Ireland more or less in its eastern form. People became hermits or anchorites – retiring to live an isolated ascetic life of prayer. Or they became coenobites: retiring to live according to a strict rule of life in a community, a community however which only assembled together on certain occasions for common worship – otherwise the devotees spent most of their time apart. The Irish enthusiasts had no Alexandria to flee from, and the impulse seems to have been to renounce not that which was bad but that which was good – in search of better – to go 'on pilgrimage for Christ', seeking perfection in pure communion with God and attempting to purge away all desires and impulses which might distract from this end. This was done by mortification of both the flesh and the spirit.

The later monastic tradition ascribed the impulse for much of this movement to the founder of Clonard (in the midlands) – St Finian. He is said to have been the teacher of many of the sixth-century founders of monasteries. This is characteristic of the neat stylizing of medieval Irish scholars. The reality was more complex and confusing.

Some of the ascetics of this time seem to have been drawn to the cemeteries where the bones of 'saints' were deposited (often themselves ascetic hermits who had acquired a reputation for sanctity or wonder-working). The custom had developed on the continent in the earlier centuries of Roman persecution of Christianity, when the bodies or bones of the martyrs had been carefully preserved in special shrines, and revered by the faithful. There was also an old Celtic custom, attested archaeologically in Gaul and Britain and linguistically in Ireland, of frequenting and worshipping at shrines – small buildings set in formal enclosures. Pagan and Christian traditions blended together, and the *cella* (box or casket) containing the revered relics became the Irish *cell* – the little church which was essentially a *martyrium*, or tomb-reliquary – that was the centre round which many of the new communities formed, often within the enclosure of a pre-existing graveyard.

There was also the more formal founding of communities gathered together to follow a prescribed rule of life under discipline and obedience. A rule of a St Finian, probably Finian of Clonard, survives, and appears to be one of the earliest. It is essentially a penitential: a table of the penances due for transgressions of the law.[8] Columba (reputed to have been one of Finian's pupils), when he sailed to Iona in 563 with twelve disciples (emulating Christ and the Apostles), was at once undertaking a 'pilgrimage for Christ' (enduring the mortification of exile from his kin and *tuath*, beyond the sea) and setting about the formal foundation of a monastery.

The monastery was ruled by an abbot (the word, like the concept, borrowed from the Near Eastern deserts, means 'father') who was usually a presbyter but not a bishop. We find abbots (or abbesses) in the sixth century in those of the fifth-century bishops' churches that had prospered, and gradually the function of the bishop as governor, or overseer, of the Christian community falls into desuetude. Bishops continued to function, ordaining and consecrating, but the direction of church affairs, and particularly church temporalities, moved away from the pattern set within the Roman empire. Recent work, in Northern Ireland and in south-western Ireland, however, suggests that the groundwork laid in the missionary period continued to be the foundation of Christian practice through the country. While the monasteries, organized in federations, came to dominate the politics of the church, its main pastoral business probably continued to be conducted by *Einzelkirchen*, which were very numerous. The survey work suggests that almost everyone living in Ireland in, say, the eighth or ninth century was within walking distance of a small church.

Map 8 Early monasteries and church sites

The impulse to self-denial brought many of the monks into exile. In a society where there was not a clear concept, in most matters, of abstract and impersonal justice or of police in any sense, the well-being of each person was so bound up with status, with membership of tribal and kin groups, and of a particular *tuath*, that exile involved a stripping away of protection and rights and probably a psychological trauma. It appears to be so regarded in the texts. There were no citizens. There were no autonomous individuals: people belonged to families – although this dependence was mitigated by the universal custom of fosterage. Children were brought up, not by their parents but in another household – forming ties of affection and obligation which were regarded as closer than those of blood. Where kinship so dominated the life of the person, fosterage was an important counter-balance, helping to bind society together in networks of intimate relationships which often reinforced the bonds and obligations of clientship. The monastery itself was thought of as a family; but separation from foster- or kin-family, as the most severe of penances, was behind the impulse to exile.

This brought about a remarkable movement of Irish monks overseas. Later medieval legend elaborates the theme and celebrates the exile of Columba, telling that his vow would allow him never more to see Ireland; that when he first made land he climbed the nearest hill and saw the distant Irish summits low on the horizon, and so was obliged to return to his curragh and continue the voyage, until he reached Iona.

Columba was a member of the inner kin-group of the then dominant segment of the northern *uí Néill*, a lineage known as *Cenél gConaill*. His founding of Iona in 563 may be taken as marking the consummation of the union between Irish society and the church. He was a poet: he brought to monastic Christianity the full apparatus of the indigenous culture, its pride of blood, its long oral disciplines, its learning based on the mythologies and memories handed down by the *oes dána*. Like Augustine straining to accommodate within the one span of intellectual grasp Virgil and Christ, Columba represents and symbolizes almost perfectly the remarkable acculturation of sixth-century Ireland. With this development the *Romanitas* of the fifth-century church fell away, and something new came into being. This new religious form was to be checked – almost exactly a century later (664) – by representatives of the Roman imperial tradition in Christianity, but in the meantime the creative spark closed the arc.

Iona illustrates two developments: the formation of ecclesiastical families and the organization of monastic federations.

It is in the Inner Hebrides, an island separated by a sound from the large, rainy, mountainous and bewitchingly beautiful island of Mull, which in the sixth century was forested and filled with red deer. Iona is a small island, rimmed with beaches of white sand over which the clear green waters of the Atlantic roll, and round which large numbers of seals bask and swim as they did in Columba's day. Between them, Adomnán's *Life of Columba* and Boswell's *Journey to the Western Isles* convey something of the sense of unearthly peace in this place of remarkable atmosphere, which must help to explain something of the monastic impulse, the sense as the Dublin expression has it, of being 'in God's pocket'.

The island in 563 was just beyond the northern limit of the colony which had been established (since the fifth century) by the chiefdom of *Dál Riata*, part of the old federation dominated by the *Ulaid*. These had migrated across the North Channel, bringing with them the Irish (Gaelic) language which still survives in parts of the Highlands. The island was at the southern limit of Pictish territory, and the ruler of the Picts granted the site to Columba.

Not only was Columba himself a member of the inner kin-group of *Cenél gConaill*, but his successors for generations were to be drawn from the same kin. Many, but not all, monasteries followed a similar pattern. It provided a mechanism by which they were closely integrated into the control-systems of the chiefdoms. As the dominant kin-groups moved towards dynastic and aggrandizing politics by means of what is, in detail, a prolonged tedium of ferocious family quarrels, the monasteries served to keep records, to produce propaganda, to provide resource-bases in various ways. They substituted, to a limited extent, for a bureaucracy, and without at least the rudiments of a bureaucracy, developments towards state-formation must have been nugatory. They played an economic part too, both through improvements in production, and by introducing means of storage and accumulation of wealth into a primitive exchange system which hitherto had depended on the circulation of goods and commodities through rents, tributes, and formal gifts and loans made by superiors to inferiors. They early acquired the 'liberties' which were to play an important part in the evolution of medieval towns in Europe – in this instance through the protection of 'sanctuary' within the monastic vallum (emphasized by Cogitosus in his account of seventh-century Kildare).

In the same year that Iona was founded, or the year before, the other main lineage of the northern *uí Néill*, that known as *Cenél Eógain*, scored a major success, marking a stage in the expansion of the *uí Néill* as dominant overlords, through a victory over the *Ulaid* in the important battle of *Móin Daire Lothair*, in what is now Co. Derry. This was followed not only by the extension of overlordship at a distance, but by the movement south-eastward of families of *Cenél Eógain* to establish themselves in direct possession and control of lands in mid-Ulster. *Cenél gConaill* and *Cenél Eógain* claimed descent from two of Niall's sons, Conall and Eógan. Their bases were, respectively, Donegal west of Lough Swilly (*Tír Chonaill* – 'Conall's country') and the peninsula of Inishowen (*Inis Eógain* – 'Eógan's island'). When *Cenél Eógain* expanded to the Bann, the country west of Lough Neagh became known as *Tír Eóghain* ('Eógan's country'). These were the origins of the great medieval lordships of Tyrconnell and Tyrone. Columba's foundation, at this time, on the shifting frontiers of *Dál Riata* (the Irish kingdom which colonized Scotland), cannot be separated wholly from these events and developments.

From Iona, other monasteries were founded, and continued to remain under its jurisdiction, in Columba's time and later. Iona became the head of a great federation, which extended into Ireland (where the chief Columban monastery was Durrow in the south midlands) and, in the seventh century, into the Anglian kingdom of Northumbria.

Non-Columban monasteries also built up large federations. Among them, Clonmacnoise, on the left bank of the middle Shannon, on a spur of *Eiscir Riada*, isolated among the vast midland bogs, presents some contrasts to Iona. It was founded somewhat earlier and its true origin is more obscure, although there are legends. Its founder was Ciarán, a joiner's son, who perhaps began as a hermit. It seems that the monastery rapidly grew in size and activity around his tomb. Unlike Iona, Clonmacnoise was not monopolized by any kin-group, nor was it an institution of the nobility. It was plebeian, and its abbots for generations were drawn from the craft-tribes, subject-tribes and suppressed peoples of many parts of Ireland. As it grew to be an ecclesiastical city, extending for several kilometres along the Shannon shore, it developed a quite distinctive character, and became a major centre of learning and art. The kingdoms which developed on both sides of the river came to give it much patronage, and Clonmacnoise gained control over many other churches. The land immediately around it was very poor, however, and the monastery was in effect autonomous – lord of its own little *tuath* of *Delbna Bethra*, although there was a nominal secular chief. It shared with other metropolitan monasteries a function and a reputation as a burial place: medieval poems on Clonmacnoise list the sonorous names of the illustrious dead. These monastic sites in fact gradually took over from some of the old hilltop resorts as assembly places: instead of gathering among prehistoric burial mounds for meetings that were at once an expression of tribal unity and a celebration of immemorial funeral games, the people came on the major pilgrimage occasions to the shrines of the Christian dead. This has outlived the monasteries themselves, by many centuries, and such gatherings still occur annually on the 'patron day' at such places as St Mullins, in Co. Carlow.

There were many continuities from pagan to Christian custom and belief. Christianity opened up ways out of the drudgery of physical labour and low status for the humble. However, long before Christianity, religion had probably offered some measure of protection, as well as providing an 'opiate', or comfort, to the poor, by providing means for limiting the arbitrary oppressiveness of the powerful. The poets and druids who were clients of the rulers had access to otherworldly power through long training and discipline. But there is some evidence to suggest that some people of much lower degree could marshal a countervailing otherworldly force through their identification with unseen powers. This appears to have been the prerogative of certain subject tribes who were prolific in thaumaturges. For example, some of the groups who were subordinate to the *Ciarraige* of west Munster (who were themselves subordinate to the *Eóganachta*) seem to have supplied a remarkable number of holy men to the early church, most of them reputed to be monastic founders. Many of these have passed into the hagiographic storytelling in a guise which makes it very difficult to distinguish them from manifestations of gods such as Lúg or Brigid.

Witchcraft is quite often referred to, and is forbidden in the earliest extant set of regulations for a Christian community in Ireland. This suggests, again, the use – probably essentially defensive – of magical or otherworldly powers, and may indicate that (at the lower end of the social scale) women were oppressed. It is perhaps analogous to the social situation of ironworkers, a low caste who were protected by fear of their mysterious powers. An old travellers' charm, superficially christianized in the form of a *lorica*, or prayer for protection, attributed to St Patrick, indicates some of the fears of the mysterious and the unknown which almost certainly served partly as a mechanism of social control:

> . . . I summon between us today all these powers against every merciless power that threatens my body and soul, against the prophecies of false prophets, against the dark ordinances of paganism, against the false ordinances of heretics, against the encompassment of idolatry, against the spells of women and smiths and druids, against every skill that corrupts man's body and soul.
>
> Christ be my guard today against poisoning, against burning, against slaying, so that I may have great reward . . . [9]

Fear of the 'mob' expressed in more straightforward ways also occasionally surfaces in the texts, which are almost exclusively concerned with the preoccupations of the upper and learned classes.

Monasteries varied greatly in size, social function and character. They catered for a range of impulses and needs. Many monks retired from the world and its possessions and praised instead, with gentle irony, nature and the provisions of Providence (note again the ideal community – one and twelve – Christ and the apostles):

> . . . *Six pairs beside myself praying forever to the King who moves the sun.*
> *A beautiful draped church, a home for God from Heaven, and bright lights*
> *above the clean white Gospels.*
> *One household to visit for care of the body, without lust or weakness or thought*
> *of evil.*
> *The husbandry I would do and choose without concealment is fragrant leeks and*
> *hens and speckled salmon and bees.*
> *Enough of clothing and food from the king of fair fame, and to be sitting for a*
> *while and contemplating God in every place.*[10]

A version of such a monastery may still be seen on the remote Skellig rock, beyond the headlands of Kerry, where, 200 metres above the Atlantic swell, six stone huts face two tiny oratories and a rough-hewn stone cross in a little enclosure which has long been deserted save for guillemots, stormy petrels and puffins. More commonly (as on the excavated site of *Inis Cealtra*, an island in Lough Derg on the lower Shannon) such a monastery would consist of round mud-walled thatched houses, and a wooden or mud-walled oratory or two, within a fenced or stockaded enclosure.

There were also, however, much larger settlements, on a medieval urban scale, like Armagh, Clonmacnoise, Kildare, Glendalough, Lismore and others. These tended to become quite complex in their functions and to play an increasingly important part in the affairs of the community at large. They housed wonder-working shrines; they catered for pilgrims who thronged to them in large numbers on the major festivals; they had houses and reception centres for the rulers who patronized them and who spent certain parts of the year in residence; they had craftsmen and artists manufacturing or repairing a large variety of objects and equipment; they controlled extensive lands and tenantry; they provided accommodation for travellers and sanctuary for refugees; they produced copies of manuscripts of both religious and secular texts and supplied schooling for students, some of whom came from overseas; they imported wine and oil necessary for the Christian services and perhaps other goods and commodities; they served as barns and warehouses and places of safe-keeping for valuables.

Figure 2   Lettering from the 'Cathach' of St Columba (Latin manuscript
of Psalms)
Source: Royal Irish Academy Library.

This type of monastery soon came under lay control, and the monks and nuns who were devoted to prayer and penance lived in separate enclaves *within* the monastery, sometimes by an irony withdrawing some little distance from it. This may have happened at Clonmacnoise. It seems to have happened at Glendalough, where there was by the ninth or tenth century a walled town, with a 'great' church and the shrine of St Kevin (the hermit founder) at the mouth of the valley which gives the monastery its name. Withdrawn in other parts of the valley are small church enclosures: places of prayer removed from the place of ecclesiastically stimulated business. By the eighth century such secularized monasteries were beginning to behave like secular chiefdoms, and were mustering their clients for war in quarrels about borders, lands and rent.

But in the sixth century, while the early monastic fervour was at its height, the impulse to penitential exile brought many Irish monks to Britain and Europe. By that time the imperial system had quite broken down in the west. The taxes were not collected, the roads and aqueducts not maintained, and many of the well-to-do had deserted the cities for country estates or mountain refuges. The Germans had moved in, annexing a generous share of the land and setting up their barbarian successor-kingdoms to rule over the former provinces. The pagan Franks accepted Christianity *en masse* at the end of the fifth century, and it was largely to their lands that many of the Irish came a little less than a hundred years later.

The best known of these monks is another Columba, usually called however, from the Irish diminutive of his church-name, Columbanus. He came from Bangor, St Comgall's monastery on the south shore of Belfast Lough, and he worked in eastern France, in Switzerland and in northern Italy. Some of his letters and other writings are extant: he is the first Irishman whose mind we can get to know in any direct way. He exemplifies some of the character which the alumni of the earliest Irish monasteries were to acquire on the continent. He was strict in his own life, stern and unbending as an Old Testament prophet in his dealing with the shortcomings of those in high places, headstrong, argumentative and very difficult to deal with. His letters, to Gregory the Great and others, show him to have been widely read – presumably in the school of Bangor, since he was not a young man when he left there – and his Latin is vigorous and good. Indeed, he makes it plain that he rates the scholars of Ireland – which he conventionally locates 'at the ends of the earth' – above those of the continent. This arises in the course of a controversy about the calculation of the date of Easter and other moveable feasts, about which there was much dispute at the time.

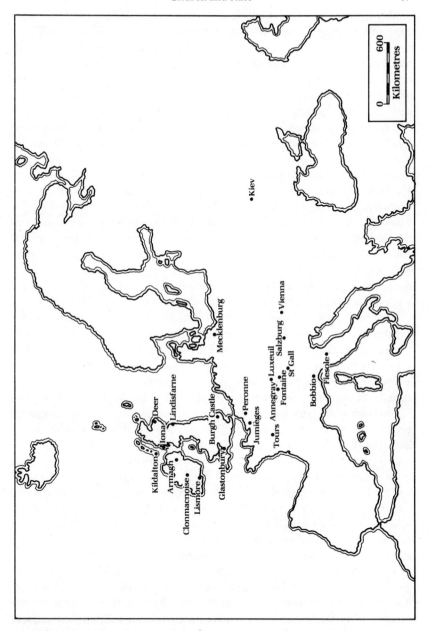

Map 9 Expansion of Irish Christianity: location of some Irish bishops, church foundations etc., from sixth to twelfth century

Monks like the two Columbas made a deep impression on their contemporaries, coming as they did from 'the ends of the earth' but displaying the huge self-confidence of people produced by a society which was enjoying the excitement of change and discovery in many areas at once. The Venerable Bede points out that they practised what they preached – they were genuinely uninterested in the things of this world – and had a moral advantage. But their enthusiasm and their impatience with certain conventions and certain kinds of social discipline made them most unamenable to the kind of order which had been imposed on Europe by the Romans and which was acceptable to the Germans now dominating western Europe and Britain. Their spiritual raids on the old Roman world were effective but stormy. In England, the southward spread of the Irish church was halted and reversed at the synod of Whitby in 664 (where the Roman style, reintroduced to England by St Augustine of Canterbury at the end of the previous century met the contrasting Irish ecclesiastical culture on the Easter issue). Irish monks continued for centuries to be welcome in Europe for their learning, but Irish monasticism gave way to the much more sober and practical version which followed the rule of the sixth-century order established by Benedict of Nursia in Italy.

The metropolitan monasteries in Ireland were forcing-houses for cultural development. The Latin letters introduced in the fifth century had evolved by the late sixth into a beautiful and clear insular script. Our oldest surviving example of it is a small Latin manuscript of the Psalms, known as the *Cathach* of St Columba, which was penned (possibly by Columba) shortly before 600. This script is an ancestor, by way of the Hiberno-Saxon miniscules which influenced the Carolingian book-hands that were revived by Italian Renaissance printers in preference to the Gothic black-letter, of the type-faces we generally use today. No doubt for a number of generations as Christian communities increased in number the scribes were fully occupied meeting the needs of the altars, with copies of the Gospels and of the Psalms especially. Then they began copying other liturgical and Christian texts. The native scholars devised a Latin orthography for the writing of Irish, and some of the lore which had been transmitted orally began to be written down, either in full or in mnemonic abbreviation. Not all of this writing was done in the monasteries, but most was.

The comings and goings of the monks as the monastic federations spread gave rise to a period of intensive intercourse between different cultures. The chief contacts were across the North Channel. Bede, writing in the early eighth century, says that in his time there were four nations and five languages in Britain. These were the Irish, the Picts, the Britons, the Anglo-Saxons, with their languages, to which was added the language of

Figure 3   Skellig buildings

the church, Latin. The Latin language itself affected the Irish language, but the Irish tradition of oral learning also affected Latin writing, particularly in verse. Even in what is now extant there is a considerable volume of Latin verse written by Irishmen from the sixth century onwards, and the verse produced in Irish is remarkable both in quantity and in quality. Some was composed by the professional poets, some by amateurs – monks whose main task was copying canonical texts but who occasionally relieved the monotony of this in creative expression.

The churches kept records. These included tables of Easter dates, which seem to have suggested the noting of occasional important events, lists of people who were to be prayed for, and, in due course, annals or chronicles. Iona seems to have maintained some sort of chronicle from its foundation. Bangor became an early centre of annal-writing and chronological computation. Chronicles like those of Isidore of Seville and Bede came to be copied, and then elaborate Irish chronicles were reconstructed by synchronism, often strained and artificial. But a historiography developed, drawing on the Bible, on the external chronicles which were based partly on Graeco-Roman history, on Irish myth and legend, and on what could be assembled from the meagre records of the churches. From this there emerged synthetic histories that were to be of long-enduring import: they were to be re-synthesized in the seventeenth century and to furnish the ideology of modern nationalism with its essential fuel. In the meantime, they served a different purpose: to help create a state.

The interplay of cultures stimulated great activity in the arts and crafts. The record here is imperfect. Woodcarving, wall-painting, textiles, leatherworking, have left little. Metalworking, stonecarving and manuscript-painting are left to represent for us an important part of the imagination and perception of the age. They serve as a corrective. Perhaps the leading characteristics of the literature are an all-pervasive unsentimental irony, the simple epic unqualified acceptance of birth, life and death, and an intense preoccupation with *wit* – the precise, exact, subtle use and juxtaposition of words within a rigidly conventional framework. The visual work shows us something else: an avoidance equally of representation and abstraction, and obsession with intricacy of pattern, drawn out of or returning to, nature, a respect for what *is*.

The carapace of imperial order in which Christianity reached the far West was dissolved, to be replaced by an order that was neither rigid nor wholly organic: the obsessive repetitions that are characterised by the serpentine writhings and coilings of Celtic visual forms. The order comes from within: this is the key to what is 'Celtic' in Irish art of the early Christian period. It cannot be imposed by T-square and set-square, or marked off by numbers like the lay-out of a Roman camp, nor even guided by a development of harmonic modules like a Greek entablature: it spirals out from the heart of the design; it expresses neither essence nor being but endless becoming, and the artist must have been as fully engaged in every veering of a line as in the planning of his overall design. A fair comparison is the calligraphy of the Far East. The master calligrapher can charge and poise his brush, stare at and absorb the blank page, and then swiftly place the right shape in the right balance in the right place. This the early Irish artist could do – with the Chi-Rho Monogram of Christ, for example, on an unsquared slab of stone, as in the Inis Cealtra grave-marker.[11]

The culture was far from isolated, however, and was subject to repeated impulses of *Romanitas*, as this revived on the continent. Irish scholars as well as Anglo-Saxon played a part in the Carolingian renaissance, and Carolingian influences are manifest in, among other things, the stone-carvings (mainly in the distinctively insular form of High Crosses) of the ninth and tenth centuries. The powerful and puritanical reform movement within the monasteries, that of the *Célí Dé* ('God's clients') which began in the eighth century, had among its objects resistance to foreign influences – although the movement itself probably owed something to them. By the ninth century, important church buildings were being constructed in stone, and one of the most remarkable achievements – and one of the least noticed – of the Irish craftsmen was the production of fine-jointed, exquisitely tooled mortared stone churches which are on the one hand an extraordinary petrification of the native tradition of modular wooden building; on the other, a brilliant pastiche of Roman ashlar. Similar originality in imitation was to be shown in the way the Carolingian free-standing *campanile* was to be borrowed, at about the end of the ninth century, to produce the distinctive Irish *cloicthech* ('bell-house') – the 'Round Tower' which still marks so many of the monastic sites.

The chiefdoms of the late prehistoric Celtic world met the challenge of Christianity because they had to. Other aspects of the Roman world had appealed to them, as to all the barbarian overlords outside the empire. Roman wealth and power called for emulation as well as exploitation. Christianity was a more doubtful boon: in principle it challenged the wealth and power of empire. It released dangerous social forces in Ireland. But, as it separated from the memory of the empire, it offered great potential advantages to the ruling groups through its religious prestige, which eclipsed that of the old hilltop sanctuaries, and through its documentary and organizational techniques. We find parallel desires on the part of upper-class laity and clergy for a unified, orderly, Christian kingdom of Ireland.

Adomnan, abbot of Iona at the end of the seventh century, writing the *Life* of his kinsman and predecessor Columba, refers to Columba's contemporary Diarmait mac Cerbhaill, king of Tara, as 'ordained by the authority of God as ruler of all Ireland', This expression[12] may be no more than rhetorical, but Columba himself ordained, or anointed, Aedán mac Gabráin as king of Scottish Dál Riata. This was in the sixth century. It is plain that by the late seventh and early eighth centuries politically minded ecclesiastical writers like Adomnán and Bede found it highly desirable that the ruck of petty chiefdoms should be superseded by some higher – and more highly organized – authority. They encouraged the notion of an 'over-king' with real capacity to govern, rather than a paramount chief acknowledged by desultory tribute and expendable hostages. We find occasional use of the term *imperator* – 'emperor' – to convey this sense of overriding authority and separate it from the much weaker sense of chiefdom which writers of that time read into a word like *rex* or *rí*.

By the eighth century the notion of the Christian kingdom was well established – the model had been provided by Constantine. The king acted as the person charged by God with authority to rule and as protector of the church and promoter of its purposes. He would maintain good order not – as in the old pagan tradition – by inherent divinity which ensured the co-operation of the Otherworld and of the elements of nature – but by being directly responsible and consecrated to God. This not only paralleled what was happening outside Ireland, but also reflected internal developments. By the time the great body of customary law came to be written down, the tracts found it necessary to distinguish three grades of *rí* – the chief who was head of a single *tuath*, the chief who received tribute from others, and the *rí* who was head of a 'fifth', or province and enjoyed the special prestige of paramountcy. By the sixth century it is clear that the autonomy of the *tuath* was breaking down, as the over-chiefs not only took tribute from it but were beginning to interfere in its internal affairs – sometimes to the extent of intruding members of the leading kin-groups of the superior chiefdom into positions of dominance in the inferior. This is the process just noted in connection with the expansion of *Cenél Eógain* families into mid-Ulster in the late sixth century. By the eighth century true kingdoms had emerged, with rudimentary structures of government.

By the same date, relations between the federations of monasteries and the counter-federation which the pre-monastic churches had formed for their own protection (adopting the monastic system itself in the process) had been settled in a general way through a series of compromises after prolonged controversy and conflict. The primacy of Armagh, in antiquity and prestige, was generally acknowledged (and its founder, Patrick, was accordingly being fitted into the legendary history of churches all over the island), but certain other churches were allowed a regional or provincial primacy: Kildare, for example, having made its own claim to primacy in the seventh century, yielded to Armagh but continued to claim a special position in Leinster; Ardmore similarly yielded to Emly in Munster.

This hierarchical rearrangement of the churches was carried out in close association with the emerging dynastic politics of the provincial kings. There is also an economic background to the pressures which were building up in the ecclesiastical and secular politics. From about AD 600 – that is, almost exactly contemporary with the expansion of monasticism – there is evidence for new agricultural practices, involving intensified cultivation and the colonization of further land. We may suspect that the monasteries, which for reasons to do with their internal organization and their ascetic direction had a somewhat different economy from the lay farms, played a large part in bringing about this change. It is associated with the introduction of the mouldboard plough, almost certainly from Anglo-Saxon England. This required a team of oxen to pull it; it was most efficiently used in strip cultivation, the strip being as long as the team could pull the plough without pausing to rest (the 'furrow-long' or 'furlong'); strip cultivation in turn tended to lead to an open-field system of one kind or another. A four-ox team seems to have become usual.

The woodlands now began to diminish at a faster rate – to the extent that the laws were required to protect the more valuable trees. We must envisage an expanding population, pushing tillage and grazing areas towards the limit of suitable land. Land accordingly will have become more valuable, and the pressure from above to find accommodation for the prolific ruling families (who practised polygyny and grew in numbers at a very fast rate) will have borne heavily on the lower orders. Times of such expansion are often very bad for the poor, and we have quite a number of hints in the texts of an enduring and quite bitter antagonism and hostility between upper and lower orders.

Cashel, probably from its origins the centre of a Christian overlordship, was an obvious claimant of the Christian *imperium* which was being envisaged. It seems that some efforts were made to put forward such a claim. But it was very difficult for a central power to arise in Munster because of the weakness of the obedience traditionally commanded by the occupier of the paramountcy and of the looseness of the succession system. The widely dispersed chiefdoms of the *Eóganachta* – among whom there was a strong east–west hostility – were all eligible to provide the provincial lord at Cashel, and indeed on occasion an outsider was admitted.

An early eighth-century ruler, Cathal mac Finguine, was to be remembered as an ideal king of Cashel. He seems (although the interpretation of the annal is not certain) to have issued the 'Law of Patrick' in Munster in 737, bringing unity to the church; and he also appears to have attempted to have the supremacy of Cashel recognized throughout Ireland.

If he did so attempt, he failed; but one of his successors a century later came close to it. Feidlimid mac Crimthainn was a *céle Dé*, a member of the ascetic order within the monasteries that had become a force in the second half of the eighth century. The movement of the *célí Dé* was to some extent a millennial one, devoted to the reading and interpretation of the Bible, preaching a strict withdrawal from the world, denouncing the wealth, power and worldly pretensions of the great established monasteries, a fraternity of evangelizing *sadhus*. It seems odd perhaps to find one of them embarking on a career like Feidlimid's but he may just possibly have seen his own violence as being like that of Christ when he drove the moneychangers from the Temple.

Feidlimid was a member of the *Eóganacht* of Cashel, a branch of the *Eóganachta* which had not held the paramountcy for two centuries. He was also an ecclesiastic, who appears to have seized the abbacies of both Cork and Clonfert before he was inaugurated king at Cashel in 820. For the next twenty-seven years, until his death, he campaigned furiously to impose his will on the great churches of the whole island and on the *uí Néill* overlords of the northern half. He plundered and burned Kildare, Clonfert, Durrow, and Clonmacnoise (repeatedly), attempted to force his own candidates on the greater churches, including Armagh, and harshly maltreated his opponents in these endeavours. He too proclaimed the 'Law of Patrick' in Munster. According to the Munster annals, the *uí Néill* kings of Tara submitted and acknowledged him as 'king of Ireland', but the other annals contain no such admission.

The *Annals of Ulster* describe one or two rulers of earlier times as *rex Hiberniae* – *uí Néill* dynasts of the seventh century; but, as F. J. Byrne points out, these annals at this stage are largely dependent on a chronicle compiled at Iona, whose late seventh-century abbot Adomnán had an interest: 'it will be clear that the annalistic testimony to the kingship of Ireland enjoyed by Domnall and Loingsech cannot be treated as independent of Adomnán's own ideas'.[13] The *uí Néill* chief who became king of Tara in 797, Áed mac Néill of Ailech, came to be known as Áed *oirdnide* – Áed 'the ordained' – an indication that he was probably the first of the *uí Néill* dynasts to be ecclesiastically anointed as king. It has been suggested that this took place at an assembly at *Dún Cuair* in 804, presided over by the abbot of Armagh. At any rate by the ninth century the idea of an *imperium* of Ireland was taking shape.

In the meantime, at the close of the eighth century, raids on the coasts began, by shiploads of Scandinavians who appeared out of the blue, pillaged what they could, and disappeared again. The first recorded was in 795, but Anglo-Saxon sources tell of similar raids on the North Sea coasts of England a dozen years earlier. The evidence suggests that the raiders who appeared off Ireland came mainly from the region around the fjords of Stavanger and Bergen in western Norway. The pressure of a rising population in Scandinavia had forced the cultivation of marginal lands and stimulated, among the seafarers of the coasts, attempts to colonize elsewhere and movements of adventurous fortune-seeking. There had for some time been colonization of Shetland and Orkney. Late in the eighth century it seems that population pressure increased, as did political pressure on the local lords from centralizing monarchies, and at the same time the development of ship design and construction and of weaponry made far-ranging freebooting expeditions possible. From different parts of Scandinavia, adventures of different kinds were organized, by great rulers on a large scale, or by independent *jarls* on a small. The Danes were in conflict with the Carolingian empire and were probing the English coasts across the North Sea.

The first raids came from the direction of the Hebrides and affected mainly the northern and western coasts of Ireland. Monasteries and churches appear to have been the chief sufferers. The attacks were at first isolated and sporadic, exploratory and opportunistic in their character. For half a century they were not much more than an occasional and alarming nuisance – although they did have a major impact on the very exposed metropolitan monastery of Iona. It was attacked in 795, 802 and 806, suffering severe loss of life: in 807 a major part of the community, bearing the relics of Columba, moved to Kells in the Irish midlands to found a new monastery.

Towards the middle of the ninth century, the Scandinavians, exploration over, began to organize expeditions on a much larger scale, sending fleets down into the Irish Sea, establishing defended base-camps, and mounting formidable raids inland. Although they plundered freely, it is probable that their main object was to win land and that they were organized under leaders who hoped to establish profitable principalities. They were partly successful and made settlements of varying density and size along the east and south coasts from Belfast Lough round to Cork. They also attempted settlements in Donegal, in west Connacht, and round the Shannon mouth.

The military equipment of the Vikings was much superior to that of the

Irish, but their initial advent was at a time when rising population, the consolidation of dynasties, and the growing struggle for power, privilege and wealth within the country, were already leading to more sustained and organized warfare in Ireland than the small-scale conflicts of the past. The Irish dynasts quickly learned from the Vikings, and learned also how to make use of them as mercenary allies. Attempts at land-taking were strenuously, and on the whole successfully, resisted, but there was a period of intensified warfare from the 840s until the 880s.

The main Norse settlement was made around Dublin Bay, and here, in Fingal – the 'country of the foreigners' – the Vikings set up a petty kingdom, which, however, soon directed its ambitions outwards towards Scotland and northern England. By the end of the ninth century the drive towards settlement in Ireland was spent. The Irish Vikings began moving out, to seek lands elsewhere – beyond the Atlantic, in Faroes, Iceland and, ultimately, Greenland (they found Irish hermits, whom they called '*papae*', before them), or across the Irish Sea in northern England.

A new Scandinavian movement into Ireland began early in the tenth century, at a stage when the Vikings were finding that their initial advantage had been eroded in various parts of Europe: it was no longer easy to move at will into the countries of western Europe and take the land they wanted. This second wave of attacks, by people who came largely not directly from Scandinavia but from the Viking colonies, resulted in the establishment of a number of trading towns. These were confined to the southern half of Ireland. The *uí Néill* of the north showed resilience and managed to check the *Ostmen* (as the Scandinavians were now coming to be called) in the course of the century. The *Eóganachta* suffered disaster in 908, as they made a determined effort to assert Munster's claim to dominion. In the battle of *Belach Mugna* in that year, Cormac mac Cuilennáin, king-bishop of Cashel, was killed in a campaign against Leinster, along with many *Eóganacht* chiefs. Early in the century the Ostmen developed their trading centres in Dublin, Wexford, Waterford, Cork and Limerick, of which the more important were Dublin and Limerick. In Ireland, as in Russia, this was the chief legacy of Viking settlement. Elsewhere in Europe and beyond they had succeeded in winning land – extensive areas in England came to be known as the Danelaw, and a large territory in western France came to be known, after these Northmen, as Normandy.

A king of Tara, Niall Glúndubh, was killed early in the tenth century fighting the Dublin colony. Another king, Maelsechnaill, of the midland branch of the *uí Néill*, crushed the Dublin Ostmen at Tara in 980, and brought them under heavy tribute. In the meantime the *Dési*, former

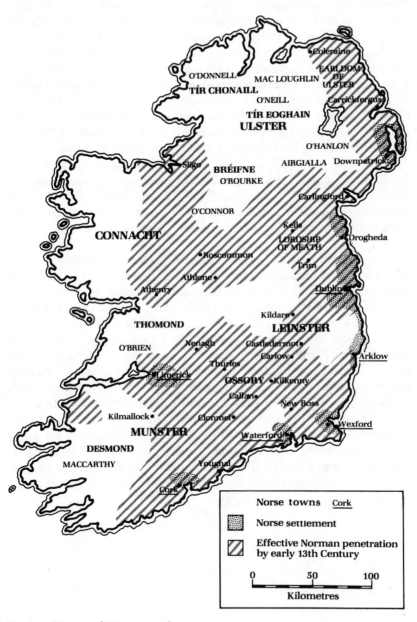

Map 10 Norse and Norman settlement

vassals of the *Eóganachta* of Munster, who had moved across the lower Shannon, took advantage of the *Eóganacht* weakness after 908. Outsiders until now in the rotation of paramountcy among the Munster chiefs and kin-groups, they aggressively pursued a new dynastic ambition. Known as *Dál Cais*, this little chiefdom in east Clare successively seized the kingship of Cashel, defeated the Limerick Ostmen and sacked their city, challenged Maelsechnaill and forced the submission, *seriatim*, of all the main lineages in Ireland. This was carried out under the leadership of their chief Cennetig, his son Mathgamhain, who was murdered at the behest of the *Eóganachta*, and Mathgamhain's brother Brian, known as Brian Boru. In the course of a long life Brian succeeded in forcing the submission of one dynasty after another. He was acknowledged as king at Cashel; Maelsechnaill submitted to him at Tara in 1002; one by one the separate chiefdoms and dynasties of the north yielded. He brought all the Ostman towns under control and tribute. He favoured and visited Armagh, where his secretary recorded the visit of *imperator Scottorum* – 'emperor of the Irish'.

In a sense, therefore, Brian achieved what had been envisaged for at least two centuries, a unified kingdom of Ireland. But only in a sense: it was achieved by receiving unwilling submission and grants of hostages from one paramountcy after another, and once Brian's presence (and that of his army) was withdrawn, his control broke down. The province of Leinster revolted, aided by the Dublin Ostmen, who found assistance among their kinsfolk in the Northern Isles and in Man. Brian, deserted by almost all of those who had yielded to him, supported only by the Munster levies and one or two from east Connacht, marched on Dublin and, outside the city, on Good Friday, 23 April 1014, fought the battle of Clontarf. In a long day's fighting he defeated the Leinster–Ostman alliance, but in the aftermath of the battle he was killed by fleeing Vikings, and the heavy losses to his family and supporters were such as to weaken *Dál Cais* seriously for a generation. The failure of the increasingly violent struggle to establish centralized power was to destabilize Irish society for centuries.

4 *The sword-land*

Clontarf revealed, not for the first time, the fragility of dynastic politics: wiping out enough members of a family in a single murderous affray could have long-term consequences. The meteoric rise of *Dál Cais*, from obscurity to the near-hegemony of Ireland in half a century, was checked. A 'high-kingship' available to the sword now appealed to every provincial dynast with ambition. What the contender had to do was, starting young, to fight his way doggedly through a daunting series of conflicts, with rivals, enemies and opponents in his own family, his own *tuath*, his own province, and the other provinces, establishing his dominance at each stage in turn. There was no other way. The *imperium* did not exist in law, and there was no customarily established succession to it. Brian's failure (for such it ultimately was) to win all Ireland by right of force had left the winning tantalizingly possible and infinitely disputable. So, in a time of stress and fundamental social change, the energies of five generations of dynasts, and a great part of the resources they could muster, were devoted to chasing this will-o'-the-wisp. The scholars rewrote the history to invent an immemorial 'high-kingship' and puff up the dynasts with the bombast they required for their vain endeavour. They attempted to supply what the law lacked: a set of rules by which the winner of the bloody game could be identified.

In many respects the small Ostman colonies, centred on the trading towns of Dublin, Limerick, Waterford, Wexford and Cork, now took over the shaping of Irish affairs. They were not politically powerful. On the contrary, they were tributary to Irish kings. But they were the dynamic element in society, founding a money economy (which, however, they were unable to maintain), engaging in an expanding trade, the staple of which was slaves, mainly from Britain, and increasingly influencing Ireland's communications with the outside world. Better supply-bases than the monastic cities, they could provide the provincial kings with silver (another staple of Ostman trade) and some gold, and with a technology which transformed warfare from a series of occasional brief brutal encounters between chiefs and their clients into sustained campaigns, spreading misery much more widely. The towns had fleets which were hired out for warfare; the provincial kings learned to use ships, coastwise and on the rivers and lakes, in their manoeuvres. They also seem to have learned from the Viking wars the usefulness of horses, mounting soldiers for swift movement: heavy horses were imported (some from Wales), again through the Ostman towns.

Dublin became an important centre in the eleventh century. It was well situated both for taking a share of the long-distance trade which linked the northern lands with western France and the Mediterranean, and for conducting business across the Irish Sea. English coins had begun to circulate in the tenth century; towards the end of the century Dublin struck its own, exact copies of the current English silver pennies obviously primarily for use in England. The Norse-speaking city paid its rents to the provincial Irish kings who were from time to time dominant, but its main business was with England, and its connections by kinship and alliance were with Man and the Isles. Wexford and Waterford also conducted a busy trade across the channel, so that communications of all kinds became much more regular.

Excavations in Dublin have revealed something of the life of the Ostman town and have shown how commodious was its trade and manufacture. The bay had first been semi-permanently occupied by the Vikings in the middle of the ninth century. Their cemetery of that time, accidentally discovered in the making of a nineteenth-century railway cutting, was inland from the site of the later trading town, but their defended base may have been down river. It is probable that the town began early in the tenth century with the construction of a *longphort* – to use the Irish term – a 'ship-camp', at the point where the river Liffey begins to widen out, and near the lowest ford. There was a sequence of three earthen ramparts, marking two extensions of the city area, and then, in the eleventh century, a further extension was bounded by a stone wall. Within the expanding wall, the city was built of wood; its buildings and layout resembling those of the trading towns which had developed at commercially strategic points in the Scandinavian homeland in the Viking age. The buildings, gable-ends presented to the wood-paved sidewalks and streets, were situated within fenced yards and, internally, were subdivided, with cubicles, sleeping-benches, porches and drainage systems. Workshops lined the streets and a variety of goods and implements was manufactured on the spot, apart from those which were imported. Some time after the middle of the eleventh century, the fine metalworkers of Dublin – and perhaps other Ostman settlements – began producing goods for the hinterland. By the

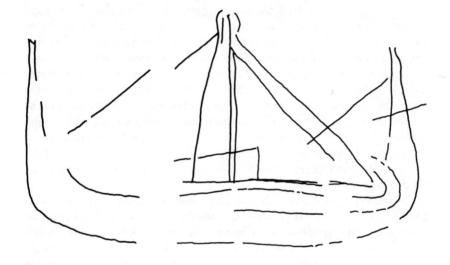

Figure 4   Viking ship. After a carving on a wooden plank *c.* AD 1100, found at
Winetavern Street, Dublin
Based on a photograph from the National Museum of Ireland.

end of the century Scandinavian styles and taste were exercising a dominant influence on Irish artwork produced in such native centres as Clonmacnoise.

Ostman Dublin was a Christian city, as were the other towns. The first Viking raiders had been worshippers of Odin and Thor but by the later ninth century most of the Scandinavians had at least included Christ among their gods. The new wave of arrivals in the early tenth century again included many pagans but by the end of that century the townsmen were mainly Christian (which no more prevented them from continuing a folk-cult of Thor than Christianity prevented the Irish from continuing a cult of Lug). Sitric, who was ruler of Dublin at the time of Clontarf, founded the city's cathedral, Christchurch. Here a problem arose. The Ostmen did not wish to fit into the Irish monastic organization of the church. Perhaps because their countrymen at home in Scandinavia had been brought to Christianity under English auspices, they looked to the English church – organized on regular European lines – and sent priests (who often have Irish rather than Norse names) to Canterbury for consecration as bishops. This, like the Easter controversy of the sixth and seventh centuries, drew attention to discrepancies between Irish ecclesiastical practice and that of the rest of western Europe. There arose within the church, largely from the Ostman initiative, a powerful pressure to change Irish practices to conform to those of the European church. The pressure of course met the obstacle of vested interest: the Irish monastic system was integrated into the dynastic political system.

There were some signs of change. Brian Boru's interest in the church, as Donncha Ó Corráin has pointed out,[1] was largely political, but he was an innovator, and was attempting to institute certain uniformities. He himself may or may not be responsible, but it seems that changes in the liturgy began in his time – poorly documented, but revealed, for example, in the addition of chancels to the numerous stone churches built or enlarged in the eleventh century. A missal, which contains a prayer for Brian and his army, appears to introduce the (southern English) Old Sarum rite of the Mass.[2]

England, like Ireland, had been troubled by political turmoil and dynastic conflict. In Brian's time it had become part of a Danish empire; then under the Anglo-Saxon kings instability continued, from disputed succession and renewed Scandinavian threats. The Irish annals note King Harold's victory at Stamford Bridge in 1066, when a further Scandinavian invasion was defeated, but fail to record his forced march to the south immediately afterwards and his defeat and death at Hastings. The duke of Normandy, William, effectively asserted his claim to the English kingdom, now more or less unified, and within the space of less than a generation had achieved a uniquely consolidated dominion, parcelling out England among his Norman and Breton followers, who conquered the country with him but, individually, owed their lands to him. The Normans took over the whole apparatus, such as it was, of English government, including the church, which they also staffed with their own men. Derived from the Viking settlement in France under Rollo, they formed a caste (not a 'race', for they were ecumenically exogamous) which specialized in the winning of land by proficiency in warfare. The conquest of England was probably their most successful enterprise. Apart from military technique there was really no 'Norman' culture. But the thoroughness of the Conquest imposed on England, for many generations, a social superstructure whose language and manners were those of northern France.

In Ireland no such clean sweep occurred. There were several rudimentary states – the provinces. None could cope adequately with the archaic subdivisions, internal feuds and long-remembered precedents that made succession to leadership a prolonged, tedious, bloody and precarious business. Each in turn succeeded in producing a king or kings who could, finally, win through by this process and gain control of a province. But the 'high-kingship' beckoned; each strong provincial ruler aimed at it and came into conflict with the other provinces.

When Brian Boru was killed, his predecessor, Maelsechnaill, who had submitted to him in 1002, resumed his kingship of Tara until he died in 1022. Then the weakness in the current political development was revealed. The provinces had superseded the archaic politico-social system of multitudinous chiefdoms grouped very loosely under vaguely paramount lords. Provincial kings now intervened directly in the affairs of all parts of their provinces; and they aimed at keeping the kingship in their own families. They also competed with other families for the provincial kingship and with other provincial rulers for the 'high-kingship'. At every stage of competition the arbiter was force. The competition now became a free-for-all throughout the whole island, among the lords who could make any sort of show of royal ancestry; among the overlordships which could make even the most tenuous claim to provincial or dominant status in the remotest past.

Two of Brian's sons who survived Clontarf contended for the kingship of Munster. One, Donnchad, had the other murdered in 1023 and went on to follow in his father's footsteps, trying to subdue the other provinces. But he first ran into the stubborn opposition of the king of Osraige, a border territory of Leinster which had recently become formidable in its own right; then, in the 1040s, into the hostility of an aspiring king of Leinster, Diarmait mac Mael-na-mBó. Diarmait saw Dublin as the key to power, seized it, expelled its ruler and made himself king of the city and its territory. He also sponsored the ambitions of Donnchad's nephew, son of the murdered man. The nephew was Turlough *ua Briain* (grandson or descendant of Brian), whom we may now refer to as Turlough O'Brien. In this period, surnames – an indicator of social change – were beginning to form, based on patronymics in *mac* or on the word *ua*, later ó. Turlough finally took the Munster kingship in 1063, packing his uncle off 'on his pilgrimage' to Rome. He himself remained faithful to his sponsor Diarmait mac Mael-na-mBó, who was killed in battle in 1072 and was described by the annals, on his death, as 'king of Wales and the Isles and of Dublin and the southern half' – a tribute more to his ambition than to his achievement.

Turlough O'Brien may have been faithful to his sponsor, Diarmait, but he owed nothing to Leinster which he now entered and divided. He too took swift measures to control Dublin, putting in his son Muirchertach as king. He took full advantage of the hostility between the different dynastic families in Connacht (emerging now with the surnames O'Conor, O'Rourke and O'Flaherty) to divide and weaken that province. In the north, internecine conflict in *Cenél Eógain* meant that the province gave him little trouble. Turlough was flatteringly addressed by Lanfrance, archbishop of Canterbury, as 'most glorious king of Ireland', but his victories had left him far short of that. However, when he died in 1086, his son Muirchertach took over the kingship of Munster with little difficulty.

The kingship was initially divided among three brothers. One died; Muirchertach banished the other, Diarmait, and gained sole control. However, he had to fight off attacks from the other provinces, which came as soon as Turlough's strong hand was removed. Munster was invaded both by an alliance of Ruaidri O'Conor from Connacht and Domnall MacLoughlin from the north (where stability had been restored) and by an alliance of O'Conor and O'Melaghlin of *Mide*, with much devastation. At one stage Muirchertach had to submit and give hostages to MacLoughlin, but finally, by taking advantage of divisions among his enemies and by continued fighting, he was able to take Dublin (banishing its king Gofraid whom his father had also banished), depose the king of *Mide*, and enter Connacht with fleets and armies, to divide and subdivide the province. From 1096 onwards he made repeated efforts to subdue the north, in expedition after expedition, making a great circuit in 1102 in which he destroyed *Ailech*, the ancient hilltop centre in Inishowen, and marched through *Cenél Eógain* and *Ulaid*, leaving churches burning behind him. Two successive abbots of Armagh intervened repeatedly to make peace

between O'Brien and MacLoughlin. The dominance built up in years of
warfare collapsed instantly in 1114 when Muirchertach fell ill and his
brother banished him (to Lismore), and attacks on Munster came from all
sides. Although he had a brief return to kingship before retiring again to
the monastery of Lismore, his power was at an end.

The struggles of the kings over the century from the death of Brian at
Clontarf to the deposition of Muirchertach O'Brien in 1114 read, in the
detail of the annalistic entries, with a deadly and depressing monotony.
Almost every year there was campaigning by fleets and armies, with the
burning and destruction of monasteries, towns and strongholds –
occasionally more widespread devastation as well. The kings and their
armies cannot have seemed to the ordinary people as anything but a
reinforcement of the plagues and famines which also afflicted them from
time to time.

Yet, change and development can be discerned. For one thing, the
turbulence of the struggle for kingship was like the violence of breakers on
a beach with a rising tide. Every now and then a wave carried farther up
the shingle than any before. Sustained energy and increasing ruthlessness
in cutting through established custom and law by deposing, banishing,
subdividing, creating arbitrary new hierarchies in the provinces; all this
was changing the system. The weakness was the lack of continuity. Each
man's achievement was his alone and died with him. This weakness was
being overcome by the emergence of a father–son succession – but such
development was, of course, fiercely resisted by the numerous interests
which ran with the older modes of succession.

Control of the trading cities – especially Dublin and Limerick – had also
clearly come to be a matter of importance. The O'Briens had been quick
to realize this and it partly explains their comparative success over a long
period. The rulers of *Osraige* and the south Leinster dynasts of the *úi
Cennsalaigh* at Ferns also grasped the point. Seizure of Dublin was an
important ploy in the chess of the high-kingship. Not only were the cities'
fleets increasingly employed throughout the century, but by its close the
overseas connections – especially of Dublin – were significant. The whole
Scandinavian world, with its far-flung connections, was interested in what
happened in both Britain and Ireland through much of the eleventh
century. Dublin sent its ships on hire across the Irish Sea, as it did to Irish
kings; with its marriage and kinship relations in Iceland, Man, Cumbria
and the Isles it must have been, among other things, a considerable centre
for political intelligence. The Norman conquest threw the outlying parts
of Britain – Wales, Scotland, the Isles – into some confusion, and tempted
other would-be conquerors and opportunists. It seems that Diarmait mac

Mael-n-mBó had ambitions in Wales. Muirchertach O'Brien involved himself in conspiratorial intrigues against Henry I in Wales and the west of England – especially with the earl of Shrewsbury. He married one of his daughters to Magnus Bareleg, king of Norway, who came to Ireland at the end of the century, and another to the earl of Shrewsbury's brother Arnulf de Montgomery. He sent aid to the revolt against Henry I, but this resulted in no more than the settlement of a few Norman knights in Munster. The alliance with the king of Norway was also fruitless, since Magnus was killed in a minor skirmish in the north of Ireland.

Muirchertach was treated, or at least greeted, as king of Ireland by the archbishops of Canterbury, who consecrated the bishops of the Ostman towns and were urging intervention in the affairs of the Irish church. The customs and organization of the church in Ireland were so different from those now beginning to prevail fairly uniformly elsewhere that to the pious standardizing and centralizing clerics of the beginning of the twelfth century they were a scandal. The anomalous position of bishops, the control of church property by hereditary lay governors of monasteries, the music and liturgy, practices such as 'incestuous' marriages within near degrees of kindred, participation in the Bristol slave trade: all were grounds for complaint, apart from the commoner abuses which for some decades had been the general object of conformist revision. Muirchertach responded, and joined the growing movement in the country for drastic change. In 1101 he gave Cashel, at a solemn gathering, to the church. By this at one blow he strengthened the church in Munster by granting it a site of ancient prestige, and weakened the *Eóganacht* dynasties (now showing some signs of emerging from their eclipse) by depriving them of their historic royal site, while depriving their monastery, Emly, of its pre-eminence in Munster. Ten years later, at *Ráith Bresail*, near Cashel, plans were drawn up for a new diocesan organization of the church. It was based on the plans for the English church brought by St Augustine from Gregory the Great at the end of the sixth century: dividing the country into two provinces (the older northern and southern halves) with metropolitans at Armagh and Cashel and twelve bishoprics in each province. This idealized scheme was to remain purely theoretical for quite a while. The existing organization involved innumerable vested interests. For example, the abbacy of Armagh for a couple of centuries had been in the hands of one family, the *uí Sinaig*.

Muirchertach was just one among a number of those who were expressing the emerging concept of kingship as state government in ways other than warfare – notably by patronage of the church. Formal patronage associated with the concept of the Christian king goes back to

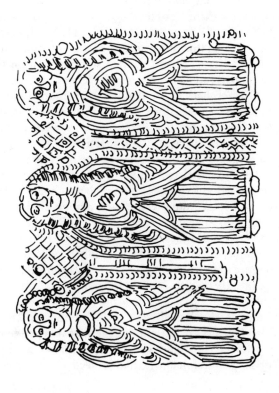

Figure 5 Figures from the eleventh-century *Breac Maodhóg* reliquary Drawn from figures in National Museum of Ireland.

the eighth century if not earlier (it is possible, for example, that the splendid set of Eucharistic vessels found at Derrynavlan in Co. Tipperary consists of royal gifts modelled on the imperial festival donations of the Byzantine east), but after the middle of the eleventh century it appears to be much more a matter of set policy. There was a great revival of the art of fine metalworking (much influenced by the Scandinavians) and a large production of reliquaries of various forms, some very splendid and of considerable size. Church-building in stone increased, and a new type of standing stone cross – which gives prominence to the figure of a mitred bishop with a non-Irish type of crosier and which borrows Crucifixion figures from north-European iconography – was erected at the centres of patronage.

Some churchmen and some rulers made attempts to implant European forms of Christianity by importing some of the continental orders of monks, a movement which, drawing on the Benedictines and the Canons Regular of St Augustine, had slow and uncertain beginnings round the beginning of the twelfth century. Cormac MacCarthy went a little farther and brought in a whole new elaborate style of building and sculpture – the Romanesque. He was a member of the *Eóganacht* of Cashel, who assumed the kingship there, with O'Brien's agreement, in 1127 and, in the intervals of ferocious campaigning (mainly against the king of Connacht) set about building an elaborately carved and painted stone church on the rock of Cashel. It was consecrated, with solemn ceremonial, in 1134. The McCarthys of Cashel had close family connections with the Irish monastery of St James in Regensburg in Bavaria, but the style of Cormac's Chapel suggests that the masons he brought in were from England, possibly Canterbury. However, it is clear that masons had been coming or returning, from England and the continent, for quite some time before. The Round Tower at Cashel, which was probably erected immediately after Muirchertach O'Brien's grant of the site to the church in 1101, has its stones dressed in the technique traditional among Irish masons. The Round Tower at Clonmacnoise, known as 'O'Rourkes', which was completed in 1119, has its stones dressed in the new technique associated with the Romanesque, a technique which rapidly displaced the older one. The craft, even more than the decorative art, is a striking illustration of the inrush of change in early twelfth-century Ireland.

The most successful organizational introduction was that of the reformed division of the Benedictine order of monks known as the Cistercians (from Citeaux, in Burgundy, the first independent centre of the breakaway). Máelmaedóc ua Morgair, better known as St Malachy of Armagh, a reforming churchman who had succeeded, against considerable

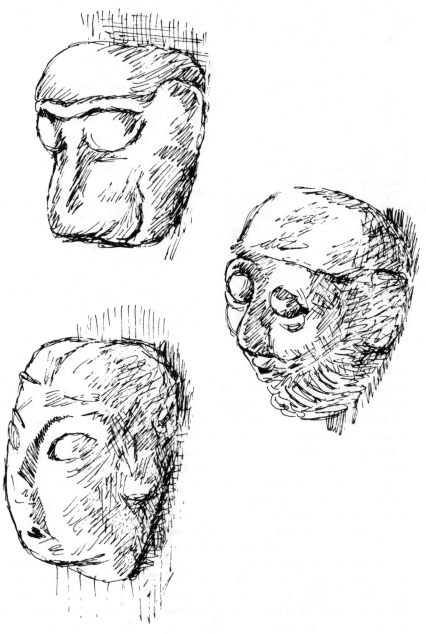

Figure 6   Faces, Cashel

opposition from the hereditary Successors of St Patrick, the *uí Sinaigh*, in becoming head of the church of Armagh, then made it his mission to go to Rome. His object was to seek approval from the pope for a reorganization of the church in Ireland, on the lines of *Ráith Bresail*, along with grants of *pallia* – the insignia of the two proposed new archbishops. On the way to Rome he spend a number of weeks in the leading Cistercian monastery, Clairvaux in Burgundy, as the guest of St Bernard. He was greatly impressed by the order, and left some of his retinue with Bernard as novices. Indeed he wished to become a Cistercian novice himself, but this the pope would not have. Instead, he was commanded to make the journey again, first returning to Ireland to organize a national request for the *pallia* and the new church order.

When Malachy came back to Ireland, he was granted land for the foundation of a Cistercian monastery by Donnchad O'Carroll, ruler of *Airghialla*. This is a good example of a medieval speculative land grant, since O'Carroll had no real claim to the land he gave. It was at the new extreme limit of his previously minor kingdom, which had expanded remarkably over the previous half-century. The monks came in 1142 – those from Malachy's entourage together with some from Bernard's community, including his master-builder, Robert – and settled in the glen of a small stream which flows into the Boyne at Oldbridge near Newgrange. It was a place called *Mel*, and, employing an onomastic pun as was their custom, the Cistercians named their monastery *Sancta Maria de mellis fonte* – 'honey-fountain' – Mellifont. Ten years later, after Malachy's death, a synod met here and at Kells to receive the *pallia* – but in the interval, political considerations had increased the number of metropolitan sees to four – Armagh, Cashel, Dublin and Tuam. The Irish church was formally reorganized. Mellifont itself prospered and sent out colonies to found new Cistercian houses throughout the land. There rose on the site a church 60 metres long – a scale new to the Irish – in the severe Cistercian version of Romanesque – yet another art-style imported in this highly active period. Mellifont had its troubles, some of which were to be endemic in the church of the Middle Ages.

Apart from the problem they encountered in exchanging the rich sunny land of Burgundy for the damp woods and countryside of eastern Ireland, the French-speaking monks found the Irish barbarous and their ways incomprehensible. The continental authorities of the Cistercian order were also to find the Irish houses extremely difficult to deal with, and in Mellifont's troubles of the late twelfth century, and the more widespread thirteenth-century revolt against the order – known as *conspiratio Mellifontis* – we have in miniature the problem of the 'two nations' in the medieval Irish church. But the consecration of the completed abbey buildings in 1157 was, at long last, a national assembly, presided over by an acknowledged 'king of Ireland', Muirchertach MacLoughlin, and attended by large numbers of lay and clerical leaders who gave donations to the new foundation.

Sweeping change is also evident in the writings of this time. There is a greater variety of material, including a proliferation of popular or vulgar themes – from folklore and romance – as well as much translation of foreign material. Ornate forms of expression come into vogue. A true vernacular literature begins to emerge simultaneously with a rearguard action on the part of the strictly trained professional *litterateurs*, scholars and poets. In consequence, an *odium poeticum* manifests itself, every bit as savage as *odium theologicum*, and as long-lasting. The vulgarization is perhaps most plainly manifest in the hagiographical literature, which goes beyond being popular and becomes infantile – it is difficult to envisage the adult audience, of any age or culture, that found some of it acceptable.

Meantime, the struggle for kingship had continued with mounting intensity. It had seemed that in the eleventh century the political, social and economic centre of gravity had shifted to the coastal towns. This was indeed what had happened; but at the beginning of the twelfth century a determined effort was made to reassert an old balance, based largely on the internal resources of the country. The illness and death of Muirchertach O'Brien coincided with the ambitious drive towards supremacy of the Connacht dynast, Turlough O'Conor. Connacht, left aside from the shared hegemony of the *uí Neill* for hundreds of years, had re-emerged in the eleventh century, but was dealt with ruthlessly by Turlough O'Brien. Now the tables were turned. Turlough O'Conor showed himself capable of marshalling all the resources of his province, and also showed that although these did not include centres of wealth created by the Norse, they were quite considerable. He was lavish in patronage: Clonmacnoise under his rule rivalled the Ostman towns and may even have been minting coins. He began to build up other centres on old monastic sites – Tuam and Cong. He emulated the Scandinavians in the construction of strongholds of stone (he is the first Irish king to be credited with the building of 'castles') and in the use of fleets, and he out-did the O'Briens in the ruthless partitioning of other provinces and in the intrusion of his own people into other kingships. He rapidly and completely superseded and replaced O'Brien as the most widely acknowledged king, but throughout his embattled career – until he died in 1156 – he was implacably opposed by the now fully revived ambitions of the northern kingdom of MacLoughlin (the old *Cenél Eógain* of the northern *uí Néill*). One of his most effective partitionings on

his way to supremacy was of Munster, which he divided into North
Munster (Thomond), assigned to O'Brien and South Munster (Desmond),
assigned to MacCarthy. Although the two rival dynasties contrived to
combine together for a while against O'Conor – when Cormac MacCarthy
became an agreed king of Cashel (that is, of Munster) in 1127 – the
partition was to have permanent effects.

So, whereas in the eleventh century, the competition for centralized rule
had been between the chief dynasties of the southern half of Ireland (the
old 'half of *Mug*'), in the twelfth century it was between the leading
dynasts of the northern half (the old 'half of *Conn*'). The southern half was
the more progressive, with its busy trade in both exports and imports, its
consequent involvement with the outside world, and its rather more
sophisticated political development. The backwardness of the northern
half was relative. Connacht under the O'Conor kings showed the capacity
to develop its own sophistication, perhaps influenced by, but independent
of, the Ostmen: there are indications that the old Atlantic link with
western France, which had once brought Merovingian princes to the
schools of Clonmacnoise, was reactivated. The north, however, whose
chief external connections were with the barbarous world of the half-
Gaelic half-Viking Western and Northern Isles, was atavistic and perhaps
actually retrogressive in economy and institutions by the twelfth century.

After the death of Turlough O'Conor, Muirchertach MacLoughlin, his
opponent in the north, moved rapidly to replace him in the hegemony of
Ireland. With the aid of the Leinster king, Diarmait MacMurrough, he
succeeded, although precariously. Turlough O'Conor's son, Ruaidri,
organized an uprising against him in the north, and in 1166 MacLoughlin
was killed and Ruaidri in turn became 'high-king'. He and his client–ally,
O'Rourke of Breiffne, moved effectively to crush the remaining
formidable opposition, Diarmait MacMurrough, who was driven out of
his kingdom of Leinster.

Diarmait decided to restore his fortunes and right his wrongs with the
help of aid from overseas. He travelled to Bristol in 1166, and later to
France. He succeeded in recruiting, from the most westerly marches of
Henry II's wide dominions, and with that monarch's slightly ambiguous
assent, groups of adventurous Normans who were prepared to assemble
companies of knights and men-at-arms and serve Diarmait in return for
solid prospects in Ireland. They were not simple mercenaries: they
expected and were promised land and position. They came mainly from a
group of families in Pembrokeshire and round Bristol – directly across the
Channel from Wexford and from Diarmait's own territory – and it is
probable that they had had previous dealings with Ireland. Land-hungry

Normans had been winning lands for themselves in Wales through the century, but for some little time now had been losing ground again to Rhys ap Gruffydd, king of Deheubarth. The Ostman fleets from Dublin, Wexford and Waterford had been active on the Irish Sea, in the service of Henry II and the Normans against the Welsh. Diarmait was now calling upon the wider contacts and resources of south-eastern Ireland to redress the upsurge of vigour in the more isolated north-west.

The advance party of his recruits fortified themselves east of the entry to Waterford harbour, resisted with ferocity the attempt of the Ostmen of Waterford to dislodge them, and awaited the arrival of reinforcements. These soon came. The fortunes of the half-Welsh Robert fitz Stephen had been failing in Wales: he came to restore them in Ireland. He was followed by his half-brother Maurice fitz Gerald and Maurice's nephew Raymond le Gros. These in turn were followed by the weightier figure of Richard de Clare, earl of Strigoil – known as Strongbow – who was not merely an adventurer of the Welsh marches but a man of property and position. They were resisted by the Ostmen but took Wexford and Waterford. In Waterford Strongbow married Diarmait's daughter Aoife. Diarmait recovered control of his province of Leinster and with the help of his allies seized Dublin and expelled its Ostman king. He died at home in Ferns in the early summer of 1171, leaving the province of Leinster to his Norman son-in-law.

This bequest was challenged immediately by his Leinster relations; but Diarmait had made a bold attempt to cut the Gordian knot of the Irish dynastic system and establish a kingdom on a foundation of military strength. His ambition probably went beyond that of ruling Leinster alone, but at least within that limit he was moderately successful. His introduction of a new, unpredictable, powerful element into the kingship struggle altered the nature of the struggle. Domhnall Mór O'Brien, who had become ruler of Thomond just as Diarmait was returning to reclaim Leinster, was a dynast of considerable capacity who, in the early stage of his career, was clearly setting out to fight his way through to the high-kingship. He made good use of his Ostman city of Limerick, and he also hired some of Diarmait's Norman allies, but within a few years he had grasped that a fundamental change had occurred with the introduction of the Norman mercenaries, and he cut his losses and concentrated, successfully, on preventing the penetration of his base in Clare. The Normans were showing both a remarkable military capacity and a singleness of purpose which was not at all trammelled by Irish custom and tradition. They wanted land and power and they began to strike out on their own.

Ruaidri O'Conor did not perceive as clearly as O'Brien that the newcomers were operating in a way new to the violent dynastic politics of Ireland. He tried to deal with them, by combat and negotiation, in a wrongly perceived context, and his efforts convey an impression of ineptitude.

Henry II, not only king of England, but through inheritance and marriage lord of many other territories as well, knew his Norman barons and fully understood the significance of their early successes in Ireland. He intervened, took what time he could from his endless peripatetic administration of his many lands, and came to Ireland late in 1171. He held, as legal pretext, a title to possession of Ireland, which had been secured for him in 1155, just after his accession to the throne – a papal grant (*Laudabiliter*) made by the English pope Hadrian IV in response to the Canterbury interest, authorizing him to take over Ireland 'to proclaim the truths of the Christian religion to a rude and ignorant people, and to root out the growth of vice from the field of the Lord'.[3] *Laudabiliter* is an interesting manifestation of papal imperialism, coming as it did within three years of the synod of Kells, where a papal legate, John Paparo, had presided over the reorganization of the Irish church.

Henry's objects were to confirm his authority over the barons, to assert his own interest in Ireland, and to set up there a system of checks and balances that would keep the country reasonably stable for the moment and reasonably amenable to control. So he negotiated with the Irish provincial rulers who came to him to complain of baronial encroachments on ancient rights, and who submitted to him and acknowledged his overlordship in return for protection. Ruaidri O'Conor, however, the high-king, withheld his submission. The leaders of the Irish church also acknowledged Henry's overlordship, at a synod convened at Cashel: in return, Canterbury was denied the jurisdiction over the Irish church which it had been trying to assert. Henry curbed those of the first Norman arrivals who showed dangerous capacity or ambition. He left most of Leinster with Strongbow, but took over the Ostman towns, granting Dublin to the merchants of Bristol, its chief trading partner. As a counterbalance to Strongbow, he granted Meath to a new arrival, Hugh de Lacy.

Henry did not return to Ireland, but he made several important later interventions. He and Ruaidri O'Conor came to an agreement, whereby Ruaidri was acknowledged as 'high-king' in those regions outside Norman control. Then, as Norman entrepreneurs pushed westward into Munster, Henry made speculative land-grants in the province, ignoring his previous arrangements with Irish rulers. He had four sons to provide for, but the territories he ruled in his own right were both extensive and varied.

Plate 1 An early Christian oratory, Gallarus, County Kerry

Plate 2 The 'Doorty Cross', bishop, Kilfenora

Plate 3 Romanesque doorway, human heads from arch, Dysert O'Dea, County Clare

Plate 4 A wedge-shaped grave, Culleens, County Sligo

Figure 7   Figure from Cambrensis manuscript
Source: Trinity College Dublin.

Reserving the English kingdom, with Normandy and Anjou, for the eldest, he decided to leave Aquitaine, Brittany and Ireland to the second, third and fourth respectively. In 1177 he announced that Ireland would go to John, who was then still a child. As it happened, the 'lordship' of Ireland, so created, was to stay with the English crown. John, although the fourth son, ultimately became king of England. A separate kingdom of Ireland did not emerge.

On the contrary, by the end of the twelfth century an important political effect of these interventions had been to reverse the centralizing tendency of the earlier part of the century. Some of the older Irish kingdoms more or less retained their integrity, if not quite their earlier extent; others had been carved up and redistributed among Norman rulers; others now had Norman dynasts in place of the Irish. After Ruaidri O'Conor, the concept of the 'high-kingship' faded but did not quite disappear. The distant supremacy of the English kings, 'Lords of Ireland' after John, often had little effect within large parts of Ireland.

Negotiations between Henry II and his successors and the Irish rulers involved cross-purposes, misunderstanding, ambiguity and, on both sides, a great amount of double-dealing. Different languages, legal systems, outlooks on succession, family and property, were in contact. However, both sides thoroughly understood that this problem existed. They also shrewdly understood the potential advantage of mutual misunderstanding: the bargains being struck were of the kind that both sides wanted to disown if and when it suited them. A tissue of ambiguities was created in Ireland with the intrusion of bold Norman land-owners, combined with the cautious background concern of the imperious, but otherwise preoccupied, English monarchs. The interventions of the English crown, even if often tardy, were effective in preventing the emergence of a single dominant power in Ireland. And, by the close of the twelfth century, the advent of the first military adventurers was being backed by a substantial colonizing immigration.

Gerald the Welshman, who arrived in Ireland about 1185, described the country. He remarks that the Irish made no use of castles: 'Woods are their forts and swamps their ditches.' He goes on to describe the economy:

The soil is soft and watery, and even at the tops of high and steep mountains there are pools and swamps. The land is sandy rather than rocky. There are many woods and marshes; here and there there are some fine plains but in comparison with the woods they are indeed small. The country enjoys the freshness and mildness of spring almost all the year round. The grass is green in the fields in winter just the same as in summer. Consequently, the meadows are not cut for fodder, and stalls are never built for the beasts. The land is fruitful and rich in its fertile soil and

plentiful harvests. Crops abound in the fields, flocks on the mountains, wild
animals in the woods. It is rich in honey and milk. Ireland exports cow-hides,
sheep-skins and furs. Much wine is imported. But the island is richer in pastures
than in crops, and in grass rather than in grain. . .[4]

From other sources we can infer that by this date, while the land was not
overcrowded, it was being fairly fully utilized, for grazing small cattle and
sheep, with pigs in the woods. Farms ranging in size from about 30 to
about 300 hectares had fenced fields, in which a variety of crops was
grown, including oats, barley and wheat – but the evidence indicates that
wheat did not do very well.

The new monastic orders, especially the Cistercians, were introducing
a more intensive agriculture, with a much greater emphasis on marketable
produce rather than self-sufficiency. Similarly, the Norman-Welsh barons
who won lands for themselves in the late twelfth century were interested
in farming as a source of income. Not sharing the Irish tradition of
reckoning wealth in cattle, they sought – and found – good broad hectares
of commercial land. In order to have this worked in the way they wanted,
some of them planted rural colonies of Welshmen or West-Countrymen,
or peasants from northern France, in the countryside. Soon, in those areas,
the whole pattern of life was changed.

Adaptable as they were, the Normans seem often to have found the
peculiarities of the Irish church (many of which persisted in spite of the
diocesan reorganization and the enacted reforms) unacceptable. Their own
variety of Christianity – very different from that of the early church – was
one which reconciled the trade of war in which they specialized with a
pious, and sometimes superstitious, religious enthusiasm. They founded
numerous abbeys in the territory they colonized, and in the towns they
founded or took over they built cathedrals and parish churches. This
reinforced the colonization. Masons and carpenters, along with other
craftsmen, came over. They shipped over the very stone from Somerset
and Pembroke, sometimes already wrought or carved for use in the Irish
buildings.

The Normans secured their lands by building castles, which functioned
first as advanced strong-points in hostile country; then as centres of
control. They built them methodically, one supporting another, at
bridges, fords and passes, according to the military procedures of the
tradition they had inherited from the invaders of England. For the first two
or three generations they built wooden strongholds on artificial earthen
mounds, leaving in the modern landscape the characteristic 'motte-and-
bailey' earthworks which map their penetration of the country. The first
great royal castles of stone were built about 1200; by this time the major

magnates had also begun to build fortifications in stone, though not quite as large. A distinctive Irish castle-type appeared about 1250, by which date castle-building in Britain had passed saturation point and such military engineers as were still in the business must have migrated to Ireland. It was about 1200 that the Normans in Leinster built the first Gothic churches – in the Early English style. By about 1250 this style, with some minor distinctive Irish features, was well established in the south and east.

Frank Mitchell has pointed out that the distribution of Anglo-Norman sites in Ireland is related to soil-types: 'On the whole . . . they did not advance beyond a line running from Skibbereen through Galway to Coleraine, and settled most densely in Leinster and east Munster. . .'.[5] The line marking the limit of comparatively dense settlement corresponds to that separating the more oceanic climate (rain-days for more than half the year) from the less, or the wet lands from the drier, and the settlement shows a preference for grey-brown podzolic soils. However, even to the east of this line, there were great variations. Norman colonization was very patchy, depending on military and political as well as natural environmental circumstances, and the sites vary greatly, from full manorial establishment and drastic innovation to a fairly thoroughgoing adaptation by the new overlord to the pre-existing Irish pattern.

What is important is that the new settlements were numerous, that there was quite extensive, if uneven, colonization, and that there was a new approach to agriculture, accompanied by very different equipment, methods and objectives. While this has left a permanent character stamped on some Irish landscapes, notably in the south-east, in others it has been obscured by late-medieval abandonment of the settlements. But it introduced a permanent contrast into the countryside; for the older approach to farming survived side by side with the new – on poorer land – as it would continue to survive beside many later colonizations.

This was largely a frontier economy, with some of the freedom which was both necessary to entice settlement and inevitable at the extreme limit of central authority. Many boroughs were formed, often remaining rural. Conditions of tenure were probably, in general, comparatively easy. Sometimes the indigenous population was displaced. More often there was accommodation. Attached to many manors were villages of native Irish betaghs (unfree workers on the land, so called from the Irish term *biatach*, meaning originally one who paid food-rent). Old towns were occupied, new ones founded, and these became places of intercourse between cultures as well as places of trade.

The rural settlements as a whole were Irish within a few generations, in language and to some extent in custom. But the lords continued to be

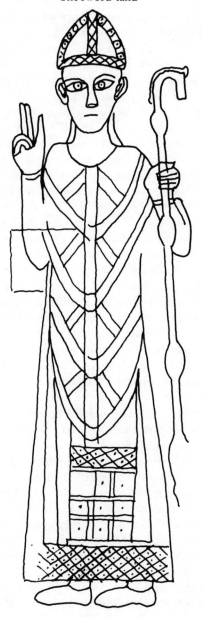

Figure 8 Figure of a bishop. From an engraved stone slab in Kilfenora Cathedral, County Clare, thirteenth century

French- as well as Irish-speaking. Many of the greater magnates had extensive interests outside Ireland, in Wales, England or France, and there were many proprietors who were largely absentees. The English connection remained important, even in the most remote settlements.

Henry II had planted Hugh de Lacy in Meath largely as a counterweight to the over-mighty Strongbow, and de Lacy acted as royal representative in Ireland. But the balance in the country was shifting rapidly through the fierce initiatives of the magnates. In 1177 John de Courcy, recently arrived, invaded the north-east and within a short time had taken over the old kingdom of *Ulaid*, founding on this base the medieval earldom of Ulster. He married the daughter of the king of Man, shrewdly took over the religious traditions of the north, including the cult of Patrick, and in general consolidated his position. In the midlands de Lacy, too, strengthened and expanded his position, took the hostages of Connacht, and is described in one Irish source, in the old fashion, as 'king of Ireland'. He was killed in 1186 while overseeing the building of a motte on the old Columban monastic site of Durrow. Strongbow also died in his maturity.

When John came on the first visit to his lordship in 1185 he had to attempt different counterpoises. He made fresh grants – in Louth and Tipperary – but he failed either to curb the Norman magnates adequately or to come to satisfactory arrangements with the Irish kings. His visit (about which information is poor) was reckoned a failure by his contemporaries. He became king of England in 1199, and his elder brothers being dead, inherited the wide range of dynastic responsibilities. Although Ireland was now far from the centre of his interests, as king he intervened more effectively. Through the agency of the second Hugh de Lacy he drove the over-powerful de Courcy from Ulster, and planted the north coast with Scots. He placed the collection of Irish revenues on a regular basis and built stone castles, including that of Dublin, the main centre of revenue collection and chief royal base in Ireland. He issued further speculative land-grants, and negotiated with Irish kings as a means of keeping the still expansive Norman lordships under a measure of control. In 1210 he was the last king of England, for almost two centuries, to visit Ireland. His reign ended in a series of disasters in France and England, and when he died in 1216, his son Henry III was still a child. There was a period of uncertainty and conflict in England and Ireland, but by the1230s this had ended.

The period of Anglo-Norman colonization coincided with the medieval climatic optimum: average temperatures reached a peak between the late twelfth and the late thirteenth centuries, and conditions for crops like wheat were better than at any other time in the past thousand years. It was, generally in Europe, a time of rising population, and there are good reasons to think that this was true of Ireland too. There is no way of measuring accurately the size of the population, but it is probably safe to guess that this was in excess of a million.

By about the middle of the thirteenth century the colonizing movements had affected most of the regions where there were large stretches of land suitable for the Norman agricultural practices, and new ventures were pushing into more difficult and doubtful areas. A complex balance had been reached, between the policies of the distant royal government, the requirements of the great magnates with concerns outside as well as inside Ireland, the interests of the smaller lords, the special position of the towns, the ambitions of the Irish rulers, and the (probably considerable) influence on events of both native and colonial populations lower in the social scale. The balance was not only complex, it was inherently unstable, and the pressures generated by a rising population alone were probably enough to upset it.

But there were other serious pressures, connected with the continuing sense that there were in the island two 'nations' with distinct identities. This was not a matter of race or blood-lines, nor was it even, to any great extent, a matter of cultural prejudice – although that was to come. Irish and Normans intermarried freely, mingled freely, entered readily into alliances, and engaged with equal intensity in the bloody intricacies of dynastic politics. The custom on both sides of tracing descent primarily through the male line and indicating patrilineage through surnames, conceals the fact that in the mid thirteenth century many of the principal Norman magnates were the grandsons of Irish twelfth-century kings, and many of the Irish kings were the grandsons of twelfth-century Normans. The distinction was probably founded more firmly on the opposition of two economies than on a contrast of cultures. It had begun to emerge at least as early as the eleventh century, as southern and eastern Ireland opened up to the European world, greatly aided by the cosmopolitan and outward-looking Ostman towns with their busy traffic and their involvement for good and ill with the growing commerce of the west.

Now, by the middle of the thirteenth century, uncolonized Irish areas survived chiefly in the west and north, although nowhere was untouched by the colonizing movement. The dynastic ambitions of O'Neills, MacLoughlins, O'Conors, O'Briens, MacCarthys and others survived; but all the dynasts were now crowded by the castle-building Normans on their reduced borders; they were driven in on themselves, and to some extent back to earlier stages of development. Irish civilization, as it had developed to the twelfth century, had already a very strange balance, compared to the romanesque civilization of western Europe. It had powerful roots in Celtic prehistory, a strong pagan tradition of mythology and folklore underlying its Christianity, marked elements of withdrawal from the world of everyday reality, an obsession with repetitive pattern-making, word-weaving, legalizing: a culture of dreams. It had, of course, its practical and everyday side as well, but by the thirteenth century, in its literary manifestations (which had added weight as the material culture was impoverished) it exhibited a remarkable duality of outlook. It ignored, for many purposes, what had actually happened. Bards, genealogists, historians, the well-rewarded companions and genii of the kings, continued to treat of a Gaelic world as if neither Norman colonists nor English monarchs existed. The everyday dealings of the kings were within – and with – the world of reality. But in an extraordinary way, a great deal of medieval Irish writing treats the profound and permanent changes which began in the twelfth century as if they were a brief shadow passing over a sunny hillside. Even as the Norman lords settled into Irish ways, and themselves took bards into their halls, these intransigent transmitters of culture found formulae to maintain the distinction. They devised an evasion for one harsh reality and praised the Normans for their 'sword-land': territory held, not by right of descent from the immemorial tribal gods, but by right of conquest.

The duality was not confined to cultural perceptions. It took legal shape. As English institutions were steadily established in the country the Irish were excluded. In spite of negotiations, agreements, intermarriages and alliances, they came to be treated differently from the colonists, in a very drastic way. Since they had their separate customs, language, laws and outlook on the world, and partly lived in their own territories or enclaves (within the lordships), it was normal medieval thought and practice to treat them as a separate 'nation'. But in the dealings of the colony, whether in the royal courts or the courts of the lordships, the external Irish were denied even their own law: they were treated as outlaws without security of person or property. This arose largely because of two circumstances: the great incompatibility in economy, property-holding, and criminal procedures between Irish society and Norman, and the precariousness of the balance between new settlers and old natives in the very broad frontier zones of the colony. An imperialist relationship, of a kind later to be familiar, was created. In spite of intimacy of intercourse, alienation went deep and was encouraged by interested groups on both sides.

The territorial division which had broadly taken place by the middle of the thirteenth century was only very roughly one between south-east and north-west. Fragmentation and decentralization were increasing as the

Figure 9   Female figure from the cloister, Jerpoint Abbey, County Kilkenny

great lordships of the late twelfth century were broken up. Leinster had passed from Diarmait MacMurrough to Strongbow by testament; Henry II had reserved the towns in making his re-grant. From Strongbow, with an interval in which it was administered on behalf of the king, the lordship passed to William Marshal. In 1245 the brothers Walter and Anselm Marshal both died without male heirs and their inheritance, including Leinster, was divided among their five sisters. The prime lords of the now divided province were absentees, but the lordship had been well settled and in many parts was thickly planted with subordinate lords and tenants. It had important towns, including Kilkenny, Carlow, Kildare and 'New' Ross, as well as Wexford. There were, however, large areas not settled or thinly settled – the Wicklow highlands just south of Dublin, and the bogs and hills of Laois and Offaly to the west, for example. In the north Wexford area, the MacMurroughs, reduced and deprived, bided their time.

The old midland kingdom, *Mide*, had already been in decline by the early twelfth century, and was being taken over by Diarmait MacMurrough when he was expelled from his Leinster kingdom. Although he recovered his position, Henry II had checked his heir Strongbow by granting Meath – as we may now begin to call the territory – to Hugh de Lacy, and he made it the basis of a great lordship. In 1241, Walter de Lacy died without male heir, leaving the Meath lordship to two granddaughters. So, this lordship, too was subdivided towards the middle of the century. It was well settled in parts, but not in the whole north-western region. A system of strong castles, including the great fortification of Trim, on the Boyne, defended it.

Munster in general had been penetrated in a much more piecemeal fashion, by somewhat lesser magnates and with much competition between them. Robert le Poer made good use of his control of Waterford, and his family dominated the old *Dési* country from Waterford to Dungarvan, while the hills to the north-west remained Irish. John gave lands to William de Burgo in south Tipperary in 1185, and the Suir valley was well settled. William had used his south Tipperary lands as the base for the remarkable northward expansion achieved by his family into Connacht and beyond. Members of the prolific family of fitz Gerald had moved out from a base in the south midlands to penetrate the valleys of west Munster, in north Kerry and west Cork, in the first quarter of the century. The MacCarthy dynasts, crowded into the south-west Munster heartlands, struggled to maintain themselves, largely by negotiation. Domhnall MacCarthy was killed by John fitz Thomas fitz Gerald in 1251, and some years later fitz Thomas was given a grant of Desmond and *Deisi*, provoking a reaction by the MacCarthys. Domhnall's son Finghin defeated the colonists at Callan in 1261, but was himself killed later the same year.

North of the Shannon, the O'Briens, following the dogged policy of the twelfth-century Domhnall Mór, struggled, also largely by negotiation with Henry III, to maintain their diminished territory of Thomond. They had long lost the city of Limerick, but early in the century established a new centre at Clonroad (Ennis). About the middle of the century Henry gave speculative grants for land north of the Shannon, provoking attacks on the settlers by Conor O'Brien and his son Tadg.

Both Henry II and his son John had come to arrangements with the O'Conor kings of Connacht, but both also came to quite different arrangements with others. John in the late twelfth century gave a title to Connacht to William de Burgo, who died in 1206. In the meantime, Normans were employed in the fierce conflicts among the O'Conors for the succession to Ruaidri, with whom Henry II had treated. Ruaidri's brother Cathal *crobderg* ('red hand') emerged as king, and to him and his heirs in 1215 John granted all Connacht outside Athlone 'during good service' for an annual rent of 300 marks. But he also gave a charter, the same day, to Richard de Burgo, William's son, as a kind of speculative reserve. John had recently had a castle and bridge built at Athlone, and the narrows and fords of the middle Shannon were well guarded with other castles. When Cathal died in 1224, the succession was contested again, and Henry III granted a new charter to Richard de Burgo. However, he reserved for himself a large part of what is now Co. Roscommon – and Athlone. By the middle of the century this royal territory was mostly leased to (Felim) O'Conor, while the rest of Connacht was parcelled out by de Burgo in large grants. Connacht was not settled as Leinster and Meath were. For the most part the land was not suitable; there was not large-scale immigration, and the Norman lords established a domination over the existing society and economy. In parts of south-east Connacht however, there was settlement, patchy and on a comparatively small scale. Maurice fitz Gerald, justiciar from 1232 until 1245, was one of those who had lands there.

Maurice also held speculative grants from his friend Hugh de Lacy, now lord of the old *Ulaid* territory (roughly modern Antrim and Down): in Sligo and Fermanagh, with a title to Tyrconnell. In 1238 he and de Lacy entered Tyrone to intervene in a succession conflict among the O'Neills. In 1242, however, de Lacy died, leaving no male heirs, and the Ulster lordship reverted for the moment to the crown. The new justiciar of 1245 – John fitz Geoffrey – devoted his attention to these Ulster lands, and in 1252 fitz Gerald, attempting to realize part of his grants, built a castle at

Caol Uisce on the Erne. This came to nothing, however. He died five years later, himself leaving a disputed heritage; and Godfrey O'Connell of Tyrconnell immediately moved south and destroyed the *Caol Uisce* castle. The greater part of the north-west continued to be dominated by the Irish dynasts, O'Neill, MacLoughlin, O'Donnell, Maguire, O'Hanlon, O'Rourke and others.

With the great consolidated lordships tending to subdivide, with difficulties increasing as the frontier moved into poorer land or more difficult country, with the intermittent checks applied by the Lord of Ireland across the sea, and with the increasingly effective counter-attacks provoked by the great pressure on the remaining Irish territories; with all these the advance of settlement slackened and all but ended. The divide between the 'two nations' widened, and in a remarkable but ineffective meeting at *Caol Uisce* in 1258, Brian O'Neill, Aed O'Conor and Tadg, son of Conor O'Brien tried to agree on O'Neill as king to lead a concerted Irish counter-attack. The Irish polity was too fragmented – and by now too varied – for that, and O'Neill soon afterwards was killed in attacking Downpatrick, the centre of the Ulster lordship.

Tensions heightened in the later thirteenth century. It was a time of increasing fortification: towns began to rebuild their walls, and the greater abbeys to begin to look like castles. Although in theory Christians in Ireland all professed the same faith and obeyed the same centralized organization, in practice there were two churches of quite different character – and the difference tended to increase. English law was published and administered in Ireland. Councils, assemblies and parliaments of the colony, held from time to time at convenient places in the thirteenth century, dealt with Irish matters. In 1297 a parliament in Dublin enacted that for convenience in applying the English common law to those who were entitled to it, and saving them from being treated in error as Irish out-laws, the colonists should maintain their distinctiveness of appearance and not wear Irish dress or hair-styles. The colony was now supplying a steady and substantial revenue, and some services, to its lord the king. Many of the colonists also sought fortune and advancement by entering the royal armies in the Scottish and continental wars.

There were some signs, round the end of the century, of renewed expansiveness, although at the same time some of the lordships were being rapidly eroded in their frontier zones. The earldom of Ulster, now ruled by Richard de Burgo, was becoming a great and extensive unified lordship. In Thomond, Richard de Clare was pursuing the last of the Norman land-taking adventures, continuing the expansion of colonies north of the Shannon estuary that had been initiated by his father Thomas de Clare in pursuit of a speculative land-grant of Edward I. But in the years 1315–18 there were disasters for the colony as a whole. It was a time of crop-failure, famine and disease. In 1314 Robert Bruce, having imposed his rule on Scotland, defeated Edward II at Bannockburn. Then he took up family claims in north-eastern Ireland, which dated from King John's plantation there and had come to the Bruces through their earldom of Carrick. Domhnall O'Neill, son of the Brian O'Neill who had been acknowledged by the other Irish chiefs at *Caol Uisce* and then killed at Down, approached the king of Scots and offered to acknowledge the overlordship of Bruce's brother Edward.

Edward Bruce landed near Larne in the early summer of 1315, was joined by large Irish contingents, and marched south, storming Dundalk. He was inaugurated and acknowledged as king of Ireland. Both the earl of Ulster and the justiciar (Edmund Butler) moved against him, but he was victorious at the battle of Connor. Most of the earldom of Ulster fell into his hands, while the extensive de Burgo lordship of Connacht began to fall apart. For several years, from the Ulster base, Bruce mounted great clumsy mauling raids and campaigns which, backed by famine, caused devastation to the colony. Robert Bruce himself joined his brother on a destructive but inconclusive march south. Meanwhile, other border wars flared up.

Domhnall O'Neill, writing on behalf of a number of Irish chiefs, submitted a 'remonstrance' to Pope John XXII, justifying the transfer of allegiance from Edward II to Edward Bruce, on the grounds of the ancient right of the kings of Ireland, the unworthy motivation of the papal grant *Laudabiliter*, the failure of Henry II and his successors to observe the terms of that grant, and in particular the denial of law to the Irish lords. But O'Neill had no more success than his father in the futile endeavour of achieving an Irish kingship by agreement among the quarrelling dynastic kin-groups. Then in 1318 Bruce was defeated and killed at Faughart in Co. Louth (an ancient battle-ground, a strategic pass into Ulster) and the enterprise came to an end. The colonists had other victories – notably at Athenry in 1316, where they managed to check the rot in Connacht – but also suffered losses – as at Dysert O'Dea in 1318, where de Clare was killed and the disintegration of his colony in Thomond began.

In the years following these calamities, the colony struggled – with some success – against increasing difficulties. Among these, the fragmentation of lordships by division among heiresses was important, and this contributed to the growing problem of absenteeism. There was some consolidation, and within a few years four earldoms were created. Edward II made John de Bermingham (who had defeated Bruce) earl of Louth in 1319, and John fitz Thomas FitzGerald earl of Kildare in 1316. Edward III made James

Butler earl of Ormond in 1328 and Maurice fitz Thomas FitzGerald earl of Desmond in 1329. The Louth earldom faded, but Kildare, Desmond and Ormond were to dominate later colonial history.

A generation after the Bruce invasion there was a greater disaster, the Black Death, the plague which raged in Ireland as elsewhere. It was most intense in the towns, and perhaps a third of the colonial population perished. Like a slow flowing tide the pastoral Irish seeped back, inching round the crumbling colonial outposts here, breaking over them there. Many villages and farms were deserted. The revenues of Ireland began to dwindle, and royal governments tried to recoup the loss by taxation of the colony. The colonials resisted, increasingly alarmed at the Irish advances, increasingly resentful of the failure of the Lord of Ireland to defend them. The English kings were distracted by Scottish and French wars and growing internal problems, and constantly found it necessary to defer taking other than stopgap action in Ireland.

Tensions between the 'English born in Ireland' and the king's agents, the English born in England, led Edward III, during a lull in the French wars, to send his second son Lionel to Ireland as his lieutenant in 1361, with an English army. Lionel found that his military establishment was too small, even with colonial increment, to solve any problem by force. He tried to deal in other ways with the problems and alarms of the colony, attempting to regulate absenteeism and to dispose the defences of the settlements as usefully as possible. At Kilkenny in 1366 he presided over a parliament which tried, among other things, to safeguard the colonial identity – both by placing the colonials on a level with the 'new English' who came over as officials or agents, and by protecting them against 'degenerate' or lapsed English and against the Irish. The Statute of Kilkenny enacted separation from 'the Irish enemy': the English should speak English among themselves, should use English forms of their names, should dress in English fashion, should give up patronizing Irish bards, storytellers and musicians – should in general no longer 'live and comport themselves according to the customs, fashion and language of the Irish enemies. . .'.

This, along with later enactments, was ineffective. By the late fourteenth century many parts of the colony, including Dublin, were paying danegelds, or protection money, to neighbouring chiefs, and were still losing ground. The Irish chiefs in turn were reviving claims and ambitions to the old kingships of the twelfth century. Finally, the last decade of the century provided another long lull in the French and Scottish wars. Richard II decided to make the major effort that was clearly needed to solve the Irish problem. He assembled a great army and fleet and sailed to Waterford, arriving at the beginning of October 1394. He campaigned into

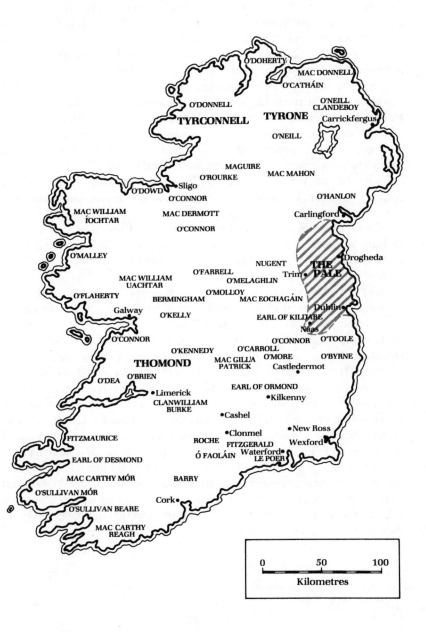

Map 11   Lordships of the later Middle Ages

Leinster and quickly defeated Art MacMurrough, the 'king' of that province. The mere showing of his great force was enough to bring most of the other Irish rulers to submission. Richard decided to revive the old compromise of giving the Irish rulers legal status and involving them in the government of the lordship. He distinguished between the 'wild Irish enemy', the 'Irish rebels' – who had been provoked into rebellion but could be brought to civility – and the 'obedient English'. In March 1395 he knighted O'Neill, O'Conor, MacMurrough and O'Brien, all of whom had put aside their Irish dress and taken English. He made grants to promote recolonization of lost territories, and, having dealt comprehensively with the problems, left Ireland in May.

Richard's policy of conciliation of 'Irish rebels' was unpopular with the colonists and broke down almost immediately among the Irish. His achievement vanished like smoke, and he returned after four years, landing at Waterford again on 1 May 1399. He marched this time fruitlessly to Dublin, where he heard of Henry Bolingbroke's rebellion in England. He sailed away again at the end of July, leaving the Irish problem unsolved, to lose both his throne and his head.

Most of Ireland now passed out of the effective control of any English monarch, and the colony was largely left to fend for itself. By the middle of the fifteenth century, the 'English Pale', a small tract of territory north of Dublin, together with more isolated patches and walled towns, represented government. The great earldoms now became the powers in the land, treating with the expanded Irish chiefdoms on the one hand and on the other with the government in England, which was preoccupied both with French war and with increasingly bloody internal dynastic struggles. As the war in France went badly, opposition gathered in England. A leader of that opposition, Richard duke of York, was removed from command of the army in France in 1446, and was appointed as lord lieutenant of Ireland, to which he came in 1449. Henry VI had no heir: York was, for the moment, heir presumptive. His status, and a considerable interest through inheritance in Ireland, made him very welcome to the colony and helped to shape the commitment on the part of the greater magnates (with the exception of Ormond) to what was to be the Yorkist cause.

Part Two

Protestant Ireland

5 The English conquest

No enactments such as the statute of Kilkenny could prevent a large part of Ireland from going native in the late middle ages. Because of the exigencies of English dynastic politics, and the other and more pressing interests of the English kings, no central direction of the Norman settlement had been allowed to develop. On the contrary, centralization had been hindered. The individual leaders of the settlement had pressed into the more attractive lands, but had slackened their efforts beyond them – or had simply found personal places in the framework of Irish society. The fragmented Irish kingdoms proved resilient. Their rulers in time came to terms with the Norman military superiority, largely by importing their own mercenaries – military tribes from the Western Isles known as gallowglass. From the climatic optimum of the thirteenth century there was a deterioration, to a low point in the late fifteenth century; then after a brief recovery, to a lower level still in the late sixteenth century, which continued until gradual recovery began in the late seventeenth century. The climatic changes appear small when measured simply in average annual temperatures (a matter of a degree or so) but in the cool damp, marginal tillage lands of Ireland they were critical, for example, for the ripening of wheat. Climate, politics, war and plague combined in the failure of the early Norman economy in Ireland. Population certainly fell drastically. The mid fourteenth-century plague recurred for many years, affecting Irish as well as colonist areas. By the early sixteenth century it is quite possible that the number of people in the country was only half that of the thirteenth century. Villages were deserted; pastoralism was resumed. Migration of the herring had made Irish coastal waters highly profitable to fish, but this source of wealth was exploited largely by outsiders. From the Irish hinterland the main products were the furs and pelts of forest animals and, overwhelmingly, what could be derived from the ubiquitous cows. Hides were exported in large numbers. Art Cosgrove draws attention to the import of 34,000 Irish hides by the Pisan leather industry in a six-month period in 1466–7.[1] Textiles in wool and linen were also exported, and timber from the forests.

By the second half of the fifteenth century conditions throughout the country were like those in the border zones of an earlier period. The governors whose responsibility it was to exercise a centralized control could do so only through a multitude of personal relationships, alliances, negotiated proxies, and diplomatic missions of persuasion. The loyal 'English' subjects of Dublin, Waterford or Drogheda might be safe within their walls. But they had daily intercourse with the Irish, for trade and otherwise, and the Irish language penetrated even into the most English strongholds.

Some magnate families, by favouring the Irish way, intermarrying with the Irish chiefs, behaving like Irish lords, contrived to maintain a kind of order among the innumerable aristocratic kin-groups. The Geraldines, or Fitzgeralds, in their two main lineages of Desmond and Kildare, and the Butlers were pre-eminent among these families, along with the de Burgos, or Burkes, who had merged much more thoroughly into the native polity. The survivors of the more ancient dynasties pursued their ways, O'Neill in Tyrone, O'Donnell in Tyrconnell, O'Brien in Thomond, MacCarthy in west Munster and many others.

However, the cultural traffic was not all one way. If the Irish language now prevailed again throughout most of Ireland, the way of life of which it was a chief expression had been greatly modified by contact with another, closely and over a long period. French and English traditions had penetrated the balladry and storytelling of the country people. English legal and administrative methods had influenced the procedures of most of the Irish lords. Gothic art, often closely modelled on distinctively English originals, more commonly deriving diffusely from French styles, prevailed throughout the island.

There were regional variations in the style of life, which correspond roughly to the social and political configurations that had developed in the course of the century. For example, a distinctive type of building was becoming numerous – the so-called 'tower house'. This is a small castle, a tower of several storeys, built of stone with machicolated parapet defences, narrow windows or loops, and other defensive devices, with an attached walled yard, or 'bawn' – the residence of a local lord, capable of withstanding a cattle-raid or border foray, the usual small-scale skirmish of the time. These are found distributed very densely on the lands of the Kildare, Ormond, Desmond, MacCarthy, O'Brien and Burke lordships, contrasting with distributions of somewhat different types of fortified buildings in the Pale – and the east generally – and with a different pattern still in the north. The orders of friars founded in the thirteenth century, especially the Franciscans and Dominicans, had been received quickly in

Ireland and established in the towns. But the friars, especially the observant Franciscans, also flourished in the non-English areas of the west and north. The Irish chiefs greatly patronized them in the fifteenth century, and the distinctive tapering square towers of their ruined churches are still a feature of western landscapes today. We may contrast these again with the great abbeys of monks, more characteristic of what had been the settled agricultural lands of the Norman thirteenth century – now for the most part fortified and absorbed into the secular interests of the lordships.

These interests were caught up in the prolonged and bloody dynastic feud in England that is romantically known as 'the Wars of the Roses', between the families of Lancaster and York. Richard duke of York, who came to Ireland as lieutenant in 1449, had a colonial Irish background and was heir to the earldom of Ulster and the lordships of Trim, Laois and Connacht – territories which had largely fallen into Irish or 'rebel English' hands. The colonial magnates liked having a royal person who was 'one of their own' as governor, and York pleased them by beginning an attempt at reconquest, although he soon ran out of money. Even when he returned to England to be embroiled in the murderous dynastic quarrel, he continued to command the support of the leading colonial magnates. Only the Butlers of Ormond, after 1452, were Lancastrian. In 1459 when York, after a defeat, fled to Ireland, was convicted of treason by the English parliament and was replaced (for the second time) as lieutenant by Ormond, there was a virtual declaration of independence by the colony. In Drogheda in 1460, a parliament summoned by York confirmed him as lieutenant and made it treason to question his authority, declaring that Ireland 'is and at all times has been corporate of itself' and that Ireland was bound only by the laws of the Irish parliament.

Although York was defeated and beheaded after his return to England, his cause triumphed in the person of his son Edward IV. Ormond was executed and his absent brothers convicted of treason. One of them invaded Ireland in 1462 but was defeated by Desmond, who was then appointed by Edward to govern the country. This was not a success. The Desmond branch of the Fitzgeralds had gone over very much to Irish ways, and the colony, especially the Pale, found the earl's rule vexatious – particularly his exaction of 'coyne and livery', that is, the quartering of troops, Irish fashion, on the king's subjects. He was replaced after some years by an Englishman, Sir John Tiptoft, who had earned a reputation at home, even among the aristocracy of that time, as a 'butcher'. Tiptoft accused the earl of Desmond, among others, of treason for his dealings with the 'Irish enemy', and had him beheaded, more or less out of hand.

This immediately sparked off uprisings both in the colony and among the Irish. Tiptoft, like other governors before and after, found himself without the means to finish what he had begun and, after attempts at compromise, was recalled and, in due course, himself executed in England. The failure of policies of force, inadequately backed, led the king back to policies of conciliation. The government of Ireland was entrusted, or abandoned, to the leading available colonial family, the Fitzgerald earls of Kildare.

In 1485 Henry Tudor successfully revived the Lancastrian cause. He returned to England from a long and obscure exile to assert in arms a claim to the throne, based on his pedigree. Richard III went down to defeat and death at the battle of Bosworth and Henry went on to London to be acknowledged king.

Throughout his reign Henry VII was concerned for the security of the throne he had taken by violence. His enemies soon put forward pretenders to the throne, employing imposters – first a boy named Lambert Simnel, whom they passed off as Edward, son of the duke of Clarence (the real Edward was imprisoned in the Tower of London), then one Perkin Warbeck, impersonating Richard duke of York (who had met his death in the same Tower). Both attempts were begun in Ireland. Simnel was actually crowned Edward VI in Dublin on 28 May 1487 and then invaded England, with English Yorkists, 2000 German mercenaries and an Irish force led by Kildare's brother Thomas – to be defeated by Henry at Stoke and to end up as a scullion in the royal kitchens. Both Kildare (whose brother was killed at Stoke) and Desmond, as well as other lords of the colony, were implicated in the Simnel episode, and Desmond supported the later attempt of Warbeck.

These enterprises made acute the question, not merely of control of the lordship of Ireland, but of the danger it could present to an English monarch when in hostile hands. From now on this was to be a growing concern of the rulers of England. The Irish colony had long been restive because, so its magnates perceived, their lord's handling of it had alternated neglect with mismanagement. They themselves had begun to alternate between appealing for firmer government and asserting their competence to govern themselves without interference.

Henry's first concern was to reassert his authority formally. He did this by sending over a soldier, Sir Richard Edgecombe, in 1488, to receive the submission of the Irish magnates and issue pardons. Then, having left Kildare in control again for a few years, the king appointed his own son, Henry, to be lieutenant and named as deputy an old companion of his exile, Sir Edward Poynings, who sailed to Ireland with 700 men late in 1494. Poynings summoned a parliament which met at Drogheda from

December 1494 until April 1495 and enacted a number of laws, the general thrust of which was to improve the defences of the colony and subordinate it more firmly to the crown. The important ninth act, later commonly known as 'Poynings's Law', decreed that if a parliament was to be summoned in Ireland, the king's lieutenant and the Irish council should first inform the king under the Great Seal of Ireland why parliament was being called and what acts were to be passed: if the king then issued his approval under the Great Seal of England, parliament might be summoned; but no parliament could validly be held in Ireland except through this procedure.

Poynings's parliament concluded its work by attainting Kildare, who was taken to England. There, Henry was satisfied that the earl had now been brought to heel and would accept the dynasty. The English parliament reversed the attainder and in August 1496 Kildare returned to Ireland as deputy – and, now, as Henry's man.

This *rapprochement* worked, after a fashion. Kildare – 'Garret *Mór*' ('the great'), as he came to be known – ruled Ireland in his own way. This was wholly satisfactory neither to the king nor to many in the colony. He had a network of alliances by fosterage and marriage which extended deep into the Gaelic Irish world as well as among the colonial families; he dominated the colony in its various parts – Pale, English towns and enclaves, and the march lands of the lordships – through his own extensive estates, through the general protection which it was his duty to supply and for which he levied various exactions, and through the special protections he issued for a special consideration. He dealt in both *brehon*, or Irish, and English law. His power, although not unlimited, was formidable, as he showed in the hard-fought battle of Knockdoe, near Galway, in 1504, when with the aid of the colonists and of the Irish of Leinster and Ulster he curbed the overexpansive Ulick Burke of Clanricard, who was aided by O'Brien and by many chiefs of Thomond and south Connacht.

Henry VIII, in 1509, inherited from his father a more secure throne, although providing an heir was to be a problem. His father had maintained some splendour, as a matter of policy, and the new king did likewise, keeping a Renaissance court, a theatre for displaying the sublimity of the state. He was affected by the remarkable shift in European perspective that was just taking place. Henry VII had sponsored Cabot's voyages. The Portuguese and Spaniards had opened up to European knowledge the coasts of Africa, the route to India and, now, the passage to the New World. While Henry VIII reigned, the Atlantic rapidly assumed a wholly new significance. He still pursued the traditional claims of his predecessors in France, but became more and more concerned with the control of the

British periphery, with the emergence of a centralized nation-state in Britain, and with adjustment to the shifting balance in the international world of power, where England's weight, although not insignificant, was still light. Like other rulers of Europe, he experienced, probably without being quite aware of what was happening, a re-orientation to the west. Ireland assumed a new strategic meaning.

The case first presented itself as a pressing need to secure more than a notional submission of the many colonial and Irish lordships and to extend the real authority of the crown. In 1519 Henry recalled Garret Óg ('the young'), who had succeeded as earl of Kildare in 1513, to answer numerous charges of misgovernment. For the next ten years he tried at intervals to manage Ireland without the semi-autonomous Kildare. The first replacement, Thomas Howard, earl of Surrey, who was sent in 1520 with a small force to obtain real submission to the king's authority and to ensure that lands in Ireland were held only by those with legal entitlement, reported that this was not feasible by diplomatic means: that Ireland could be subdued only by conquest, requiring an extremely large force, and that, since this was impracticable on grounds of cost, Kildare should be reinstated.

Finally, in 1532, the king came to the same conclusion. But by then he was deeply involved in his attempt to secure a divorce from his queen Catherine of Aragon, incurring the hostility of her nephew Charles V. In 1533 he married Anne Boleyn. This involved a breach with Rome and the reorganization not only of the English church but of the administration and bureaucracy. The enacting of independence in ecclesiastical matters brought much property and patronage into the king's hands. Thomas Cromwell, who supervised the revolutionary change, extended his bureaucracy into Ireland, disconcerting Kildare, who anticipated dismissal and began preparing to cause trouble that would show that he was indispensable. After some procrastination, Kildare obeyed a summons to London, leaving his son 'Silken' Thomas in charge of government in Ireland. Thomas apparently became alarmed about his father's fate and attempted again to demonstrate that Ireland was ungovernable without Kildare. He was led into an extreme, however, probably by the opportunities apparently provided by Henry's breach with Rome, since this troubled some consciences and involved England, although aberrantly, in the rapidly widening religious division in Europe. He rose in open rebellion in June 1534, associating his cause with that of the papacy and apparently hoping for help from Charles V. His father died in September; in October Sir William Skeffington arrived at the head of a large army and crushed the rebellion. Thomas surrendered on terms but was executed, together with his five uncles. Although his half-brother, then a child, escaped with MacCarthy's help and was much later recognized as earl, the Kildare rule was at an end.

Because of this and of the new complexities and dangers of the international situation the English commitment to Ireland became greater. The king and his government abandoned the policy of ruling Ireland through a resident magnate. Henceforth English governors were appointed. This meant much greater expense, since they had to bring their own force with them. The number of officials from England functioning in Ireland increased. Many of these urged that really firm control of the country – by force – would yield a large profit. Similar arguments – that great revenues could be raised in this or that part of the world – were heard at other European courts at this time, and were often founded on illusion or deceit. Competitive imperialism was in the European air, its objectives first formulated by the Portuguese: 'Christians and spices' – that is, the imposition of European views and the making of profit. Ireland began to be regarded as if it were part of the non-European world. It presented, no longer merely a problem in government, but an opportunity for a new breed of adventurers. They were different from the Normans who had come to win fortunes long before. Many were honourable servants of the state – and of their religion; some were dishonourable but fearless conquistadors; others were riff-raff. They belonged to a new age of bureaucracy and money, when lawyers, spies, assassins and executioners flourished, and the conflict was joined in earnest between the world of rational calculation and organization and the world of tradition.

The government wished to implement the new religious policy in Ireland. This seemed comparatively easy at first. The Palesmen co-operated. They had the example of Kildare's destruction and feared expropriation since, although they had not actively helped, they had failed to oppose him. Skeffington's successor, Lord Leonard Grey, held a parliament in 1536 which passed a declaration of the royal supremacy, with a denial of the pope's authority, in line with what had been done in England. More sweeping measures, including the suppression of monasteries, met with delays, and the king decided to speed up the process of change by appointing a special commission, headed by Sir Anthony St Leger. The commissioners arrived from England in 1537 and carried through a thorough programme of reorganization; of parliament, of the administration and of the church. The dissolution of the monasteries was begun in earnest, and this was linked to a process of piecemeal conquest now initiated: the vacated monastic houses in the Pale area were to serve as forward strongholds for a new advance. From the proceeds of dissolution patronage for co-operative lords became available.

By now the doctrinal disputes which had been disturbing Christendom for the previous twenty years were hardening into ideological confrontation. Sides were being taken all over Europe, on the basis of conscience, conviction, interest and social and political pressures. Those decisions which were strictly of informed conscience may be taken to have been a minority – and to have balanced out. It was the calculation of rulers that, by and large, decided which areas went which way, and patterns of interest and politics were emerging in the map of the religious divide. Henry had opposed the reformers. His basically jurisdictional quarrel with the papacy cut across the much more fundamental divisions in belief that were beginning to take shape. It impinged confusingly on an Irish church which was already culturally rather than doctrinally or even jurisdictionally divided and on an Irish civic polity which was in disarray after the fall of Kildare. And it came as part of a much wider revision of policy. Now, sustained government, by royal officials and soldiers rather than by resident lords, was simultaneously attempting to subdue the country, to raise a greatly increased revenue, and to replace the authority of the pope by that of the king. Reformation and conquest had the same face.

The church in Ireland in the early sixteenth century had many of the defects which challenged reform in Europe as a whole; it also had features, good and bad, which were its own. Hereditary control of ecclesiastical office and benefices was common; many of the clergy were sons of clergy or otherwise illegitimate, so that many required papal dispensation for their offices; disputes between rival kin-groups and individuals over benefices were so common that for a long time past 'Rome-running' (of the rivals with their claims and complaints to the pope) had been one of the striking abuses. The great monasteries, as elsewhere, had become secularized and the monastic ideal and purpose were largely dead. Things were better among the friars, especially the observants. But it seems that pastoral care was weak. Outside the comparatively narrow area of English control it was common for the pope to make provision to vacant sees and other offices, a situation that in other countries at this date led to many appointments of well-connected foreigners. But Irish livings were too poor to be attractive to Italians with friends at court in Rome, and locals were usually named. The papacy therefore could quite commonly seem a distant benefactor rather than (as elsewhere) a distant oppressor. For Irish ecclesiastical families, on the other hand, to have the king provide to vacancies could be seen as a threat.

The sharp division between the Irish and the colonists continued to be marked in the church: they went their separate ways, even when a single diocese (like that of Armagh) straddled the divide – although the concept and theory of unity were maintained. To disturb this system, as the administration now attempted, without first having firm control of the whole island, was to give rise to at least some conflict and resistance. But the Irish areas were no more open to the first stirrings of the counter-reformation than to the Henrician reorganization. Two Jesuits, founder-members of the new order, who came to the north of Ireland in 1542, instructed by Ignatius Loyola himself, were received by none of the Irish lords and returned with a very poor opinion of the Irish church.

While Henry VIII and his government, under a variety of new pressures, felt it necessary to bring Ireland to full obedience, Henry no more than his predecessors could afford the great expense and trouble of a campaign of military conquest. He aimed, after a show of firmness, at conciliation and diplomacy: conquest by negotiation. But the new situation required, among other things, new formulae for the relationship between the monarch and Ireland. For one thing, the title 'lord of Ireland' was widely interpreted as stemming from the papal grant *Laudabiliter* of the twelfth century, and the king had now denied the pope's authority. For another, the Irish still remembered the 'kingship of Ireland' which had once had meaning and a nebulous reality. Its revival was occasionally mooted as an alternative to the English lordship, with the current O'Neill as presumptive high-king. Henry decided that he would take the title 'king of Ireland' instead of 'lord'. A declaratory act of parliament in Dublin in 1541 ratified this, although the king was at pains to make it clear that his authority did not derive in any way from the Irish parliament. At about the same time the 'new' kingdom received its enduring emblem: the crowned golden harp on a blue field appeared as the arms of Ireland.

Henry attempted to reinforce his title by reviving, with modification, the policy of treating directly with Irish rulers and establishing formal relations between them and the crown – a policy that had ever been regarded with jealous disapproval by the colony. Autonomous authority such as the Irish rulers enjoyed was abhorrent to the English system of government. Henry's system, which has been called 'surrender and regrant', was put into force mainly by St Leger (who had a number of spells as deputy). The Irish chiefs, along with some gaelicized colonial magnates, were encouraged to come in and surrender their territories, abandon their Irish titles, disown the pope, and acknowledge Henry as their king. In return they received their lands back from him by feudal grant, and English titles of nobility were bestowed on them. So they were supplied with title, office and property, all neatly within a framework of English law.

This was a formula which begged some questions. Although the Irish succession system by this date had moved so far towards the English mode of primogeniture, that it was now customary, while a ruler was still alive, to nominate his 'tanist', or successor (often his eldest son), Irish law was still very different from English. Neither his office nor his territory was within the gift of an Irish ruler to surrender to the king. The regularization achieved from the government's point of view was reached by ignoring the legal right on the Irish side. *Laudabiliter* appears to have carried some weight with the Irish, but if the king's right did not derive from the pope, it was difficult, in Irish terms, to derive it from the actions of those who surrendered what they did not own. But by this date, alienation was increasing fast: the English administrators had no perception of the Irish legal view.

Besides, the policy was expedient. The king's right, as it was taking shape in the minds of the officials, was really right of conquest – but the conquest had not yet happened and would be costly: surrender-and-regrant bought time. The Irish lords who conformed, as most did, found it expedient too. It gave them the security of possession which outlawry denied. The security was spurious, partly because many territories were subject to competing claims, arising from earlier, often inconsistent, grants; partly simply because the Tudors and their agents were not to be trusted.

Once the intention of reducing all Ireland to obedience had been formed, it must and did seem to the administrators that the chief difficulty of the enterprise lay in the areas outside their law – largely the Irish-ruled territories. These presented in an acute form the general problem of extending full centralized control into peripheral areas (such as the north and west of England) that was a major preoccupation of the Tudor reigns. But with hindsight we can see that the crucial failure – in a policy which had considerable success – lay in the handling of the colony, and arose from the government's generally inadequate means for its task.

The problem of the 'English born in Ireland' was more complex than that of the marcher lords in Britain. It was unique. They were now of ancient establishment but had retained their distinct identity – and were continuing to maintain it as distinct not only from the Irish but also from the growing numbers of new English arrivals. Their position had long since been diminished through the loss of many of the territories their forebears had settled (and which they still claimed). They had maintained the king's right in Ireland, but on their own terms. Frustrated by English neglect, they had asserted, and formed the habit of assuming, a considerable measure of independence. They occupied the bases from which Ireland must be reduced, but in those bases they were now superseded by the king's agents and servants coming in from England. The unsureness of the government's touch showed in the great tensions which developed between leaders of the colony and the English chief governors. But the longer-term weakness arose from the government's failure to manage in the colony its shifts of religious policy.

The people of influence in the Pale had gone along readily enough at first with Henry's religious changes, partly perhaps because they were cowed by the destruction of Kildare. Obedience to the secular power was acceptable teaching for churchmen. The papacy had long been a supporter of the English monarchy in Ireland; the breach between the two now was as much a political as a religious matter. Henry's reforms were not fundamental revisions of belief, and initially the response to them was largely based on political calculation. Indeed the sudden shifts of favour and fortune resulting from his successive marriages must have been almost as upsetting to the colony as his church policies, since the Irish parliament, often receiving the news belatedly, had to cope with rapid changes in the royal succession, in English court factions, and in the status of such Irish families as the Butlers, cousins of Anne Boleyn – who was bedded, married, queened, rejected and beheaded by the king in quick succession.

In spite of his six marriages, Henry failed in one of his main objectives: to make the succession secure. When he died in 1547, he left a male heir, but a minor. Government fell into the hands of a group who, among other things, strongly favoured the protestant reformation and for a few years gave English policy its direction accordingly. Somerset, the regent who first acted for Edward VI, appointed as chief governor in Ireland a soldier, Sir Edward Bellingham, who had given satisfaction in military command. Bellingham believed that force would solve the Irish problem – and bring in an increased revenue. As for religious policy, he simply ignored the fact that while in many ways England was prepared for the full reformation, Ireland was not. In the districts under his control he applied the same changes as were being introduced in England. The conservative and slow-moving colony was deeply disturbed. Soon there was turmoil throughout the country, and the situation became dangerous for the government. Widespread uprisings threatened, with the likelihood of French intervention in the south. Although Bellingham was replaced, he left the country in a state of war.

When the young king died and his catholic half-sister Mary, Catherine of Aragon's daughter, came to the throne, she set about restoring relations with the pope and undoing the reformation in England. Otherwise she followed her father in being determined to secure the dynasty and the kingdom, but her methods were inept. In Ireland, she inherited an administration of convinced protestants, a colonial establishment unnerved by viceregal policies of treating with the Irish and by tactless pushing of the reformation from outside, and a hinterland of increasingly alienated, alarmed and mistrustful Irish lordships. Her restoration of the Mass and reversal of the reformation were generally welcomed by the colony. She made no changes in the Irish council. She dismissed some married bishops and other clergy and a few more fled; but in general the proponents of the reformation were also, by and large, the agents of the government and representatives of England, and circumspection was necessary in handling them. Mary burned no protestants in Ireland. Most of what she did should have been pleasing to the colonials, but they resented her appointments, ecclesiastical and otherwise. The mounting of increasingly costly military and other ventures bore very heavily, especially on the Pale, through billeting of troops and mulcts of other sorts, so that there was great discontent. By the end of the short reign settlers were migrating from the Pale and its oppressive exactions to place themselves under the government of O'Neill.

In the two reigns, of Edward and Mary, the shift from conciliation towards a programme of aggressive attack on the problem of the areas beyond English control took place with little break in continuity and the process of conquest was effectively initiated. The wholesale destruction of the Irish and a repopulation of the country from England had been considered and rejected. It was beyond the government's means in money, soldiers and spare people. But a modified version of this extreme was tried, with plans for a limited replacement of the inhabitants in selected troublesome regions. Mary's marriage to Philip II of Spain, who had the benefit of Spanish experience of state-sponsored colonization beyond the Atlantic, encouraged her in more modest imperialist ventures across the Irish Sea.

Two areas were considered: east Ulster, where the government, very concerned with Scotland, was anxious to check the inflow of settlement from the MacDonald lordship of the Isles, and the south midland region of bogs and wooded hills in Laois and Offaly. The earl of Sussex, sent as deputy in 1556, abandoned an attempt to penetrate east Ulster, but succeeded in moving settlers into Laois and Offaly, where Bellingham had built fortifications. These were placed on the better lands as a screen for the impenetrable redoubts of O'More, O'Conor, O'Dempsey and others who menaced the Pale and the communications between Dublin and the south-west. This half-measure was to be a continuing expense for the government and a misery for the settlers (some of them brought from the Pale) who

Map 12 Tudor Ireland

were harassed by the displaced proprietors. It was in itself a failure, but a beginning.

Mary's policies seemed foreign both in England and Ireland. Anne Boleyn's daughter Elizabeth, who succeeded her in 1558, restored Englishness to government in England. Much more adaptable, moderate, sensible and enterprising than Edward or Mary, she had the capacity, had she known it, to woo the Irish rulers and, in the theatre of her court, to play the part of the goddess of sovereignty to them. But she had to play her part among her own courtiers, and to operate through the calculating intelligence of the solid statesmen who surrounded her, served her faithfully, enriched themselves and, in their methodical way, enlarged the state, while at the same time handling the dangerous aristocrats left over from the medieval polity. In Ireland, her servants plodded on with the reduction of the country, by trial and error, estimating stage by stage the minimum necessary effective expense. There was some initial delay, because the previous reigns had left treasury, church, foreign relations and domestic affairs all in a bad state.

Henry VIII's 'surrender and regrant' policy was giving rise, in the second generation, to a rash of succession disputes and of questions about the earlier or current surrenders. This was partly because of its comparative success, which had extended the area in which central government could function, if in a limited way. There was also now an incursion of opportunists taking up half-forgotten claims to lands granted in the distant past and subsequently lost, through absenteeism or otherwise, to the returning Irish. There were specialists in discovering such claims – a Wexford lawyer named Synott, for example, who traced the titles of Leinster lands derived from William Marshal through heiresses, and was able to advise pleasantly surprised gentlemen in England that they could learn something to their advantage in Ireland. One of the most immediate and important surrender problems arose from the death of Conn O'Neill in 1559. He had been given the title of earl of Tyrone. His nomination of Matthew as his eldest son had been accepted with his surrender, and Matthew created baron of Dungannon and designated Conn's successor. But Conn was polygynous in the Irish aristocratic fashion (both simultaneously and successively) and Matthew was the offspring of one of his alliances which had not been formalized by a marriage ceremony. Further, Matthew died in 1558 – before Conn – leaving children but also leaving confusion. Shane O'Neill claimed to be Conn's eldest legitimate son and rightful successor. While the question of legitimacy hardly arose in Irish custom, it did in English custom and law. A tangle of cross-purposes, disingenuous pleadings and temporizing

Plate 5   A late eighteenth-century small landlord's house with a thatched roof, Derrymore, County Armagh

Plate 6   A 'station': one of the spots at which prayers were recited during the pilgrims' 'rounds' of a holy place on a patron day, Glencolumbkille, County Donegal

Plate 7   The interior of a house, County Armagh, by Cornelius Varley

Plate 8   Meeting between Art MacMurrough and the Earl of Gloucester, from French metrical history of Richard II

ensued, in the course of which central Ulster slipped out of even a semblance of English control.

The real issue was whether the ruler of Tyrone was to be 'O'Neill', with all ancient rights, or the queen's earl. And the government regarded the control of Ulster as important, partly because of the Scottish connection and settlement there. The question of Scotland was urgently vexatious. Mary queen of Scots, who had a good claim on Elizabeth's throne, married the dauphin of France in 1558, creating a Scottish–French danger in which Ireland might play a part. The government handled the O'Neill problem clumsily but, as it transpired, safely. The deputy, Sussex, learned to his frustration that Ulster, beyond its natural defences of drumlin hills and winding streams, lakes and bogs, was impossible to subdue by the campaigns he could afford to mount. Shane was given a kind of recognition, the earldom remaining vacant. Sussex's successor Sidney decided to return to the attack, and with much and prolonged difficulty Shane was overcome – defeated by O'Donnell of Tyrconnell and killed by the Antrim Scots with whom he sought refuge. They pickled his head in a barrel and sent it to Dublin where it was spiked on the castle along with other exemplary relics of Irish treason; but nothing much changed in Ulster.

Early in 1560 the Irish parliament, following the English, undid Mary's ecclesiastical legislation. Protestant faith now became official again, although not pushed as hard as under Edward. It was still the religious policy brought from outside, in the persons of ecclesiastics and officials from England. The distinction between these and the old colonials was sharpening. As new colonization brought larger numbers of immigrants, the distinction was to be registered as that of 'New English' and 'Old English'. The old colony remained largely catholic; but it was the base from which the government must hope to attack the hydra-headed independence of the lordships.

When this endeavour was resumed, it began with an attempt to curb private war among the queen's subjects: the earls of Desmond and Ormond were both summoned to London after Ormond defeated and captured Desmond in a battle in 1565. The government decided to resume a proposal that had been considered in Henry's time. When Sidney was appointed deputy he was instructed to set up decentralized administrations in some of the old colonial lordships. Undertaking a survey, he found that parts of the south-west were at present ungovernable and that there were rebelliously independent factions in Ormond and Connacht. He had Desmond consigned to the Tower of London in 1567. Meanwhile, adventurers arriving from England in pursuit of land claims were spreading

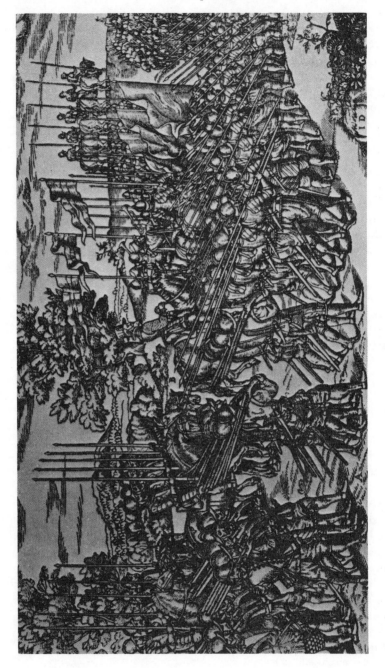

Figure 10 Sidney on the march
Engraving from *The Image of Ireland.*

even greater unease in the south in the absence of the earls. Ormond's brother, Sir James Butler, rebelled and James Fitzmaurice Fitzgerald, Desmond's cousin, led a revolt to which he gave a religious character. The earl of Ormond, 'Black Tom', a relation and friend of the queen, returned to Ireland and quickly placed the Butlers firmly in the government camp. Sidney proceeded to subdue ruthlessly the Munster rebellion, which was scattered and uncoordinated. He pressed on, against the reluctance of the colonial parliament, with plans for the reconstruction of the major lordships.

The queen and her advisers also decided on more colonization. The experience of Philip and Mary in the midlands, however, suggested that for the state to undertake this would be both difficult and costly. They preferred the mercantilist, or early capitalist, device of state-backed private enterprise, and proposed again to begin in the north-east. The mode of procedure had its own difficulties because in backing without fully controlling a private enterprise of this kind the state was setting up a rival to its own officials and, to some extent, to its own authority.

Several schemes were drafted, one of which involved Sir Thomas Smith, a secretary of the queen, who published the plan prematurely but was allowed to proceed. He and his son were granted a huge tract of the old earldom of Ulster, now reverted to the crown but occupied for generations by the O'Neills of Clandeboy (*Clann Aodha Buidhe*, from the thirteenth-century Aodh *buidhe* – 'the yellow' – O'Neill). The Smiths were to take the land as tenants of the crown, drive out the proprietors of all grades and retain the labour of the lower orders. Sir Brian MacPhelim O'Neill, the incumbent, had been loyal to the crown but resented the arbitrary decision to take over his country. He routed the intruders, who had landed with an inadequate force. The queen now granted a large part of Antrim, outside the government-held fortress and town of Carrickfergus, to Walter Devereux, earl of Essex. She and Essex were joint shareholders in the enterprise, which employed a force of 1200. Essex's only achievement was to bridge the Blackwater beyond Armagh – to open the way into Ulster. Otherwise he was unscrupulous, inhumane and unsuccessful.

Sidney, returning as deputy in 1575, forced through his regional reorganization against growing opposition, creating two 'presidencies', in Connacht under Sir Nicholas Malby and in Munster under Sir William Drury. By 1578 Malby had quietened southern Connacht through a programme of burning and destruction and was trying to show a profit in new revenues. Munster was thrown into confusion again when James Fitzmaurice Fitzgerald renewed his religious war in the midsummer of 1579. He landed at Smerwick in west Kerry with 700 soldiers, made

contact with Desmond (who had been allowed, against official advice, to
return to Ireland five years before) and made a general appeal for the
defence of 'our country'. He had obtained minimal (and easily disowned)
help from the pope and from Spain, and counted on the alarm and
foreboding being spread by government actions to secure him allies in
Ireland. Although he was soon killed in a skirmish, the rebellion attracted
support.

Drury, the new president of Munster, died, but English forces, making
use of the command of the sea which had become a feature of their Irish
wars, converged on Munster. Malby, from Connacht, defeated 2000 men
fighting under papal colours and led by two of the Geraldines. Perrot
patrolled the coast by sea. Pelham, the lord chief justice, proclaimed
Desmond a traitor, and the earl abandoned his towns and castles and took
to the woods and hills 'to defend the faith'. In the Pale, James Eustace,
Viscount Baltinglass, took up the papal cause, joined with Fiach MacHugh
O'Byrne of the Wicklow hinterland, and tried to rouse rebellion
throughout Leinster. A new deputy arrived, Baron Grey of Wilton, a
puritan who offered no quarter to the pope's supporters. He slaughtered
the little force of Spaniards and Italians at Smerwick and then conducted
campaigns of methodical devastation in Munster, burning the corn,
driving cattle, destroying all food, to induce famine. By the time he was
recalled in 1582, he had succeeded: famine was everywhere and the
rebellion was crushed. The earl of Desmond was finally hunted down and
killed in Kerry in the winter of 1583.

The reduction of the country proceeded. In Connacht Sir Henry
Docwra completed the chasing out of Scottish mercenaries and went on
with the work of inquiring into titles, assessing crown rents and mapping
the property and power of the proprietors, in what was a logical sequel to
the old surrender-and-regrant policy. The 'composition' of Connacht,
negotiated with the western lords in 1585, was intended to end
autonomous power west of the Shannon and to produce a sizeable
revenue.

In 1585, the parliament in Dublin agreed to huge confiscations in
Munster, and to the attainder of the dead earl of Desmond. Following the
rebellion the province had been garrisoned and secured. Now a vast area
came to the crown, and a further plantation was carefully planned, to bring
in large proprietors who would sub-let their lands and make the area safe
for regular royal government. The confiscated lands, partly depopulated
by war, famine and disease, were divided into large lots and the new
landowners and their tenants began to move in – to the number of about
10,000 settlers by 1598.

Sir John Perrot, lord deputy in the middle 1580s, again proposed tackling the difficult problem of Ulster. Turlough Luineach O'Neill, who had succeeded Shane as paramount lord, although he was cautious and quiet, maintained the Irish style of independent rule. The deputy was concerned about him and about the large numbers of Scottish mercenaries in the north, about the kinship alliance of the Macleans of Mull with the sons of Shane O'Neill, and about the Antrim interests of the MacDonalds of the Isles. Using the sea, he seized the castle of Dunluce, on the north coast, which was being held for James VI of Scotland. Sorley Boy MacDonnell retook it shortly afterwards, but in the following year, 1586, the treaty of Berwick ended these concerns by settling matters between James and Elizabeth. Sorley Boy received the Route, in Antrim, and Angus MacDonnell the Glens. When the Scots re-entered Connacht, however, under Donald MacDonnell (Angus's brother), Bingham slaughtered 2000 of their men, women and children in Co. Mayo.

The government, for its northern plans, had its own O'Neill, Hugh, the second son of Matthew. He had been taken to England as a small boy by Sidney and brought up at court, succeeding to his father's title of baron of Dungannon, and on his return to Ireland had co-operated with the queen, not only in the north but in the suppression of the Desmond rebellion. He became the second earl of Tyrone and attended the upper house of the Dublin parliament that approved the Munster settlement.

The advance of government control was shown in the crisis of 1588 when Ireland gave no cause for alarm. This was the year that the Spanish Armada sailed, the great fleet of transports, carrying an army for the assault on England, that was scattered by the English in the Channel. Some of the Spanish ships that made their way through the Dover straits sailed northward along the British east coast, round the north of Scotland, and turned south for Spain, to be wrecked on the northern and western coasts of Ireland. The queen's agents had orders to give no quarter to the soldiers and sailors struggling ashore: they were to be killed at once. And only in the north and north-west were a few given shelter and help.

Ulster remained outside the new system, but the pressure was begun with increased garrisoning of its approaches. Hugh Maguire of Fermanagh reacted when the pressure came along the Erne in 1593. O'Donnell of Tyrconnell was his cousin; Tyrone was his father-in-law. In response to government requests Tyrone gave help against Maguire that was evasive and ineffectual. Under the direction of Sir Henry Bagenal a ring of forts was closing in around Ulster, and Maguire's country in particular, and in 1594 the English took Enniskillen castle at the narrows of the middle Erne. In the following year, Turlough Luineach died; the earl of Tyrone was

The Civill Irish Woman

The Civill Irish man

The Wilde Irish man

The Wilde Irish Woman

Figure 11 Figures from Speed's *Atlas*
Source: National Library of Ireland.

inaugurated, Irish fashion, as O'Neill at the inauguration site of Tullaghoge near Dungannon. Maguire, with O'Neill's cautious help, retook Enniskillen. O'Neill began arming and training soldiers, acquiring arms largely from the Scottish lowlands. He and his fellow earl, Red Hugh O'Donnell of Tyrconnell sent to the Isles for mercenaries. He sent his brother Art to retake the Blackwater fort, and in the summer of 1595 he attacked Bagenal at Clontibret as that commander was re-supplying the frontier garrison at Monaghan. O'Donnell meantime took Sligo and began to move on northern Connacht.

O'Neill was proclaimed a traitor in June 1595. He had weighed carefully the developments of the preceding decades and saw the end of the ancestral sovereignty of the O'Neills approaching. He hoped to prolong it either by building a position of strength from which he could negotiate with the government – or by other means. So, he was in communication with Philip of Spain, expressing the grievances of 'the whole Irish nobility', and offered Philip the crown of Ireland. But he also negotiated with the queen's government, receiving a pardon in 1596. In that year Philip II sent arms which safely reached Ulster and in the autumn dispatched two expeditions, one bound for south-west England, one for Ireland, both of which were driven back by storms. O'Neill and O'Donnell now sent appeals south to Munster, and tried to make a common cause to resist and undo the English conquest. More parleying with the government followed, and in 1597 O'Neill formally submitted to Ormond, then in military command. But when a new field fortification was placed on the Blackwater and Bagenal, with 4000 men, was sent north to supply it, O'Neill met him at the Yellow Ford. Bagenal lost his guns, half his force and his life.

Pressure, steadily exerted through the century, had consolidated a desperate resistance of the old Irish polity. O'Neill, on the base of an Irish lordship, had practised diplomacy, organization and methodical war. A generation earlier Shane O'Neill, in his wars against the English, had been described by their intelligence as the first Irishman to make use of the ordinary people, and not merely the warlike propertied class, in his military organization. Hugh used all the resources of a province which was moderately rich, employing *bonnachts* – or native paid soldiers – gallowglass, and the normal Irish levies in a numerous, well-armed, trained and organized army. He also succeeded in holding together an alliance of Irish lords who had a tradition of mutual family and territorial enmity.

For the government, the profit of conquest seemed always to recede before its ever-increasing cost. But this was a familiar dilemma by now, and if the end was in doubt it was also in sight. A large effort was needed, and the queen made Robert Devereux, earl of Essex, her lieutenant, and sent him to Ireland in her cause in April 1599 with 16,000 troops. By now, government had collapsed in Connacht, Munster and parts of Leinster: fire and sword were being turned back on the colonists. Essex's expedition, to the queen's fury, was a fiasco. He was recalled (to join the great roster of the servants of the Tudors who ended their careers with the loss of their heads) and was replaced at the beginning of 1600 by Charles Blount, Lord Mountjoy, a level-headed administrator and soldier. Sir George Carew, as president of Munster, quickly pacified that province. Mountjoy methodically organized a large-scale amphibious operation. He sent Sir Henry Docwra from Carrickfergus with 4000 men to O'Neill's rear, to dig in at Derry on Lough Foyle. He himself marched north overland, but was checked at the Moyry pass and retired. He settled down to the process of steady devastation, to induce famine and destroy the potential bases of O'Neill's war. O'Neill on the other hand knew that to win he had to go on the offensive, outside Ulster, and that to do that successfully he had to have Spanish help. He and O'Donnell negotiated – with difficulty because of the slowness and uncertainty of communications and because Ireland, as ever, was only a marginal element in the calculations of European diplomacy – with Philip III for a Spanish expedition of sufficient size to an advantageous part of the country. The expedition finally arrived late in 1601, too far south, at Kinsale in Co. Cork. O'Neill, O'Donnell and their allies marched south, but on Christmas Eve were defeated by the English cavalry before they could link up with the Spaniards, who then surrendered without having been engaged. O'Donnell departed to Spain, where he died shortly afterwards, but O'Neill retreated to the north again, to the heartland of his country, where he was invested by Mountjoy. Eventually, negotiations began, and in March 1603 O'Neill travelled south to Mellifont, formerly the Cistercian abbey, now the house of an old friend, to meet Mountjoy. He submitted and was granted terms. He retained his earldom and his property but lost his independence: royal government was to move into Tyrone. Similar terms were agreed for Rory O'Donnell, the new earl of Tyrconnell. Mountjoy knew, but did not inform Tyrone as they parleyed, that the queen had died six days before. James VI of Scotland, whose mother Mary queen of Scots had been beheaded (although reluctantly) by Elizabeth, was now James I of England, and of Ireland.

The military phase of the conquest was complete and English authority was effective in some fashion in every part of Ireland. The warfare by which this had been accomplished had grown increasingly savage – not fundamentally different from the wars which had been endemic both in the

Irish and in the colonial lordships, but much more extensive in its effects
and much more bitter, as religious, ethnic, racial, cultural and political
prejudices gathered strength. Some historians have seen the beginning of
nationalism in this period, and it is true that, for example, James
Fitzmaurice Fitzgerald and after him the northern earls made appeals for
a national resistance to the English. But it would be rash to equate this with
the nationalism of later times, aimed at the achievement of an independent
nation-state and animated by a romantic ideology. The distinction
between the Irish 'nation' and the English 'nation' within Ireland was
maintained throughout the Middle Ages and was descriptive, of two
groups with different customs and habits – as it might be, age-groups or
class-groups in a modern society – which therefore, in politics, could
constitute distinct and often conflicting interests. But medieval political
relations were between the prince and a hierarchy of 'orders', 'estates' and
kin-groups: there was not a 'general will' of the atomic individuals, but a
prescriptive order. In the sixteenth century the aggressive and voracious
drives of early capitalism and imperialism were at work, immensely
destructive of traditional cultures, but also creative and productive. What
was perceived in Ireland was that one 'nation' within the country had
developed a tendency which was proving to be destructive of the social
fabric of the other. The transmitters and guardians of Gaelic culture
sounded warnings and began to politicize the long-recognized differences:

> Shame on the foreign grey gun;
> Shame on the golden chain;
> Shame on the court without language;
> Shame on the denial of Mary's son.
> Nobles of ancient Art's island,
> Your transformed status is not good;
> Misguided cowardly company –
> Speak nothing henceforth but 'Shame!'[2]

Nationalism in a later sense could develop from this perception (and the
poem just quoted was to be printed, for example, by Patrick Pearse in the
twentieth century as part of the testimony of Irish nationality down the
ages); but that would take time.

   The destruction was very evident as the wars came for the moment to an
end. Some large areas had been devastated by fire and famine and were
temporarily depopulated. Yet it seems certain that the overall population
had increased and was, perhaps with brief setbacks, continuing to increase.
War and migration had caused much dislocation of people – some towns,
for example, are described as being waste and all but deserted at this time

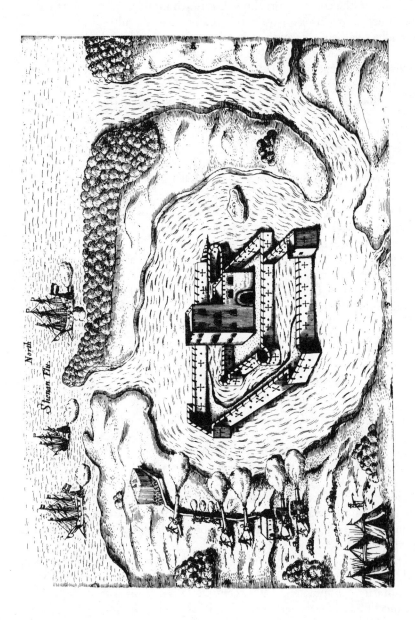

Figure 12   Castle of Carrigfoyle (from *Pacata Hibernia*)

– but on the whole the late-medieval settlement patterns had not greatly changed. Some contrasts had been sharpened by developments of Tudor times – for example, the clearance of the woods in the colonial areas (especially the old Pale) and in large parts of the east and south-east added to the distinction between these lands and the wetter country of west and north-west, including many of the regions of Irish polity now newly opened up to English government. Within those north-western regions an old way of life had continued until now. Edward Tremayne, clerk of the Irish privy council, summed it up as it showed itself, in governmental terms, to Tudor eyes:

The Irish government . . . is that one great lord possesseth and ruleth a Country, sometimes as big as an English shire, sometimes more, sometimes less, as it happeneth. He attaineth unto it rather by choice and election than succession. In which election they observe to choose him of the kindred (which they call 'septe') of such as have been used to rule them. Such are Oneale, Odonell, Oreley, Ocarroll and such others. And for the most part he that hath showed himself most mischievous in murdering, spoiling, and burning doth soonest attain to the government, first to be 'thaniste' (which is as it were heir in succession), and afterward to be the ruler when the lord in possession dieth. When this great lord is thus in possession of his Country, he is followed of all the warlike people of the same, viz., horsemen, gallowglasses, and kern, and with these multitudes he useth the inferior people at his will and pleasure. He eateth and spendeth upon them with man, horse, and dog. He useth man, wife or children according to his own list, without any means to be withstanded or again-said, not only as an absolute king but as a tyrant or lord over bondsmen. For deciding of causes in controversies he hath a judge of his own constitution and useth the law called the Brehon Law, nothing agreeing with the laws of England. If any of his people commit an offence, he is punished or pardoned as pleaseth the lord. If any of his people receive wrong or any offence be done against his Country, this great lord useth the revenge according to his own will, without making any stay for commission for the Queen or her governor. . . .[3]

The system here (in 1573) observed sharply but without full understanding of its complexities – and in particular of the legal and customary limitations on power – was one against which the military campaigns and the attempted plantations had been directed. It was not just the independent authority of the Irish chiefs which offended, but the whole unregulated foreign and un-English character of the way of life. In England itself the developing polity was harshly authoritarian, sternly opposed to idleness and vagabondage in particular and approving of order, regulation, centralization and method. These all seemed to be lacking in Irish society, with its 'booleying', or transhumance, when the young people moved to the hills or bogs for the summer months with the cattle, with its shifting tillage patches with bewilderingly movable fences, with its intense close-knit kin loyalties and feuds, with its whiskey-drinking, oatcake-eating, musicians, bards, doctors, brehons, chiefs, women, who wrapped themselves in their shaggy mantles and seemed independent of all good order and discipline.

But there was a rooted contradiction in the government's approach to Ireland. It could not decide whether it should aim at tidying up an extremely untidy country by anglicizing it – compelling and teaching the people to behave like English – or whether it should aim at transplanting the Irish to some distant colonies, in the Americas or the West Indies, and wholly replacing them with civil and amenable folk. And in the meantime, the agents of government struggling with the realities of everyday contingency, many of them looking to their own fortunes, drove a course somewhere in between. Mountjoy in the last days of his war against Tyrone expressed the wish that 'I should . . . either have made this country a rased table, wherein she [the queen] might have written her own laws, or have tied the ill-disposed and rebellious hands till I had surely planted such government as would have overgrown and killed any weeds that should have arisen under it'.[4] But in practice, Mountjoy found that he had not the means for any such drastic solution; his victory over O'Neill was a negotiated one and his handling of the north after Mellifont was conciliatory.

Tyrone, pardoned in the autumn of 1603, managed in the next two years to establish extensive rights of property in Ulster under the new dispensation. Then, however, Mountjoy was replaced by Sir Arthur Chichester, a 'servitor' (one who had served in the war) who came as lord deputy hoping to see a presidency of Ulster established on the model of Connacht and Munster and that he should be its lord president. He was ill disposed to O'Neill, as was Sir John Davies, the attorney general, an intellectual who was full of ideas about the government of Ireland, how it had been mistaken in the past and how it might be managed for the future. Davies, who regarded the position of Tyrone as an anomaly dangerous to the state, argued his case in London, where a commission was appointed to consider the reconstruction of Ulster. As English law was overlaid on Irish law and custom, there were disputes in many parts of the province. In east Ulster, meantime, on the lands of Clandeboye a Scottish enterprise was transforming the country. Sir Arthur Chichester had joined with Hugh Montgomery and James Hamilton to acquire extensive lands from Conn O'Neill (a befuddled sot) and were settling them with immigrants from Scotland – a comparatively dense settlement on partly depopulated territory in north Co. Down and an extensive settlement also in Antrim.

O'Neill of Tyrone, as he enlarged his authority and resumed something of his old status, came into dispute with his main subordinate chief, O'Cahan. He found the new government pressure disquieting and knew that he was under suspicion, partly because his son Henry was serving with the Spaniards in the Netherlands. This was one of the loose ends left after the late war. Government policy had been, more or less, in favour of the departure from the country of the trained soldiers who had fought against them, but had misgivings about their future movements. Mountjoy had summed up the problem for the privy council:

I find the Irishry at this time to affect some journey into the Low Countries, or to the Indies, or to be led to any other place of service. Unto which if it be objected that they will return more able soldiers and more dangerously affected, I can assure your lordships there is no experience can better the knowledge they have already attained to. . . .[5]

Now it was known that O'Donnell, earl of Tyrconnell, was planning to go to the continent and that Cúconnacht Maguire of Fermanagh had already slipped away there on a mission. Maguire appeared on board ship in Lough Swilly late in August 1607 to take Tyrconnell into exile. Tyrone, who had no doubt matured in his mind thoughts very similar to those he harboured before entering in the war against Elizabeth: the calculation that his enemies were closing in and that the old O'Neill sovereignty was at an end, quickly decided to join them. The earls sailed from Rathmullen on 4 September 1607.

The government took its opportunity, declared that Tyrone had ruled oppressively and had been engaged in conspiracy and, in December, confiscated the earls' lands. Then Sir Cahir O'Doherty, who had been protected in his lands of Inishowen by Docwra – at Derry – rose in revolt when Docwra was replaced by Sir George Paulet, who harassed him. The revolt spread, and after its suppression and O'Doherty's death, the government decided on much more extensive confiscations. The assessment of the area to be confiscated was done on the principle of *Vae victis*, without scruple in respect of many proprietors who had been involved neither with O'Neill nor with O'Doherty. It was decided to colonize the confiscated lands and to abandon the half-hearted programme of anglicization of the Ulster Irish.

From late in 1608 a committee (which included Davies) sat in London to prepare a scheme of plantation. Its report, submitted in 1609, was modified and put into effect in 1610. The principle of the plan was that planters should outnumber the native Irish in the colonized areas and should be segregated in their own districts. Land was to be granted to three kinds of person: 'Undertakers', who undertook to move in from England or Scotland with imported tenants to land which would be completely cleared of natives; 'servitors', who might keep Irish labour on payment of a 50 per cent rent surcharge; and native 'deserving Irish' who would be moved from their present land to new allotments. Land was to be distributed in 'proportions' of 2000, 1500 and 1000 acres together with bog and woodland, the proportions being grouped in large 'precincts'. The precincts were to be the units of segregation – Scottish undertakers on one, English on another, servitors and Irish mixed on another. In each, one undertaker was to be granted an extra large proportion of 3000 acres, which carried with it administrative and supervisory responsibilities. Terms of letting were easy: common socage of £5⅓ *per annum* for each small allotted proportion. The undertaker must stay five years on his portion, must have twenty-four able-bodied males drawn from ten or more families for each small proportion, must build a strong 'bawn' and maintain a supply of arms, and must have no Irish on his proportion. Undertakers and servitors were required to take the oath of supremacy. Irish grantees, excused the oath, must build houses and bawns and practise tillage and husbandry after the manner of the Pale, and they had to pay double rent. The county of Coleraine, which included O'Cahan's country, was omitted from this general scheme. It contained the two walled towns of Derry and Coleraine and presented other problems. The city of London was persuaded, on very favourable terms, to be a corporate undertaker in its plantation.

As this elaborate and ambitious scheme – covering the six counties of Donegal, Coleraine (which came to be known as the county of Londonderry), Fermanagh, Tyrone, Armagh and Cavan – went into operation it was greatly modified in practice. The hasty surveys were inaccurate and the parcels of land actually granted were considerably larger than the scheme envisaged. The Irish were not moved off the undertakers' land in advance of the plantation. They were found to be indispensable in practice and, after a series of compromises, the segregation principle was finally abandoned within about twenty years. The same happened on the London companies' holdings. Meanwhile, many of the dispossessed withdrew to the woods, hills and bogs, to harass the planters, who had to live like frontiersmen, constantly on the watch for attack. The 'bawns' they built were mostly defended farmsteads, with strong stone walls pierced by musket-loops. There were occasional stronger buildings, and the planters laid out some new towns.

In the south, where the Munster plantation had been overrun in the wars, resettlement went on in the early years of the century; but it was a patchy and incomplete business. Elsewhere, the searching out of defective titles – especially those where a royal interest could be argued – proceeded at an increased pace, leading to great unease and uncertainty which affected most landowners. Partly in connection with this, an extensive system of bribery and corruption developed among the English officials of the Irish administration.

The succession of James VI of Scotland to the English throne inspired here and there some naïve hopes. One or two Irish poems greet the Stuart king as representative of the 'Milesian' Celtic world. Others hoped that the son of the catholic Mary queen of Scots would be more kindly in his dealing with catholics. But such ideas widely missed the reality of what was involved in the union of crowns and of the considerations which moved James in his decisions. The large Scottish element in the plantation of Ulster was a truer reflection of the new significance of the union.

6 *The protestant settlement*

The end of the war against the Irish and the accession of James laid bare a crucial problem, that of the old colonists, or 'Old English' as they were now known to distinguish them from the increasingly numerous 'New English' brought in by the conquest. The 'Old English' were Irish who had sustained the English connection in Ireland since their forebears came over with Henry II. In the Irish language they were commonly referred to as '*Gaill*', a word which had been applied to the Vikings and the Normans. They were distinguished from '*Sacsain*', which was applied to the English and to the 'New English' of Ireland. And they were distinguished from '*Gaedhil*', the word applied to the native Irish, or 'Old Irish' as they were coming to be termed. But occasionally another word was used – '*Éireannaigh*' ('Irish') – to apply to those born in Ireland, both *Gaedhil* and *Gaill*.

These distinctions are reflected in the ambiguous and unsure status of the 'Old English' in the reign of James I – but their real problem arose from another distinction. They wished to think of themselves in the old way as England's colony in Ireland, but they were so regarded neither by the new colony rapidly forming nor by the new government in England. They could not simply merge into the new colony, or absorb it, because they were catholic and it was protestant; and their own attempts to argue that being catholic was compatible with loyalty to the crown ran contrary to the whole feeling and thought of the age and were regarded with cold disbelief by those they sought to persuade. James himself told a deputation from them in 1614 that they were only half-subjects of his: 'For you give your soul to the pope, and to me only the body and even it, your bodily strength, you divide between me and the king of Spain. . . .'[1]

At the same time, within catholicism itself, the old division in the Irish church between the colonists and the natives was, if anything, enlarged by the events of the reformation and, more particularly, of the counter-reformation. The tridentine reforms, like the policy of English government, were directed towards uniformity, centralization, regularity, order and accountability, and placed central emphasis on the training of priests and the organization of the church on diocesan and parochial lines. Counter-reformation catholicism, perhaps even more strongly than early protestantism, shows the outlook of the dawning age of capitalism. This fitted well with the mind of the Old English and poorly with the mind of the Old Irish, whose church was integrated into native custom, tradition and kinship.

Elizabeth had been excommunicated by the pope and her subjects released from their allegiance. The question of the allegiance to be given by catholics to a sovereign who was a 'heretic' was a thorny one, as indeed was the question of the organizational structure of the church in a country with such a sovereign. In the last years of Elizabeth's reign, Rome had consulted O'Neill and had appointed four archbishops to the Irish provinces, three of them his nominees. These included Peter Lombard, an Old English townsman, from Waterford, who, as archbishop of Armagh and primate, addressed the problem of accommodating Irish catholicism to the sovereignty of James I. His final formula was that James might be accepted as lawful (but not Christian) king provided he ruled justly; but the penal laws against catholics constituted unjust rule. Since there was no question of the repeal of these laws, this left the political–religious question unsolved. There was a tendency for the Old English catholics to go on looking for some such formula, while Old Irish churchmen remained more intransigent on the allegiance question just as they tended to resist reconstruction by the counter-reformation. Rome in the 1620s decided on the fixed policy of maintaining a full episcopal system in Ireland. This distinguished Ireland from other lands ruled by protestants, where a 'missionary' organization was usually favoured and normal church organization suspended. It represented, essentially, an irredentist view and set the terms for a long-enduring contest. The civil authorities had already established an episcopal church: the established church was now matched by a church-in-waiting which, given the numerical proportions of the adherents of the two, constituted a formidable reversionary interest.

The New English settlers and a good deal of opinion in Britain were very much against reaching the kinds of accommodation that the Old English sought. The king, too, was unprepared to compromise on the constitution: it was a protestant kingdom. But, for its own ease and convenience, the government was obliged to offer some concessions in practice from time to time, while yielding nothing in principle. Ireland was not governed as a kingdom with interests of its own, but as a resource for the management of Britain. In this light the government tried to manipulate Irish affairs to obtain what the king needed in his English business.

Increased revenues were required from Ireland and a parliament was necessary once the sweeping confiscations in Ulster had begun. Parliaments, however, required careful management and preparation. The Old English were entitled to representation – which would give a catholic majority and the opportunity to air numerous grievances. The king in 1611 sent over Lord Carew to intimidate and gerrymander. Recusancy laws were sternly enforced for a while, one elderly bishop was executed, and the electoral system was skilfully revised to return a packed parliament with a narrow protestant majority. Even so, the Old English, forming a solid opposition, succeeded in creating impediments to government policy. The administration fell back on other means of raising revenue. It attempted further plantations, in Wexford, the midlands and elsewhere, with limited success. With even less success it tried to check leakage through corruption in the Irish government. And it squeezed the Old English through the regular imposition of heavy recusancy fines.

Slap-dash and improvised Irish policies continued through the later years of James and the early years of Charles I. In England there were consistent efforts to raise money without having to go to parliament: the king would be absolute. In Ireland this effort partly took the form of bargaining, chiefly with the Old English, for money subsidies to the crown in return for 'matters of grace and bounty to be rendered to Ireland'. This meant that the government would apply the law – mulct the catholics with recusancy fines; inquire into the title of the New English protestant settlers to their lands – unless the money was forthcoming. The issue was complicated by the desire of the Old English to be treated as loyal subjects and allowed, for example, to take part in the defence of Ireland (the war against Spain being a test case). But neither the government in England nor the New English wanted to see arms in catholic hands; instead they expected the Old English to pay for (protestant) soldiers.

The attempt to govern without parliament was to be more significant in English than in Irish politics, but it led the king to send one of his most trusted and capable associates to Ireland in 1632 as lord deputy. This was Thomas, Viscount Wentworth, whose purpose, as Aidan Clarke has put it, was 'to create a new source of power for the crown in Ireland . . . to fulfil the real purpose of his deputyship by showing how Ireland could be used to redress the balance of power elsewhere in the king's favour. . .'.[2]

Wentworth's purpose was political, but as always, the first and most pressing need was for money, and there was something of an impasse. Considerable subsidies had been granted to the king, largely by the Old English community, in return for 'graces'. More were now needed, but the Dublin officials and the New English settlers were firmly opposed to the toleration of catholicism for money and argued that as much could be raised through swingeing recusancy fines. Wentworth came to an understanding with the Old English; to the protestant party, led by the earl of Cork, he offered the sop of a parliament in return for subsidies. He showed his capacity in the preparations he made for election and in his management of the parliament. His aim was to withhold undue concessions but to persuade parliament to vote money. He managed the election so that a small group committed to official policy held the balance between Old and New English factions; he arranged the parliament in two sessions, the first to vote money, the second to consider grievances; he interpreted Poynings's law, with its requirement of an advance submission to the crown of the proposed legislative programme, to keep firmly in his hands the business to be dealt with; he sided with the Old English in the first session, with the New English in the second. In the sessions of 1633–5 he could boast a success in parliamentary management that otherwise was to elude Charles I.

Wentworth was equally successful in other ways; but it was in the long run an unprofitable success. He was a tireless administrator, whose dealings with the various groups in Ireland were devious as well as tough. He partly misled, partly bullied all sides, while he searched out all possible ways of raising funds, including new plantations and customs farming. He played upon the greatest anxiety of the landowning class (who at that time had a virtual monopoly of political influence) – the old question of defective titles. Ulster planters were heavily fined for failing to observe the terms of the plantation; London's charter in Derry was revoked, extinguishing the security of the tenants; and these were then rack-rented by the royal commission which replaced London. These devices to raise money failed to take account of other requirements of policy. The concessions gained by different groups for the funds they provided proved to be evanescent. However, the exercise in absolute government continued in Ireland unchecked until it collapsed in Britain.

Wentworth imposed uniformity on the Irish protestants. The Ulster Scots were presbyterian, and the New English, although they were of the same confession as the established church in England, also inclined to calvinism. Wentworth, like many English observers, had a low opinion of them, partly because of their lack of zeal in propagating their faith, partly for what he saw as their self-serving: he required them to conform, liturgically and otherwise, to the English norm.

Meanwhile, across the Channel, the effort to enforce conformity in Scotland led to the crisis which began in 1637 with the signing of the covenant by which the Scots bound themselves to one another to resist.

The covenant was promulgated in Ulster, but there the Scots were on the whole content – without pledging – simply to abandon conformity and revert to their preferred liturgy (which consisted mainly, according to reports to the government, of listening to sermons). Wentworth, however, acted with characteristic vigour. He moved the army into Ulster and had an oath of abjuration of the covenant administered to all adult Scots (the 'black oath', as it was soon known among them) in the critical year of 1639.

The king moved an army to the Scottish border, where the Scots met him in arms. An inconclusive agreement was reached.

Charles sent for Wentworth, who urged coercion of the Scots. Money was needed for this and it was decided to summon parliament, in Ireland for March 1640 and in England for April: Ireland would show the way. Wentworth prepared the ground carefully, and again succeeded in managing the Irish parliament – for its first session, which he attended. He had now been promoted to lord lieutenant and created earl of Strafford. He went across to attend parliament in England, but the April session there refused to supply the king until he should first attend to their 'liberties'. The king dissolved parliament and decided to invade Scotland, raising the money through prerogative powers. Strafford told him that money and an army were available in Ireland. But in fact the government was already losing control of the Irish parliament too; money was scarce and the army in Ireland was far from ready. In England, the opposition, once parliament was dissolved, entered into collusion with the Scots, who crossed the border. Charles met them at Newcastle but had no army to resist them. He had to temporize and was forced to summon parliament again: it met in November. Meanwhile, a further session of the Irish parliament in October had spent its time rehearsing its grievances against Strafford's government and presented a petition, reciting these complaints, instead of supplies to the lord lieutenant. The English parliament listened to reports on the Irish situation, where, it was told, the settlers had been ill-treated, the catholics too much tolerated, and now a catholic army was being raised for use in Britain. An attack was mounted on Strafford. Charles threw his servant to the closely pursuing wolves to gain time. The English Commons tried Strafford, failed to prove its case, and then abandoned the pretence of justice and condemned him to death anyway. Charles signed the death warrant and Strafford was beheaded on 12 May 1641. The king was forced to make concessions to both parliaments.

In Ireland, discontent was greater in the Irish areas, especially Ulster, than perhaps anywhere else. The Old Irish rulers, many of whom survived with diminished property and deprivation of power, had been expected by the terms of the conquest to accommodate to overwhelming change. Their religion was outlawed, with their language and the style of state they had kept; they were required to change their way of farming, of dealing with their tenants, of thinking and of looking at the world. Not surprisingly they failed to do this, to put off all the intimate paraphernalia of one culture and put on those of another. After the space of a generation most of them were in distress, financial, psychological and otherwise, and were in a state of desperation to nerve them to extreme enterprises. As the conquering state now began to show signs of disintegration, some of them met to plan action. The chief leaders were Rory O'More, of the old midland family, now with territories in Co. Armagh, and Conor Lord Maguire of Fermanagh. They were in touch with Sir Phelim O'Neill, the head of the name, and with others, including Owen Roe O'Neill in the Spanish service in Flanders. A group came together in Dublin in May and planned to take arms, as was being done throughout the three kingdoms in that year of crisis. Their hope was to take control of the country in October. The main blow was to be struck in the north, but it was planned to seize Dublin castle, the centre of administration, simultaneously. They found some support among Old English families, since these by now were beginning to despair of their position. They hoped for papal and other continental support.

Until the last moment this conspiracy remained unknown to the government. In July the king ordered the earls of Ormond and Antrim to keep in being the undisbanded elements of Strafford's army in Ireland and to begin fresh recruiting. The conspirators saw in this no conflict with their own plans: they attempted contacts with Ormond, which were rebuffed. They held a final meeting on 5 October and decided on 23 October as the day of action, including the seizure of Dublin castle. But just a few hours in advance the plan was betrayed in Dublin, and Maguire, along with some others, was captured. In the north however, on 23 October, the insurgents took over a large part of central Ulster. Sir Phelim O'Neill issued a proclamation: they were not in arms against the king but in defence of their liberties; no injury was intended to the king's subjects. But once the rising took place, spontaneous actions occurred throughout the north. For the space of a generation the dispossessed, high and low, had watched with hungry hatred as the planters reshaped their land: now they settled the score. The plantation forts and towns held out. The farms and villages succumbed. There were hundreds of murders, often brutal in the extreme, and thousands of refugees took to the autumn paths and tracks. Many of them died, of wounds, of exposure and of hunger. The leaders of the insurgents tried to prevent this terror, but it took them time to gain control. Although many of the Irish helped and sheltered the planters, there had been a great explosion of hatred. Reports of what had happened sped ahead of the refugees, swelling into wild rumour, and the story soon fed the propaganda pamphlets of the civil war in Britain. The episode was to be presented as a planned massacre of all protestants, carried out without mercy and with the utmost savagery. It added to the great dislike of Ireland and the Irish already widespread in seventeenth-century Britain, and persuaded many honest puritans that the Irish were outside the pale of ordinary humanity.

On the day the outbreak began the lords justices in Dublin proclaimed a state of rebellion which, to the alarm of the Old English, they blamed on 'evil-affected Irish papists'. They sent commissions to raise troops in Ulster where, within a matter of days, the Scots assembled their veteran soldiers and went over to the offensive. Parliament in England voted money for troops and the king appointed Ormond to command. He began recruiting immediately, especially among the Ulster refugees who were thronging into Dublin. But the first contingent sent north from Dublin was defeated near Drogheda. The insurgents then met representatives of the Old English at Knockcrofty and Tara. Having satisfied themselves of the Ulstermen's loyalty to the king, the Palesmen agreed to join them. This was a momentous conjunction. The old medieval colony had allied with the older Ireland on the common ground of Roman catholicism – or, rather, of protestant threat to catholic property.

At the beginning of 1642 the king issued a proclamation calling on those in arms in Ireland to surrender. Both the Dublin government and the New English wanted more than that: revenge and confiscation. The English parliament also opted for confiscation, passing an 'adventurers' bill' in March to encourage investment in the reconquest of Ireland as a speculative venture. At about the same time the catholic bishops of the Armagh province, meeting at Kells, declared that the insurgents' war was just and was being waged against puritans whose aim was the destruction of the catholics and of the Irish. They excommunicated those who continued to support the 'puritans'. This was followed by a more widely based meeting at Kilkenny in May, which repeated the excommunication, called for an end to provincial rivalries and proclaimed that there should be no difference between the Old English and the Old Irish. The clergy were joined by lay leaders and the meeting then drafted an oath of association which was the counterpart of the Scottish covenant. It proclaimed allegiance to the Roman church and a determination to defend and maintain the king's just prerogatives and the power and privileges of the parliament of 'this realm', the fundamental laws of Ireland and the free exercise of the catholic faith; and it included a pledge to obey the orders of

'the supreme council of the confederate catholics of this kingdom'. Lord
Gormanston was appointed commander of 'the army of the Pale' and the
revolt spread.

The insurgents were doing badly in the field, losing ground in west
Ulster. Then, on 15 April, General Munro landed in the east at
Carrickfergus with 2500 men from Scotland and on 1 May he captured
Newry. Dundalk was recaptured and Drogheda, which had held out
against insurgent siege, was relieved. The insurgent cause was on the point
of collapse when, in midsummer, the exiled Irish began to return with
help. Owen Roe O'Neill landed at Castledoe, the old stronghold of the
MacSwineys, gallowglass of the O'Donnells, in north Donegal, with men
and arms. He had long experience of command in the Spanish army. In
September the veteran Thomas Preston, Gormanston's uncle, landed at
Wexford from Flanders, along with John Burke, a relation of Clanricard.

The council at Kilkenny set up an assembly which began its first session
on 24 October. This repudiated the title of parliament, because of the
confederate insistence on the royal prerogative, but went on to act in many
ways like a parliament. In Dublin, the chief protestant stronghold, the
regular parliament was meeting through the summer but, apart from
expelling its forty-one catholic members in June, it marked time as the
confrontation between parliament and king in England moved to its
climax. It was in recess when the English civil war began on 22 August. In
the autumn the English parliament sent delegates to Dublin. There were
many sympathizers there, but they were cautious. In England the die was
cast. In Ireland, faced with a catholic confederation in being and in arms,
the officials and protestant settlers were slow to open up in their own ranks
the division now being tested by war across the Channel.

Events in Ireland in the following years were conditioned by the
fortunes of war in England. The king faced the puritan English, the
presbyterian Scots and the catholic Irish, all of them concerned to impose
their will on him or to resist the imposition of his will on them. Now that
he was at war with the forces of parliament in England, he had two
concerns in Ireland: to retain control of the government there, keeping it
from going over to the parliament; and to neutralize the catholic
confederation. Ormond, as commander of the government forces, was an
important figure. Brought up as a ward of court he was therefore, unlike
most of his family, a protestant – a puritan. He was steadfastly loyal to the
king. He took part in prolonged and tortuous negotiations with the
confederation, directed first towards a truce and then towards a peace
settlement. These dealings with the catholics were seized on by the English
parliament as evidence of the king's leanings towards the papists and were

made the occasion of a barrage of propaganda directed at the Irish
protestants to bring them over to the parliamentary side.

In his negotiations Ormond played on the divisions within the
confederation, which were deep and tended to widen. Dislike and distrust
grew between the Old English and the Old Irish. There was also a division
within the Old English which, ideologically, might be summed up as the
difference between the clerical view and the lay view of allegiance to the
protestant monarch – hence of the terms that might be acceptable from the
crown. In this division, the clerical view, which tended to be supported by
the townspeople, especially of Waterford and Wexford, was the more
radical and unyielding. The problem of the Old English, however, was all
but insoluble: they were in a position which was contradictory to the point
of absurdity. They clung to the king. His prerogative government for years
had given them the 'graces' by which they uneasily survived, but had
maintained them in insecurity under constant threat of the court of castle
chamber. Now they were involved in an effort to put the same kind of
pressure on him as the English parliament had attempted. But while trying
to pin down the king to some binding agreement on the penal laws –
appealing to *Magna Carta* (for the 'privileges and immunities' of the
Roman catholic church) and other ancient liberties – they still continued
to proclaim the royal 'prerogative'. What they needed to satisfy their
aspirations was a catholic monarch; but one faction was so anxious to
display allegiance to the crown and rejection of any (including papal)
foreign overlordship in secular matters that they seemed to be looking for
a Henry VIII. The townspeople, who had formed close contacts with the
continental counter-reformation, aimed at something more like a treaty
with the king which would in effect establish the Roman catholic church
in Ireland, something wholly unacceptable (indeed in all the circumstances
of the time quite impossible) for the crown. The Old Irish wanted to
recover their independent life. Their allegiance, although offered, was not
committed but was available as part of a bargain. They had no commitment
to English political culture, but there are hints in their formulations of the
influence of the more radical and democratic political background of
Spain. Spain and France both showed some slight interest in the Irish
confrontation but were neutralized by their mutual suspicions. The
papacy was the most active in intervention, and the church in Ireland
played a major part in the politics of the civil wars. In Ireland these wars
essentially took the form of devious and complex bargaining punctuated
by (usually indecisive) military episodes.

After a few such episodes a year's truce was concluded in September
1643. Shortly after accomplishing this, Ormond was made lord lieutenant.

The armistice with the catholics shook the loyalty of the protestant commanders of government armies and garrisons – Coote in Connacht, Thomond in Bunratty, Inchiquin in Munster. When the English parliament formed its league with the Scots in September, this created a situation in which the Ulster Scots were at war with both Ormond and the confederation, while these were at peace with one another. In July 1644, shortly after the king's defeat at Marston Moor, the parliament appointed Munro commander in Ulster; Inchiquin in the south declared for the parliament. When the king suffered disaster at Naseby in June 1645 he attempted through an agent (Glamorgan, whom he later disowned) to offer very favourable terms, including establishment of the catholic church, to the confederation in return for an army. However, this became impossible, and in the peace concluded between Ormond and confederate delegates in Dublin at the end of March 1646 much less favourable terms were involved.

The pope, Innocent X, had sent a nuncio to the confederation. John Baptist Rinuccini, archbishop of Fermo, arrived in Kilkenny in November 1645. He and the greater part of the clergy were opposed to the dealings with Ormond. The situation changed rapidly in 1646. In April the king threw himself on the mercy of the Scots, and in June, Owen Roe O'Neill inflicted a decisive defeat on the Scots in Ulster at Benburb on the Blackwater. Garrisons and territory came into the hands of the other confederate armies. In Waterford, in August, a legatine synod of the Irish bishops rejected the Dublin peace terms and issued excommunications and interdicts to hold the catholics to the terms of the Kilkenny oath of association. The delegates who had dealt with Ormond were imprisoned in Kilkenny. In the meantime, Ormond himself, after the collapse of the king's cause in England, was now forced to negotiate with the parliament. A winter assault on Dublin, attempted by the confederation, failed because of political and military command divisions, and the assembly that met in Kilkenny at the beginning of 1647 was in bitter disarray.

Early in 1647 the Scots handed the king over to the parliament; then the army, increasingly opposed to the parliament, took him. In June, as a result of half-a-year's negotiations, Ormond surrendered Dublin to the army. The city was taken over by Col. Michael Jones who arrived from England with 2000 men. Ormond signed a treaty with parliamentary commissioners who replaced him, and sailed for England. The army moved in and set up the puritan regime: the liturgy of the established church was now proscribed in Dublin. In August, Jones defeated Preston in Co. Meath, while Inchiquin at the beginning of winter destroyed the Munster army of the confederation.

In London, the king, hoping for advantage from the rift between the parliament and the army, and the divisions within the army itself, reached a new agreement with the Scots in December. He directed Ormond to make what terms he could with the Irish catholics. Ormond went to Paris, where the queen was busy with her own negotiations on Charles's behalf. Then, in Ireland, with some success, he tried to swing the Irish protestant commanders back to the king. Inchiquin, although he had some trouble with his officers, declared for the crown again in April. Then he made a truce with the confederation, which was opposed not only by his puritan officers but, on the other side, by Rinuccini, who issued further excommunications. The truce split the confederation. The Old English supported it: O'Neill and the Old Irish supported Rinuccini.

Following their new arrangement with the king, the Scots invaded England but Oliver Cromwell defeated them at Preston in August. Ormond came back to Ireland the following month. He went to his manor house in Carrick-on-Suir, and there began another round of negotiations with confederate delegates. In December he stated terms, which were rejected by Kilkenny. But almost immediately the situation changed with news that the army in England was proposing to try the king.

This finally shattered the confederation. A majority rallied to the imperilled king and made a peace with Ormond which gave the catholics little but vague and useless promises from Charles. Rinuccini and O'Neill dissented. The confederate government was now dissolved and the majority leaders placed themselves under Ormond, as did the Scots in Ulster, in accord with the Scottish reaction to the army's move. The king was executed at the end of January 1649 and these forces were now at the disposal of his son the exiled Charles II. Rinuccini sailed from Galway and Ormond faced an English republican army whose hands and swords were freed from the business of war in England.

The republican forces held a small part of Ulster under Monck, and Dublin, under Jones. The royalists invested the parliamentary positions, but Jones received reinforcements before they closed in and then defeated Ormond at the battle of Rathmines and secured Dublin. Cromwell landed there in midsummer with 8000 foot, 4000 horse and a train of guns. He moved north to Drogheda. The town, which had successfully withstood siege by the 1641 insurgents, was made to pay for their deeds. It refused Cromwell's call to surrender but after a week his men stormed the walls and carried out a massacre, the 'marvellous great mercy' which avenged the 'slaughtered saints' of 1641. Cromwell sent a force to subdue the north and himself turned south, taking Wexford early in October. Here there was another slaughter in the streets, but this one was not, apparently, premeditated. Cromwell failed to take Waterford and moved westward to winter quarters at Youghal. Meanwhile, Ormond had succeeded in bringing O'Neill's Ulster forces back to the royalist cause, but Owen Roe himself died in November.

The Roman catholic bishops held a winter meeting at Clonmacnoise, largely to deal with the bitter quarrels in the catholic ranks, which had been made worse by Rinuccini's parting excommunications. They issued expressions of unity and warnings about Cromwell's intentions. Cromwell in reply, in a verbal broadside from Youghal, confirmed their misgivings and then, in the spring, resumed his progress through a country which was now afflicted by bubonic plague. He took Kilkenny in March. The citizens paid £2000 to have their lives and property spared, but the puritan soldiers excepted the churches from this dispensation. In May Cromwell departed, leaving his son-in-law Henry Ireton in command. The conquest proceeded, more slowly. By now Ormond had virtually none but catholic troops to resist the Cromwellians. The bishops met again at Jamestown in Co. Leitrim, where they declared – with more excommunications to back their view – that Ormond's leadership could no longer be accepted. This was immediately followed by news from Dunfermline that Charles II, in order to placate the Scots, had repudiated the 1649 peace terms with the catholics and agreed that there should be no terms for 'Irish rebels' – reneging not only on the catholics but on Ormond, who finally sailed from Galway in December. By 1653, the mopping-up operations of the Cromwellian conquest had accounted for the last remnants of resistance except for the outlaw swordsmen 'on their keeping' in the hills and woods. 'We came, by the assistance of God', as Cromwell put it, 'to hold forth and maintain the lustre and glory of English liberty in a nation where we have an undoubted right to do it.'[3]

After the exemplary treatment of Drogheda and Wexford, Cromwell had given quarter and made it plain that he intended a settlement of stern justice according to his lights. It was clear that this would be both punitive and comprehensive. The Irish were widely regarded in England as being collectively guilty of the 'massacres' of 1641, and Cromwell's conquest was seen as a vindication:

He to the Commons Feet presents
A Kingdome, for his first years rents:
And, what he may, forbears
His Fame to make it theirs:
And has his Sword and Spoyls ungirt,
To lay them at the Publick's skirt. . . .

Demands for freedom of catholic worship were described by Cromwell as 'abominable'. He believed in freedom of conscience but saw certain institutional and liturgical forms of rebellion as intolerable in a Christian and well ordered state. 'I meddle not with any man's conscience', he had said at New Ross – and meant it – 'but if by liberty of conscience you mean a liberty to exercise the mass, I judge it best to use plain dealing, and to let you know, where the parliament of England have power, *that* will not be allowed of.'[4] And, over and above the ideological considerations, there was the practicality that the parliament had financed the conquest by pledging the land of Ireland.

In the course of the fighting enormous destruction had been done. By the end of the war, tillage had greatly diminished and livestock numbers had been seriously depleted. Sir William Petty, in connection with the Cromwellian settlement, carried out the first really detailed surveys of Ireland. He reckoned the population in 1652 to be about 850,000 – an underestimate by present-day calculations. The probable true figure is a little over a million. Petty also estimated that over 600,000 had died since the beginning of the war in 1641. His 1652 calculation placed protestants at between 15 and 20 per cent of the total.

A settlement act for Ireland was passed by the English parliament in August 1652. The temper of the time is shown by the preamble, in which it was necessary to state that genocide was not the intention. The act extended pardon to 'the inferior sort' and set out to break down the structure of Irish polity by destroying the pre-existing property and influence of the country. In principle, almost everyone of power or property in Ireland was threatened by the act, including the New English settlers and the Ulster Scots. But in practice the parliament was using its power mainly against the catholics. The act scheduled the groups excluded from pardon: all who had helped the rebellion of 1641, all Jesuits and priests involved in the rebellion, all guilty of the murder of civilians, all who failed to lay down their arms within twenty-eight days, and a list of named people, starting with Ormond. Officers who had fought against the parliament were to be banished, although their families might be granted the equivalent of a third of their estates. Everyone else who fought in the war was to forfeit his estate in return for the regrant of the equivalent of a third. Those who, without fighting against the parliament, had not shown 'good affection' were to surrender a fifth of their estates. This act gave effect to the puritan emotional need for making an example of Ireland, but it also served other, more down-to-earth, purposes. Under its provisions, theoretically, about half the adult male population could have been condemned to death. But it was not used in this way. A special high

court, set up in October to try murders, was used as a political weapon.
Some hundreds of executions were carried out, including that of Sir Phelim
O'Neill, but the threat of death was chiefly intimidatory.

Confiscation and plantation were the real effects of the act. The
parliament had raised money for the Irish wars by pledging Irish land. The
adventurers' act of 1642 had intended to raise £1 million for 2.5 million
acres in the four Irish provinces. Bonds were issued which ultimately
brought in a little over £300,000 after the terms had been eased – a
'plantation acre' ultimately was a good deal more extensive than an
ordinary acre. Merchants of London and elsewhere bought the bonds as a
speculative investment; by the end of the wars many had been sold to third
parties. In 1643 it was enacted that soldiers serving in Ireland might receive
their pay in the form of debentures for land on similar terms. Then, in
1644, parliament had begun to charge the Irish war to English public
finances as a loan to be discharged with Irish land. By the time of the
settlement parliament in fact owed more Irish land than it could repay even
by the most comprehensive confiscation imaginable.

There was a period of frantic surveying, since the amount of land
available was unknown. But distribution went ahead of the survey, causing
much confusion and giving endless opportunities to rogues and cheats
who, of course, appeared on the scene in numbers. There was by now an
established custom of allowing defeated soldiers to go abroad to serve in
foreign armies: 34,000 of the Irish did so. A more recent custom, begun
with the defeated Scots after the battle of Preston, was also followed:
numbers were transported as indentured servants (slaves in effect) to
Barbados. A section of the army wanted a total clearance of the Irish off
the land, and the government would have liked a wholly new settlement
of protestant yeomen, but Ireland was not attractive to new settlers. The
New English – now beginning to be known as the 'old protestants' to
distinguish them from the still newer Cromwellian settlers – had a period
of unease when it seemed that their lands too were at risk.

There was much confusion and corruption in implementing the
settlement. Catholic landowners were directed to transplant to Connacht
and Clare, where they received an equivalent of somewhat less than half of
their holdings. Most of the soldiers disposed of their land debentures,
often at a greatly devalued price. By and large the beneficiaries from this
were the officers of the Cromwellian army, and these in consequence
became a very large element in the new landowning class which was created
throughout most of Ireland. In June 1657 an act 'for the attainder of the
rebels in Ireland' in effect affirmed that the transplantation was complete.
There was not enough land to go round and, even though the parliament

met its obligations only by scaling them down in a devaluation, it had to call a halt to the redistribution. In just a few years almost all the catholic land had been handed over to new proprietors. A whole propertied class was uprooted and bodily removed westward, in the form of numerous caravans of middling or lordly households, with their valuables, retainers, and dependants – including poets:

> Our sole possessions: Michael of miracles,
>   the virgin Mary, the twelve apostles,
> Brigid, Patrick and Saint John
> – and fine rations: faith in God.
>
> Sweet Colm Cille of miracles too,
>   and Colman Mac Aoidh, poets' patron,
> will all be with us on our way.
>   Do not bewail our journey West. . . .
>
> . . . Consider a parable of this:
> Israel's people, God's own,
>   although they were in bonds in Egypt,
> found in time a prompt release. . . .[5]

In religious matters, independency was triumphant in the Cromwellian regime, so that there were disadvantages in Ireland for both the Church of Ireland and the presbyterians. As for the catholics, their public worship was prohibited and there was a hunt for priests and schoolmasters to deprive them of ministry and instruct them in what was seen as their errors. P. J. Corish points out that 'it was certainly in this decade that the tradition of the "Mass-rock" stamped itself on the Irish experience', having quoted the sources which 'agree in describing the ministry of the catholic clergy as intermittent and extremely furtive. They could not turn to the laity for shelter and support, for this would have exposed their hosts to too much risk. They lived in huts in the bogs, in the woods, or on the mountains. They were probably safest in towns, where some are known to have carried on a rather daring ministry under one disguise or another'.[6] The towns had suffered heavily in the war, in which there had been many sieges, and some attempts – ineffectual for many reasons – were made to prevent catholics from living in them.

Charles Fleetwood succeeded Cromwell as commander-in-chief in Ireland in 1652 and was appointed principal parliamentary commissioner of government. He was to apply the laws of England in Ireland and spread the Gospel and the 'power of true religion and holiness'. The following year the union of Ireland and England was decreed by parliament, with thirty Irish members seated in a house of 460 at Westminster. But that year parliament was subordinated to the military dictatorship of the 'lord protector', as Cromwell became. The lord protector's son Henry came to Ireland in 1655 and was appointed lord lieutenant in 1657. However, the new dynasty of republican absolute monarchs did not long survive its founder Oliver, who died in 1658. In England, the section of the army dominated by Monck, which was working towards a compromise with Charles II, came to the top in a struggle for power. On their behalf in Ireland Sir Theophilus Jones seized Dublin castle, Sir Charles Coote took control in the west, and Lord Broghill in Munster. Charles was proclaimed king in Dublin in May 1660, the rule of the saints came to an end and royal government and the Church of Ireland were restored. Coote was made earl of Mountrath and Broghill earl of Orrery for their services, and both were appointed lords justices (along with the lord chancellor Sir Maurice Eustace) under the absentee lord lieutenant, Monck.

Catholics now expected toleration and a restoration of their lands. Many had fought for Charles in exile overseas. They hoped at least for the terms of 1649, which Ormond had concluded with the confederation. But the balance of the restoration precluded such a drastic upheaval: those who supported the return of Charles Stuart to England made sure that this would not undo the settlement that had taken place.

Ormond returned, was raised to the rank of duke, and served two terms as lord lieutenant – 1662–9 and 1677–85. Under the restoration an old problem of government in Ireland revived: the country was looked on as an easy source of pickings for courtiers and officials with land-grants and patronage schemes of various kinds. Both Ormond and the earl of Essex, who was lord lieutenant from 1672 to 1677, were unable, though they tried, to check this, since those in England who were closer to the king were involved.

A prolonged political struggle regarding the disposition of Irish land now took place, chiefly between the Cromwellians and the catholics, with Orrery as the leading figure on one side, and on the other Richard Talbot, 'agent-general of the catholics of Ireland'. There was some redistribution, leading to intensive lobbying, influence-peddling and corruption: important or influential people obtained special grants or exemptions; others did very badly. The English House of Commons supported the protestant interest, especially against the proposals of Talbot, who went into exile in 1671. At the end of all the redistribution processes, the share of the land in catholic ownership, as studied in detail by J. G. Simms, was just over a fifth – it had been about three-fifths in 1641.

In the matter of religious toleration, too, the catholics were disappointed, again largely because of the attitude of the restoration parliament in England. Within the church the bitter disputes which had marked the affairs of the confederation continued. Oliver Plunkett, of an Old English Pale family, who was appointed archbishop of Armagh, was involved in disputes with the Old Irish northern part of his diocese, and also with Peter Talbot (Richard's brother) who was appointed archbishop of Dublin. Against this background of internal quarrels, the church undertook the process of reorganization after the severe persecution of the Cromwellian period. The training and supply of priests was a problem, fairly vigorously tackled. Then, as a growing anti-catholic mood set in in England, a proclamation was issued in 1673 expelling bishops and religious orders from the country. The 'popish plot' agitation of 1678 was English, but the prejudice of the time required Ireland to be involved in any such machination. A 'French plot' was accordingly concocted, under the influence of Shaftesbury and with the assistance, on the spot in Ireland, of Orrery. Peter Talbot was arrested and died in Dublin castle. Oliver Plunkett was also arrested in connection with the contrived 'plot', was tried and acquitted in Dundalk and was then taken to London, tried and executed at Tyburn in 1681. Irish friars, from his diocese, gave evidence for his conviction. After this, however, the agitation against catholics died down again.

Petty reckoned that in 1672 there were 300,000 protestants in Ireland, of whom at that date about 100,000 were presbyterians. It is probably something of an underestimate; but soon afterwards there was a further significant migration from Scotland into Ulster, resulting from friction between Scottish bishops and the covenanters in the later years of Charles's reign. In 1672, the *regium donum* offered as an annual payment to presbyterian ministers was widely accepted in Ulster, and with the access of population the presbyterian church became very solidly established by the end of the century.

Charles had ruled without parliament in the later years of his reign, giving him greater freedom of manoeuvre in these matters – he had subsidies from France which enabled him to dispense with parliamentary supply. When he died in 1685 and was succeeded by his brother James, duke of York, another serious constitutional crisis began. James II was a catholic. However, he had no son and would be succeeded if he died by his protestant daughter Mary, married to William of Orange. His accession led to renewed catholic hopes in Ireland, but James was also king of England and Scotland: even if he was a catholic his subjects were mostly protestant. He recalled Ormond, but replaced him with lords justices who were protestant themselves and acceptable to Irish protestants. However, he began issuing commissions in the army to catholics. He made Richard Talbot earl of Tyrconnell and gave him command of the army in Ireland. When Tyrconnell began replacing protestants with catholic officers in the army in Ireland great friction arose between him and the new viceroy, Clarendon, and alarm spread among protestants in both Ireland and England. Clarendon was suddenly recalled in January 1687 and – against strong opposition – Tyrconnell was appointed in his place (as lord deputy). He now extended his activity from the army to the civil polity, appointing catholic judges, sheriffs and other officials, revoking and replacing the charters of corporations to put catholics in place of protestants. He began working with the king on a new land resettlement, by which perhaps half of the land of previous confiscations would be repossessed. This was reflected in a general revival of catholic activity throughout the country – for example, in many attempts, in which catholic landowners and regular clergy co-operated, to begin restoring ruinous abbeys, friaries and churches.

Then in June 1688 a son was born to the queen, James's second wife, and the way seemed open for the foundation of a catholic dynasty. James, fearing a *coup d'état*, began moving troops from Ireland to southern England – and helped to precipitate what he feared. Protestant alarm increased and the English army joined the magnates who were already plotting against the king. The plot succeeded. James had to flee to France, and William of Orange, with James's daughter Mary, came over, in the 'glorious revolution' to be offered the crown on terms which left much of the substance of power in the hands of the conspirators.

Tyrconnell in Ireland was without money, and a large part of his military force had been moved to England. However, he acted vigorously in support of the king. He raised a new army by offering colonels' commissions, with hopes of a considerable increase in fortune, to those who would maintain regiments. Priests acted as recruiting sergeants to bring in the numbers. Protestants in general were alarmed and on the defensive. Their support, overwhelmingly, was for the 'glorious revolution' and many of them went over to England, where they urged William to invade Ireland. He however was preoccupied with the onset of continental war – against France – and preferred to negotiate with Tyrconnell. Meantime, Tyrconnell disarmed the protestants outside Ulster, while law and order broke down. In November, Louis XIV declared war on the Dutch, and his government soon saw in Ireland a useful opportunity for diverting William and drawing forces away from the continental war. They gave support to James, who landed at Kinsale

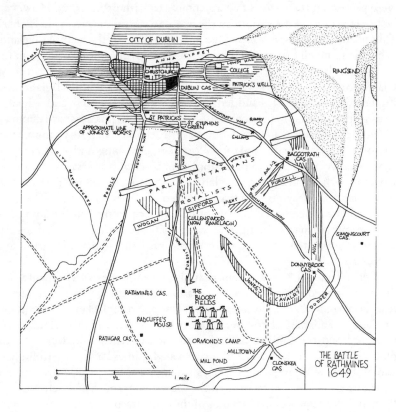

Figure 13 The Battle of Rathmines, 1649. Ormond, a slow and cautious
commander, was besieging the more dashing and aggressive Jones in Dublin when
he received word that Cromwell was about to sail for Ireland. At sunset on 1
August 1649 he sent Major-General Purcell with 1500 men to re-fortify
Baggotrath castle by night, in order to deny Jones grazing for his horses east of
Trinity College and to provide cover for batteries of guns to command the river
approaches from Ringsend. Purcell was misled by his guides, went astray, and
reached Baggotrath only an hour before daylight, to be expelled from the
incomplete work by Jones's cavalry. Jones's centre advanced on foot from Dublin
due south to Cullenswood. Meantime, his cavalry rode 3 km through
Donnybrook to Milltown, wheeled north over the high ground above the Dodder,
and struck Gifford's rear as Jones's foot engaged his front. By the end of 2 August,
Ormond had been driven from the Dublin area. A good account of this battle was
published by F. E. Ball in the *Journal of the Royal Society of Antiquaries of Ireland*
for 1902, but this map is based on a re-examination of the evidence

in March 1689 with Irish, French, English and Scottish solders. James was met at Cork by Tyrconnell, whom he made a duke, and they proceeded to Dublin. Here James summoned a parliament, which met in May.

It was largely catholic in composition, although James summoned protestant, not catholic, bishops to the upper house, and some came. This parliament passed a declaratory act affirming that the parliament of England could not legislate for Ireland; but the king blocked an attempt to repeal Poynings's law. He was also unwilling to establish the catholic church in Ireland, offering instead 'liberty of conscience'. He resisted passage of an act of attainder which would have made thousands of protestants liable to charges of treason. In return for a subsidy of £20,000 a month for thirteen months he reluctantly agreed to an act of repeal of the acts of settlement and explanation – which opened up wide again the whole question of the confiscations. In general, the parliament, which was prorogued on 18 July, attempted to turn the tables on the protestants – except that it favoured religious toleration. The monies voted however proved to be insufficient and the Jacobite government had to devalue the currency through the issue of 'brass money'.

Most of the north remained in protestant hands and went over to the 'glorious revolution'. William sent money and arms to Londonderry, where the new reign was proclaimed. A force was sent to reduce the city in April, and James decided to appear in person. But the besiegers were short of equipment for their task and had a raw and untrained army which was not very well led. A Williamite force of three regiments, also badly led, arrived in Lough Foyle on 13 June, but delayed ineptly because the Jacobites had put a hastily-made boom across the river below the town. The city held out not because of its military leadership but because of the spirit of its people, who endured starvation but refused to surrender. At the end of July the Williamite commander Kirk plucked up courage and initiative to break the boom; the city was supplied and the siege was lifted in a few days. Enniskillen also not only held out but mounted sorties against the Jacobites, which led to a remarkable victory at Newtownbutler on the day the siege of Derry was raised. These events dismayed the Jacobites, and the French were for falling back from Dublin to the south and west. Their interest in Ireland, however, was to divide and divert William's resources. Tyrconnell exerted himself rather to reorganize the Jacobite forces and return to the attack.

William was now forced, whatever his other preoccupations, to take action in Ireland, and he did so vigorously. He decided to raise new regiments in England, mainly commanded by Irish protestants who came over to join him. He placed in overall command the 74-year-old duke of

Schomberg, a protestant veteran of the French army who had joined the Dutch after the revocation of the edict of Nantes. Schomberg arrived in Bangor in August, entered Belfast and, after a week's siege, took the Jacobite-held town of Carrickfergus. He moved south, received supplies at Carlingford, and made a winter camp north of Dundalk. Here reinforcements, including a large body of Danes hired from their king, arrived in the spring. Finally, William himself sailed to Carrickfergus with 15,000 soldiers. James marched north from Dublin to Dundalk, and then fell back to the Boyne, followed by William, who now had about 36,000 men. James, with 25,000 (Irish loyalists and French allies) failed to hold the line of the river in the battle of 1 July (12 July new style) and William was able to enter Dublin.

Tyrconnell and the French thought that peace should now be negotiated. The Irish army opposed them and prevailed. Their chief spokesman was Patrick Sarsfield, of an Old English Pale family but through his mother a grandson of the 1641 leader Rory O'More. The Jacobites fell back on the Shannon, which they held at the crucial points of Limerick and Athlone. James had now departed, but William himself came to Limerick, which, like Derry earlier, successfully withstood a royally supervised siege. William then left Ireland. So did Tyrconnell and the main body of the French. Schomberg had been killed at the Boyne and a Dutch general, Ginkel, took over the command of the Williamites, and opened the campaign of 1691 with attacks on Athlone. Finally the river crossing was forced and the Irish fell back to the hill of Aughrim where, under the French general St Ruth, they faced the Williamites in fairly evenly balanced force on ground of their own choosing. When St Ruth was killed by a cannon-ball they were defeated. Sarsfield, in command of the reserve, covered a retreat to Limerick, which came under siege again.

Ginkel was anxious for a quick resolution in Ireland, and negotiated terms. The 'treaty of Limerick' had two parts. Under the military articles, all the soldiers in the city who wished to go to France might do so, Ginkel being responsible for the provision of transport. Under the civil articles, catholics were to be allowed freedom of worship 'consistent with the laws of Ireland or as they did enjoy in the reign of Charles II' – a remarkably unclear formulation. To the Jacobite troops who surrendered in five counties, stayed in Ireland and took an oath of allegiance to King William, there was a guarantee, whatever their religion, of pardon and of retention of their lands. Noblemen and gentlemen might carry arms. The same guarantee applied to those under the protection of the Irish army in the same five counties. Those leaving for France, however, would lose their lands. About 11,000 soldiers sailed, to form the nucleus of the 'Irish

Map 13   Late seventeenth-century Ireland

brigade' – regiments of the army of the exiled Stuarts, wearing British uniform but usually serving the king of France.

The treaty was criticized by both Jacobites and Williamites. Its military articles, however, caused no great problem: they were observed on the spot. William and Mary ratified the civil articles almost immediately, but that was not the end of the matter. The revolution of 1688 had greatly changed the powers of the king. Many of the crown's prerogatives were renounced, and parliament now had greatly enhanced power. The Scottish parliament had quickly followed the English in asserting greater independence. The Irish parliament was to be in a more difficult position. The protestants, now coming into ascendancy again, had had a most bitter fight for survival and regarded it as essential to their security that the catholics be prevented from ever gaining power again. It had been necessary to accept William's leadership, virtually without question. Now they found cause to question it, because of what they saw as an absurd squandering, through the leniency of the Limerick terms, of the hard-earned fruits of military victory. But the protestants were in a weak position. They expected English support in being master in their own house, but now had to depend on the English parliament to defend their position against the king; while at the same time they attempted to fend off the English parliament from establishing a position of supremacy over them. They were deeply dissatisfied both with the land settlement and with the religious settlement in the articles of Limerick. The first meeting of the Irish parliament under William and Mary refused to pass the peace settlement and it became necessary to compromise with both parliaments.

On the whole the land provisions of the Limerick articles were honoured, in spite of the two parliaments. J. G. Simms estimated that in 1703 catholics still held about 14 per cent of Irish land. But, frustrated on this side, the Irish protestants succeeded in using the vagueness of wording of the religious provisions to create for themselves the impregnably secure position they sought. This was done chiefly through the series of enactments known as the 'popery laws' or 'penal laws'. 'The purpose of the penal laws', as F. G. James summed it up, 'was to ensure the protestant ascendancy by destroying or debasing the catholic upper classes rather than by eliminating catholicism.'[7] Indeed, the elimination of catholicism had not been in the interest of either of the 'old protestants' of the Elizabethan and Jacobean settlements or the more recent Cromwellian and Williamite settlers, and this may help to explain the inertia of the reformers in Ireland, who tended, rather than evangelizing, to stay in the comfort of what Edmund Spenser had called their 'nests'. Protestantism defined the élite, and dilution was not wholly welcome. But the catholic ruling class was a rival élite, one which had shown powers of resilience and resistance. It was the élite rather than the mass that was the object of the new colony's '*delenda est*'.

An act of 1691 began the political elimination of the Roman catholics by making it impossible for them to enter parliament; thirty-six years later this process was completed when they were deprived of the vote. The Irish parliament addressed itself particularly to the prevention of any expansion of catholic property and to the diminishing of that which still existed. There was a series of laws to prevent catholics from buying land or renting large amounts on long leases. Protestants were prohibited from marrying catholics (unless the catholics converted). It was provided that catholic estates should be divided among all male heirs unless the eldest converted to the established church, in which case primogeniture would apply. No catholics, except those protected by the articles of Limerick, might bear arms or possess a horse worth more than £5. Other laws attempted to weaken the professional and commercial classes among catholics. The army was closed; several acts were designed to exclude catholics from the legal profession; catholic tradesmen were forbidden to have more than two apprentices; in 1659 catholics were forbidden to educate their children abroad, while catholic schools were prohibited at home; there were attempts to drive out the higher and regular clergy. Local communities were also made responsible for the restitution of property stolen or destroyed by 'tories, robbers and rapparees', and there were fines for those refusing to work on certain days of the year 'on the pretence that the same is dedicated to some saint or pretended saint'.

This sytem was effective. As it went steadily into operation in the space of about a generation after Limerick, it destroyed what remained of the catholic landowning and ruling class, leaving ultimately only a comparatively inconsequential remnant. Some of the landowning catholics were absorbed into the 'protestant ascendancy' through conversion. Many sank to a lower level in society, through subdivision of estates, to create a stratum of middling farmers whose tradition was a mixture of radical discontent and tenacious conservative memory; some drifted into exile. The protestant ascendancy ruled over a conquered country, but not by its own strength alone: it was *Anglo-Irish* both in its origins and in its dual relationship with England: maintaining England in Ireland; being maintained by England in Ireland. This was a very difficult relationship, whose problems dominated the opening years of the new order.

7 *Ireland in the British Empire*

The principal actors in the conquest and annexation of Ireland had been governments, soldiers and landowners. The changes involved, however, were drastic enough to affect the whole population. This occurred in several ways. The late Elizabethan attempts at 'total war', with the deliberate inducing of famine by destroying food resources, had an obvious effect on all classes in certain areas. Settlers on confiscated land often lived precariously and at times were subject to terrifying upheavals, as in Ulster in 1641. But warfare in the later seventeenth century was on the whole less inhumane in its conduct, although at times highly organized and destructive. At Drogheda and Wexford, Cromwell had earned an enduringly evil reputation in Ireland but in general his conduct of war compares not unfavourably with that of the late Elizabethan commanders. But the successive settlements involved displacement of population and, at times, extensive migration. The cultural change, which was one of the objects of the conquest, also penetrated ultimately to the lowest layers of Irish societies.

'Anglicization' had been one of the broad aims of royal policy, at least from the time of Henry VIII onwards, but it had been pursued in an uncertain and erratic manner. Sometimes the main purpose – in so far as this was ever clarified in the confusion and cross purposes of policy-making – seems to have been to *change* the Irish, to turn them into Englishmen, as Macaulay was to propose in his famous nineteenth-century education memoir for the Indians. This was the approach made (rather half-heartedly) to Ulster for a year or two after the treaty of Mellifont. But this approach alternated with attempts at replacement and it was the ambition of successive governments to plant an English or Scottish yeomanry, protestant and loyal to British political tradition, in place of the Irish, not merely to impose a new ruling class. This was nowhere successful, but it approached success, patchily, in parts of Ulster. Elsewhere, the confiscations and plantations and transplantations ended by creating an ascendancy, a new colony which was top-heavy in its class balance, and which did not displace the earlier inhabitants.

The conquest was consummated in the middle years of the eighteenth century. The new colony, having secured its own position as best it could, put down its own roots and began the process of transformation. After centuries of recurrent war there was peace. The different communities who, in one way or another, laid some kind of claim to Ireland had a breathing space to observe one another and come to what accommodation they could. In spite of plague and war the total population had been increasing, and the landscapes had been changing, not merely from increased pressure on land but from such activities as intensive iron-working which had stripped large tracts of the surviving forests for charcoal. Handsome undefended houses had been built here and there since the Stuart restoration, and the small medieval city of Dublin was being replaced by the beginnings of a new monumental capital.

Among the peoples of varied traditions now living in the country the most obvious distinction, which had marked the struggles of the preceding decades, was that between protestants and catholics. After Limerick there was no longer a possibility – short of another Stuart restoration – that the old catholic ruling class, whether of Irish or of colonial background, could again command a formidable power in the land. But catholics were still numerous, to the extent of more than three-quarters of the population; they had a compelling common interest by being all, to greater or less extent, affected by the popery laws, and their church retained its diocesan and parochial organization.

Another very clearly marked divide was one of language. There are no exact figures, but a considerable majority of the inhabitants of Ireland at the beginning of the eighteenth century were Irish-speakers, many of them monoglot. Some parts of the country, mainly in the east and in the older towns, had been English-speaking for centuries. English was now the language of law, government, commerce and affairs throughout the island. It was the language of the ascendancy, although many of the planter landlords after a generation or two could speak Irish to their tenants. English, including the Scottish dialect, was the language of the Ulster settlers' descendants and there was a distinct demotic English speech in the north-east; but in the cultural patchwork created by the plantations in the north, Irish also survived vigorously.

The political and social framework of Gaelic culture, had, however, been shattered, its political structures in the sixteenth-century wars, its social forms in the seventeenth-century confiscations. The upper social order of the 2000-year-old culture had been extirpated; the institutions concerned with its continuity had been demolished. It is true that, at least since the thirteenth century, the Gaelic polity had been fragmented. The regions had developed separately and distinctively in some respects, although unity of culture continued at the level which included literature and the transmitted myth and consciousness of formal learning. Life in sixteenth-century Thomond, Ormond, Tyrone and the Western Isles, while it showed certain close and exact similarities from a shared heritage of language, learning and law, yet showed many differences founded on varieties of experience, economic development and divergent attitudes to the outside world. Now, for the remnants of the old polity, which were still very extensive, the violent impact of conquest was succeeded by the steady pressure and attrition of a superimposed new order.

The cultural transformation of the originally Irish-speaking catholic masses is one of the most important processes of the eighteenth and nineteenth centuries, if not the most important. In this period, democracies emerged in the western world, a real and effective pressure from below, for the first time. In Ireland this happened in circumstances unique for Europe (although there were some parallels, in part, in America): we must try to understand the emergence of two distinct, and to a large extent opposed, democracies, one catholic the other presbyterian, both in different ways in conflict with an anglican colonial establishment which represented the anti-democratic system set up by the new British oligarchy.

Of the old Gaelic polity there remained, at the upper social level, a scattering of landowners, greatly reduced in number and under steady pressure from the penal laws. They had a considerable overseas connection through the numerous Irish officers and gentlemen – their relations in large part – in the service of France, Spain, Austria and other countries. But not all of the landlords who belonged to old Irish or Norman families were catholic. Those who were protestant still had a cultural standing in the world of Gaelic culture, in so far as it survived; there were also some protestant planter families who, like the Normans of the twelfth and thirteenth centuries, accommodated to some extent to Gaelic culture, even in its last decline, patronized poets and harpers, and took some interest in the antiquities of the land their great-grandfathers had settled in.

Down to the seventeenth century, a modern version of the ancient *oes dána*, or 'class of learning', survived more or less intact, and was of great importance in maintaining the consciousness of Gaelic culture. The shrewder Elizabethan and Jacobean officials and soldiers had singled out this class for attack, seeing in it a most important moral resource for the society they were trying to subdue. Thomas Smith in 1561 had given his, the English, view of them:

There is in Ireland four septs in manner all rhymers. The first of them is called the Brehon, which in English is called the Judge.

The second sort is the Shankee which is to say in English, the petigrer. . . . They make the ignorant men of the country to believe they be descended of Alexander the Great, or of Darius, or of Caesar, or of some other notable prince; which makes the ignorant people to run mad, and caring not what they do: the which is very hurtful to the realm. . . .

The third sort is called the Aeosdan which is to say in English, the bards, or the rhyming septs; and these people be very hurtful to the commonweal. . . . Their first practice is, if they see any young man descended of the septs of O or Mac, and have half a dozen about him, then they will make him a rhyme, wherein they will commend his father and his ancestors, numbering how many heads they have cut off, how many towns they have burned . . . and in the end they will compare them to Hannibal or Scipio or Hercules, or some other famous person; wherewithal the poor fool runs mad, and thinks indeed it is so. . . .

The fourth sort of Rhymers is called Fillis which is to say in English, a poet. . . .[1]

This politically important class finally disintegrated in the early years of the eighteenth century. The law-schools were broken up in the seventeenth century and the law that had for centuries provided an alternative to English could no longer be either administered or even expounded – even in the remotest parts. The medical schools and tradition – derived largely from Arabic learning of the Middle Ages – were broken up at about the same time. The poets, all but a few, shared in the ruin of the order that had patronized them for hundreds of years, and their elaborate system of training came to an end. Their bitterness fills the writing of the turn of the century – bitterness at the downfall of the Gaelic aristocracy, which is also bitterness at the uppityness of the lower orders now that the old aristocracy is laid low. Ó Bruadair's is a typical late seventeenth-century expression of these feelings:

O it's best to be a total boor
  (though it's bad to be a boor at all)
if I'm to go out and about
among these stupid people.

It's best to be, good people,
  a stutterer among you
since that is what you want,
  you blind ignorant crew. . . .[2]

Ó Rathaille, reluctantly writing for the planter Brownes rather than for the

MacCarthys, the ancient rulers of his native Kerry, summed up, as one of the last professionally trained in the old style, the change in the world in his death-poem of 1729:

No help I'll call till I'm put in the narrow coffin.
By the Book, it would bring it no nearer if I did!
Our prime strong-handed prop, of the seed of Eóghan
– his sinews are pierced and his vigour is withered up.

Wave-shaken is my brain, my chief hope gone.
There's a hole in my gut, there are foul spikes through my bowels.
Our land, our shelter, our woods and our level ways
are pawned for a penny by a crew from the land of Dover. . . .[3]

The significance of these transmitters of the ancient culture is that they passed on – to people whom they largely held in contempt and through modes of expression and communication which, in their beginnings, they also held in contempt – a view of the new order which was to have enduring effects. In this view, the new lords of the land, no less than the peasants who were the unworthy audience of the last of the professionally trained poets, were boors: they lacked, above all, what was of supreme importance in the ancient scheme of things – ancestry.

A famous description – the last first-hand account – of the old system of training is given in 1722 by the editor of the *Memoirs of the Right Honourable the Marquis of Clanricarde*:

Concerning the poetical seminary, or school . . . it was open only to such as were descended of poets, and reputed within their tribes. And so it was with all the schools of that kind in the nation, being equal to the number of families, that followed the said calling. But some more or less frequented for the difference of professors, conveniency, with other reasons, and seldom any come but from remote parts, to be at a distance from relations, and other acquaintance, that might interrupt his study. The qualifications first requir'd, were reading well, writing the mother tongue, and a strong memory. It was likewise necessary the place should be in the solitary recess of a garden, or within a sept or inclosure, far out of the reach of any noise, which an intercourse of people might otherwise occasion. The structure was a snug, low hut, and beds in it at convenient distances, each within a small compartment, without much furniture of any kind, save only a table, some seats, and a conveniency for cloaths to hang upon. No windows to let in the day, nor any light at all us'd but that of candles, and these being brought in at a proper season only. The students upon thorough examination being first divided into classes; wherein a regard was had to every ones age, genius, and the schooling had before, if any at all; or otherwise. The professors (one or more as there was occasion) gave a subject suitable to the capacity of each class, determining the number of rhimes, and clearing what was to be chiefly observ'd therein as to syllables, quartans, concord, correspondence, termination, and union, each of which were restrain'd by certain rules. The said subject (either one or more as aforesaid) having been given over night, they work'd it apart each by himself upon his own bed, the whole next day in the dark, till at a certain hour in the night, lights being brought in, they committed it to writing. . . .

Every Saturday, and on the eves of festival days, they broke up, and dispers'd themselves among the gentlemen and rich farmers of the country, by whom they were very well entertain'd, and much made of, till they thought to take their leaves, in order to resume their study. . . .[4]

In the early years of the present century Daniel Corkery pointed out that Lecky and other historians of eighteenth-century Ireland had missed, in their concentration on the politics and concerns of the Anglo-Irish establishment, what he called in the title of his book *The Hidden Ireland*. Historians by and large find in the past what seems to be significant or interesting for the present. Nineteenth-century historians, seeing the ascendancy as the outcome of Irish history, tended to treat it as *the* significant element of the eighteenth century, and the remnants of Gaelic culture as, by that date, insignificant. This balance is no longer so clear, since the ascendancy is, as Kipling foresaw for the British empire as a whole, 'one with Ninevah and Tyre'. Its legacy has been much affected by a rediscovery of the Gaelic past and by political and cultural realignments, so that some reinterpretation was required. But, as Louis Cullen has shown, Corkery in turn, writing from the viewpoint of early twentieth-century nationalism, got the balance wrong too: he romanticized and sentimentalized; it might be added that he bowdlerized.[5]

With the destruction of the old propertied class and of the learned professional class, the recording and transmission of the matter of art in Gaelic culture passed down into the keeping of a lower order of society. Material culture was transformed by migration, by impoverishment and by the introduction of new elements and techniques. The tradition of the élites moved into closer intimacy with folklore and gradually lost most of its institutional base.

The gentry continued, here and there and more in some parts of the country than others, to patronize poets and musicians until after the end of the eighteenth century. After the old order had been finally defeated in the closing years of Elizabeth's reign, a tremendous effort was made to save its heritage at least as an archive. Much of this took place in the Irish colleges and other overseas centres to which the catholic clergy, especially the regulars, had resort after the conquest. These included Paris, Rome, Salamanca, Douai, and, of special importance in this matter, Louvain in the Spanish Netherlands. The bulk of the work was done in the earlier seventeenth century, and included much research on hagiography and other ecclesiastical matters and a great deal of investigation of Irish history. Part of the object of this was conservation of the records of a mortally assaulted civilization; part was its vindication, so that the historical works in particular are propagandist in tone. Some of the hereditary scholars had joined religious orders, especially the Franciscans, and played a large part in this undertaking. Part of the early organization of what became in effect an institutional endeavour to recover and record the materials bearing on Ireland's past was done by Old English churchmen from the towns – Henry FitzSimon of Dublin (a Jesuit), Luke Wadding and Peter Lombard of Waterford, David Rothe of Kilkenny, Stephen White of Clonmel (another Jesuit). The college of St Anthony in Louvain was founded by a member of a Connacht family of hereditary historians, Flaithrí Ó Maíl-Chonaire, a Franciscan who became archbishop of Tuam, who died in 1629, and this Franciscan college became a workshop for members of similar families, now educated at Salamanca, Paris, or Louvain itself, to collect historical materials of various kinds, edit and collate them and – so it was intended – print them. A great deal of the work of collection had to be done in Ireland, and there a major part of the burden was borne by Brother Michael O'Clery and a group of colleagues, including members of his own family. O'Clery and several others, known collectively as 'the four masters', produced in manuscript a great collation of annalistic materials which they entitled *Annals of the Kingdom of Ireland*. The 'annals of the four masters', as they were more popularly known, did not come into print until the nineteenth century, but much else that went back to Louvain did. There John Colgan, of a family attached to the church of Donaghmore in Inishowen in Donegal, edited and published much hagiographical matter. Interestingly, he shows a good and detailed knowledge of early church sites in many parts of the country as well as a mastery of the contents of the texts.

By the second half of the seventeenth century such scholarly organization was no longer possible. The schools in Ireland were broken up one by one, and professional training in the old learning became less and less easy to come by. However, new kinds of literature adapted to more popular taste and more political purpose, began to appear. An important early example was a lively narrative of Irish history to the time of Henry II, drawn from a wide range of sources in Irish, written in Irish in the 1630s

by Geoffrey Keating, a member of an Old English family of
Co. Tipperary, who was educated at Bordeaux. This soon achieved a wide
circulation in manuscript copies. *Foras Feasa ar Éirinn*, as Keating's work
was called, was to have a long-continuing influence. It provided the basis
for semi-popular, semi-learned interpretations of the country's past that
were to appear right down to the present century.

Fragmentation continued through the eighteenth century. The
cultivation of the old literary tradition died in Connacht and Donegal,
where it had been active throughout the seventeenth century (although
folk-music, folk-poetry and folk-tale survived vigorously). In Munster
and in an extensive area spanning the Ulster–Leinster borders, the literary
tradition in a 'debased' form continued (Daibhid Ó Bruadair, a poet of the
ancient tradition who died in 1698, called the new popular metres
'sráidéigse' – 'gutter poetry'). There were still 'schools' of poetry, but
these, by the later eighteenth century, were often no more than occasional
gatherings in taverns.

But in the areas where the tradition survived there was extraordinary
activity in the copying and circulation of manuscripts. It was a kind of
samizdat publication, except that most of the contents were traditional.
The copying was a means both of publishing new work (mainly poems)
and of providing farmhouses throughout the area with anthologies of
material old and new, including tales and romances, poetry, genealogies,
religious matter, lives of saints, charms, spells, medical texts, histories,
prophecies and other lore. There was comparatively little overtly political
material, but the composition of a type of Jacobite poem called '*aisling*'
('vision') continued until late in the eighteenth century. This followed a
formula related to a very old theme. The poet describes how he fell asleep,
almost always in the open and in a place very often with some traditional
associations. In his sleep he is visited by a beautiful woman – described
according to received formulas of beauty – who reveals to him that she is
Ireland, that she has been forced into marriage with a boorish husband
without breeding or blood, but that the true prince, over the sea, is coming
to rescue her. There are many variations on the theme and it seems that it
was possible for the poets (at least among themselves) to conduct a
discussion of current political developments, less purely fanciful than all
this seems, through their possession of the code of references embodied in
the poetic images. It was dangerous to express openly, even in Irish,
sentiments which might threaten the protestant establishment and
government.

Such sentiments were undoubtedly widespread, but almost wholly
underground. They took several forms. Jacobite revanchism, with

overtones of cultural resistance, was only one of them, largely expressed in Irish. There was also rejection of the pretensions of the established church, which in time came to be widely shown in opposition to the payment of tithes. And there was resentment at the exactions of the propertied ascendancy: this, later in the century, gave rise to violent activity by rural secret societies.

Although Irish was the language of the majority, this, in the early eighteenth century, was of little advantage to it. It was not the language of power, commerce, or even, in any important sense, religion, and it was in slow but continuous ebb. Catholicism on the other hand, the religion of the majority, was not in retreat at all, although its existence was barely acknowledged by law. On the contrary, at a time when, throughout Europe, it was taken for granted that the religion of the people was a primary concern of the state, the state in Ireland, through the penal laws, by recognizing only the religion of its colony and by withdrawing recognition from the religion of the excluded mass, abdicated this concern and left it to the shadowy 'titular' bishops and their clergy. These proceeded with the reorganization of their church, quite untrammelled by and independent of the apparatus of the state – except in so far as this apparatus forced them to work with secretive discretion – and went on to replace the secular leadership which the penal laws destroyed. The catholic Irish became Jews, their religion beaten into their culture, their culture into their religion, between the hammer of the ascendancy and the anvil of deprivation.

The penal laws were more stringently applied in the earlier part of the century than in the later. In the first half of the century catholic Ireland expended its efforts at resistance overseas. The armies and navies of France and, on a much smaller scale, Spain and Austria continued to recruit soldiers and sailors from parts of the country (especially in the west), but, domestically, the catholic communities were so leaderless as to present no serious threat to the government, even in the crises of 1715 and 1745 when attempts were made at a Jacobite restoration. Irish Jacobites faced the Hanoverian armies on continental fields, but not, except in token numbers, in Britain; and Ireland itself in the times of alarm remained quiet.

Although the penal laws were colonialist rather than religious in their primary purpose, they bore very heavily, especially in the early decades of the eighteenth century, on catholics as such. King William, a calvinist, was not personally intolerant, but Queen Anne, although she too made some effort to see that the articles of Limerick were observed, was something of an anglican bigot and in her reign this gave scope to the extremists in the establishment. In 1704 an act applied to every catholic clergyman coming into the kingdom the penalties already enacted for bishops and regular clergy, and another act required the registration of all the priests already in the country. In theory this might have led to the complete dying-out of the catholic clergy within a generation; in practice it led merely to increased harassment for a period. Where – chiefly in Dublin and the other larger towns – priest-hunters were active, exposing clandestine catholic activity for reward, they were not greatly encouraged by the authorities and they were greatly discouraged by riots which were a real danger to their lives. In Ireland as in eighteenth-century England the mob was an effective check on the excesses of power.

The penal laws led to interesting displacements of catholic activity. In the seventeenth century, when they were more directly applied against worship, there was a great realignment of popular devotion from the regular services of the church to older forms of demotic religion (often with a large content of ancient paganism) such as annual gatherings at traditional shrines, the cult of holy wells and local 'saints', and a resort to *lares* and *penates* which was hardly even superficially Christian. This was balanced, however, by the growth of a largely urban and domestic devotion based on mature counter-reformation developments and making use of literary works of piety such as the writings and translations of Bishop Challoner. By the middle of the eighteenth century, without formal easement of the popery laws, the numbers of the clergy were increasing, the hierarchy had been fully restored, and the catholic church was beginning to address itself to long-term problems of organization such as the education of catholics within the country (still formally prohibited). Deprived of property and professional advancement, catholics of some means turned more and more to trade, and a commercial middle class grew rapidly, to become a significant element in the politics and society of the later eighteenth century.

The other element in society which grew in size and significance was at the bottom of the social scale. Records and observations make it clear that landless labourers and cottiers formed a numerically large class in the seventeenth century. In the eighteenth century their numbers seem to have increased both absolutely and relativ ly, in spite of major set-backs such as the great famine of the early 1740s. This may have caused (relatively, in a much smaller population) death and devastation as great as did the much better documented famine of a hundred years later. The potato, brought from the New World, was already beginning to be established as a cheap and widespread staple diet by the end of the seventeenth century. 'Whoever travels through this kingdom', wrote the young Edmund Burke in 1747, 'will see such Poverty as few Nations in Europe can equal. . . .

Indeed Money is a Stranger to them; and were they as near the *Golden Age*
in some other Respects, as they are in this, they would be the happiest
People in the World. As for their Food, it is notorious they seldom taste
Bread or Meat; their Diet, in Summer, is Potatoes and sour Milk; in
Winter, when something is required comfortable, they are still worse,
living on the same Root, made palatable only by a little Salt, and
accompanied with Water: their Cloaths so ragged, that they rather publish
than conceal the Wretchedness it was meant to hide; nay, it is no
uncommon Sight to see half a dozen Children run quite naked out of a
Cabin, scarcely distinguishable from a Dunghill, to the great Disgrace of
our Country with Foreigners, who would doubtless report them Savages,
imputing that to choice which only proceeds from their irremediable
Poverty.'[6] The gross maldistribution of wealth which was to breed several
generations of misery was already a part of the colonial scene – more
readily noticed by 'foreigners' indeed than by Burke's fellow-countrymen.

In the north, plantation and migration had produced a distinctive social
and religious pattern. The seventeenth-century plantation of Ulster,
although it fell short of intentions, had established not only a new class of
landowners and a protestant ascendancy such as were to be found by now
throughout the island, but also a substantial protestant settlement of
tenant-farmers, craftsmen and others. Following the pattern of the
plantation these were partly anglican, partly presbyterian. There were also
a few presbyterian landowners of some substance. In the east Ulster
counties of Antrim and Down presbyterians had settled extensive tracts.
These counties, especially Antrim, had ancient connections with Scotland
and the settlement pattern was complex. King John had settled Scots in
Antrim; later, relations had been intimate with the MacDonald lordship of
the Isles; and the Jacobite side of Scotland, in the late seventeenth-century
wars, had been represented by the 'redshanks' – the wild soldiers of the
Scottish–Irish archipelago.

Viewed from the Rhinns of Islay, just south of the MacDonald
stronghold in Loch Gorm, the Antrim island of Rathlin (attached to
Scotland in the Middle Ages) lies low on the southern horizon, a blue
shadow on a clear day. From the north Antrim cliffs near Ballycastle,
Rathlin is in plain view, the first of the Isles. It was from these cliffs in 1575
that Sorley Boy MacDonald's men watched helplessly as an expedition of
three frigates commanded by Sir Francis Drake on behalf of the earl of
Essex, put parties ashore to murder the women, children and old men who
had been left for safety on the island. On the east coast of Antrim a
different Scotland comes into view: Kintyre and the approaches to the firth
of Clyde. It was from the country south of Glasgow that a large part of the

seventeenth-century immigration came, from Galloway, Ayrshire and the Lothians, although there was also some continued admixture from the Isles. The immigration was overwhelmingly English-speaking, although it is to be borne in mind that Galloway, for example, was Gaelic-speaking in part until well into the seventeenth century, and the culture of the Gaelic world was not remote from the background of the Scots whose colonization of Ulster at this time was to give that province much of its modern character. The geography of the archipelago which screens the North Channel underlies the recent history of northern and eastern Ulster: Glasgow became the great regional centre, drawing presbyterian ministers in training to its university and migrant workers to its slums.

The initial immigration, like most colonizing ventures, had drawn a mixed lot of people.

Although amongst those whom Divine Providence did send to Ireland, there were several persons eminent for birth, education and parts; yet the most were such as either poverty, scandalous lives, or, at the best, adventurous seeking or better accommodation had forced thither, so that the security and thriving of religion was little seen to by those adventurers, and the preachers were generally of the same complexion with the people.[7]

So wrote Robert Blair, a Scottish minister of the kirk, himself an early migrant to Ulster. Presbyterianism in its later forms emerged from the less clear-cut distinctions of the early seventeenth century by stages. The early settlers were calvinistically inclined and were broadly opposed to 'prelacy', but accepted the formal shape of established religion. It was the massacres and perils of 1641 that threw them back on their own resources and reinforced their inclinations with renewed impulses from Scotland and especially with the widespread adherence to the Covenant.

Non-covenanted protestants were allied with covenanters in the upheavals of the seventeenth century when, in spite of the complexities and shifts of policy, a broad protestant interest was identified. This was especially true of the Restoration period. Charles II had signed the Covenant at Dunfermline, and it was possible for the presbyterians to be sincere royalists – which was their abiding instinct – while at the same time satisfying themselves that the state was founded on an original compact, acknowledged and joined in by the king, by which they had bound themselves to one another and to God. In its passage to Ireland, presbyterianism suffered something of a sea-change, very marked in the important migrations of the late seventeenth century. The migrating Scots separated themselves from the remnants of feudalism, and to some extent colonized in Ireland a New World, as the Pilgrim Fathers did in America, where, to a degree, social forms and institutions had to be created.

The presbyterian communities were resolute and tenacious. They came through the seventeenth-century wars with a clear sense of distinct identity (locating their separateness very firmly in Ulster: the 'north of Ireland' already assumes an exclusive character in their seventeenth-century documents) and with an outlook and habit of self-reliance. David Miller, in his study of the *Queen's Rebels*, has stressed the importance of protestant 'public banding', a custom of Scottish origin by which, in the absence of strong central government, the nobility and gentry (initially) had entered into 'bands' for mutual protection. The confederate catholics of the seventeenth century had covenanted with one another too, but had tried to organize on centralist and authoritarian lines. They attempted to enforce their covenant not through the private conscience of the plighted confederates but through the directions and excommunications of the dominant prelates, and their military organization was mortally weakened by lack of the central authority which by its design it required. The protestants, but particularly the presbyterians, solved this through the device of allegiance qualified by private judgement and stated reservation, and through the expedient of the public band.

In Britain the presbyterians had functioned as a catalyst in the politics of the seventeenth century, sparking off the civil wars. In Ireland their position was not so central but their resistance in Ulster was most important. They exemplified the tensions and dynamics of the religious politics of the age: a church, but always poised on the edge of the descent into sect, because of the conflict set up between private judgement and the acceptance of an agreed formula of belief, and the conflict between rejection on the one hand of a priesthood of all the faithful and on the other of the hierarchy of prelacy; a disputatious community expounding texts and awed by the dreadful divide between the elect and the reprobate; the perilous adventure of the reformation. After the glorious revolution the laws both of Britain and of the episcopalian establishment in Dublin discriminated against the Ulster presbyterians – most severely in the reign of Queen Anne – but the solidarity of the presbyterians with the protestant cause combined with their energy and contentiousness to maintain for them a strong position in the north.

The close connection with Scotland continued. Young men went to the university of Glasgow (and some few to Leiden, that other resort of eighteenth-century presbyterianism) to learn theology and be equipped as ministers of religion. But eighteenth-century Scotland was not only presbyterian. The union of 1707, linking Scotland with England in a new single kingdom, set in train social, economic and cultural changes. One of its aftermaths was the 'Scottish Enlightenment', the exposition of political and philosophical ideas which, among other things, offered new interpretations of the constitutions of states; to evade the prescriptions of absolute monarchy and found politics on the consent of the governed and on attempts at a satisfactory affirmation of the public good. Versions of the 'social contract' and of 'the greatest good of the greatest number' were expounded in Scotland side by side with the sterner theological preoccupations of calvinism, and became part of the background of intensive theological and philosophical debate which went on among the endlessly disputing presbyterians of eighteenth-century Ulster. The debate, being conducted to an extent in pulpits, impinged on the populace at large. Francis Hutcheson, one of the early utilitarians in Glasgow (where he was professor of moral theology, and the first to lecture in English rather than Latin), and who was also, as Garry Wills has shown, an important intellectual ancestor of the American Declaration of Independence, was the son of a minister of Armagh. We are told that when he preached in Armagh in place of his father one cold and rainy Sunday, he provoked the comment from one of the elders, a native of Scotland:

We a' feel muckle wae for your mishap, reverend sir; but it cannot be concealed. Your silly son, Frank, has fashed a' the congregation wi' his idle cackle; for he has been babbling this aboot a gude and benevolent God, and that the souls of the heathern themselves will gang to heeven, if they follow the licht o' their own consciences. Not a word does the daft boy ken, speer nor say aboot the gude, auld, comfortable doctrines of election, reprobation, original sin, and faith.[8]

Issues like that raised by Hutcheson's sermon engaged the presbyterian congregations of Ulster throughout the eighteenth century. A prolonged dispute hinged on the willingness or unwillingness of ministers to subscribe to the fairly fundamental Westminster declaration of faith as an instance of true presbyterianism. The divide was between 'old light' fundamentalists and 'new light' latitudinarians. It was at times bitter, and led to the formation of factions, schisms and sects. It had political as well as theological aspects and implications; for the 'new light' ministers and congregations, who were theologically liberal, tended to be more questioning in their approach to the constitution and political institutions.

The *regium donum*, or royal bounty, had first been paid to the Irish presbyterians by Charles II, to give some recognition of their loyalty and allow them a quasi-established position. The amount given was £600, to be divided among the ministers for their subsistence. This half-recognition of the presbyterian church in Ireland was in effect an acknowledgement of a distinct political and religious situation in Ulster. This initially was a precarious grant and neither Charles nor James II in general favoured the presbyterians. William renewed the *regium donum*, increasing it to £1200 per annum. But the test oaths and other devices which were intended to bar catholics from public life and landed property acted also as a restriction on presbyterians. Their chief grievance arose from a bill, originally directed against catholics alone and transmitted from the Dublin parliament with enthusiastic presbyterian support in 1703. The new ministry of Queen Anne in England modified it to include a sacramental test which would also exclude presbyterians from 'any office, civil or military, or receiving any pay or salary from the crown, or having command or place of trust from the sovereign'. In this form it was passed in 1704, and a promised toleration act, such as applied to dissenters in England, failed to materialize.

Although the *regium donum* continued as a charge on the Irish exchequer (in spite of attempts to put an end to it) it was inadequate, and some presbyterian communities, including their ministers, suffered economic hardship in the early eighteenth century. There began a migration, almost wholly presbyterian at this time, from Ulster to the West Indies and North America. Many of the emigrants travelled not as free people but (to raise the means of travel) as indentured servants, going voluntarily into this form of slavery. There was some resistance to the immigration in the longer settled parts of America (such as Boston) but as the migration continued over a long period, the numbers built up, and the eighteenth-century Ulster people made a considerable contribution to the populating of the American colonies. Simply 'Irish' at the time, they were retrospectively designated 'Scotch-Irish' in the early nineteenth century, when it was felt necessary to point up Irish religious differences. They left a considerable imprint on parts of what was then the frontier of European settlement, whose traces remained in some distinctive and picturesque enclaves, such as those of the 'hill-billies'.

Not all the migrants were presbyterian; not all were indentured servants. Economic pressures and dissatisfactions of different kinds impelled people of various social strata in Ulster to move. From catholic Ireland there was migration on a much smaller scale, mostly from the poor, and the anti-Irish feeling that began to manifest itself in America, where the Irish were already thought of, loosely, as a catholic people, was in origin anti-catholic.

The trans-Atlantic movement marks a significant change in Ireland. Until the eighteenth century, there had for hundreds of years been movements of settlers into Ireland but little migration from the country (apart from that of small groups that were highly specialized – like the monks and scholars of pre-Norman times). Now the movement into the country was reduced to a trickle. There were one or two final attempts at plantation, on a very small scale and chiefly in an endeavour to strengthen protestantism or introduce skills or useful habits, like the introduction of some thousands of Palatines into Co. Limerick in 1709 (these failed to act as a leaven but were gradually absorbed into the surrounding population). English officials in small numbers continued to arrive. But a certain stability was achieved by about 1700: for some considerable time there was to be no notable new admixture to the Irish population. Instead there was a diaspora. This had already begun in the seventeenth century with an outward flow of catholics. At the end of that century large numbers of men left Ireland after the signing of the treaty of Limerick and took service overseas, mostly in the Jacobite cause. In the early decades of the eighteenth century considerable numbers of young men continued to leave for France, Spain or Austria. Official policy opposed this, but not very effectively. And the migration to America and the West Indies continued, now strongly, now weakly, throughout the century.

One of the last significant introductions before this change was manifest was that of Huguenot settlers, mainly refugees. A few arrived early in the seventeenth century, but the chief settlement derived from the revocation of the edict of Nantes in 1685, when, deprived by the revocation of toleration in France, some hundreds of thousands of protestants left that country of whom perhaps as many as 100,000 came to England and Ireland. Stuart policy did not welcome them, but William of Orange did, and they in turn supported his cause. Five largely Huguenot regiments served him in the Irish war, under La Melonière, Du Cambon, La Caillemotte Ruvigny, Schomberg and Miremont. William offered titles and grants of forfeited lands to these allies and undertook to 'do our endeavour in all reasonable ways and means so to support, aid and assist them in their several trades and ways of livelihood as that their living in this realm may be comfortable and easy to them'.[9]

The Huguenots were calvinistically inclined but were encouraged to conform to the established church; many did so. They settled in a number of places in Ireland and had four churches in Dublin (two non-conformist and two conformist), two churches in Cork, and other churches in Waterford, Carlow, Portarlington and Lisburn. They brought industrial skills and habits of industry and maintained these in Ireland. Some of their settlements had the character of industrial plantations. For example, in 1697 a bill was passed 'For the encouraging the Linen Manufacture of Ireland' and the king invited Louis Crommelin from the Low Countries. He arrived at Lisburn with seventy-five French families and 1000 looms, and began the linen manufacture there under state auspices and with a state salary – on the system so widely operated under Louis XIV. Elsewhere, too, textile industries were established by the Huguenots. They also prospered in other businesses. In Dublin, for example, the chief centre of Huguenot settlement, the La Touche family established a silk and poplin weaving industry but also founded an important bank. Within a century or so, the Huguenot communities lost their French distinctiveness and blended into protestant Ireland.

The general change in patterns of migration and settlement which began about the beginning of the eighteenth century took place in association with another change, at first unmarked by contemporaries but gathering force through the century until, after about 1780, it was impossible not to take note of it. This was the growth of population from around 2 million in 1700 to around 5 million in 1800. This important change underlies many other developments of the time.

The anglican protestants were the dominant body in eighteenth-century Ireland. They formed what came to be known as the 'ascendancy', which consisted of the landowning and governing class (amounting to perhaps 3 or 4 per cent of the total population), which was extended by professional, mercantile, manufacturing, military, tenant and even working-class groups of conforming protestants. Until late in the century, these alone had full political rights. They did not form a homogeneous group, either in political opinion or in social status, but they were united in a common consciousness of their somewhat anomalous colonial situation. Their leadership, to put it perhaps oversimply, had dispossessed the catholic leadership. Their security in their privilege lay in a bargain which was partly explicit, partly implicit. They supported the constitution as established by the glorious revolution and they maintained the king's dominion in Ireland. In return, the monarch maintained them in their special position and in their property.

That was the essence of the bargain, but it did not lead to easy relations between the Irish ascendancy and the English parliament and government. The constitutional relationship between Ireland and England was obscure, and efforts to enlighten it (as by declaratory acts) only served to set off the impenetrable darkness of certain corners of the constitution.

The glorious revolution which had replaced James II by William III in England in 1688 had greatly modified the balance between crown and parliament in England and had set in train a new style of government. This affected Anglo-Irish relations. The clear link between the two countries was the shared crown. The nature of the relationship between the two parliaments was uncertain, but became important now that parliament in England, *vis-à-vis* the crown, had acquired much greater weight. As cabinet government, founded on parliament, began to replace royal government, the powers of the English parliament in relation to Ireland came into question.

The problems were not merely constitutional, however. After the drastic reversals of fortune of the late seventeenth century, the Irish protestants tended for some time to feel extremely insecure and to feel that government in England must be brought to understand their precarious position. William III was conciliatory to catholics, which alarmed the Irish protestants, who turned to the English parliament for defence against the king. At the same time, the Irish parliament (wholly protestant now) wished to resist the tendency of the English parliament to attempt to extend its jurisdiction over Ireland. An early conflict of interest arose, for example, in connection with the wool trade, when in 1698 the English Commons proposed to protect their own wool production (still the basic English industry) against exports from Ireland. It is in this context that the Irish protestants succeeded, with some help from the English parliament, in having parts of the treaty of Limerick abrogated and in beginning the system of penal laws directed against the catholics.

There were two contrary views as to the relationship between the two kingdoms, both turning on interpretations of history but springing from current politics. One view was that Ireland was a conquered country. The protestant ascendancy then was a garrison, or colony, holding Ireland for the crown. This view lent itself readily to the assertion of the competence of the English parliament to legislate for Ireland and to control an Irish executive. It is perhaps implied in the Act of Recognition passed by the Irish parliament in 1692 which stated that Ireland was 'annexed and united with the imperial crown of England, and by laws and statutes of this kingdom is declared to be justly and rightly dependent upon, and belonging, and forever united to the same'. But there is no explicit reference to the English parliament in this wording.

The alternative view was that Ireland was a separate kingdom (originating in allegiance voluntarily offered by Irish 'captains of their nations' to English kings in the past) for which the English parliament was not competent to legislate except in very limited ways. It was conceded that the common law of England applied in both kingdoms and that the English parliament could define this, for Ireland as well as England, by declaratory acts. Ironically, this was a view which had first been formulated (by Patrick Darcy) for the catholic confederation of Kilkenny and had been revived by James II's Irish parliament. It was re-stated on behalf of protestant Ireland by William Molyneux, in a pamphlet of 1698, *The Case of Ireland's Being Bound by Acts of Parliament in England*

Stated. This pamphlet was burnt by the common hangman in England, and English parliamentary reaction to its argument was quick and effective. The protestant ascendancy was in too weak and precarious a position to defend successfully a position of independence. It continued, however, to resent its dependence, and Irish parliaments as in the past were difficult for English viceroys to manage.

Molyneux was a friend of John Locke, whose influence is manifest in the reasoning of the pamphlet, and some of the political principles hotly debated in Ireland as in England were not connected with the constitutional question of the relations between the two kingdoms. Several other debates cut right across this. There were whigs and tories in Ireland as in England, although Irish circumstances produced different emphases and, by and large, the ascendancy had a strong whig bias, at least in political matters. For, in Ireland even more than in England, a distinction must be made between the ecclesiastical and the political aspects of these labels. It was anglican protestantism that the Irish ascendancy was determined to maintain, and the ecclesiastical toryism of Queen Anne's reign suited them well, in so far as it enabled them to strengthen greatly the popery laws. On the other hand, the inclination of Irish anglicans was against high-church ideas on the whole: they were surrounded by catholics, and depended for their security on whig political principles. A powerful opposition developed during Anne's reign, and succeeded in defeating the government's careful arrangements (although narrowly) in the election of 1713. The parliament then elected was adjourned after a month by the viceroy, the duke of Shrewsbury, who was concerned to restrain the Irish parliament from intervening in the succession question that agitated the later part of Anne's reign. He was told that the Irish parliament was determined to secure the protestant succession and had as much right to legislate for Ireland as the English parliament for England. Before parliament met again the queen died. Shrewsbury, whom she had appointed just before her death Lord Treasurer of Great Britain, proclaimed George I king. With the advent of the Hanoverian dynasty the protestant succession was secure and the whigs dominant.

The question of Anglo-Irish relations, however, remained unresolved, in spite of an attempt by the English parliament to settle it. Before the Act of Union of 1707, which united the kingdoms of England and Scotland in the new kingdom of Great Britain, there had been some pressure from the Irish ascendancy for a similar union of Ireland and England. This was the alternative to parliamentary independence which some of them advocated and sought in the endeavour to secure themselves in the management of Irish affairs. However, the English, and then the British parliament

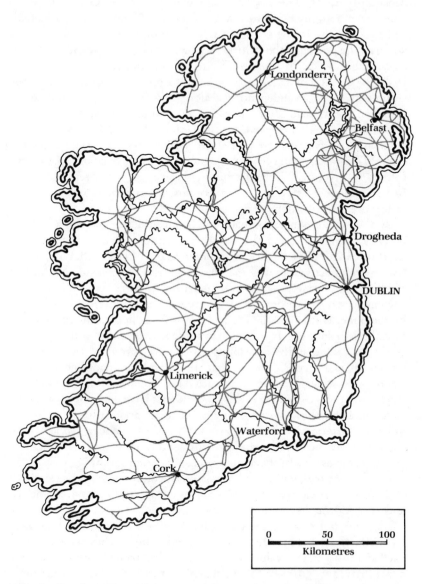

Map 14 Road system, 1778
Based on Taylor and Skinner, *Maps of the Roads of Ireland*, London and Dublin,
2nd edn, 1783.

preferred a different view of Ireland's situation. This was expressed in the declaratory act of 1719 – usually known as the Sixth of George I – which arose from an inheritance case which had come before both parliaments and exposed the ambiguities of the constitutional relationship. The act declared the power of the British parliament to legislate for Ireland 'in all causes whatsoever'. It was possible to enforce this, but not to make the Irish colony accept it. A new war of pamphlets began, with further arguments for Irish independence along with a revival of Molyneux's. Jonathan Swift, dean of St Patrick's cathedral in Dublin, was one of the first to join in with a *Proposal for the Universal use of Irish Manufacture in Cloaths and Furniture of Houses, etc. Utterly Rejecting and Renouncing Every Thing that comes from England*. A body of 'patriot' opinion was formed in protestant Ireland whose cohesive force was rejection of the British parliament's assertion. This opposition for the moment could be little more than verbal; but it was persistent.

By this stage a generation had passed since the perilous reign of James II. The ascendancy and the revolution settlement had survived. The Jacobite danger was still alive, as the attempt of 1715 showed, but the penal laws were effective, as was the almost paranoiac vigilance of the Irish protestants. Overseas, thousands of Irishmen wore the uniform of the Pretender, who was protected by the king of France and recognized as king by the pope. Until 1760 the Pretender was consulted on the appointment of catholic bishops to Irish sees. Until the middle years of the century it might be said that the possibility of an overthrow of the revolution settlement was a consideration that the ascendancy could never ignore. There was widespread fear, towards the end of Anne's reign, that government was conniving at this, and the first Irish parliament of the new reign, in 1715, took swift action against tories and censured the second duke of Ormond, several times lord lieutenant under Anne. In the circumstances, however great the resentment, it was extremely difficult for the colony to assert effectively its pretensions to autonomy.

Besides, the Irish parliament was a poor medium for the expression even of Irish protestant opinion. 150 constituencies (the thirty-two counties and 117 boroughs) returned two members each to the House of Commons. For most of these the electorate was tiny, and the boroughs were effectively the private property of individuals. They were treated as such and had a market value. Management of parliament – that is, securing a majority for government measures – was, therefore, a matter of persuading a comparatively small number of people to employ their parliamentary property in the government's interest, and this was done by the exercise of patronage. The majority was required, even before the act of 1719, for bills to pass. The effective constitutional legislation was Poynings's law of 1495, as amended in the reign of Mary I, and as modified by custom. The Irish parliament could introduce legislation in the form of a proposal, which was submitted to the Irish privy council. The privy council could change or reject the proposals, or 'heads of bills'. Those they accepted became 'bills' and were sent on to the English (later the British) privy council, which also might change or reject. If they were accepted they were sent back to the Irish parliament, which could accept or reject, but not amend, the bills. It was a chief function of the lord lieutenant (the viceroy) so to manage the parliament in Dublin that bills coming from England would pass. In the long absences of the eighteenth-century lords lieutenant, they were replaced by a panel of three lords justices with similar powers of patronage and management. When corruption is as institutional as this, it is not certain that it should be called 'corruption'; but many contemporaries did so call it. It was, however, the commonplace of eighteenth-century politics, particularly galling in Ireland because it regularly operated against the general interests even of those who – for an immediate consideration – collaborated.

In Britain parliament became more important during the eighteenth century; public financing gradually became more regular; government became slowly more widely effective. Ireland reflected this, and since the Irish parliament, while gaining in importance, remained subordinate, it became necessary to devise a system for its continued and effective management by natives of the country who knew the ropes, acting on behalf of the lord lieutenant (the viceroys came over from England, but did not spend much of their terms residing in Ireland). The system was to farm out patronage to managers in parliament, who undertook to steer government business through the House of Commons (the House of Lords, with its bishops appointed by government, was much less of a problem) and were consequently known as 'undertakers'. This system worked after a fashion. But the undertakers tended to adopt an independent stance of their own, knowing the British government to be, to an extent, dependent on them. They had something to sell: their skill and experience in handling the difficult Irish parliament.

The 1740s mark a point of change in Irish economy, politics, society and demography. The decade opened with famine, followed by epidemics. Like all such visitations, the famine was uneven in its incidence, but it was extremely severe in the west and may have killed, proportionately, as many people as the better remembered famine of just over a century later. Like the later famine, it marks a stage in the decline of Gaelic culture, raging as it did most furiously in the areas where this was still preserved.

After 1741, for many decades, there was no severe famine in the country. On the contrary, there was an improvement (with some setbacks) in general prosperity. The population began to increase, slowly at first, then, after about 1780, very rapidly.

In 1745 Charles Edward Stuart unfurled his banner in the Scottish highlands and began what was to be the last serious attempt to unseat the Hanoverians. The following year, after he had invaded England and retreated again, he and his cause were finally defeated at Culloden. Although there were Irishmen in the prince's company, Ireland remained quiet. After Culloden Jacobite nostalgia sustained a kind of dream-politics for thirty or forty years, but the cause was plainly lost. The remnants of the Irish catholic gentry began to adjust to the prospect of Hanoverian permanence, and the next generation began to produce, very tentatively at first, a view which attempted to accommodate that reality but also to advance their own cause in other ways. The officers wearing British uniform abroad, but in the French service, became willing to transfer their allegiance to the Hanoverians – but on conditions:

Your publick Papers [writes Colonel Daniel O'Connell from Paris to his brother in Co. Kerry, on 5 October 1778] have transmitted here the pleasing account of the New Laws in favour of the Roman Catholicks. A Revolution so unexpected and so long wished for must needs procure, in course of some years, an accession to the power and prosperity of the Kingdom of Ireland, and unite in one common Sentiment of loyalty the hearts of that long opposs'd and long unfortunate Nation. One step more still remains to be made – I mean the Liberty of spilling their blood in defence of their King and Country. I doubt not 'twill soon be granted, tho' no motive cu'd ever induce me to bear arms against France, where I early found an Asylum when refused one at home. I still wish the prosperity of the country, and at the same time that I pursue with inviolable fidelity that of my adopted King, Nature, stronger than reason or principle, still attaches my heart to Ireland.[10]

At home in Ireland, a new direction was taken, round the middle of the century, by catholic leaders, mostly aristocrats and gentry who had contrived to weather the storm. They accepted the conquest and the defeat of the Stuart cause, but were concerned to show that Gaelic Ireland had not been uncivilized and that catholic Ireland was worthy to be admitted to the political nation. Charles O'Conor, of Belnagare near Cruachain, descendant of the O'Conor kings of Connacht, John Curry of Dublin, and some others, wrote pamphlets and papers to sustain these views. They opened a debate on the interpretation of Irish history which was to continue for decades; their exposition was to be of great importance in giving shape to Irish nationalism. The contrary exposition, expressing a view widely held by the ascendancy of the day, may be illustrated briefly from the work of one Dr Smollett:

Setting aside the ridiculous legends and fables of the Irish with respect to their antiquity and origin, it seems highly reasonable to conclude, that the country was first peopled from Britain. There is no good reason to induce us to believe that it was ever conquered by the Romans. Towards the decline of the Roman empire, a colony of Scots began to make a great figure in Ireland, whence it acquired the name of Scotia. The island was afterwards often harassed by the Danes, Norwegians and Saxons; but never entirely subdued, till Henry II, King of England, made himself master of it in the twelfth century.[11]

The response may be illustrated from Sylvester O'Halloran, an historian whose work was widely read and accepted at the end of the eighteenth and the beginning of the nineteenth century:

Having a natural reverence for the dignity and antiquity of my native country, strengthened by education, and confirmed by an intimate knowledge of its history, I could not, without the greatest pain and indignation, behold on the one part, almost all the writers of England and Scotland (and from them of other parts of Europe) representing the Irish nation as the most brutal and savage of mankind, destitute of arts, letters, and legislation; and on the other, the extreme passiveness and insensibility of the present race of Irish, at such reiterated insults offered to truth and their country: instances of inattention to their own honour, unexampled in any other civilized nation.

For, though unhappily for this antient kingdom, *unnatural* distinctions have but too long been kept up by artful and designing enemies, to the almost entire ruin of the whole; yet are we in fact, but *one* people, and as unmixt a race as any in Europe. There is not at this day a Milesian, or descendant of Strongbow, whose bloods are not so intimately blended, that it would be impossible to determine which should preponderate. . . .[12]

These intimations of a catholic ideology, drawing on the Gaelic past, began to appear round the middle of the century. They were widely influential by the 1770s, but their important effects were further delayed.

In the meantime, the post-Revolution ascendancy, freed from the Jacobite threat to their property and privilege, enjoyed a brief period in which they conceived of themselves as the nation. In the first half of the century, their hostility to catholics was directed chiefly at the aristocracy and gentry they had replaced. They paid much less heed to the lower orders of catholics. At times in the early part of the century there seems to have been a view that these belonged to a dwindling species, and some perhaps regarded them, as the American colonists in places were beginning to regard the American Indians, as no more than a temporary inconvenience. By the last quarter of the century, however, such a perception was no longer possible: catholic numbers, which included many of the very poor, were plainly increasing.

But the protestant nation was transforming the country. Ireland emerged from its medieval wars only after the glorious revolution, when houses ceased to be fortified. The ascendancy tamed the land, stage by stage. In 1730 their parliament began to improve the country's commercial communications by appointing provincial Commissioners of Navigation to build canals. The work so initiated continued until the end of the century. About the same time systematic road-building began, with the aid of parliamentary grants and private investment. Many of the gentry, in tune with what was happening in Britain, were anxious to 'improve' their properties and had an obvious interest in systems of communications which would enable them to develop a market agriculture. They began reorganizing their estates and building elegant houses.

The great age of improvement, which can be measured roughly by the number of enclosure bills for the benefit of private individuals passing through parliament, was the 1770s and 1780s – the maximum decade in respect of the number of such bills was in this period. Here Ireland again, but palely, reflected England, where the chief 'improving' decade was that between 1770 and 1780.

There, a progressive, extravagant, arrogant, ruthless class was sweeping aside immemorial custom along with the old common lands, relentlessly changing the face of the countryside, causing unparalleled hardships to the rural poor, and in the process laying the foundation for new and unprecedented industries and new, improved, and vastly more efficient agriculture: making the modern world. In England there was provision by law for the poor: at the very beginning of the revolutionary process, in the sixteenth century, the parishes were charged, each with the maintenance of its own poor. There was no such provision in Ireland.[13]

Arthur Young, who visited Ireland in 1778, describes a number of the improvers. He saw, for example, the beginnings of the woods at Coole, about which Yeats was to write, more than a hundred years later:

The trees are in their autumn beauty,
The woodland paths are dry. . . .[14]

He wrote: 'Mr Gregory has a very noble nursery, from which he is making

Plate 9   Emigrant ship, Dublin Bay, by Edwin Hayes

Plate 10   Volunteers on College Green, by Francis Wheatley

Plate 11   Festival of St Kevin at Glendalough, by Joseph Peacock

Plate 12   Linen bleaching, Cullybackey, County Antrim

plantations, which will soon be a great ornament to the country.' The Robert Gregory of 1778 had 500 or 600 acres, which he was busy improving. He was building many miles of walls 'dry, six feet high, 3½ feet thick at bottom, 20 inches on top, costs 2s 6d the perch. Piers in mortar with gates and irons complete, £1. 14s'. Young goes on:

He has fixed two English bailiffs on his farm, one for accounts and overlooking his walling and other business; and another from Norfolk, for introducing the turnip husbandry; he has twelve acres this year; and what particularly pleased me, I saw some Irishmen hoeing them; the Norfolk men had taught them. . . .[15]

'Improvement' provoked resentment, although it did in fact improve, on the whole. But parliament, in Ireland as in England, was drawn predominantly from the aristocracy and gentry of the country and, given their head by the revolution constitution, they looked after their own interests in country matters. The larger landowners, unless they were experimentalists in the new crops, tended, for their own farming, to ranch. In the west in particular, much of the tillage was carried on, according to Young, 'by little farmers, from £20 to £100 a year, but most of it by the poor labourers, who are generally under-tenants, not holding of the landlords'.[16] This distinction runs back through the eighteenth century. In 1735, the Dublin House of Commons resolved that enforcing the tithe of agistment (tithe on grazing lands) was calculated to impair the protestant interest and cause popery and infidelity to flourish. Afterwards, this tax, nominally at least for the support of the established church, was borne chiefly by the tenants, who were catholic, and evaded largely by their landlords, who were protestant. It reinforced the class distinction between graziers and tillers and for a time led to an agricultural regression.

Apart from the planting and organization of large estates, other work and other colonization was transforming the country. To take the example of northern Co. Clare, in the west, the region around Ennistymon down to the middle of the century was effectively beyond the reach of British civilization. The roads were next to impossible and the wild coast offered no harbours or jetties. The medieval parishes – Kilmanaheen, Killasboglenane, Kilmacreehy, Kilshannig – still functioned around their ancient centres, and the present-day towns and villages, Liscannor, Lehinch, Ennistymon, Ballyvaughan, and so forth, had not yet taken shape. But the organization of Gaelic civilization had been broken by Elizabethan, Cromwellian and Williamite expeditions and by the hangings and confiscations which followed them. Enormous tracts of land had come into the hands of newcomers at the beginning of the century. For example,

Lord Clare, of the senior branch of the chief Clare family, the O'Briens, who remained true to James II, lost 57,000 acres. The last efforts to re-edify the medieval churches had been made by landowners during James II's brief tenure of the throne; these were now in ruins. Other parts of the old order of the Middle Ages had also been, comparatively recently, destroyed. The O'Davorens's school of Irish legal learning, maintained for centuries at Cahermacnaghten, for example, was no more. Many of the castles and tower houses of the old gentry had been slighted. The stone cahers of the Burren district were deserted. Up to the mid century, the country, around Ennistymon was Jacobite, and the young men were still going to France and Spain. Ennistymon was the location of a tower house, built by Turlough O'Brien in 1588 and still the seat of one of the main branches of the O'Briens. Thirty years later, about 1780, this district was just beginning to be brought under the full dispensation of Hanoverian rule. This can be illustrated by the fact that the establishment of the anglican church, other than on paper, proceeded very slowly in Co. Clare. Lecky points out that in mid century, in sixty-two of seventy-six parishes, no protestant church existed. By 1780, however, the first protestant church in Ennistymon was nearing completion, on a grant of £300 from the Board of First Fruits. The Rev. James Kenny, archdeacon of Kilfenora, collated to the parish of Kilmanaheen in 1775, was also fining down 40 acres of rough ground, about half a mile from the church, and building on it a glebe house and offices, the first in the county. By 1780 he was making his garden, in which he cultivated balm, sage, thyme, pennyroyal, rosemary, camomile, horehound and other herbs. In this remote place in the west a process of centuries' duration was reaching a consummation of a kind towards the close of the eighteenth century.[17]

The ascendancy built elegant towns and, in Dublin, what became in their time one of the chief European cities in spaciousness and style. Medieval Dublin had been small, crowded within walls round Christchurch cathedral (also small) on the south shore of the Liffey's tidal stream at a point where it could easily be bridged. To the south of the walls there was an overspill with an oddity, a second cathedral, the result of a medieval dispute. On the north shore there was a secondary settlement beside the great Cistercian abbey of St Mary. To the east of the city was another great priory and, in the south-east angle of the walls, the castle. Expansion began towards the end of the seventeenth century. The new city lay mainly down-river from the old, on both sides of the Liffey. Its focus was College Green, where the university (founded by Queen Elizabeth I) occupied the site of the medieval priory, south of the river. Opposite the university was the parliament house, a great Ionic-columned building,

Figure 14 The Damer House, Roscrea, County Tipperary: an early eighteenth-century town house

begun to Sir Edward Pearce's design in 1728. It was extended handsomely in 1785 by James Gandon. Trinity College (the only college of the university of Dublin) was itself rebuilt in the course of the eighteenth century, with a monumental arcaded library, a series of courtyards, and a great grey Palladian façade facing the parliament house. The castle was also remodelled, mainly in brick, during the century. By the end of the century the city extended in all directions from this focus to a radius of roughly a mile. In 1757 the parliament appointed a body called the Commissioners for Making Wide and Convenient Streets, and under their supervision the city assumed a spacious character, with broad and well-proportioned streets, alternating straight stretches with pleasing curves, with squares and fountains, rows of four-storeyed brick houses punctuated with the stone façades of the grander houses of the aristocracy. Apart from the focal area there were numbers of splendid public buildings, notably the custom house, downstream, and the four courts, upstream, both on the north bank of the Liffey. To the west of the city, also on the north bank, extended the hundreds of acres of the great Phoenix park. This capital city, which proclaimed the aspirations of the protestant nation, reached its grandest state in the last two decades of the century. It housed, of course, as well as the elegantly designed streets and squares of the new building, the crowded alleys of the old medieval core, and could display all the extremes of splendour and misery, of squalor and luxury, that characterized the eighteenth century. It also possessed, like London and other eighteenth-century cities, a volatile and dangerous mob, dandies and criminals, satanic clubs and charitable societies.

The evidence suggests that in the second half of the century prosperity was increasing, and this also appears to have been a fairly general contemporary impression. But it was a precarious prosperity, readily affected by the fluctuations in trade and subject also to erosion by deeper processes of change. The Irish economy remained closely dependent on the land, and efforts to develop manufactures met with limited success. Many Irish landowners wished to emulate their fellows in Britain, who had proceeded from a transformation of agriculture to that great expansion of manufacture which we call 'the industrial revolution'. So, for example, enterprising gentlemen attempted to introduce the 'Manchester system' into Ireland, and as well as Norfolk experts on the farms we find Manchester mechanics being imported to Dublin, Cork and Limerick. Production of cotton indeed flourished in the 1770s and 1780s. Restrictions on trade, imposed by British protectionism (especially in respect of woollen cloth and goods) gave rise to frustration and hence to exaggerated expectations of the prosperity that would ensue were they to be removed.

The activities of those displaced persons termed 'rapparees' and 'tories', resulting from the wars and upheavals of the seventeenth century having diminished in the early eighteenth century, the incidence of crime and indications of unrest in the middle years of the century seem not to have been remarkable, by the standards of the time. But in 1759, when the import of Irish cattle into England was permitted again after a long period of prohibition, there was a movement by landlords to form new pasture, enclose common land, and in some cases demolish houses and villages. This provoked an outbreak of agrarian crime, which began in Tipperary and spread to other parts of Munster and to Leinster and Connacht. Bands of men, wearing white smocks over their clothes, gathered at night to level fences and attack cattle. They were known as 'Whiteboys' and their movement became a virtual rebellion in Tipperary. Soon they began to issue threats connected with a number of other longstanding grievances. They attempted to control and diminish payment of tithe and the payments exacted by their own catholic clergy, and they also sporadically protested at rents. The movement, once begun, was very difficult for the government to control. The members of the Whiteboy gangs were mostly cottiers, it would seem, but they included many people of more substance, and they enjoyed the sympathy of a large part of the rural population: it was almost impossible to obtain evidence to convict them. One attempt at exemplary punishment had the effect of alienating a large section of the people and spreading Whiteboy activity. This was the execution, unjustly, of Father Sheehy, parish priest of Clonmel, in 1766 for a Whiteboy murder. The Tipperary landlords attempted to combat the Whiteboy movement by taking the law into their own hands, forming troops of horse from chosen tenants. But the activities of Whiteboy gangs continued into the nineteenth century, in spite of repeated attempts at repression by government. Separate but similar outbreaks occurred in Ulster. In 1763 landlords in Derry, Tyrone and Armagh, availing of a law which empowered them (in their capacity as grand jurors) to use forced labour in making roads in their own interests, provoked outbreaks by gangs who wore oak sprigs in their hats and called themselves 'Oakboys', or 'hearts of oak'. They too went on to protest against tithe. In Co. Antrim, in 1770, 'hearts of steel', or 'Steelboys' revenged themselves when leases fell in on Lord Donegall's estates and he demanded for the renewal large fines which many of his tenants were unable to pay. The Ulster outbreaks did not last long, but Whiteboy activity, especially in Munster, was to cause alarm to the authorities for many years.

These grievances were local and particular. In Dublin, after the middle of the century, the wider constitutional grievance began to come into focus again in parliament. As resentments against British governmental control

Map 15   The shiring of Ireland: counties and provinces

accumulated among the members of parliament, the very loose 'patriot' grouping began to cohere into a more persistent faction or party which kept up against government measures a harassing opposition. Only one general election (on his accession) was held in the thirty-three-year reign of George II, but there were many by-elections, which helped to increase the opposition. The government's system of parliamentary management held through the reign, but came under increasing strain. The question of the constitutional relationship between Ireland and Great Britain combined with a more subtle problem – of the relationship between a strong executive and a weak legislature – to cause the trouble. The Irish parliament was frustrated, and expressed its frustration in anti-British, or more exactly, anti-English rhetoric. Public opinion on the whole backed it in this, and since some British legislation had in fact imposed restrictions on Irish trade, the defects of Irish society and of the economy tended to be blamed on the British. The importance of mobs in eighteenth-century cities should not be underestimated, and the Dublin mob too played its intimidatory role, all the more effective because its fury could as readily be directed against members of the Dublin parliament as against England. Riots were not infrequent. Some were factional, with one trade and quarter fighting another (the Liberties weavers against the Ormond market butchers), some were religious (catholics against priest-hunters or methodists), but some were political (often to demonstrate approval or disapproval of parliament). There was serious political rioting in 1752 and in 1759 the mob broke into the parliament building itself and enthroned an old woman on the lord chancellor's chair.

When George III succeeded to the throne in 1760, parliament was dissolved and a general election was held, in an atmosphere of great excitement. Whatever startling changes may have been expected from the election, nothing very startling happened, but over a number of years the old system of parliamentary management broke down. There was a quick succession of viceroys in the opening years of the reign, but the government continued for a time to manage its parliamentary business fairly smoothly. George III came to the throne in the middle of the seven years war against France (1756–63). Indeed Ireland was invaded in the year of his accession – a somewhat absurd episode, when the French admiral Thurot captured Carrickfergus castle (which was defended by brickbats). The conflict as a whole, however, the 'first world war', was far-flung and important. It was costly, but it confirmed British sea-power, added enormously to the territories under British rule (including Canada and Bengal), transformed British status in the world, and raised very difficult questions about the relationships of the different countries in the British sphere.

The concept of the 'British empire' was emerging and developing, given different meanings and different emphases at the time by different people. It was applied to Great Britain itself (which Lord Charlemont, however, referred to as 'the seat of empire'), to British dominion of the oceans, or, increasingly, to British rule over a growing number of colonies and possessions around the world. 'Trade, shipping, the Navy – not colonization – were the true imperial interests of Englishmen in the hundred years after the restoration of Charles II', according to C. E. Carrington.[18] These interests now involved Ireland, but in a somewhat perplexing way. They were shared by the ascendancy and its followers, but Irish interests could not be quite identical with the 'interests of Englishmen' since some English laws and regulations intervened to make a distinction. Irish wool could be exported only to England, not to the plantations or to foreign countries; Irish cattle similarly could not be exported. Broadly, the emerging British concept of what we might nowadays call the 'settlement empire' was one of a division of function: the plantations would produce food and commodities, to be sold to Britain; Britain would supply them – along with as many other parts of the world as possible – with manufactured and luxury goods. Ireland was looked on, not quite as a plantation or colony, not quite as a potential constituent of a British nation-state. The confusion affecting both British policy-makers and Irish representatives was as great as that affecting Anglo-American dealings (if not greater) in that seminal period when the bills for the seven years war came due. It was becoming clear that some policy other than benign neglect was necessary for the colonies. The post-war British ministries blundered, through what were initially not much more than adjustments of administrative arrangements, into disputes that swelled to great issues of constitutional principle in America. These issues had been raised in Ireland. The declaratory act of 1766, which threw down the gage to the American colonials, was copied verbatim in its main clause from the Irish declaratory act of 1719. And some of the ideas put forward by the Americans on the maintenance of the 'rights of Englishmen' in the colonies had been rehearsed by the Irish colonists earlier in the century.

As the American dispute proceeded in the 1760s, members of the Irish ascendancy continued their own constitutional debate. Like the Americans at the beginning of the trans-Atlantic quarrel, they identified themselves with 'the British empire' and its emerging symbolism and concepts. Its trade, largely was their trade; differences about participation in that trade, resentments against mercantilist restriction of it, could still be viewed as an internal family matter. The 'empire' was rapidly becoming a popular idea, and images derived from an imperial rather than a purely local patriotism were current among the lower as well as the middle orders of society, in Ireland as well as in England. But in Ireland the currency was among protestants, not catholics. One set of images, for example, exalted the sailors, who were the heroes of the recurrent wars against the French and of what was (in much later terminology) to be known as 'the old colonial system'. Since the seventeenth-century civil wars, soldiers continued to be regarded with some reserve by popular opinion, as potential dangers to liberty. Sailors, on the other hand, were its brave defenders. Hence, 'hearts of oak', a good protestant nautical libertarian title for societies which banded themselves in defence of rural freedoms. Other armed Ulster gangs styled themselves 'fleets' and did their jibbing and tacking in the country lanes of Armagh.

In Ireland, as in America, trade, taxation and representation were the matters of dispute giving rise to constitutional issues. In parliament the growing opposition caused a major modification of the system by which the executive in Dublin castle had managed legislation. The dole of patronage ceased to operate smoothly: the undertakers were becoming more difficult to handle, and politicians whose votes had been brought were inclined to renege in such numbers that government was finding it difficult to replace them. It was decided to depart from precedent and have a resident rather than a visiting lord lieutenant. The five-year administration of Lord Townshend (1767–72) presided over changes which both arose from and re-emphasized the peculiar weaknesses of the Irish parliament. Periodic elections were instituted by the Octennial act of 1768 – something of a victory for the 'patriots' – and the government reluctantly accepted in practice the initiation of money bills in the Dublin Commons. However, the now resident lord lieutenant continued, although with difficulty, to manage the passage of government legislation.

The imperial crisis of the 1770s caused considerable political instability in Great Britain, and in Ireland broke (for a short while) the deadlock in constitutional relations. That state of disequilibrium with which we must contrive to live in the modern world – a dizzying acceleration in economic, technical, social and demographic change – was already affecting England. Food production had been drastically transformed since the beginning of the century by a combination of radically new farming methods and new transportation systems for bulk commodities. The average weight of both oxen and sheep sold at Smithfield, as J. H. Plumb has pointed out, more than doubled between 1710 and 1795.[19] This revolutionary change was associated with a whole complex of other changes in farm organization and management and the provision of animal feed. For example, to take the case of two villages in a remote Irish county, it is associated with the opening of factories in Scarriff and Newmarket-on-Fergus for the manufacture of oilcake for feeding (mainly English) cattle. The oilcake was made from rape seed. Rape was a first crop used on land newly brought under cultivation as the population of the west of Ireland expanded. But the transformation of agriculture, and its accompanying revolution in transport and communications, blended in with the beginnings of revolutionary change in the production of textiles, pottery and other goods, and with a runaway expansion in long-distance trade. Governmental and business communications expanded too. In England the system of post coaches had just begun to provide a possible speed of travel by road that for the first time began to match that of the Roman empire in the age of the Antonines. And, in the aftermath of the seven years war, people began to discern the lineaments of the worldwide thalassocracy of which England was now the centre. But they weren't quite sure what to do about it. The king viewed the aggrandisement of the imperial crown in one way, parliament somewhat differently. Parliament still represented overwhelmingly the landed interests of the country. One of its chief functions, in practice, especially since the prerogative of the crown had been diminished, was to pass measures that would profit the members of the Lords and Commons and the interests they represented, frequently at the expense of other interests. Those other interests now included a fast-growing commercial and manufacturing bourgeoisie, whose overlap with the aristocracy and gentry, although significant, was not sufficient for them to feel that they were adequately represented in parliament. The elder Pitt, in his manic intervals, had (as a few people have in every generation) an insight into what was really happening and conducted a single-minded drive towards the promotion of 'trade, shipping and the Navy', which won him the plaudits – along with countless gold presentation snuff-boxes – of the English merchant towns. Their burghers' eyes were increasingly on the West Indian plantations, the waters of the Hooghli and the slave-coasts of Africa rather than the shires, and they desperately needed a voice to speak on their behalf.

If there was confusion of policies and interests in England, it was confounded further in Ireland. There, commercial and landed interests were less at cross-purposes: the situation and circumstances of the Irish colony drew it together into a (quarrelsome) community. It was an energetic, active, eloquent community by the late eighteenth century, and many of its members were furiously pursuing the kinds of profits which could now be made in England. That they were less easily to be made in Ireland was only in small part due to English restriction, but English restriction was a ready-made and familiar grievance. The general tendency was to associate entrepreneurial problems in Ireland with limitations on trade, and limitations on trade with the subordination of Ireland's parliament to Britain's. In the new Irish parliament which assembled after the accession of George III in 1760, there were numbers of young men who dominated the political scene twenty years later. They represented a brilliant generation such as, happily, occurs every now and then in most civilized communities. Some of the brightest, including Burke, Sheridan and Goldsmith, made their careers in England. But the Dublin parliament retained some others.

There were, of course, differences of approach to the pressing problems of the day. John FitzGibbon, later earl of Clare, was to pursue the maintenance of the English connection, being a realist who held that the ascendancy could not survive independently in a country the great majority of whose people were catholics. He was prepared to point out bluntly and coldly to his colleagues that 'the Act by which most of us hold our estates was an Act of violence – an Act subverting the first principles of the Common Law in England and Ireland'.[20] For him, the Irish colonial grievances against British policy were small compared with the protection the colonials received from Britain. Henry Flood, a 'patriot', wanted to have the best of both worlds. He aimed at Irish colonial independence from Britain and advocated the freeing of the Irish catholics from all religious restrictions. But he did not advocate admitting them to the political nation: he realized that this would mean the end of protestant privilege.[21] Henry Grattan, a more pliant man in the sense that he took shrewd political heed of currents of public opinion – an orator – was generous in his proposals for the catholics. He envisaged, dimly as it may be, a kind of pluralism (as we would now put it) for Ireland, a new nation compounded of protestants and catholics, with its independent parliament under the crown. He was very reluctant to endorse notions of 'British empire' at this stage (later, in the nineteenth century, he was to change). As an example of a more typical parliamentarian, leaving the outstanding leaders aside, we may take Sir Lucius O'Brien, the senior member of the Irish Commons from Clare, a 'patriot' and leading country supporter of Grattan. O'Brien was protestant but of the old Gaelic family descended from Brian Boru. He was an improving landlord, a smuggler, a 'fixer', a tireless committee member (with a special concern for law-and-order), an indefatigable lobbyist, a plausible talker. Arthur Young solemnly prints, as part of his account of landholding and agriculture in Co. Clare, a pack of lies provided for him by O'Brien (who entertained him with hospitality and blarney) with the intention, undoubtedly, of influencing the British government and impressing them with the sorry state of Irish landowners.

There were both similarities and differences between the grievances of the Irish colonials and the Americans. Among the occasions of the American revolt were two issues, important at the time (but in historical hindsight diminished in favour of more respectable causes). Those arose from British concessions to the French – and catholic – governmental arrangements in Canada, and from British attempts to protect Amerindians against the expansive aggression of the colonials. The Irish colonials, on the other hand, were accustomed to depend on British support against catholics and natives. But protestations against taxation without representation, arguments against the right of jurisdiction of the British parliament (as distinct from the king) over colonial affairs: these met with sympathy in Ireland. Ambiguity characterized the Irish colonial response to the American colonial revolt. When the revolt led to rebellion, the Dublin parliament – with some opposition – supported the crown. When rebellion led to war, and war to the entry of France and Spain into the conflict, the Irish colony found itself facing both ways at once. The largest military expeditions ever to leave British shores had gone to the American war, stripping both Britain and Ireland of soldiers: large numbers of mercenaries and others (from the king's Hanoverian dominions and elsewhere) had to be employed. With the French entry into the war, Ireland's shores were again in danger of invasion.

The ascendancy reacted to this danger by raising companies of volunteers, and the government, unable to supply adequate troops itself for the defence of Ireland, gave the volunteers acknowledgement. The peril was immediate and real. In 1779 the French not only prepared for the invasion of Britain, but gained naval control of the Channel. That year's fleet of India merchantmen, unable to reach British ports, had to shelter for weeks in the Shannon estuary, and Irish waters were subject to the hazard of privateers, including the American John Paul Jones and two Irish ships (with privateering warrants issued by the Americans at Dunkirk), the *Black Prince* and *Black Princess*, operating on the Irish Sea.

The volunteer army was first raised in 1778; within two years its numbers were sufficient to be a force in the land, all the more powerful since it was the only effective military force, the regular army being on the far side of the Atlantic. Raised to defend Ireland from the French, the volunteers were soon used to back the Irish parliament's case against the English parliament. More than that: they acted as an extra-parliamentary force to put pressure on the Irish parliament in favour of independence. In its extreme difficulty, with the French intervention swinging the American war against it, the British government made concessions to Dublin, beginning with free trade, granted at the end of 1779. There followed concessions on other disputed matters, culminating in 1782 in an amendment of Poynings's law and a repeal of the declaratory act of 1719. The Irish parliament became, apart from a few remaining restraints of which the royal veto was the most important, an independent legislature. But it did not produce an independent executive; it remained loyal to the crown, to the British connection and to the British cause in the war: the constitutional relationship of Ireland and Britain became, if anything, more obscure.

Outside parliament, however, the volunteers, having in the briefest period helped to force through what the parliamentarians had failed to achieve in three-quarters of a century, became a political body in their own right. Some leading parliamentarians took part in their proceedings, but most became alarmed. The seventeenth century was still a vivid example to eighteenth-century politicians: armies were feared by parliaments unless they were very securely under legal and financial control. The volunteers, an overwhelmingly protestant body, were strongest in Ulster, where protestant discontent had become somewhat radical. They brought into focus the growing demand for the ending of the patronage system of politics and for reform of the electoral system. They had allies within the Irish parliament, notably Henry Grattan and, with reservations, their own commander-in-chief Lord Charlemont. They held conventions, in Dungannon in February 1782 and in Dublin in November 1783, at which not only were demands for those reforms put forward, but also resolutions in support of 'the right of private judgment, in matters of religion to be equally sacred in others as in ourselves'. There were 100,000 of them under arms; they represented, essentially, colonial discontent, and although it was their armed threat that secured colonial legislative independence in 1782, that same threat was to lead to the suppression of colonial autonomy in Ireland.

First, the Dublin parliament resisted the demands of the volunteers. No eighteenth-century parliament could claim to be more 'representative' than a body like the volunteers (the Irish parliament was probably less so), but it could fall back on the cant of its time – 'liberty' and the sacred constitution. In impassioned speeches it did so. Reform was rejected. On the catholic question, even some of the radicals were cautious: this offered the government a lever to prise asunder the protestant autonomists.

On the question of relations with Great Britain, on the other hand, the Dublin parliamentarians tried to push too far too fast. They had succeeded so far partly because they enjoyed some sympathy in the British parliament, where there were many who favoured conciliation of the colonies and an arrangement whereby people of British origin settled in different parts of the world might live as political equals. But the Dublin 'patriots' pressed for rhetorical as well as real concessions. Flood put forward the demand, conceded under the pressures that a failing war imposed on the British parliament, for an act of 'Renunciation'. Then, influenced by an economic depression induced by bad harvests, some parliamentarians in Dublin began to ask for protective tariffs against British goods. This stimulated those in Britain who had had the vision of a more or less federal empire to try to reach a permanent agreement with Ireland that would settle, for Britain's commercial and strategic security, relations between the two kingdoms on matters of mutual commerce and common defence. The Rockingham whigs had been dealing with their factional counterparts in Ireland (notably Lord Charlemont), and these dealings were taken over by Lord Shelburne, a political protégé of the elder Pitt. He was briefly prime minister, succeeded by the younger Pitt who addressed himself to a settlement. An Anglo-Irish treaty was prepared in draft, an ostensibly commercial agreement whose intention, as Pitt put it, was that of 'relinquishing local prejudices and partial advantages, in order to consult uniformly and without distinction the general benefit of the empire'.[22] The balance of the draft treaty embodied a major concession to the Irish side and a comparable demand. The concession was a departure from the mercantilist principles embodied in English commerical legislation since the Navigation act of 1651: Great Britain and Ireland were to constitute a common market; Irish ships and merchants might carry colonial produce to British ports; the produce of each kingdom was to be accepted freely in the other; duties would be kept to the same level in the two countries. In return Ireland was to contribute to imperial defence by making payments in support of the navy. 'There can be but one navy for the empire at large, and it must be administered by the executive power in this country'.[23] Pitt wrote to the duke of Rutland, lord lieutenant in 1785, in briefing him on the negotiations with the Irish parliament. Britain had by now lost the American colonies, and what Pitt was proposing was no less than the remodelling of 'our reduced and shattered empire, of which Great Britain and Ireland are now the only considerable members',[24] as he put it in a speech to the House of Commons. On the basis of the proposed treaty he was prepared to modify the system by which the British executive carried measures through the Irish parliament.

The negotiations were carried on through Grattan, the chief spokesman of the 'patriots' and now the dominant figure in the Irish House of Commons. Grattan obtained one or two further concessions – giving the Irish parliament independent control over its naval payments – and the treaty was passed in Dublin and was sent on to Westminster. Here it met

Figure 15 Dublin castle: Bedford tower and record office

with a storm of opposition, in pamphlets and press, on behalf of British manufacturers and merchants. Fox and Burke spoke against it in the house. It finally passed, but with twenty amendments which sought to impose British trade and shipping regulations of the future on the Irish parliament. In this form it was rejected in Dublin. 'Our lives are at the service of the empire', said Grattan, 'but our liberties? No.'

With this failure to reach a mutually acceptable arrangement between the two kingdoms, there also failed the attempt at Irish colonial self-determination. Legislative independence continued for the moment but British executive control was strengthened, with a renewal of the old system of managing parliament. In Dublin castle the ruling group backing the lord lieutenant, led by the lord chancellor, John Fitzgibbon, coldly dismissed the rhetoric of 'liberty' and observed with penetrating accuracy the weakness of the 'patriots' – their inability to reconcile the continuation of their own perceived position as leaders of the nation with the aspirations and the inescapable fact of the existence of close on 4 million catholics. Grattan had protested that if forced into the 'false dilemma' of having to choose between the empire and Irish liberty he would choose Irish liberty. He did. Pitt chose the empire, abandoned the idea of treating with an independent colonial Ireland, and, among his many other concerns, began to steer Irish policy in quite a different direction.

Part Three

Divided Ireland

8 *The United Kingdom*

Ireland enjoyed a modest prosperity in the later eighteenth century, but the country became more and more agitated by the action of social forces which were the more alarming as their origins were obscure. The declamations of the aristocrats and gentlemen of the anglican Dublin parliament had their immediate counterpoint in the violent demonstrations of the catholic Dublin mob. That the population was rapidly increasing had become evident by about 1790; some of the effects of this increase, even before their cause was known, had already begun to cause concern. Among these were agrarian outrages and, in the most densely populated rural areas (such as Co. Armagh) a developing rural civil war between catholic and protestant peasants.

What was happening is easier to understand today than it was at the time: we have many comparable examples in 'developing' countries, where the effects of colonialism and neo-colonialism, and the transition from various kinds of traditional societies to 'modern' systems have been quite intensively studied by sociologists, economists and others. Ireland in the late eighteenth century was subject to powerful forces of change which were both endogenous and exogenous, and the balance between the two was uneasy and unstable. The Irish parliament passed laws; the British government administered them, pursuing its own policy as far as possible. In Britain, what we now call 'the industrial revolution' had begun. People at the time knew that something was happening, but could have no clear idea as to what it was. What did seem clear, however, to contemporaries (although it was subsequently obscured by capitalist myth) was that control of the legislative and executive apparatus of the state was the way to profit. The initial accumulation of capital which made the industrial revolution possible arose largely from governmental action, backed by innumerable public and private bills which expropriated domestic property (such as that of the monasteries in the time of Henry VIII or the lands of defeated opponents in the civil wars or the common lands and the customary perquisites of the poor in the eighteenth century) or foreign property in the colonies. Government also provided monopoly and protection.

The colonial establishment in Ireland benefited from this but was aggrieved since its interests, in the long run, were subordinated to British interests. It was unable to develop Ireland as Great Britain was being developed because Ireland lacked the necessary infrastructure and available natural resources. The country lacked good harbours, the canal system was inadequate, and although there was much road-building in the last few decades of the century, the roads were not good and the network was exiguous. Besides, while some members of the Irish ascendancy were vigorous and enterprising, too many were content with the slothful exploitation of their privilege and lived dissolute and useless, if colourful, lives in the style picturesquely described by Jonah Barrington.[1] The society, like many colonial societies, was insufficiently mobile. The penal laws, coming after centuries of warfare, had done their work of erecting a formidable barrier between the privileged colonials and the excluded natives. Poverty, in spite of increasing general prosperity, not only remained widespread and squalid but tended to increase as the population grew. There was a deep structural fault. No tradition of ancient dependency tempered the alienation of tenants from their landlords, of catholic artisans and merchants from protestant placemen, over most of the country. The thousand petty humiliations of a resentful subservience could be met only with the glib deference and the placating comicality that masked hatred. This hatred was directed against the ascendancy, so many of whose members were at the time proclaiming their devotion to Irish liberty. And, as the island became more crowded, its fragile order dissolved.

The face of the country changed drastically in the course of the eighteenth century. The clearance of the virgin forests, which had been in progress for centuries, accelerated, and extended to remote parts. By the closing decades of the century the old fortified or defended houses of the gentry and aristocracy had given way everywhere to large-windowed houses, many of them elegant and ample and set in parks and walled demesnes. The modern network of 5- to 10-acre fields, with thorn hedges grown on banks had begun to characterize many landscapes, and by the end of the century marginal lands were being colonized in most parts. Within the landlords' estate walls trees were planted, often including exotic species, and laid out for aesthetic effect, but otherwise timber was scarce, and the maintenance of supplies of fuel took up a good deal of the energies of the countryside. The isolated farmstead in the middle of its fields was becoming much more common, especially in the lowlands, but cluster villages, each occupied by two or three interrelated extended families, were widespread in the hill country in the west and also in parts of the east. These were generally associated with rundale cultivation: small infields for tillage at or close to the village, larger outfields and rough grazing farther from it, with commons and often with turbary (peat-cutting rights) extending up the hills. Such villages tended to be unstable, swelling and dwindling within the space of a generation or two as families grew or hived off. The pattern was very old; the network of rights and obligations within the village and its fields was complex; and the villages were usually reserves of the Irish language, of folklore and folk-music and of ancient tradition. In the hills the old custom of transhumance, called 'booleying' in Ireland, survived widely.

The upper stratum of rural society was, of course, the protestant ascendancy, to which most of the large landowners belonged. There was also a scattering of catholic landlords of substance, chiefly in the west. There were also catholic farmers of much smaller property whose families, through the operation of the popery laws directed against catholic property, had sunk in the world through subdivision or otherwise. These were tenacious of the memory of former glory and represented that combination of conservative tradition and radical discontent that was to characterize the catholic rural population for many decades to come. Most of the farmers were tenants, either holding their lands directly from a landlord (often on a short lease and at a high rent), or from a land-jobber, who had rented a large farm to sublet it in small parcels at exorbitant rents. Grazing land was often let on conacre (an eleven-month lease). The farmers employed labour in and out of the house, and there was a very large class of landless labourers, itself subdivisible into several grades. James Caldwell in 1780 distinguishes between cottiers who 'hold at will a small take of land, seldom more than an acre, and grass for a couple of cows, at an exorbitant rent which they work out at the small wages of four of five pence a day without diet' and 'persons who have short leases or leases of uncertain tenure at high rents' and 'inhabitants of cottages in the neighbourhood of towns and small villages and are supported by daily labour'.[2] But there were numerous people below even this last category, destitute, homeless, often half-starving. Another witness refers to the 'middling class of people who live on potatoes, milk and butter and have a good healthy appearance'. These contrasted with the destitute, suffering from scurvy and skin diseases, dying young.

The antiquary Edward Ledwich, who was vicar of the parish of Aghaboe in Queen's County (now Laois), published in 1796 a survey of his parish, carefully compiled, and (although designed to show how modest his own income was) probably reasonably accurate. He provides an interesting ideal table, for this, one of the better parts of the country, to show the annual economy of a cottier, 'by which we may appreciate the situation of the lowest class in the parish'. His account of the cottier's income and expenditure may be summarized as follows:

220 days' work at 6d a day	£5.	10.	0
Supply from tilling 2 acres of garden	5.	0.	0
A pig	1.	10.	0
Three-quarters of a hundred of butter	2.	2.	0
'Two of his family spin 6 skenes a day a 1d each, and work 260 days, not being prevented by the seasons'	6.	10.	0
	£20.	12.	0

(Ledwich comments: 'I might add twenty shillings more for eggs, fowl, and ten shillings for a bauneen or young pig, and five shillings for a calf.)

2 acres of garden	£3.	0.	0
Grass for a cow	1.	10.	0
Hay	1.	0.	0
Soap 13 pounds at 8d a pound		8.	8
Candles 3 pence a week for half a year		13.	0
A coat, waistcoat, breeches and making	1.	14.	1½
Shoes, 2 pair		12.	0
Stockings, 2 pair		5.	5
Shirts, 2 of bandle linen		6.	6
Hat		4.	4
Tithe		6.	6
	£10.	0.	6½

Ledwich says he has not the information to calculate the cost of clothing the cottier's wife and four children (the wife's business) but estimates it at not more than 4 pounds. A further 4 shillings go to the parish priest. A surplus of 6 pounds and just over 7 shillings is left. 'We see here the excess of his income over his expenses is nearly the industry of two females of his family, and it evinces the immense value of manufactures. What I have now detailed exhibits the exact state of my labouring tenants. As soon as the cottier gathers a few pounds, he takes potato-ground in the neighbourhood, and retails the crop the next spring at considerable profit, and after some time commences a small farmer, reckoning much on the aid of his children, who are then grown up. From such small beginnings, I have known many arrive at opulence.'[3] The 'many' may be doubted. Most did not.

Spinning (of wool or linen) was widespread; weaving somewhat less so. It seems that by the late eighteenth century, the provision of spinning wheels for the daughters of his more reliable tenants was the sign of a benevolent landlord. A true peasant society was coming into being. That is to say, the sub-tenant farmers, in order to survive, were coming under increasing pressure to produce for a comparatively remote market – to pay the rent, for which privilege they increasingly had to compete – as well as providing subsistence for themselves and their landlords.

Weaving, especially of linen, became important in this respect in Ulster. By the 1770s, the highest density of rural population in Ireland was in Co. Armagh. Here linen-weaving became extremely important. The work was 'put out' by factors, and was done in cottages throughout the area, where the looms, worked by men, women and children, were active from first to last light. The linen was not of the finest kind – that was supplied from other sources – but it catered for a widening mass market, largely in England. The industry had become firmly established, largely *faute de mieux*, with the English restrictions on Irish wool. Flax was grown quite widely in eastern Ireland, but linen-weaving was especially characteristic of Ulster. The craft of weaving had been brought in here by planters, both Scottish and English.

Much of the Armagh plantation had been English, and in parts of the county (especially the north-eastern parts) had been fairly dense. English farmers, in the plantation, had brought in customs and practices of their native country, including, for example, the large-scale cultivation of apples, but in the drumlin hills that run through Monaghan, Armagh and Louth on the Ulster borderlands, very old ways survived cheek-by-jowl with the plantation. And in among the more rugged ranges of Slieve Gullion in south Armagh, the Cooleys in Louth and the Mournes in south Down, the old Irish tradition, in language, storytelling, poetry, music and outlook, was still vigorous in the late eighteenth century and had indeed made considerable impact on the descendants of the settlers.

In this region the pressures of a growing population were reinforced by the new economic pressures. Expanding textile markets affected the already semi-industrialized countryside in the form of a demand for more and more production from a growing number of looms. More and more linen had to be turned out to pay the rising rents. And competition for subsistence became intense, with the perpetually clacking looms at its centre.

By the last quarter of the century, these social, economic and demographic pressures were being given expression in protestant–catholic violence. There was, independently, an intensification of inter-denominational prejudice associated with the easing of the popery laws and the consequent improvement in catholic competitiveness in society as a whole. This was also associated with the stirrings of evangelical protestantism and the new emphases on 'sincere' and 'true' Christianity that marked the time, not only in England but in Ireland. Both John Wesley and his brother made numerous tours in Ireland and their methodist movement offered a challenge not only to the Enlightenment laxity that had begun to characterize much of the established church and its ministers (as well as a section of the presbyterians) but also to the Roman catholic church. One of their leading coadjutors was a native speaker of Irish named Walsh and they made a determined effort to make converts among the catholic masses. Among the more fervent presbyterians in Ulster there was also a movement at this time to provide Irish-speaking ministers. The reaction, especially to the methodist preaching, was sporadically violent. Catholic mobs had attacked the preachers in Dublin, Cork and Limerick.

In several parts of Ulster, but especially in Armagh, rural violence became, as it were, institutionalized. Armagh had been the centre for one of the agrarian secret societies of the early 1770s, the 'Oakboys'. Their activities were stimulated when the leases on the huge Chichester estate fell in and the landlord, the Marquess of Donegall, refused renewal on the comparatively favourable terms that had obtained since the plantation. He replaced many of his protestant tenants with catholics who were prepared to endure a greatly less favourable arrangement.

The Oakboy agitation didn't last very long, but it left a heightened hostility between protestants and catholics. It should be added that, at the level of tenant farmers and labourers in particular, it would be a mistake to take the protestants simply as descendants of the plantation tenants and the catholics as descendants of the indigenous natives. There had been a good deal of admixture through inter-marriage. But whatever process of merging had been going on, it was now in reverse and the opening divide was marked by religious affiliation. This was because religion was a most important legal distinction.

The hostility at this social level was a reflection of the conflicts of interest, of attitude and of judgement among the superior classes at this time of extreme confusion in politics. The confusion was largely caused, in Britain and by extension in Ireland, by the appearance of a new political force which threw into some disarray the forces that had become used to a more venerable dispensation. The new political force was the bourgeoisie, now increasingly asserting its interests, which frequently ran counter to the established interests of the landowners. Frequently, but not always. The ruling classes, actual and potential (to include the bourgeoisie), still formed a narrow segment of the whole population. In Britain there was in the 1780s what might be described as a bloodless replay of the great seventeenth-century conflict. It was in 1780 that Dunning's famous resolution was narrowly carried in the Westminster Commons: 'that the influence of the Crown has increased, is increasing, and ought to be diminished'.

In Ireland the religious question, the peculiar problems of a mature colonial situation and the anomalies created by the legislative independence of 1782 added to the confusion. And everything in western politics was transformed by the thunderclap of 1789. The fall of the Bastille and the subsequent events in France brought all political questions into a new focus.

At first, very large numbers of those, both in Britain and in Ireland, who desired fairly drastic changes in the established order of things welcomed what was to come to be known as the French revolution. But events moved rapidly in France, and to extremes unprecedented in the other revolution, in America, which had appealed to similar sentiments and interests. A political crisis of narrower scope had developed in 1788 in Britain, when the king suffered an illness which affected the balance of his mind. In Britain a regency, which was in question, would have brought in the king's heir, who was politically opposed to his father, and would surely have replaced the young Pitt by Fox, leader of the 'friends of the people', whose coalition with the tory, Lord North had been ousted when Pitt, at the age of 24, became prime minister with the backing of George III. In Ireland, the question of a regency gave rise to a more dangerous question involving the royal succession; for the 'patriots' in the Dublin parliament wished to push an independent right (as the legislature of a separate, distinct and independent kingdom) to make their own nomination.

In the event, the king recovered. Pitt remained in office. Ireland was increasingly perceived, in its present state, as a danger to the constitution.

The volunteers welcomed the upheaval in France which appeared to be replacing an absolute with a constitutional monarchy. In 1790, the first anniversary of the taking of the Bastille (14 July) was celebrated with parades, toasts and speeches. Change was in the air. It seemed that the fustian of the lawyers and the entrepreneurs might justly replace the silks of the landed aristocracy and gentry. But change in France went too far too fast. The emergence of the *sans-culottes* and the onset of the Terror – above all, the killing of the king and queen – gave pause to many. In the meantime, many radical clubs and societies were formed. In 1791, the first Society of United Irishmen was founded in Belfast, by a group, mainly of Ulster protestants, which included Wolfe Tone from Dublin and Thomas Russell from Cork. Belfast at the time, a business city approaching 20,000 in population, was dominated by a mercantile Enlightenment of broad presbyterian background which contemplated with equanimity the union of catholics and protestants in a new liberal Ireland. The Society started off from the radical wing of 'patriot' political opinion. It sought the foundation of a new nation based on the union of catholics and protestants (but in particular presbyterians) against the old oligarchy, and it aimed initially at parliamentary reform, doing away with the system of rotten boroughs that gave the English executive power over the Irish government.

Such aspirations were echoed elsewhere, and similar societies were founded in Scotland and England, and gave Pitt's spies much to do. But, when the crisis came, Ireland proved to be different. The onset of war with revolutionary France raised the old bogey of a French invasion of Ireland. Pitt attempted conciliation. He was responsible for a relief act in 1793 which repealed a number of the popery laws and allowed the vote to catholics who were freeholders of 40 shillings or more – to the chagrin of some whigs who had professed to support the catholic cause, but not to this extreme. In October 1794, Pitt had his first meeting with Grattan at a dinner given by the whig leader, the duke of Portland. One of those present was Sir John Parnell, who, with the Speaker of the Irish House of Commons, John Foster, represented the colonial business interest among the landlords who made up the government party in Dublin. Parnell spoke in favour of the coming together of catholics and protestants in the United Irishmen. Pitt answered, 'Very true, sir; but the question is, whose will they be?'[4] Parnell indeed had opposed some of the concessions to catholics, while Pitt knew that the United Irishmen were moving towards outright French republican ideas: 'Whose will they be?'

The great war against the revolution had now begun. Government control was extended over both the colony in Ireland and the mass of the increasingly disaffected people. In 1793, along with catholic relief, there were other significant measures. The volunteers were disbanded and replaced by militia (with a largely catholic membership in the rank-and-file). This alarmed protestants, especially in Ulster.

Catholics, in law, were forbidden to carry arms. The prohibition indeed was implicit in the Bill of Rights. Protestant gangs, or 'fleets', were formed, and were most active in Armagh, whose ostensible object was to raid the cottages of catholics suspected of possessing weapons. They tended to concentrate, however, on cottages where there were working looms, which they smashed. Catholics organized their own secret societies in response. The protestant gangs were known as 'Peep-o'-day Boys' from the usual time of their operations. The catholic gangs became known as 'Defenders'. The catholic groups developed in an unusual way: local gangs formed ties with one another which began to form a widespread federal organization. The gangs no longer operated in isolation but could call in help from one another. Many Defenders were recruited into the militia, causing great alarm to protestants. Now protestants too attempted to organize a federate league, in imitation of the Defenders. James Wilson, a presbyterian farmer in Tyrone, proposed such an organization in 1793, an oath-bound society to be known as the 'Orange Boys' (after William of Orange, who was forever to be remembered for the foundation of the protestant constitution).

In 1795, when Defender gangs were very active, an armed band near Loughgall, Co. Armagh, spent a week looting protestant farms, with running skirmishes. This led to a rally of protestants and to a pitched fight at a place called 'the Diamond'. In the battle of the Diamond the protestants were victorious: more than thirty Defenders were killed. As soon as the fight was over the protestants met to organize themselves more effectively. James Wilson, who was present, declined to join the new organization because his radical political ideas were rejected. Instead, James Sloane, an innkeeper of Loughgall, became the first head of what was to be known as the Loyal Orange Order.

The order was to be organized in lodges, after the manner of the Freemasons. But it was a specifically protestant, religious, organization. Flushed with the triumph of the Diamond victory it mounted a violent campaign in Co. Armagh to drive catholics from their homes. They fled to Connacht, or to thinly populated areas nearer home, such as north Longford. Many holdings were taken over by protestants. The government and the local landlords were slow to react to this lawlessness, largely because they were confronted with the danger of revolution by radical protestants of a different stamp in Antrim and Down. Orangeism in its origins was a lower-class rural movement, almost wholly anglican. In times of disorder rents tended to fall, and landlords didn't normally welcome violent agitations. But these were not normal times.

The landlords were losing confidence in the militia, largely catholic in membership. They observed that on 12 July 1796, only a year after the foundation of the Institute, about 5000 Orangemen paraded unarmed at the Diamond. With whatever distaste, the landlords recognized that this was a force which, in the troubled times possibly lying ahead, could stand to the state.

The gentry began organizing 'loyal associations'. These were closely associated with the Orange lodges and were forerunners of the yeomanry regiments that the gentry, mistrusting the militia, raised with government permission in 1796 and 1797. They encouraged animosity between the Orange lodges on the one hand and the Defenders and United Irishmen on the other, and the gentry and middle classes themselves began joining the Orange Institute. A Dublin lodge was founded in 1797, and on 12 July of that year General Lake reviewed Orange parades in Lisburn and Lurgan. The movement was widespread throughout the country and was strong not only in Ulster but also in the midlands.

Meanwhile, the United Irish organization moved towards a revolutionary extreme. Outside Ulster it was fairly weak, although there was an active centre in Dublin directing the affairs of Leinster (and well penetrated by government spies). Under pressure from the law it became a secret oath-bound organization, which soon had a doubly secret military command and structure. Its objective became the setting up of an Irish republic with French help. Its leaders made contact with the Defenders in order to bring in the disaffected mass of people in the country. It attracted not only radical members of the middle classes but also a few eccentric noblemen, notably Lord Edward Fitzgerald, fifth son of the leading Irish magnate, the duke of Leinster.

Wolfe Tone went to France to negotiate an alliance, and a powerful expedition, under Hoche, sailed to Ireland from France in the winter of 1796. Adverse weather prevented a landing and invasion, but a part of the fleet arrived in Bantry Bay in the south-west. The British navy failed to intercept the French either on their outward or on the return journey, and the government became extremely concerned about the danger which Ireland now presented in the great war against France. A bitter spirit of faction was spreading through the country, while it was plain that large numbers of the common people would welcome an invader because they detested and despised those who ruled over them.

To those masses, the message of the French revolution came largely as a millenarian promise: the world turned upside down and the end of rent and tithe. But the government was most concerned about east Ulster, especially Antrim, where the United Irish movement was strong, where literacy was comparatively high, where some presbyterian ministers had joined the revolutionary society (although they were a small minority) and large numbers of the protestants were, for the moment and with misgivings, prepared to embrace the catholics as equal fellow-citizens.

The government response was to send soldiers into disaffected areas and institute a regime of brutal searches and inquisitions, with summary and exemplary punishment. Ulster, where the largely catholic militiamen were used against the protestant United men, suffered most. It was also decided to break up the military and planning structure of the United Irishmen by arresting the leaders. This was done. There was ample information from spies and informers.

However, in the early summer of 1798, uprisings took place anyway, partly sparked off by the government's repression. In the south-east, centred on Co. Wexford, the insurrection was formidable. It involved some gentry, some catholic priests, and numbers of artisans and tradesmen who had read Tom Paine. But in large part it had the character of a jacquerie, with a strong anti-protestant bias intensified by a series of atrocities perpetrated by troops led by local gentry during the government's repressive campaign. Here and there the insurgents took brutal revenge on local protestants, innocent as well as guilty, whom they saw as their oppressors. The fighting was ferocious and bloody. The rebels stood up staunchly to trained troops and for a time controlled a large tract of country. Eventually General Lake moved in sufficient force to defeat them. Savage reprisals followed.

The north had been fairly effectively terrorized by the government's determined and ruthless preventive measures. In particular, those with property had found it wise to back away hastily from any involvement with the United Irish movement. Nevertheless, in Ulster too there was an uprising, mainly protestant, in Antrim and Down. It was quickly put down.

There were further French expeditions; but these were not large enough, went to the wrong places and were at the wrong times. One modest force landed at Killala in Co. Mayo. It was joined by a body of Mayo peasantry, fought skilfully and marched inland, to be defeated by General Lake at Ballinamuck, Co. Longford. Later, a larger expedition was intercepted on Lough Swilly, Co. Donegal. Wolfe Tone was aboard, in French uniform. He was taken to Dublin, and since he regarded it as a dishonour to be hanged, rather than shot in deference to his status as an officer of the republic, he cut his throat in his cell.

Much blood was shed in '98, the year that was to be remembered in numerous ballads. Perhaps 50,000 people suffered violent deaths, in battle or otherwise. But it seemed for a time almost as if the bloodshed had only begun. After the defeat of the rebellion led by the United Irishmen there was further, disorganized, violence all over the country, countered by repression. This had happened under the independent Irish parliament, and many of the gentry were in a vengeful mood. But the British government looked to wider interests, including the wider war. The French had made their chief effort in 1798, not in Ireland, but in Egypt, where Napoleon landed; but Ireland, plainly seething with discontent, continued to be an obvious danger. Pitt and his colleagues decided on a new approach to the country. Even while the uprisings were happening, they sent to Dublin as viceroy and commander-in-chief the soldier, Lord Cornwallis, a man experienced in both the lost American colonies (to his discomfiture) and the growing Indian empire. He restrained the ascendancy's fury and began to restore some discipline to their savagely rampaging troops.

Pitt had decided that a full parliamentary union with Great Britain was the answer to the obviously grievous problems of Ireland. His chief concern in this was the war. He had allies in Ireland, led by Fitzgibbon, now Lord Clare. Clare saw union as essential to protect the protestant privilege against the masses of the people. Many, more detached, observers also favoured union. Adam Smith, for example, saw it as offering protection to, not against, the masses. But most of the Irish ascendancy were against it. They valued their independence, cherished their own parliament in College Green in Dublin and believed that, working out their own destiny, they could best keep control in a country in which they were a wholly dominant, if comparatively small, minority. They had to be won round to the idea. This could not be done in sufficient time by the slow processes of persuasion. Cornwallis was charged to do it by a gross inflation of the usual means of parliamentary management – bribery and patronage on a scale of excess. Even so, it was only on a second attempt, and with the help of fears aroused by the widespread violence, that the Dublin parliament was induced to vote its own extinction, in 1800.

The Act of Union had an obvious and well-noted precedent in the parliamentary union with Scotland of 1707. But there were very great differences. The Scottish union was seen to complete a process by which a long-independent kingdom steadily grew closer, with at least a semblance of voluntary assent, to another kingdom, on terms of equality, to form an enlarged nation-state. Reality might be different, but the Scots were happy to be 'Britons' (or some of them were), and the English had to be happy to be 'Britons' too. And Scotland retained much of the symbolism and something of the substance of national independence – its laws, for instance, and the presbyterian church, now established.

No such arrangement was possible with Ireland. The 'two nations' of the Middle Ages in that country had not been drawn together. On the contrary, for a century they had been harshly separated on terms of inequality by law and custom, and now were further separated by the mutual spilling of blood. Pitt thought that he could deal with both sides in setting up the union. But he was prevented from doing so. He wished to embody in the act clauses giving catholic emancipation; that is, to remove almost all the remaining legal disabilities of Roman catholics, and in particular to enable them to sit in parliament. But the political managers in Dublin on whom he had to rely to force through the union would have none of it. He had to fall back instead on planning, and promising, that catholic emancipation would follow, once the union was achieved.

Pitt was conciliating the Roman catholics, the better to secure Ireland in the danger that now confronted the British empire. Most of the catholic representatives went along with him. The bishops, in particular, although they were deeply mistrusted by the protestant ascendancy, were themselves anxious to conciliate. They abominated the French revolutionary principles of the United Irishmen; they sought freedom for their religion within the British constitution, and they supported the union. Only a handful of leaders of catholic opinion opposed it, although most members of the protestant parliament in Dublin were against it and had to be bought. Most Orangemen were also against it, although the institute, committed broadly as it was to support of the government in perilous times, decided not to pronounce one way or another on the matter. The bill passed, by a scandalous piece of management, and the union became law on 1 January 1801.

Ireland now lost its parliament. The ascendancy could no longer legislate independently on its own affairs. The 'protestant nation' of the eighteenth century ceased to be: by asserting a self-contradictory autonomy in 1782 it had provoked its own fatal crisis.

Under the terms of the union, Ireland returned 100 members to the House of Commons at Westminster. Representation was reformed, since there was no more need of rotten boroughs for the management of Irish legislation. Each of the thirty-two counties was to elect two members. The larger cities and towns returned the remainder. The country also had representation in the House of Lords. It was not now a separate kingdom, but simply a part of the new United Kingdom of Great Britain and Ireland, and there could no longer be any question of a separate voice in the royal succession. The United Kingdom was, after a stated interval, to be a free trade area, and the Act of Union had various fiscal and financial provisions to rationalize the pooling of resources between the two islands.

But the merger was not quite complete. Some anomalies remained. In spite of the union, Ireland was to continue to have a resident viceroy and a separate executive in Dublin. The majority church in Ireland was not to be established. Instead, the anglican church was merged in the new established Church of England and Ireland.

To many people at the time, the union made little difference; but to some it made much. Dublin society was immediately affected, with the end of the assembly of Lords and Commons in the handsome parliament buildings in College Green – which became the headquarters in due course of the Bank of Ireland. In particular, the Irish peerage soon ceased to play so large a part in the life of the city.

At the time of the union the population of Ireland was nearly 5 million souls. The number had been increasing very rapidly since about 1780 (when the total was probably roughly 4 million). Just why the population had begun to expand so fast is uncertain, but it was a time when populations were expanding elsewhere (including England). By this time potatoes formed a staple food for great masses of the people. This crop was easily grown on marginal land and provided in itself most of a balanced healthy diet. It enabled hundreds of thousands of people to subsist on small scrapes of land which otherwise could not have supported them. More and more people came to live so; many with hardly more shelter or clothing than beasts of the field, with only their 'lazy beds' to sustain them (plots laboriously, not lazily, heaped up by the spade for the cultivation of the tubers). The potato was subject to blight and other diseases, and the crops sometimes failed. When this happened, the people who lived at the level of subsistence went hungry.

The fast-growing population was largely rural. Mud cabins increased and multiplied. Parts of the country least able to sustain numbers, especially in wild and rocky regions of the west, were becoming overcrowded rural slums. But numbers increased on the better lands too, and the towns showed the two faces of a society where wealth coexisted with abject destitution.

A Scottish visitor, Henry Inglis, wrote in his description of *Ireland in 1834:*

In walking through the streets of Dublin, strange and striking contrasts are presented between grandeur and poverty. In Merrion Square, St Stephen's Green and elsewhere, the ragged wretches that are sitting on the steps, contrast strongly with the splendour of the houses and the magnificent equipages that wait without: pass from Merrion Square or Grafton Street, about three o'clock, into what is called the Liberty, and you might easily fancy yourself in another and distant part of Europe. I was extremely struck, the first time I visited the outskirts of the city in the direction of the Phoenix Park, with the strong resemblance to the populations of Spanish towns, which the pauper population of Dublin presented. I saw the same rags, and apparent indolence – the result of

Plate 13   Girls setting seed potatoes, breaking clods with spade, Glenshesk, County Antrim

Plate 14   Ulster Day, Belfast – U. Clubs and Orangemen marching into City Hall to sign the Covenant

Plate 15   Janet, an Irish dulse seller and her seaweed thatched cabin, Antrim Coast Road

Plate 16   Tulla, County Clare – an Irish country town, 1971

a want of employment, and a low state of moral feeling: boys with bare heads and feet lying on the pavement, whose potato had only to be converted into a melon or a bit of wheaten bread, to make them fit subjects for Murillo; and houses and cottages in a half-ruined state, with paneless windows or no windows at all. . . .[5]

The grandeur, indeed, had already diminished in Dublin by 1834 as a result of the social change deriving from the union: lawyers and doctors were replacing gentry, and were to provide a different tone to the capital – one of witty urbanity which was largely founded on grasping insecurity. The union had a number of unexpected consequences. The protestant ascendancy, which had been opposed to it because it would deprive them of the control of affairs they had enjoyed through the Irish legislature, soon found that they were deprived merely of responsibility. Control remained, through the separate Irish executive, which the union retained and on which they kept a grip. And Pitt and his agent Castlereagh had failed in one of their chief purposes, to provide catholic emancipation with the union. Clare, whose services and co-operation were essential for the passing of the act, had refused to accept a simultaneous emancipation act. Pitt had promised to introduce emancipation immediately after the passing of the union, but opponents both in England and in Ireland succeeded in blocking it. George III considered that to sign on emancipation bill would be to contravene his coronation oath. Pitt and Castlereagh resigned, but emancipation failed, and Ireland continued to be represented exclusively by protestants in the parliament of Westminster as it had been in the parliament of Dublin.

This was to have important consequences. The catholic leadership provided by the remnants of the old Irish aristocracy had proved quite ineffective; the catholic bishops who had supported the union on the understanding that it would be followed immediately by emancipation were rebuffed. On the other hand, a group of catholic lawyers had opposed the union. They included a young member of an old landowning family from Kerry, Daniel O'Connell.

But for a number of crucial years, the significant changes that occurred in Ireland happened largely without benefit of politics. The war against France, after the brief interval of the peace of Amiens, dragged on until 1815. This had a distorting effect on the Irish economy. On the one hand it created a demand, which would not be permanent, for supplies. On the other hand its great cost made an undue demand on the revenues of Ireland. The Act of Union had fixed Ireland's contribution to the imperial exchequer at the not unreasonable proportion (for 1800) of twoseventeenths of the total. This could not be fully supplied from revenues as the costs of the war mounted, and it had to be met by borrowing. Interest, and rents to absentee landowners, were to drain monies out of a country which could not afford them.

Even before this process became inexorable, grievance was widespread in the country like an endemic disease. After 1798 there was only one brief violent gesture that was politically directed – Robert Emmet's attempted uprising in Dublin in 1803. But violence continued, local, particular and uncoordinated. Rural secret societies – often referred to in general as 'Whiteboys', although they had many different regional names – continued, by burnings, killings and the maiming of animals and humans, to express resentment at the oppressive burden of rent, tithe and other exactions. People frequently enough acted in protest at the payments required by their own pastors; but tithe, exacted by the proctors as a state tax, nominally for the maintenance of ministers of the established church, was doubly resented. The government met this violently expressed discontent with a series of coercion acts and other measures of repression. Within little more than a decade of its passing it was clear that, whatever else it might achieve, the union had failed to make Ireland a peaceful and unexceptional part of an enlarged United Kingdom.

The religious question stubbornly persisted, although in a somewhat different form. The protestant ascendancy, having given up their own legislative autonomy, very quickly began to cling to the new intimacy with Britain that they had unwillingly entered. They observed the rising tide of both catholic numbers and catholic demands, and increasingly saw the union as the safeguard of their position of dominance. Meanwhile, there had been a general, and remarkable, change in religious sensibility. In the eighteenth century the agnostic deism of the Enlightenment had been shared by many among the ruling classes of Europe and America. It gave them a somewhat detached attitude to particular enthusiasms, and tended towards a spirit of tolerance. But within the space of a generation, at the beginning of the nineteenth century, this gave way to a new enthusiasm founded on revealed religion, and to the cultivation of 'sincerity' rather than detachment. At the same time, other ideas, developed from the Enlightenment, began to spread (notably utilitarianism) giving rise to a spirit of reform. Devotion to Christian duty, and to a kind of interfering benevolence, began to characterize the policies and actions of imperial rulers at home and abroad. For the 'sincere' Christian, tolerance was a dereliction of duty; for the conscientious liberal, tolerance was a virtue but improvement was a duty. Both were unsympathetic to and suspicious of Roman catholicism on ideological grounds as well as on the grounds of the practicalities of governing a large disaffected population in Ireland.

In the context of these emergent changes the movement for catholic emancipation floundered for about twenty years after Pitt's failure to deliver it with the union. Political arguments against admitting catholics to full political life were reinforced by renewed religious prejudices. It was not only Ireland that was involved: an emancipation bill would also apply to Great Britain. Yet there were many in parliament who felt such a reform to be just, or necessary, or both.

Initially the supporters of emancipation at Westminster (notably Henry Grattan) proposed to introduce with the measure some government control of the Roman catholic church in the kingdom through a veto on the appointment of catholic bishops and perhaps through state payment or subvention of the salaries of priests. The Holy See was prepared to accept this arrangement, and the handful of aristocratic lobbyists who supplied a very timid leadership to the catholic cause at the beginning of the century was also prepared to acquiesce. But after some uncertainty the Irish bishops opposed it. They were backed by vocal repesentatives of the newly assertive catholic middle class in Ireland. A leader of this group was Daniel O'Connell.

O'Connell brought to the cause a considerable forensic talent and a wholly new aggressive and unapologetic approach, but he was not able to bring these to bear for some years. Immediately after the union the catholic case had been argued through a succession of committees, the last of which, the Catholic Board, constituted in 1811 and dissolved at the instance of the chief secretary (head of the Irish administration) Robert Peel, in 1814, was fairly broadly based. At this point the dilemma of Irish political agitation – a classical political dilemma in colonial situations – was put to O'Connell in advice given him in a letter from his uncle, Count O'Connell, in Paris:

I cannot refrain myself from congratulating you on the fair opportunity the late proclamation [abolishing the Catholic Board] affords you of bidding farewell to the late Catholic council or committee of Dublin, as well as to all your political pursuits, and to confine yourself in future to the practice of your profession in which you are sure to reap both honour and profit. . . . It has always been my steady opinion that the only way to gain that desirable end [emancipation] can only consist in gaining the good will and confidence of government and those of the Established Church by a prudent, peaceable and loyal deportment, and that tumultuous assemblies or meetings of what denomination soever, intemperate speeches and hasty resolutions are better calculated to defeat than to promote that object. Governments don't act on abstruse principles but from practical experience. . . .[6]

It was, however, precisely through 'tumultuous assemblies' that O'Connell was to proceed, after an interval in which he appeared to follow his uncle's advice. A further unsuccessful effort was made in parliament in 1819 and 1821. In 1823 O'Connell founded a new body, the Catholic Association, whose object was to further catholic interests in all areas of life, including the political. An amendment to its rules, made in 1824, transformed this association into a new and unprecedented kind of political machine. The comparatively poor were admitted to the association (to which the full subscription was a guinea a year) by subscribing a penny a month. The catholic clergy were *ex officio* members, and were employed in the recruitment of associates and the collection, at the churches on Sundays, of what became known as the 'Catholic rent'. At a stroke, O'Connell had recruited and involved a great mass of the ordinary people in what was in effect a political party. Soon the pennies had added up to £1000 a week. Mass democracy, in a crude but formidable form, had arrived. The admission of Roman catholics to parliament (the main object of emancipation) might have been of little immediate significance to these masses, but their own admission to a political process, giving some opportunity for expression of burning resentments, was of great significance to them. O'Connell had become, and was to remain, as *Punch* described him, 'king of the beggars'.

The government immediately became alarmed. It tried unsuccessfully to indict O'Connell for incitement to rebellion. It suppressed the Association in 1825, but this was promptly restored under another name. The strength of the new movement was shown in the general election of 1826, after another attempt to pass an emancipation bill had failed in parliament (being rejected by the Lords). The association supported selected candidates in a few constituencies who were in favour of emancipation, and these were elected. Tenants, the '40-shilling freeholders' who had been given the vote in 1793, voted openly and courageously against their landlords, most notably in Waterford, where the Beresford family, although detested locally, had been safely returned for many years but were now defeated.

In the meantime, Great Britain, having led reactionary Europe against revolutionary Europe, was itself suffering the consequences: a growing discrepancy between the political power of the landed class and the needs and demands of the class newly powerful economically, the bourgeoisie. A parliamentary crisis was developing; there were rapid changes of ministry; and the new administration, under Wellington, that was appointed in 1828 was in a weak position. Wellington nominated to the board of trade a popular MP for Co. Clare, Vesey Fitzgerald, who then, according to the custom of the time, had to stand for re-election. He was in favour of emancipation, but O'Connell decided to challenge the whole political system by standing against him. O'Connell won. As a catholic he couldn't take the oath of supremacy in going to occupy his seat, but his election was backed and followed by organized and drilled demonstrations by great crowds throughout Ireland. The government, weakened and divided on other issues, decided that it would be prudent to yield. The king (George IV) was persuaded, and catholic emancipation was placed on the parliamentary agenda for 1829. The victory was won, however, at the expense of the 40-shilling freeholders, the franchise qualification being raised to £10.

There had in effect been a yielding to the force of mobilized opinion in Ireland, the opinion not only of those accustomed to an active part in politics, but of the multitude. This was a new force. It had acted, in this instance, on divided parliamentary opinion in Westminster.

This force gained from the great swelling of the population and from the growing instability associated with it. Peasants subdivided and further subdivided their holdings. There were hundreds of thousands without any land. Misery was accentuated by the return of famine – as in 1817, after failure of the potato crops in some areas. The scale of the growing problem began to be revealed through the action of an administration which in many respects was both vigorous and beneficial in its operations.

The first attempt at a full and accurate census of population was made in 1821. In spite of admitted defects it gives us a more reliable estimate than any previous attempt. The total population it shows is about 6 million and, even allowing for error, this indicates an increase of considerably more than 1.5 million in the twenty years since the union. By far the greater part of these lived on the land, but an alarmingly high proportion of the rural population – approaching half – could not feed themselves from the land they held. A tenth or more were at or below the limit of destitution. The census figures for 1831 and 1841 show a continued explosive rise in population – although there is some reason to suspect that the peak may have been passed by 1841 – the figures indicating, for 1831, about 7.75 million people, and for 1841 something over 8 million.[7]

Such numbers could not be sustained even by the most intensive agriculture (of the kinds practised in Ireland). Potato cultivation made large rural populations possible only in favourable conditions and only by the employment of sub-marginal land. The country was steadily stripped of timber (for fuel) outside the estate walls. Inside the walls planting, of broad-leafed and ornamental trees and shrubs, continued, and the walls themselves, as well as access roads, outbuildings and other constructions were extensively built in the early nineteenth century, labour being superabundant and cheap. In many parts, especially in the west, almost barren mountain slopes were colonized. Rundale strips ran up the hillsides beyond the limits, not only of economy but almost, it would seem, of sanity. On the rocky crags, beyond any landlord's land worth reckoning, squatter families built foxes' earths of sods, planted their potatoes in the peaty scree, and lived brief lives without clothing (other than a rag or two), without light by night, without domestic furnishings, without utensils or vessels – a sub-human existence beyond the imaginings of Hobbes.

A memorial to the lord lieutenant from Paddy M'Kye, schoolmaster of Gweedore, describes the circimstances of a much less deprived community in west Donegal in 1837, in the parish of West Tullaghobegly:

There is about 4,000 persons in this parish [an under-estimate: it was at least twice that], and all Catholics, and as poor as I shall describe, having among them no more than – one cart, no wheel car, no coach, or any other vehicle, one plough, sixteen harrows, eight saddles, two pillions, eleven bridles, twenty shovels, thirty-two rakes, seven table-forks, ninety-three chairs, two hundred and forty-three stools, ten iron grapes, no swine, hogs or pigs, twenty-seven geese, three turkeys, two feather beds, eight chaff beds, two stables, six cow houses, one national school, no other school, one priest, no other resident gentleman, no bonnet, no clock, three watches, eight brass candlesticks, no looking glass above 3d. in price, no boots, no spurs, no fruit trees, no turnips, no parsnips, no carrots, no clover, or any other garden vegetables, but potatoes and cabbage, and not more than ten square feet of glass in windows in the whole, with the exception of the chapel, the school house, the priest's house, Mr Dombrain's house, and the constabulary barrack.

None of their either married or unmarried women can afford more than one shift, and the fewest number cannot afford any, and more than one half of both men and women cannot afford shoes to their feet, nor can many of them afford a second bed, but whole families of sons and daughters of mature age indiscriminately lying together with their parents, and all in the bare buff.

They have no means of harrowing their land, but with meadow rakes. Their Farms are so small that from four to ten Farms can be harrowed in a day with one rake.

Their beds are straw – green and dried rushes or mountain bent: their bedclothes are either coarse sheets, or no sheets, and ragged filthy blankets.

And worse than all I have mentioned, there is a general prospect of starvation, at present prevailing among them, and that originating from various causes, but the principal cause is a rot or failure of seed in the last year's crop, together with a scarcity of winter forage, in consequence of a long continuation of storm since October last, in this part of the country.

So that they, the people, were under the necessity of cutting down their potatoes and give them to their cattle to keep them alive. All these circumstances connected together, has brought hunger to reign among them to that degree,

that the generality of the peasantry are on the small allowance of one meal a
day, and many families cannot afford more than one meal in two days, and
sometimes one meal in three days.

Their children crying and fainting with hunger, and their parents weeping,
being full of grief, hunger, debility and dejection, with glooming aspect, looking
at their children likely to expire in the jaws of starvation. . . .[8]

The end of the war against France had reduced the profitability of
agriculture, particularly in tillage, and the large rural population, even in
the more prosperous areas, lacked sufficient employment. Once the war
was over, the government showed some awareness of the problem, but
Ireland, in spite of the union, remained peripheral to its concerns. Assisted
emigration to the colonies was suggested – it was a fashionable idea. But
this was not taken up. Sums of money were voted for relief work. The war,
while it lasted, had provided some work. Martello towers and other
fortifications were built along the coasts and rivers. And there had been
very heavy recruitment, especially into the navy. A very high proportion
of the seamen who served against revolutionary and imperial France was
Irish.

The pattern, established since the sixteenth century, of large-scale Irish
recruitment for military or naval service overseas, was to persist through
the nineteenth century, in another way. After the French revolution
the recruitment was almost wholly to the British forces, but with a social
difference. Officers in the British forces were supplied by the protestant
gentry – it was one of the obligations of their caste – and soldiers and sailors
by the catholic lower class: The classes of tenant farmers and artisans on
the whole resisted recruitment, and soon came to despise it and those who
'took the shilling'.

The canal system was more or less completed by the beginning of the
nineteenth century, but road-building continued, under landlord or state
patronage. In the early decades of the nineteenth century there was a great
deal of building. The Roman catholics, emerging from the penal
constraints, were already supplying themselves with new churches and
cathedrals even before the enactment of the final emancipation bill of 1829.
The established church, partly as a result of reorganization consequent on
the union, had a building programme in the 1820s and 1830s.

The modernization of Ireland proceeded, accompanied by
anglicization, with considerable direct involvement by the state. The
building of roads, harbours and public buildings was only part of this.
Wider changes were affected by political influences and shifts of party
advantage in Britain as well as Ireland. A large part of the ascendancy class
in Ireland had reacted atavistically to the changes that followed the union.

They found that if they went to parliament in Westminster, they cut no figure but were unimportant provincials. At home, the growth in catholic numbers, the politicization and defiance of their tenants, the irrepressible rural violence that threatened their lives and property, and now the phenomenon of O'Connell's mass democracy disconcerted and alarmed them. Hubert Butler wrote sympathetically of their dismay:

I doubt whether the era of aristocractic rule ended so dramatically in other countries. But the defeat of the Beresford candidate in Waterford, through the interposition of Daniel O'Connell, was a sensation of even greater magnitude. The Irish landlords of the ascendancy had loathed Wolfe Tone, but he spoke a language which they understood and abhorred, as later, in the same way, they were to loathe Parnell. Yet I think their real detestation was for Daniel O'Connell, whose powerful influence was outside their comprehension. There were qualities in him which should have warmed their hearts, if narrow self-interest alone had been consulted, his hatred of revolution, his loyalty to the young queen, his indifference to Irish culture. But I believe it was from their contact with O'Connell and the deep mass-emotion which he organised against them, that they first began to feel themselves irremediably alien. And they minded far more being called alien than being called blood-suckers or parasites. . . .[9]

Those of the landlords who felt most strongly this way tried to resist unwelcome change by attempting to assert the authority that was already slipping from them. They sponsored and took part in the activities of the Orange order, organized or approved of intimidatory displays and parades, called frequently on the Crown's military force for the protection or promotion of their interests, and made ruthless use of their privileged position in relation to the law in order to use its courts and systems on their behalf. Some of them were beginning to look north, to Ulster (extending patronage, for example, to the presbyterian, Rev. Henry Cooke) for a protestant alliance. In most of this, these members of the Irish ascendancy had the support of the still-powerful reactionaries of Great Britain. But many British politicians were increasingly impatient with them.

Not all of the ascendancy felt this way. There was a large body of moderate protestant opinion. Some had supported catholic emancipation. But the diehards had an easier choice to make: simply to dig in their heels. Those who sympathized with, or admitted, the demand of catholics for a more equitable system had to face a series of choices, on finely balanced issues, and had to face in the end what a liberalizing process must make inevitable – given the numbers involved – a *catholic* ascendancy.

There was a moderate catholic opinion too, mainly middle class. Its moderation was perhaps chiefly due to caution. There were now increasing numbers of catholic professional men, catholic merchants, catholics aspiring to wealth or status. If there were not many catholic landlords, there were many catholic families with tenure or ownership of some land but with a belief that they had been deprived by ancient wrong of their full birthright. For all of these, emancipation, either symbolically or substantively, opened up the possibility of making the advances they desired. But O'Connell had won it with the aid of quite a different group – who stood to gain much less from it in the short run – the peasants whose pennies had involved them in a mass movement with millenarian overtones. O'Connell's object now was the overthrow of what he regularly designated the 'Orange' hegemony in Ireland, an object fully consonant with long-term middle-class catholic aspirations. But he had discovered that the engine of accomplishment of such political aims was the much larger mass of rural catholic people whose menace had backed his oratory in the emancipation agitation. Repeal of the Act of Union – too daring for the one group but sufficiently dramatic for the other – became his declared objective after emancipation. But repealing the act would not, after what had elapsed since 1800, be simply a return to the constitution of 1782. A restored Dublin parliament would now inevitably be catholic.

Emancipation had been achieved by pushing, in Westminster, if not an open door, at least one that was not locked. Repeal was a different matter: for this there was no likelihood of a Westminster majority. O'Connell for the moment did not push too hard. Instead he made use of the parliamentary crisis – the Reform Bill – to press for reforms in Ireland.

Independently of the conflict of conservative and liberal interests in Great Britain a bureaucracy had been called into being by the growing complexity of political life. Merely administrative decisions, often forced by circumstances, were anticipating the great reform. In Ireland, Peel, before 1820, had tentatively begun some important developments – a scheme for elementary education and one for an all-Ireland police force. But it was in the 1830s that these began to be effective. Ireland, unlike England since the sixteenth century, lacked a poor law, and this, as the state of the country deteriorated, became a subject of frequent debate. After 1830, a reconstituted Board of Works, a new 'National Schools' scheme, a rebuilding Church of Ireland, a new constabulary force, and a new poor law, all began transforming the country, under English direction but in ways that were interestingly un-English. Perhaps the most interesting difference from England was the marked tendency in Ireland to have centralized control of these developments and the correspondingly small part played by parochial and other local government.

This, among other things, made Ireland convenient for social and

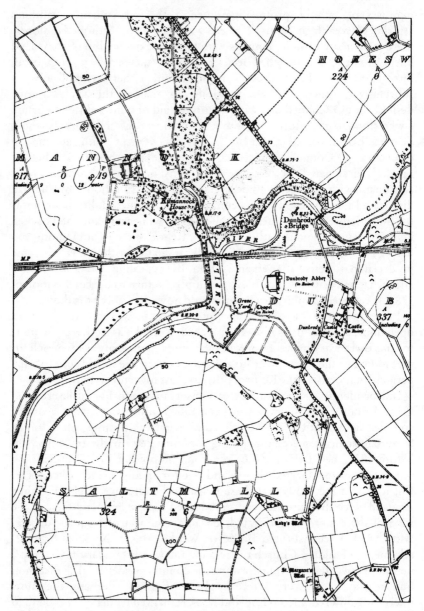

Map 16   Specimen Ordnance Survey 6 inch sheet, Wexford, sheet 39
Reproduced by permission of the Director General of the Ordnance Survey
Office, Dublin.

governmental experiment. The country, being considerably smaller than England both in land area and in population, and providing less obstacle to innovation in the way of rooted local institutions and interests, offered an opportunity to the reforming and managing spirit of the age.

One programme that was tried out in Ireland was the large-scale mapping of the country carried out by the Ordnance Survey. A survey to the scale of 6 inches to the mile had been recommended by a parliamentary committee in 1824. The main purpose was to establish accurately, for rating purposes, the boundaries of land divisions, in particular the small traditional Irish unit, the 'townland'. The scope of the survey was soon extended far beyond this. The officers in charge, Colby and Larcom, attempted to provide a comprehensive picture of the country. They hired an Irish scholar, Edward O'Reilly, to advise on the forms of place-names, in 1830, and, when he died within a few months, they employed John O'Donovan. Larcom himself took the trouble to learn Irish, and at first the survey set out to provide, not only maps, but detailed descriptions, field by field, of the archaeology, history, topography and toponymy of the whole island. Parts of the scheme had to be curtailed, because funds were not made available. A detailed memoir was published on only one parish (that which included the city of Londonderry) but, besides producing a full series of beautiful maps which record every house, every little field, every copse and stream, the surveyors left a detailed record of Ireland in the 1830s and early 1840s. They also brought together two traditions of learning. Through the survey, the old Irish tradition of scholarship, passed down through the schools since the beginning of history, was brought into contact with the Anglo-Irish tradition of the ascendancy.

The fields and hillsides over which the engineers tramped with their chains and spy-glasses were the scene of growing conflict in the early 1830s, as more and more of the people refused to pay tithe, and police and soldiers were deployed in large numbers to collect it. The conflict grew extremely bitter. The determined refusal to pay was effective. The clergy of the established church were deprived of their livelihoods and the government had to come to their rescue with grants of money. To the violence and bloodshed the government replied with another, draconian, coercion act in 1833. At the same time it attempted a reform of the church, but furious anglican and conservative opposition to the bill so modified it that when it was passed (the Irish Church Temporalities Act, also of 1833) it added to the catholic grievances rather than diminishing them. But after the election of 1835, the Melbourne administration, supported by O'Connell under the so-called 'Lichfield House compact', took a much more conciliatory line in Ireland. Thomas Drummond, the under-

secretary for Ireland under this administration, had worked in the field
with the survey and knew the country and its people. He was largely
responsible for directing the new policy; in particular for seeing to a less
partial administration of the law. O'Connell for some years abandoned the
demand for repeal of the union, and, in alliance with the whigs, indicated
that the people he led were prepared to be 'a kind of West Britons' (that
is, to occupy a position similar to that of the Scots under the union).

But the government failed to pass measures that would meet this
requirement. Its reforms, embodied in acts to reduce the incidence of tithe,
to provide for the relief of the poor and to reform local government – in
particular to open further offices to catholics – fell short of what
O'Connell wanted. He voted against the poor law, which set up the
English workhouse system in Ireland (he realized that some measure was
necessary because of the widespread destitution but in principle believed
that the relief of the poor should be a matter for private charity rather than
state provision, and he found the bill unsatisfactory). He was elected lord
mayor of Dublin in 1841, the first catholic to fill the office for a century
and a half – a personal triumph. By then he was already campaigning again
for repeal of the union, having founded the National Repeal Association
the previous year.

O'Connell conducted his campaign for repeal in the way that he had led
that for catholic emancipation in the 1820s. He used the same kind of
organization, and collected a 'repeal rent'. He summoned huge mass
meetings of his supporters – as demonstrations of strength – and held some
of them, calling on the growing spirit of romantic nationalism, at places
associated with what had come to be thought of as the glories of Ireland's
past. One of the greatest of these gatherings assembled on the hill of Tara,
the seat, as all his better-informed hearers would have been certain, of the
high-kings of Ireland for centuries:

> When Malachy wore the collar of gold
> Which he won from the proud invader;
> When her kings, with standard of green unfurled
> Led the Red Branch knights to danger,
> Ere the emerald gem of the western world
> Was set in the crown of a stranger.[10]

Tara was part of the apparatus of antiquarian symbolism that had been
assembled over the previous half-century, had been popularized in
middle-class drawing-rooms by Tom Moore's *Irish Melodies*, and was
widely diffused as visual images in political propaganda like that of
O'Connell. Shamrocks, round towers, wolfhounds, sad young women

(symbolizing Ireland, or 'Erin' as the more romantic terminology had it) with stringless harps, and sunbursts, to represent the coming dawn of national independence: all were gaining wide currency. They were an indication of the kind of nationalism that was by now established in many parts of Europe.

Such nationalist imagery helped to unify a multitude of diverse grievances. O'Connell was firmly opposed to physical violence, but he practised verbal violence. The physical violence had considerably diminished during the years of conciliation in the late 1830s. It resumed in the 1840s, when the rural secret societies, notably those known as 'Ribbonmen', became extremely active. O'Connell, in the course of his repeal agitation, made a bid against them for the support of the country people, matching the Ribbonmen's deeds with violent words.

But the ill-defined menace – the menace of the crowd – that had worked in his favour in the agitation for catholic emancipation was now being called upon to aid what the government saw as the 'break-up of the empire'. In refusing to acquiesce in this, British opinion was united: there was no such parliamentary division as there had been on emancipation. And although O'Connell's vast but disciplined and peaceful meetings – a new phenomenon in world politics – embarrassed the government by advertising abroad the strength and solidarity of Irish opinion, Peel, the prime minister, and his colleagues made it clear that they were prepared to face not only that, but civil war in Ireland if necessary, rather than yield.

Irish solidarity, however, was not quite what it might have seemed from the oceanic crowds that turned up to cheer at the repeal mass meetings. The menace of the masses disturbed not only the government but even many of those for whom O'Connell spoke – not the friese-clad peasants who formed his audiences, but the merchants, doctors, lawyers, clerks who also stood to benefit from self-government. They looked for such civil rights as would improve their opportunities in bourgeois society, not an upheaval of such anarchic force as would respond to the miseries of the multitudinous poor. O'Connell's aim was theirs; but he spoke as 'the liberator' to the great masses.

And there were others even more disturbed. Emancipation, although the agitation for it had relied on an organization largely manned by priests, had been supported by many protestants. It had been a matter of justice. Repeal, depending on a similar organization, had little protestant support, especially in the north.

In Ulster, a liberal tradition had survived the horrors of 1798, but republicanism and separatism had soon died. The distinct regional identity of the north-east was already being reinforced by economic change in the

Figure 16   Repeal meeting at Tara, 1843   *Source: Illustrated London News.*

late eighteenth century. The first significant point of change was about 1780, when attempts were made to introduce the 'Manchester system' to Ireland, in Dublin, Limerick and elsewhere. But it was only in the Belfast area that the complex of techniques and practices associated with the early industrial revolution became established. At about the same time the pattern of trade began to shift, forming a new focus, again around Belfast.

This was of special importance. It showed clearly in the linen industry. There were four stages in the processes involved in linen manufacture. Farmers grew flax, which the women of the household spun into yarn. This was woven into cloth. The cloth was bleached, at first at home, but later by 'drapers' who bought it from the farmer-weavers. The cloth was then brought to the government-founded linen hall in Dublin and there sold to merchants, chiefly for export.

The main centre of the industry was the north-east, whose weavers worked not only their own yarn but also yarns spun in other parts of Ireland. The finest linens were finished in Lisburn, where the Huguenot refugees had established the business. When bleaching became a specialized and not a home industry, this too centred on the Lagan valley, between Belfast and Lurgan. In 1780 the drapers in Ulster built linen halls in Newry and Belfast. By the end of the century, the communications system in the whole region was beginning to centre on Belfast; separate financial and banking arrangements had been developing in the north-east, and there was a growing direct trade with Great Britain. The area from east Donegal to the North Channel, and from the Boyne northwards, was developing a distinct economic identity.

The 'Manchester system' contributed to this process. By 1780, entrepreneurs from Lancashire and east Ulster had introduced the cotton-spinning jenny to Belfast, and were building water-powered spinning mills. The Lagan valley, with its fast-flowing streams, was well suited to this. In 1790, one of James Watt's steam-engines was brought from Glasgow and installed in a Lisburn spinning-mill. Cotton cloth, based on power-spinning, began in part to replace linen in the textile industry. Both raw materials and fuel now had to be imported, and this stimulated the growth of Belfast both as a port and as an industrial centre. The cotton industry was not to last against British competition, but it played a major part in transforming the economic character of the Belfast area, by introducing industrialization and by bringing numbers of industrial specialists and workers from Britain. By the end of the 1820s, east Ulster was becoming more and more closely integrated into the new British economy, as those clauses of the act of union came into effect which ended the protective and other measures that had distinguished the Irish economy from the British. New banks, catering for Ulster, were founded with the ending of restrictions. And a new wet-spinning process made possible the mill production of fine linens. In east Ulster, the textile industry shifted back from cotton, now uncompetitive, to linen.

In this context of economic (and therefore social) change, middle-class protestant opinion involved itself, politically, in the movements that exercised its counterpart opinion in Britain. The liberals concerned themselves, not with an Irish republic, but with the pressure to pass the great reform bill in the United Kingdom. For them, O'Connell, for all his interest in civil rights, was suspect. His efforts to carry his campaigns into Ulster were opposed most effectively and he suffered significant defeats, especially in Belfast. In these early decades of the nineteenth century a new and different polity was coming into being in the north. The area was being ideologically as well as economically integrated, not only into the economy of Britain, but into the economy of the British empire.

A clear indication of this re-orientation was given by the climax of the long-continued dispute between 'New Light' and 'Old Light' presbyterianism. The first tended to be both theologically liberal (moving towards unitarianism) and liberal politically. In the 1820s the attack on such liberalizing tendencies was led by Rev. Henry Cooke; they were defended by Rev. Henry Montgomery. The two fittingly symbolized contrasting Ulster presbyterian traditions. Cooke, conservative, eloquent, resistant to liberal secularism in educational and other reforms, patronized by the aristocracy, was proud of a calvinist ancestor who had defended Derry's walls, and advocated unreserved subscription to the Westminster Confession of Faith – which included among other strong doctrines a condemnation of the pope as anti-Christ. Two of Montgomery's brothers had taken part in the United Irish uprising in Antrim in 1798; he had supported catholic emancipation and had stood side by side with the catholic bishop in 1829 in the catholic church of St Patrick in Belfast to address a gathering of protestants and catholics. In that same year, however, Cooke carried the great majority of presbyterians in the Synod of Ulster against Montgomery, who then formed a separate, non-subscribing presbyterian church. Cooke went on, encouraged by the patronage of the gentry, to speak at a great rally at Hillsborough, Co. Down, in 1834, where he urged, essentially for political reasons (in support of the union) an anglican–presbyterian alliance: 'Between the divided churches I publish the banns of a sacred marriage.'

Another kind of middle-class opinion was forming, however, which supported the repeal movement, at least after the failure of the whig conciliation policies of the late 1830s. A group of young men in Dublin, responding to the spirit of the age, came together in 1842 and founded a newspaper which they called *The Nation*. Its editor was an Ulster catholic, Charles Gavan Duffy, but its principal writer was a protestant from Co. Cork, Thomas Davis. John Blake Dillon was a third member of the small group that was soon to make this paper the most widely read in the country, circulating throughout the land, deposited in the 'repeal reading rooms', passed from hand to hand, read aloud to groups, functioning generally as another voice of the repeal movement, complementary to that of O'Connell. *The Nation* was propagandist: it set out to preach a doctrine, which is embodied in its title; that Ireland is a nation and should be independent. It accepted the ideas then current in Europe which gave a mystical sense to the idea of nationality; it accepted the arguments which had been advanced since the demise of the old Gaelic order in the seventeenth century for the values and virtues of Ireland's ancient civilization; it adapted these to the aspirations of the Dublin parliamentarians of the late eighteenth century to Irish independence; and it took up the United Irishmen's concept of a new nation founded on a merging of the identities of catholic, protestant and dissenter.

There is much internal contradiction in the teaching of *The Nation*, but it succeeded in providing for a great mass of people a myth, a romantic history and an aspiration. Davis contributed essays in which he explored and developed a sense of Irish nationality. For him it was a real exploration. He had begun with an interest in British politics – of a somewhat radical bent – but was troubled by the sense, common to people in colonial situations, of being neither one thing nor the other; half-English, half-Irish. He resented feeling provincial and peripheral and looked, partly to antiquity, partly to the great movement led by O'Connell, · for an imaginative centrality. He wrote ballads, which appealed not only to people like himself but to the foot-soldiers of repeal, the rural masses who found their grievous discontents given an idealistic expression:

> When boyhood's fire was in my blood,
> I read of ancient freemen
> For Greece and Rome who bravely stood
> Three hundred men and three men.
> And then I prayed I yet might see
> Our fetters rent in twain
> And Ireland, long a province, be
> A nation once again.[11]

The group that founded *The Nation* was termed, at first ironically, 'Young

Ireland' (the reference was to 'Young Italy'), and then this appellation was applied commonly to them. Its members included protestants and catholics and were chiefly drawn from the urban middle class although there were some landowners. They differed from the essentially pragmatic O'Connell in that they lived much more in the imagination and were caught up much more in the ideology of romanticism, but like him they employed a heady and often war-like rhetoric. Unlike him, they were greatly intrigued by what was just beginning to be discovered about the early Irish and 'Celtic' past. Davis advanced beyond the antiquaries and began to treat of the Irish language not as itself merely an antiquity but a living evidence of nationhood: 'A people without a language is only half a nation.'[12]

O'Connell's greatest meetings were held in 1843, which had been advertised as 'the repeal year'. Each gathering was greater than the one before, until he stood on the ancient mounds at Tara and addressed hundreds of thousands who blackened the rolling green countryside around. In the meetings which followed during the autumn, the discipline of the huge crowds became more military in character, with squadrons of 'repeal cavalry' and platoons of stave-wielding 'O'Connell's police' acting as stewards for the throngs. Then a monster meeting was announced for Clontarf, on the outskirts of Dublin. The place was chosen because it was the site of Brian Boru's victory in 1014, which the romantic history of the time represented as the glorious battle in which Irish arms broke once and for all the power of the (Scandinavian) foreigners in Ireland. The symbolism was well understood. The government, deeply perturbed by the alarming manifestations of the summer and autumn, proclaimed the meeting, the day before it was to take place. O'Connell called it off and, displaying the discipline he had imposed, his democratic army dispersed peacefully.

Peel's government followed through by prosecuting O'Connell and some others for conspiracy. The repealers were tried in a hostile court and convicted by a packed jury. However, after a period of comparatively luxurious imprisonment, O'Connell, having successfully appealed to the House of Lords, was released. But his energy and spirit were diminished, and there was no return to the huge meetings; he seemed instead to lose his commitment to repeal. And there were new divisions. Sharman Crawford, MP for County Down, a liberal, had suggested an alternative to repeal of the union: a federal system under which an Irish parliament would deal with internal Irish affairs while the Westminster parliament would deal with external and imperial affairs. There was an amount of support for this idea.

The Young Ireland group also began to move away from O'Connell, essentially because they sought a pluralist Ireland, while the movement he led had an overwhelmingly catholic character. He himself, it is true, especially at this time, made some efforts to indicate that Ireland after repeal would not be wholly dominated by catholics; but the attitude of the O'Connellites on such matters as education gave a different impression. In an atmosphere of anti-climax and uncertainty politics became confused.

Then debates on constitutional matters were reduced to insignificance by the calamity, long half-expected or feared, that overtook the country. In 1845, a bad season caused crop failures over a large part of Europe, with great hardship ensuing in the countryside. The potatoes were affected by blight, which caused them to rot in the ground, or – even more dismaying – to come to fruition and then putrefy after harvesting. What brought hardship to other countries brought destruction to many parts of Ireland. The blight struck again in 1846 – all over the country. This crisis tested the union and the union failed the test.

Peel was still prime minister when the blight began. He acted quickly enough, and staved off total disaster. He bought maize in America and shipped it to Ireland to be sold cheaply, to hold down food prices. He established a relief commission to organize the landlords and the middle classes in voluntary committees which would bear responsibility for distributing food. He organized public works to provide employment.

Peel, however, belonged to the older conservatism. The younger generation of the British ruling classes was largely dominated by utilitarian or evangelical ideologues. The chief bureaucrat in the handling of the Irish crisis was an exponent of *laissez-faire*, Charles Trevelyan, extremely hard-working and fully possessed of righteous bourgeois insensitivity. He was concerned that the starving destitute people in Ireland should not be demoralized by becoming dependent on government hand-outs. Peel's measures, however, tided the country, in a fashion, over the disasters of 1845. But, having just carried through the repeal of the corn laws in 1846 – so incurring the hostility of the protectionist landlords – he was defeated when he tried to pass yet another Irish coercion bill to put down the agrarian disturbances consequent on the famine. Lord John Russell replaced him, at the head of a whig government, which applied the principles of political economy, and respected the sacred rights of private property to the extent that public relief works, such as they were, were designed not to enter into competition with private property and enterprise. In 1846 and 1847 the wretched people who had lived on the very margins of society died in their tens of thousands.

The population of the island had risen, from about 4 million in 1780 (by present-day estimates) to considerably more than 8 million in 1841 (according to the census of that year). Possibly a decline in population had already begun by the mid 1830s, but by then the Irish countryside was extraordinarily densely inhabited. Half the total population subsisted on potatoes, and in parts of the west this dependence was at a much higher rate. There were glens and hillslopes in Cork, Kerry, Galway, Mayo, Donegal and elsewhere, where the shanties and turf shelters of a scarecrow people crowded in among cesspools, dung-heaps and tiny potato gardens: a sight that never failed to astonish and appal European visitors. It was in such places that the visitation was most terrible.

The potato blight of 1845 had been extensive but irregular in its distribution. What appeared, virtually until the time of harvest in July, to be a fine flourishing crop in 1846, suddenly – often overnight – putrefied into stinking pulp. In a strange summer of storms and gloomy cloud, all over Ireland blight destroyed the potatoes. In 1847, when the blight eased, little had been sown, and the hunger was even greater.

The total failure of the food of the poor brought them unspeakable suffering and death. It affected everybody else too. The landlords, already inconvenienced by the endless subdivision of their tenants' holdings and by the over-population of their estates, suffered the further inconvenience of a drastic loss of rent. Most landlords by now were absentees. Their agents frequently took the opportunity of the failure of rent to clear the land of unwanted tenants by evicting the defaulters from their cabins, which were demolished. Other landlords, in pity, remitted rents and bore a great diminution of their standard of living. But they were a minority. Many saw the famine as God's intervention. The disaster showed how tenuous was the bond of Ireland to Great Britain. An advanced nineteenth-century economy and polity, linked to a society that was much more archaic, could not avert a disaster that seemed to belong to another age. The force of the current dogma of the beneficence of the free market was too strong in spite of the evidence of what was happening in Ireland, until it was too late. Food (for corn and cattle were not blighted) continued to be exported from Ireland, under guard, because it was privately produced for private gain. The government put people fainting from hunger to labour on works that were designed to be useless to avoid competition by public enterprise with what was profitable and private.

But some landlords, some members of the middle class, some civil servants laboured desperately for the stricken people, often at the cost of their own lives, as they were infected by the typhus which soon accompanied starvation. Some groups, notably the Society of Friends – the Quakers – made a huge effort to cope with the disaster. The Quakers in

Figure 17   Famine victims: Bridget O'Donnell and family
Source: Illustrated London News.

particular rallied American help. Initially the government would allow foreign food aid into the country only in British ships, but by early 1847 world opinion, together with the obvious scale of the disaster, caused the lifting of this restriction, and the Americans sent large amounts of food, some on naval vessels which were stripped of their guns to allow more space for their cargoes.

Too late. Perhaps, by 1845, there was no possibility of averting some kind of disaster. Disaster had long been foreseen. But what actually happened was beyond prediction. Within a few years the population was reduced, by death from starvation and disease and then by the great emigration which followed, from considerably more than 8 million people to considerably less than 7 million. And the decline in numbers was to continue for a century. There was hunger everywhere in the 1840s, but in some of the rural slums of the west, where the cottiers and squatters were doomed once there were no potatoes, many populations were reduced to less than half their numbers of 1841. In those areas, the scenes were witnessed that were to become a vengeful memory for 100 years, especially among the exiles.

One of the many descriptions written at the time, will serve to illustrate the conditions in the west of Ireland in 'black '47'. William Bennett, in March of that year, reported on a visit to Belmullet, Co. Mayo:

Many of the cabins were holes in the bog, covered with a layer of turves, and not distinguishable as human habitations from the surrounding moor, until close down upon them. The bare sod was about the best material of which any of them were constructed. Doorways, not doors, were usually provided at both sides of the bettermost – back and front – to take advantage of the way of the wind. Windows and chimneys, I think, had no existence. A second apartment or division of any kind within was exceedingly rare. Furniture, properly so called, I believe may be stated at *nil*. I would not speak with certainty, and wish not to with exaggeration – we were too much overcome to note specifically – but as far as memory serves, we saw neither bed, chair, nor table, at all. A chest, a few iron or earthen vessels, a stool or two, the dirty rags and night-coverings, formed about the sum total of the best furnished. Outside many were all but unapproachable, from the mud and filth surrounding them; the same inside, or worse if possible, from the added closeness, darkness and smoke. . . .

We entered a cabin. Stretched in one dark corner, scarcely visible, from the smoke and rags that covered them, were three children huddled together, lying there *because they were too weak to rise*, pale and ghastly, their little limbs – on removing a portion of the filthy covering – perfectly emaciated, eyes sunk, voice gone, and evidently in the last stage of actual starvation. Crouched over the turf embers was another form, wild and all but naked, scarcely human in appearance. It stirred not nor noticed us. On some straw, soddened upon the ground, moaning piteously, was a shrivelled old woman, imploring us to give her something – baring her limbs partly, to show how the skin hung loose from the bones, as soon as she attracted our attention. Above her, on something like a ledge, was a young woman with sunken cheeks – a mother I have no doubt – who scarcely raised her eyes in answer to our enquiries, but pressed her hand upon her forehead, with a look of unutterable anguish and despair. . . .[13]

9   *Revolution*

Too late the whig government came to realize that 'political economy' was not a panacea for all ills; that Adam Smith's 'hand' could turn to malefaction. Nearly a million people died of hunger and disease; the government swallowed its principles and began giving direct relief. In due course it was feeding 3 million people a day, although, since the machinery for distributing the state ration had to be improvised hastily, the efficiency of the scheme – and the consistency of the soup doled out to the starving people – varied greatly from place to place. But by then the trauma was deep. People in their thousands were fleeing what seemed to be a doomed island. The union was seen, by millions, to be a mockery. Had Ireland suddenly become independent it could not have coped any better with the calamity than the British government did at the end of the 1840s – but it *was* a British government that presided over a disaster unparalleled in modern western Europe, and that had presided over what led to it.

This famine greatly accelerated processes of change. The chronic malaise of the rural economy – exemplified by the subdivision of tiny holdings, debt-bedevilled estates, absenteeism, rack-renting and a squalid, all-pervasive poverty – came to sudden crisis. A huge social redistribution took place. The fringe class of destitute squatters was wiped out, as was a large proportion of the very smallholders and cottiers. Two of the remedies for the ills of rural Ireland that many people had advocated in the first half-century of the union were now applied in panic and despair. One was consolidation of landholdings. The other was emigration.

The pattern of emigration formed in the eighteenth century had been modified in various ways, but throughout the first half of the nineteenth century there had been a steady movement out of the country. Until well into that century the north continued to contribute significantly to this movement. About a third of the emigrants in the decades just after the union went out through the port of Derry. But that balance shifted as the other three provinces became much more heavily involved. The Irish went in some numbers to industrializing Britain but in larger numbers to north

America, including British America. The St Lawrence gulf and the ports of Boston, New York and Baltimore and Philadelphia received the westward flow of migrants. On some of the north American coasts nearest to Ireland, for example at St Johns, Newfoundland, the distinctive accents of south-eastern Ireland may still be heard, from the pre-famine settlement established by people from Wexford and Waterford who had gone out with people from Bristol and the English west country to hunt the cod on the Grand Banks.

But immediately after the visitation of the 1840s, the stream of emigration (which had reached a level of about 50,000 a year) swelled to a great flood. In 1851 250,000 left Ireland to cross the Atlantic, and the flight continued in later years in only gradually diminishing numbers. Very many had barely the passage-money, and even that was often supplied by others, out of charity or expediency (as when landlords took the opportunity to clear their estates). The fares were low: the famine passengers sometimes replaced ballast, as on the timber ships whose regular trade was bringing American timber eastward (for building lumber, ships' masts or other purposes). These and other cargo-vessels were hastily adapted to meet the new huge demand for accommodation. Many died on the way in the crowded holds of the inferior ships run by profiteering companies, and to the bitter memories of the famine that these millions brought to the new world was added the legend of the 'coffin ships'. The Irish, weak, fever-ridden and often penniless, were discharged on to American shores, to form instant slums in the eastern cities, and to survive the understandable alarm of the previously established inhabitants by developing tightly cohesive communities that exercised mutual self-help and a disciplined political vote.

Even before the famine the emigration was in general not positively motivated. People, especially the tenants and cottiers of the countryside – the peasants – were mostly reluctant to go, but chose to do so when it became too difficult, or impossible, to survive in Ireland. After the famine the emigration, for a while, was a headlong flight.

Within Ireland the famine mortality was very uneven in its incidence, being far more severe in a number of western areas than anywhere else. But its effects operated throughout the country. There was considerable internal migration as people struggled from the stricken countryside into the towns. The sudden decline in population had numerous and complex effects. The psychological shock of the great disaster had effects which were perhaps even more important. Attitudes and style of life in the countryside changed radically. The traditional rural systems and expectations of mutual help, which derived from earlier polities, had been placed under great strain. As the famine persisted and widened, those people who had a little food to spare had found their good will towards their less fortunate neighbours overwhelmed by the insatiability of the demand. In numerous instances in the accounts of this well-documented period we find the hand that had been stretched out to help drawn back in fear or despair.

The whole weight of an ancient rural tradition had enjoined on people to help the poor, and especially to welcome the homeless stranger who came to the door. Now, those who survived had watched the poorest class in the country destroyed, while they themselves, many of them, profited from the famine. The ramshackle Irish economy of the mid century had some of the characteristics of a zero sum: one person's loss was another person's gain. Zero-sum thinking is in any case common in peasant societies (that is, societies in which the primary producers have to deliver up in rent virtually all of their produce beyond what they need for subsistence), because in such societies individual peasants tend to prosper often by gaining advantage from their neighbours' distress – through lending at interest, for example.

The number of small or tiny holdings sharply diminished. In the ten years between the census of 1841 and that of 1851, the number of holdings of between 15 and 30 acres nearly doubled. The number of over 30 acres trebled. This consolidation of holdings in itself marked a notable change in the pattern of the countryside, although of course it was to be many years before the pre-famine pattern was wholly altered. In many areas the landlords were weakened because of the failure of rents. It might be said that, to some extent, the position of the tenant farmers was strengthened at the expense both of those above them and those below them.

To the festering discontent which continued to express itself in (mainly rural) violence were added additional fear, shame and hatred arising from the experience of the famine. It helped to shift the focus of these emotions from local landlords, agents, tithe-proctors or magistrates to the government whose remoteness now became an additional grievance. The emigrant ships carried westward hundreds of thousands who were to teach their children that it was English rule that was responsible for the famine. And the English were seen to have been not merely indifferent or callous, but malevolent. One of the strongest impressions produced by the many reports sent back by the exiles, in letters or otherwise, is that they were greatly struck by the egalitarianism of America. There it was no longer necessary to bow to the arrogance of aristocrats or landlords. When a man worked he could earn a living, rather than have the product of his labour taken away by a system which, at home, he had not regarded as part of the nature of things but as an alien tyranny. An enduring heritage the famine exiles left in the new world was a hatred of England.

In Ireland the politics of repeal had ended just before the famine in some confusion and in a division between O'Connell and Young Ireland. His long experience of bargains and expedients in courts and in parliament led him to frequent changes of course and to a willingness to compromise and to be ready to accept limited reforms. He employed a grand rhetoric but was shrewdly pragmatic. The Young Irelanders' rhetoric, on the other hand, expressed their commitment. They had developed the ideal of the Irish nation and they believed in it romantically. While they had supported O'Connell's repeal campaign, at no stage were they uncritical or unquestioning followers of his, and they elaborated their own views in the pages of *The Nation*. They came to part with him chiefly on two issues: the use of force to achieve political ends, and the religious question.

Their chief spokesman in the early 1840s, Davis, was a protestant, as were many of the group. They hoped for an independent Irish nation in which people of all religious persuasions would have equal status and equal rights. This was a central part of their teaching. The education question made this an issue.

The Peel administration, knowing that coercion alone could not satisfactorily govern Ireland, had attempted a number of measures designed to encourage the emergence of a catholic middle class that would be bound to the union and to the existing system of rule by ties of obligation and by the prospects of advancement and of the fulfilment of ambition. The government made a substantial increase, in 1845, to the grant to the Royal College of St Patrick at Maynooth, where most of the country's Roman catholic clergy had been trained since before the beginning of the century. This was a development of Pitt's policy of the 1790s – to conciliate the catholics by measures which would give the government some influence on their affairs. On the whole this had succeeded reasonably well in the first half of the nineteenth century, subject to the very serious setback of the delay of catholic emancipation for nearly thirty years. The bishops, with some exceptions, had been willing to co-operate with the government and with the union. Now, however, after emancipation, and with the evidence, provided by O'Connell's campaigns, of how forceful the opinions of common people could be, the Roman catholic church was becoming a power in the land. The government wished to check as well as to conciliate it.

They also, if the union was to have any meaning, had to provide facilities by means of which Ireland could share in the rapidly changing life of the United Kingdom as a whole – now an industrializing and urbanizing society. Educational reform was one essential. Here the claims of the churches, in an area which they regarded as peculiarly and importantly theirs, had been causing problems for some time. There had been opposition, at times fierce, to the establishment of institutions of education, whether public or private, which were secular in spirit or in their teaching. There had been much presbyterian agitation, for example, in 1814–15 concerning the establishment of the Belfast Academical Institution.

Now the government proposed to extend the system of university education in Ireland – up to this confined to the single, protestant, University of Dublin (which had one college, Trinity College, Dublin). It was decided to establish colleges at Dublin, Cork, Galway and Belfast which would be federally linked. This would supplement what Trinity could do to provide an educated middle class, both catholic and protestant, such as was needed in growing numbers to meet the requirements of the modernizing state. The government wished these to be non-denominational. This was in accordance with the liberal spirit of the age – which was in conflict and competition with the evangelical spirit of the same age, but was often preferred even by evangelical Christians when it was a matter of checking the pretensions of Rome.

The Young Irelanders favoured the scheme. The O'Connellites, in line with the views of most of the bishops, opposed it. Davis, who was involved in this controversy, died in 1845 at the early age of 31. Then, when the whigs came into office again, O'Connell's apparent willingness to abandon repeal in favour of reform led to further division. O'Connell forced the Young Irelanders out of his Repeal Association by presenting them with a motion to the effect that the use of physical force to win Ireland's freedom could not be justified, a proposition that was unacceptable to them, although they had no physical force at their disposal or in prospect in 1846. They set up a rival Irish Confederation.

O'Connell himself died in 1847, and his son John, who took over the leadership of his organization, was unable to emulate his successes. But by then the famine had set in. Some of the Young Irelanders, notably John Mitchel, a radical protestant from County Down, who founded in 1847 a journal which he named the *United Irishman*, wanted an uprising. For Mitchel, this seemed wholly justified in the light of what was happening to so many tens of thousands of people. Although the country, outside the areas so grievously stricken that the population was beyond acting for itself, was seething with bitter violence, it was uncoordinated. Most Young Irelanders at first were opposed to any resort to arms. But in April 1848 the government succeeded in having a treason felony act passed which gave them powers to impose heavy penalties on instigators of rebellion. Mitchel was arrested, tried, and sentenced to transportation for fourteen years. All the Young Irelanders were at risk. They were encouraged by the successful uprising in France early in the year, and by other stirrings in Europe, to believe that the downfall of tyrannies was at hand and that they should lead an insurrection rather than await arrest and transportation to Australia. Their badly-timed attempt to organize one (before the harvest) in County Tipperary and elsewhere led to little more than a few skirmishes, to further arrests and transportations and to a consequent collapse of their movement.

However, by now the widespread grievances of the countryside were being allied to the grievances of urban artisans under the banner of nationalism. Most of the endemic rural violence was local and separate. It was often still, as frequently happens in circumstances of great deprivation, turned inward, as in the custom of 'faction fighting'. Or it was directed, as it had been for 100 years and more, to address local grievances. But the many secret organizations, which formed an effective counter-force to the power of the law and the landlords, had some wider terms of reference. The 'Ribbonmen' of south Ulster and the north midlands, and other organizations farther afield in the nineteenth century, followed the pattern of the eighteenth-century 'Whiteboys'. They were oath-bound and they were able in general to depend on whole communities to keep silence before the authorities about their activities. They cherished a kind of mythical history of their own districts, going back to the confiscations of the sixteenth and seventeenth centuries, and they regarded the existing possessors of the land as usurpers. Many quite poor peasant families held to the belief, whether based on some foundation of fact or merely on fiction, that they were the rightful owners of estates which had for two or more centuries been in other hands.

More ancient concepts also entered into their curiously formal lucubrations. The Whiteboys of Tipperary and the south midlands in the eighteenth century had declared themselves to be the children of *'Sive Oultach'* or *'Siobhán Meiscil'*, figures of folk-myth who represented the ancient goddess of place or of sovereignty. She had two chief manifestations, as a hideous hag or as a beautiful young woman. She was known in Scotland too: Burns, in 'The Vision' names her *Coila*. *Sive Oultach* sometimes had as consort the king of England, the current ruler of the land. In her name the murders of landlords or their agents were carried out, or the midnight houghings of cattle or burnings of property.

Similar myths and legends imbued the deeds of the nineteenth-century secret societies. They provided some basis for the spread of a pseudo-

The stippling shows the areas where a minimum of 50 per cent of those born 1861–71 were Irish-speaking

The stippling shows the areas where a minimum of 50 per cent of those born 1771–81 were Irish-speaking

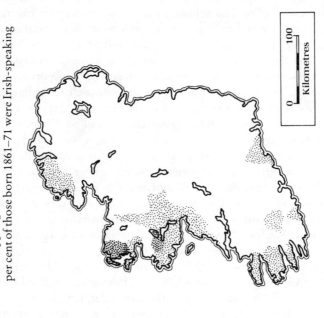

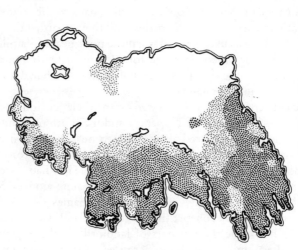

Map 17 The decline of the Irish language
Based on the more detailed maps in Garret FitzGerald, 'Estimates for baronies of minimum level of Irish-speaking amongst successive decennial cohorts, 1771–1781 to 1861–1871', *Proceedings of the Royal Irish Academy* (Section C), vol. 84 (1984), pp. 117–55.

ideology of millenarian nationalism among the oath-bound rural bands. The activity of these bands was commonly a response to some landlord initiative that threatened to upset the precarious and already grossly inequitable economic balance of the countryside. An effect of the modernization of Irish society was to unify these manifestations and subsume the local grievances in a national grievance.

This kind of activity took place, not in the regions of desperate destitution, but in more prosperous areas. By the time of the famine, the distinction between the two was heightened by a linguistic divide. The retreat of the Irish language before the advance of English had proceeded steadily for centuries by now. Garret FitzGerald, in a detailed statistical study, has shown the stages of the retreat. From the tables and maps he provides it can be seen that only in parts of the coastal regions of the south and west were more than half the children born in the famine decade (1841–51) to be brought up Irish-speaking. It is precisely in these regions that the effects of the famine were most terrible.

There was some Irish spoken over most of Munster and Connacht. Leinster, except in its south-western and north-eastern borderlands, was all but wholly English-speaking. Irish was still the majority language of west Donegal; otherwise Ulster was English-speaking except for three pockets where some Irish was still spoken: north Tyrone, parts of the Glens of Antrim, and the Ulster–Leinster borderlands in the hinterland of Dundalk Bay and Carlingford Lough.

The famine did not immediately change the percentages within these areas. But it did cause a sudden fall in the total number of Irish-speakers in the country, and therefore a sharp decline in the proportion of Irish in the overall linguistic pattern. Population loss was far more severe in the Irish-speaking areas than elsewhere.

The great psychological shock of the famine also appears to have affected attitudes to language, among so many other matters. Irish was associated with poverty and starvation: to survive in this anglicized world of the nineteenth century it was necessary to know English. The speakers of the Irish language, both the educated and the uneducated, had had a powerful attachment to the language. But this, like the attachment to Ireland itself, was overwhelmed by the grim reality of starvation. For several generations after the famine a combination of the anglicizing intention and effect of the new national school system, with the determination of Irish-speaking parents that their children should learn English, led to an extraordinary endeavour. A silence fell between parents and children in poor households throughout the south and west. The parents would not speak their own language to their children; the children, at the primary school, learned another language. In some schools, the 'tally stick' was used. A child wore a cord around its neck, from which was suspended a small stick. Each time the child broke into Irish, a notch was placed on the stick, and the child was punished at the end of the day according to the number of notches on the stick.

But, however determined, this was a reluctant purpose of the Irish-speakers, and its necessity was resented. The diarist, Amhlaoibh Ó Súilleabháin, writing in Irish in the little village of Callan, Co. Kilkenny ('wretched beyond description', according to one of the poor law guardians in 1845), on 5 January 1828, reported that:

Some of the people of the village were organizing a circulating library. It's been in existence for a year. Each member of the society pays a crown a year. Alas! Who will found an Irish library? English is triumphing every day over our own sweet basic tongue. This, and a thousand million other defects or deficiencies that we suffer since the day that the English got a grip on our own dear land, poor persecuted Ireland. . . .[1]

There were before the famine a few sporadic and scattered suggestions or attempts to reverse the decline of Irish. Among the political writers, Davis had touched on the matter. The nationalist ideology that stemmed from Fichte and the German romantics of the beginning of the century laid great emphasis on language as a diagnostic of nationality, and this argument had an appeal for the Young Irelanders. However, many of them were at a disadvantage compared to the Germans: they did not themselves speak Irish. Among those who did, the appeal was not so much to the romantic ideas imported from nineteenth-century Europe as to older Irish ideas going back at least to the Gaelic polity of the seventeenth century.

On 17 March 1862 (St Patrick's Day) one Richard D'Alton published in the town of Tipperary the first number of a paper called *An Fíor-Éireannach*, which described itself on its title-page as the 'first move to the restoration of the Irish Language. To be printed in weekly numbers, containing Catholic prayers and selections from the poetry and history of our country'. D'Alton also printed an exhortation, headed 'To the lovers of the old tongue':

One of the mathematicians of old said 'that if he had a place to stand on he would move the world'. I have Irish type, press and heart, and should you possess a tithe of the respect for the Old Tongue, which the Frenchman, Spaniard, German, Jew, Indian and a thousand others have for their mother language, then with God's blessing we will restore it to its position as the medium of intercourse amongst us, we will procure for it that *universal* respect which its richness, melody, and primitiveness claim; and thus win for it the first place amongst the languages of the earth. . . .[2]

At that time, such exhortations had no hope of prevailing against the widespread conviction that a knowledge of English, not Irish, was essential not only to prosperity but to mere physical survival. However, sporadic efforts in this direction continued, and in relation to other matters too there were, in the ensuing years, to be quite a few Archimedes seeking a purchase so that they might move the earth.

Meanwhile, the famine coincided with, and probably greatly helped to accelerate, other major changes in the culture of large sections of the population. The redeployment of the institutional forces of the Roman catholic church proceeded apace. The Royal College of St Patrick at Maynooth had replaced the continental seminaries for the training of most Irish priests. The significance of the influence of some Jansenist professors in the early years of the college's existence has been exaggerated, but Maynooth, for various reasons, did begin to exercise a stern if not harsh influence. Perhaps the main reason is that it was in competition, from the early nineteenth century, with evangelical protestantism for respectability in bourgeois society. In Ireland, the catholics, struggling to achieve a place in anglicized society, had to display protestant virtues.

Before the famine, the catholic churchmen, apart from campaigning for emancipation and then for repeal, directed much energy to attacking the very considerable residue, still existing, of medieval religion. By the end of the Middle Ages catholicism in Ireland had been syncretistic, like popular hinduism, embodying very large numbers of customs and beliefs that stemmed from a great (and often pre-Christian) antiquity. For a mixture of religious and temporal reasons the parish priests in the 1820s and 1830s vigorously followed through efforts, that had been initiated in the previous century, to stamp out many of the customs associated with 'patrons' (pilgrimage gatherings at ancient church sites), wakes and other convivial gatherings. They began to exercise considerable control over the sexual lives of their flocks, insisting, for example, on a ceremony of church marriage for sexual partners. They attacked the remarkable mélange of superstitious beliefs and customs that had come down in rural tradition; but attacked this fairly gently, for superstition helped to make the priest a figure of magical power and, consequently, of great authority. They tried, in their fashion, both to lead their flocks to God and to lead them, in temporal matters, to an improved life in the secular United Kingdom – relying on the spreading liberal values of Victorian England to overcome the prejudices of the protestant state.

To the state as such, different bishops in the first half of the nineteenth century had shown different attitudes. Some, like MacHale of Tuam, were resistant to the modernizing and anglicizing tendencies of government, on behalf of older Irish values. Most were more willing to co-operate, hoping to win acceptance for catholics through compliance with the government and, up to a point, with the spirit of the age. But from about the middle of the century, a third force began to be manifested in the church, less willing to compromise with nineteenth-century secularism, but comparatively uninterested in the ancient inheritance of the Irish church. Paul Cullen, who came to Dublin as archbishop in 1852 after twenty years at Rome, and ruled there until 1878, personified and symbolized this third, ultramontane, tendency. His policy showed a frequent willingness to ally with liberal ideas – although in fundamental principle he was opposed to them – but his aims were to see the protestant anglican church in Ireland disestablished and to see the education of Irish catholics in catholic hands. Before he came to Dublin he was present in 1850 at the synod of Thurles, as apostolic delegate, and there helped to secure the rejection by the assembled catholic bishops of Peel's university scheme – the 'Queen's colleges'. The bishops decided instead to establish a catholic university. A catholic university was indeed established, under papal authority, in Dublin in 1854, with John Henry Newman as its rector, but his views were not those of Cullen, and for various reasons this experiment was not a great success.

The church did, however, gain a much closer and more detailed control over large masses of the people. The rural tradition after the famine was very different from what it had been before. Subdivision of holdings was replaced by consolidation. Previously, especially among the poorest classes, marriage had been undertaken at a very early age. Nothing was to be gained by waiting. Now, marriage tended to be deferred. The holding was to go to one son: he waited until it came to him before marrying. A puritanical and cautious ethos prevailed, and a system of values greatly at variance with those of the past.

In Britain, the reaction to the famine on the part of politicians and shapers of public opinion was a mixture of guilt, resentment (at the Irish who had given rise to the guilt-feelings by dying of starvation) and hope that the famine, however drastically and horribly, had put an end to the chronic hopelessness of Ireland. On a slightly more popular level, as shown, for example, in the pages of *Punch*, the guilt began to be discharged by depicting the Irish as sub-human and evil. Within a few decades, as social Darwinism and the crudest racial prejudices began to inform the attitudes of the highest as well as the lowest in England, these stereotypes for a while acquired a remarkable influence.

Initially, there was a need to come to the aid of those who had suffered, not most, but most persuasively: the landlords. The tedious, cumbersome and expensive process of selling land was felt to leave many of them in an embarrassed position, with estates that they could neither manage efficiently and profitably, nor sell. Two acts were passed, one in 1848, and the other, the more radical Encumbered Estates Act, in 1849, to bring land, like other commodities, into the free-enterprise system of the age by facilitating its disposal by sale. It was hoped that new capital might flow into the land of Ireland to revitalize an economy that had revealed an obvious defect. But the legislation was not very effective. Tenants had not the capital to buy out their holdings; entrepreneurs of the industrial revolution in Britain were not on the whole interested; merchants, lawyers and other speculators in the Irish towns bought most of what came on the market, and created merely a new and worse class of absentee landlords.

However, the tenants had begun to organize, and a number of their associations came together in 1850 in the 'league of north and south', the Irish Tenant Right League. Its stimulus came largely from the north; it sponsored candidates in general elections; but the catholic church was at best suspicious, at worst hostile to this attack on private property. It was a failure.

Most of Ireland in the 1850s was in a state of aimless depression. The government ruled by a series of coercion acts. There were numerous evictions. Violence was widespread.

The north-east was somewhat different. Its connection with industrialized Britain was maintained, although Ulster lacked raw materials such as coal. The early impetus of industrialization had carried Belfast from a population of about 20,000 in 1800 to about 45,000 in 1835, and to about 90,000 in 1850. The famine helped to swell this number: people had crowded in, mainly from west Ulster, and many of them were catholics. They came into the west of the city, settling along the Falls Road, and soon upsetting the balance of creeds. With a third of its population catholic by mid century, Belfast was out of line with most of east Ulster, which was much more predominantly protestant in the city's hinterland.

It was about the middle of the century that a series of significant changes took place contemporaneously in the city. Linen finally fully replaced cotton, and, as the supply of raw cotton to the Lancashire mills was greatly diminished in the 1860s by the American civil war, linen boomed. Power-looms replaced hand-looms very rapidly after 1850. And, in 1851, part of the Queen's Island in Belfast was leased to Thompson and Kirwan to build

TWO FORCES.

Figure 18   'Two Forces'
Source: Punch

ships. Their business was taken over by Hickson, who hired Harland as a manager in 1854. Harland, who had come from the Clyde, in turn hired Wolff, from Liverpool, and between them they founded a new and important ship-building industry on the Lagan. As an adjunct, an engineering industry developed in due course. In the second half of the nineteenth century, Belfast became a major manufacturing city.

It also underwent significant social changes. Its population growth was achieved as people crowded into what was inevitably inadequate housing. Protestant and catholic, they came in from other parts of Ulster as well as from Scotland and northern England. The Ulster influx brought with it attitudes, prejudices and conflicts that had troubled mid Ulster for eighty years. In Sandy Row, in west Belfast, there was an Orange enclave that reflected the inter-denominational factionalism of County Armagh. The Sandy Row people at mid century combined being militant protestants (in a factional sense) with following old native Irish superstitions. Many of them were descended, not so much from seventeenth-century planters as from native labourers who had accepted, in a superficial way, their planter landlords' religion. The city was a paradigm of the stresses and distresses of the early industrial revolution – with an added, factional, Irish dimension. Half the population was under 20 years old at mid century, but the average expectation of life was nine years.

'But, having ventured across the Blackstaff, let us enter Sandy-row', wrote the Rev. W.M. O'Hanlon (of the congregationalist church in Upper Donegall Street, Belfast) in 1852:

This locality is not unknown to fame. Although in none of our walks had we met with the slightest insult, I confess it was not without a momentary trepidation that we penetrated into this region. I had heard of its bludgeon-men, and, even though on a peaceful mission, I thought it just possible we might fare ill among men of blood. But our fears were groundless; and, from the tranquil aspect of the people, it may be concluded, that were it not for that deep, deadly curse of our country – the spirit of party – upon which men on both sides know too well how to operate at times, we should have less to disgrace and make us a by-word to the nations. . . .

One might have supposed that a belief in magic spells and fairies had all died away, and that in this very vulgar, materialistic, and somewhat sceptical age, none could have been found, at least in this part of Ulster, to credit the tales of our grandmothers. But there are some people in Sandy-row who still retain the elder faith on these subjects, and, if works can prove the sincerity of conviction, theirs must be sincere indeed. Night after night, and month after month, in the midnight hour, Oberon and Titania, Puck, Peas-blossom, Robin-goodfellow, and all the rest of those little gentry, whom Shakespeare has immortalized in his immortal 'Dream', have found willing followers in this neighbourhood, and led them to a mystic dance for gold to Cave-hill.[3]

The spirits, we may be sure, did not bear these Shakespearian and English names; but the Rev. O'Hanlon's point, which he reiterates, is that the people of Sandy Row were not really Christians. Like their catholic counterparts, the rural protestants crowding into mid century Belfast needed evangelizing – and this was soon to come. But in the meantime, their 'bludgeon-men' were already upholding protestant faction in the sort of affray that had by now become common. The set-tos of the Ulster countryside had by now been transferred, with the influx of population, to Belfast, and protestant–catholic riots were beginning to become commonplace.

Elsewhere, as the country slowly came to a new adjustment after the famine, a small but significant number of people tried to follow Young Ireland in its nationalism. Some of them were themselves Young Irelanders. Others belonged to a new generation. In the south-west of Ireland clubs were founded which soon began to provide a framework for a wider organization. The 'Irish Republican Brotherhood' was founded in 1858. It linked up soon with other organizations, in America, in Australia, in South Africa and in Great Britain. Several organizations with different names soon came to be known under the umbrella-name, 'fenians'. The fenians, essentially, were a federation of clubs and societies which came to band themselves together, under oath, in a dedication to the achievement of an Irish republic. The fenians were composed of urban artisans and clerks and rural labourers and tenant-farmers, united in opposition to the system of government and economy in Ireland. They were oath-bound and fitted easily into the long-established pattern of rural conspiracy, but with a difference. They had a large urban element; their leadership, at the top, was chiefly urban and was ideologically interested in French and other continental patterns of revolution; and they came in due course to swear allegiance to an 'Irish republic, now virtually established'. They planned violent revolution.

Fenian organization was greatly reinforced by its American connection, and after the American civil war, which provided military training and experience to tens of thousands of Irishmen, this connection became potentially formidable. At its height, the fenian organization included tens of thousands of Irishmen and united, even if very loosely, a large part of the rural secret bands in the service of a common cause. It supplied, with motivation, status to its members, as people who were no longer involved merely in activities directed to local and *ad hoc* grievances, but were in the service of a *nation*. 'It was well known among the Irish police', writes R.V. Comerford, 'that fenians had an "independent look" about them. Because of their consciousness of America as an easily accessible refuge, because mentally so many of them were already on their way there, they could dare to run the risks inherent in "cocking a snook" at priests, policemen and magistrates in the cities, towns and villages of authoritarian, post-famine Ireland'.[4] Their concept of revolution included a confiscation and redistribution of the land of Ireland. The means they envisaged included subversion of the Irish soldiers (a high proportion) in the British army, and an uprising in Ireland armed and supported from outside – chiefly from America. But the government, through spies and informers, had their measure. When insurrection was attempted, in 1867, it was as much a fiasco as the much less well organized attempt of the Young Irelanders in 1848. But the brotherhood, as a conspiratorial association, remained, even while many of its members were serving long terms of imprisonment in British jails, or were in exile in America and elsewhere.

By the 1860s, it was plain to the government that Ireland, under the existing system, was all but impossible to rule. In 1868, one of the most remarkable of British prime ministers, William Gladstone, began his first ministry at the head of a liberal government. Gladstone was one of those rare people whose personality can significantly deflect the course of events. He had in full measure the English gift of being able to match his interests exactly to his principles, and he saw Ireland as a major problem in British politics. 'My mission', he said, 'is to pacify Ireland.'

This involved, for him, in the first place, a notably drastic modification of the Act of Union. He disestablished the church (in 1869) and, with suitable compensation, made a major transfer, partly to the state, of church lands and properties. He followed this, in 1870, with a land act which introduced the revolutionary principle of government responsibility in the relations of two sets of private individuals, landlords and tenants, and government intervention in a matter concerning private property. The act itself had little practical effect to modify the existing system, but it and the church disestablishment act signified, first, a fundamental departure from political principles previously adhered to, and, second, a radical change in the government's view of Ireland's relations with Great Britain. The Act of Union was in effect so altered as to be no longer concerned with true *union*. In 1869 and 1870 Gladstone began to treat with Ireland as a separate country.

In Ireland itself, both conservatives and radicals saw the union, in its existing form, as having run its course. The conservative landlords saw with some concern the liberalizing drift of England away from their interests. One of them, Isaac Butt, a protestant lawyer, founded in 1870 the 'Home Government Association'. He held that, because of its distinctive character and institutions (and he was thinking, in part at least, of the protection of the distinctive Irish ascendancy), Ireland would fare better with its own parliament, to deal with internal affairs only and to remain subordinate to Westminster. This was a symptom of the revolutionary changes that were stirring in Ireland, under the influence of the realignment of forces within the country – consequent on the catastrophe of the 1840s – jointly with the liberalizing and reforming policies of the British government.

Butt's idea was that Ireland's special and distinctive problems should be given recognition through a measure of devolution. But 'home rule' was taken up by a large body of opinion which was really interested in repeal of the union – self-government if not outright separation. It would seem that, within a few years, all sides looked beyond what was formally proposed, and took 'home rule', not at its face value, but as a code or trigger for a move away from the union. Otherwise it is difficult to understand the passions with which so mild a measure was to be both supported and opposed in the following years. In 1874 the first general election was held in which the ballot was secret. Butt had formed a loose alliance, or party, of home rulers, and sixty of these were returned to Westminster.

In 1875, a protestant landlord from Co. Wicklow, Charles Stewart Parnell, was elected to the House of Commons in a by-election. He was a descendent of the Parnell of 'Grattan's parliament' of the late eighteenth century, and a home ruler. Within a few years he was to be leader of the party. Where Butt was cautious, he was daring. Parnell rapidly acquired a position of national leadership which has been compared to that of O'Connell, but he was a very different sort of person. He was incurious and read little. He was not an orator, although he could command a crowd effectively by the force of what he sometimes said. He was far from gregarious, aloof and often scornful or disdainful of his colleagues. He was English in his accent and his manners. He hated England. This proudly passionate man was to dominate the scene for ten years or so, but he was riding the whirlwind that was compounded of Irish social and political forces with an acceleration of English reform.

Parnell's skill, at odds with the impression he gave, was in diplomacy. He managed for several years, especially after he became formal leader of the Irish party in the early 1880s (after Butt's death) to exercise a measure of control over three Irish movements simultaneously. One was the agitation for home rule, largely a parliamentary business. Another was the 'land war'. At the end of the 1870s, economic depression in Europe gravely affected Ireland, at the same time as famine was threatened again in the west. In Co. Mayo in 1879, Michael Davitt, a fenian, whose family had been evicted from their holding when he was 4, who had worked (and lost an arm) in the Lancashire mills, and who had been in prison from 1870 to 1877, founded the 'Land League' to protect the people against rack-renting and eviction. He invited Parnell to be president of this new agrarian organization.

At the same time Parnell came to an agreement, largely tacit, with the third force, the revolutionary fenians. They would let him try, for a while, the parliamentary road to radical reform, and would support him. This became known as the 'new departure'.

Parnell introduced to Westminster the political strategy based on a tightly disciplined party whose members learned to become lobby-fodder (the lesson was well taught and the British parliamentary system was changed forever). He treated with contempt the traditions, customs and civilities of the House of Commons. The Irish members ceased for a while to be clubbable. They were an alien, unamenable, opportunistic force, prepared to filibuster or to cause disorder. And they found more, not less, electoral support in Ireland through such tactics.

But the parliamentary agitation floated on a rising tide of popular organization. The Land League managed a variety of tactics directed against the old land system. These were in due course to include the withholding of rents that were deemed excessive; the effective resistance to evictions, partly through the encouragement of a solidarity that prevented one tenant from taking advantage of the misfortune of another; and the treatment given to such as Captain Boycott, of Lough Mask house, Co. Mayo, that gave a word to the English language: shunning the landlord's agent judged to have been unjust; depriving him and his family of all services, all human contact, all supplies, all labour. Most of these tactics worked only intermittently and uncertainly. But rural organization of resistance was more broadly based than before, and had a considerable overall effect.

In 1881 Gladstone, prime minister again in succession to Disraeli, introduced a land bill which conceded many of the demands of the Land League, notably those described as the 'three Fs' – fair rent, fixity of tenure, and freedom of sale (of the tenant's occupancy). Land courts were established to enforce some of the provisions of this act. The act was welcomed in Ulster, but Parnell and many of his supporters treated it as no more than an interim concession to their just demands.

An attempt to handle Parnell's campaign through the use of a coercion act failed. Parnell was arrested; rural violence and resistance to rent immediately increased; a compromise was reached, including the release of Parnell in 1882. He undertook to curb his supporters and was widely criticized for 'surrendering' to the government. Then, later that year, the newly appointed chief secretary, Lord Frederick Cavendish, was murdered in the Phoenix Park in Dublin, along with the under-secretary, T. H. Burke, by a breakaway revolutionary group known as the 'Invincibles'. Parnell vehemently denounced this; but it had become clear that, as he put it himself, the government had to deal with him through parliament or deal with 'Captain Moonlight' – the violence of secret societies.

A reform act of 1884 gave household franchise to Ireland, increasing the electorate (which was tripled) to the extent that it began for the first time clearly to reflect the full range of public opinion. A general election on the newly enlarged franchise was fought in 1885, with home rule, in Ireland, as the main issue. Eighty-six supporters of home rule were returned to the House of Commons, an unequivocal indication of the support of most Irish opinion for this measure. Gladstone announced that he would introduce a bill.

However, the election returns had revealed plainly, not only that there was a large majority in Ireland for home rule, but that there was a clearly defined minority against it. In the province of Ulster sixteen opponents of home rule were elected as against seventeen who supported it. The strength of the opposition was concentrated in east Ulster around Belfast. Elsewhere in Ireland unionist opinion was everywhere locally in a minority, except in one or two urban middle-class districts and in Trinity College. But in east Ulster there was a large local majority for the union, overwhelmingly protestant, and, as it was to show, determined not to come under a catholic government in Dublin, however limited its powers might be.

In April 1886, in an immensely long speech which was one of the most masterly of a remarkable career, Gladstone introduced his home rule bill. Under this measure, the union was to continue, and Westminster would have ultimate legislative authority and would continue to be directly responsible for matters relating to the crown, for war and foreign affairs, and for basic money matters. An Irish executive in Dublin would be responsible to a subordinate Irish parliament with responsibility in internal Irish affairs. This was far short of independence, but it was acceptable to Parnell and his tightly disciplined party. Gladstone, in his long speech introducing the bill, indicated that the draft measure was for discussion and that he was open to consider substantial amendments. He

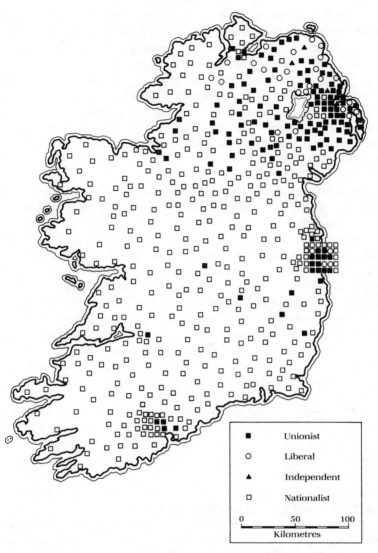

Map 18   The 1885 election: map showing supporters and opponents of Home
Rule. Not all the Ulster constituencies in 1885 were contested. To preserve the
pattern of the distribution of political opinion, I have assumed a 75 per cent vote
for the unopposed candidates, based on a notional 65 per cent turnout. The results
of later elections, in which these constituencies *were* from time to time contested,
suggests that this procedure is reasonable, given the steadiness of the pro- and anti-
Home Rule vote in Ulster over a very long period

showed that he was well aware of the strength of Ulster feeling against the measure, and he appealed to it to give the bill a chance; but among the possibilities he envisaged within the scope of possible amendments was the exclusion of Ulster – that is, partition of the country.

The bill failed. In mobilizing and appealing to Ulster opinion against it, Gladstone's conservative opponents widened the field of argument and involved the discussion of home rule in the impassioned debate on the character and future of the British empire which was then engaging the attention of British politicians. Gladstone's party divided, and the 'liberal unionists' (or 'liberal imperialists' – they were almost the same group) voted against home rule.

In mobilizing opinion against home rule, the conservatives discovered the strength of feeling that had been aroused in protestant Ulster. It was an obvious tactic to 'play the Orange card', as one of their number, Randolph Churchill, put it, and this they proceeded to do. Churchill, who came to Ulster before Gladstone's bill was introduced, landed at Larne to be greeted by a huge and enthusiastic crowd whom he told that 'Ulster will fight, and Ulster will be right!' He went on to Belfast, to address a multitude inside and outside the Ulster Hall in a meeting reminiscent of O'Connell's mass rallies. Like O'Connell, he used menacing language, assuring the tens of thousands roused to furious opposition to what the government was proposing, that, although home rule might come like a thief in the night, yet: 'in that dark hour there will not be wanting to you those of position and influence in England who are willing to cast in their lot with you'.[5]

Belfast was seriously disturbed that spring and summer, as it had been increasingly, at intervals, since the second quarter of the century. The fast-growing city had been swept by fundamentalist revival movements, and the spirit of religious fanaticism, expounded by ranting preachers, was added to political faction. Riots had recurred since the 1830s. There were many deaths and injuries in armed clashes in the streets in 1857, 1864, 1872, 1876 and 1878. The Orange order, suppressed for a time by the government earlier in the century, was gathering force again, and its parades and displays in challenge of catholic parades and displays, sparked off some of the outbreaks. These could go so far out of control as to require for their suppression the services of large bodies of troops, with artillery, in aid of the police. In 1886, the riots, which assumed the scale of a minor civil war, began with a quarrel between two labourers in the Belfast docks, one of whom, a catholic, told the other, a protestant, that after home rule none of the 'Orange sort' would get work again in Belfast.

But for the moment, home rule had failed. In Ulster, organization to

meet the next threat was intensified, and there was soon in being the broad
province-wide base of an effective political machine to maintain the union.
Meanwhile, another general election followed the defeat of the bill. It left
Gladstone's liberals in a minority, and Parnell's nationalists, who were
now tied to them, in a difficulty. The land war continued, with a rent-
withholding 'plan of campaign', but there were to be conservative
governments with little break until 1905.

In 1890 a bitter dispute occurred that was to have a considerable and
enduring influence on home-rule politics. Parnell for a number of years
had been living with a woman who was the wife of a member of his party.
The husband, who had been complaisant, ceased to be so, and the matter
came to the divorce court. Gladstone, leader of a party with a strong non-
conformist support, decided that since the business had become public he
could not continue to be allied with a party whose leader was morally
tainted. He so informed Parnell's party, which met to consider its
position. Parnell, although urged to do so for the sake of the cause, refused
to resign his leadership because of a matter that he believed to be outside
politics, and the party split. Only a minority stayed with Parnell. The
Roman catholic church, faced with the same problem of publicity that had
troubled Gladstone's conscience, supported Parnell's opponents. The
politics of the next year or so were notable in particular for the malevolence
and wounding gibes of Parnell's chief antagonist T. M. Healy, and for the
fury of the moral mobs that opposed his leadership in public meetings: at
Kilkenny, quicklime was thrown in his eyes.

Parnell died in 1891. In 1893, in a brief final interval of office, the aged
Gladstone brought in a second home rule bill (slightly different in its
provision from the first) which passed the Commons but was decisively
rejected by the Lords.

It has often been said, or suggested, that the bitter division in the Irish
party and the early death of Parnell led to great disillusionment with
politics and turned people's thoughts and energies to non-political matters
that were to occupy the 1890s and the opening decades of the new century.
It is not quite so simple. Very significant new developments were taking
place before the Parnell split: they can be described as 'non-political' only
if politics is given a narrow interpretation. Westminster was the political
club of the aristocracy (still largely in command), the gentry and the upper
middle classes. For most other people, especially in Ireland, it was only
one of a number of possible media of political expression.

Since the foundation of the Royal Irish Academy in 1785, there had been
a steady and consistent application of scholarship to Ireland's early past.
The Academy interested itself in what it called 'Science, Polite Literature

and Antiquities'. 'Antiquities' included the Irish language and the history and material remains of early Ireland. These began as, and continued to be, ascendancy interests, but by the middle of the century (partly through the dedication of the Ordnance Survey staff) those interests had made contact with the remnants of the old native Gaelic tradition of learning, as represented, for example, by Eugene O'Curry from west Clare. O'Curry, incidentally, ended up as a professor in the newly founded catholic university in Dublin. At about the middle of the century too 'Celtic studies' began to acquire a solemn academic respectability. The publication of Zeuss's *Grammatica Celtica* was probably the turning point, and as a great deal of work in the late nineteenth century was done by German-speakers, in German, it could not be lightly regarded by the late Victorians to whom the language of Prince Albert was the medium of the most respectable scholarship. The foundation was laid for the acceptance of early Ireland as a civilization in its own right, and the discovery in the nineteenth century of such remarkable works of antiquity as the 'Tara brooch' and the Ardagh chalice gave a very solid backing to the cultural nationalism that made such claims. Conservatives who approached the culture of early Ireland with other motives – to assert an ascendancy claim to pristine Irishness at a time when the signs of the social revolution were patent – only added to the nationalist case, in spite of themselves.

In 1884, in Co. Tipperary, the Gaelic Athletic Association was founded. In Ireland, as everywhere else, there were traditional games which had been played from time immemorial between neighbouring villages and parishes. Hurling, a ball-game played with large sticks of ash, shaped roughly like a golf-club (and golf is a somewhat distant relation of hurling) was a very ancient game, which figures in the early Irish sagas. To it was now attributed a special status, as belonging to the old native civilization. At a time when industrial culture was standardizing all sides of life for the new urban masses, it had become respectable to have regulations for games, and an organization with rules for orderly competitions. The GAA was in origin a modernizing system which brought traditional Irish games into line with the kind of organization that was being applied to English games such as cricket and football. It adapted, or improvised, its own kind of football, which came to be called 'Gaelic football'. It organized inter-county and inter-parish matches of hurling, Gaelic football, handball and some other sports on a regular, and largely rural, basis. And within a few years the GAA had provided a framework, respectable and legal, for the traditional banding of young men in rural communities, and an all-Ireland medium through which the local bands could meet one another and acquire an all-Ireland ideology. It was as important (in the same sort of way) as the *oes dána* of the early middle ages in stimulating unification of culture. Its rules soon forbade its members to play 'foreign games'. Thereby the soldiers of the numerous garrison towns were excluded, as were the gentry, many of whom had earlier taken an interest in the 'gentlemanly' sport (which football was not) of hurling. The GAA formed a country-side network of 'non-political' nationalist clubs. It was in fact a major expression of the new democratic non-parliamentary politics.

The Gaelic League, a society devoted to the cultivation and restoration of the Irish language, was somewhat different in character, although it too was to become part of the new politics. It was founded in Dublin in 1893. Twenty years later, Patrick Pearse, who had long been a member, was to write:

For if there is one thing that has become plainer than another it is that when the seven men met in O'Connell Street to found the Gaelic League, they were commencing. . . not a revolt, but a revolution. The work of the Gaelic League, its appointed work, was that: and the work is done.[6]

This, however, is argumentative hindsight. The Gaelic League was intended, at least by most of its founder-members, to be 'non-political'. Its purpose was cultural: to restore the Gaelic Ireland that by 1893 was being swamped by anglicization. But nothing in the public sphere is non-political. In its first few years the League was patronized by many of the Anglo-Irish. As landlordism was demolished piecemeal by revolutionary English land laws; as the arts and manners of the industrial world penetrated Ireland; as the bonds of the United Kingdom of Great Britain and Ireland were slackened one by one, the old ascendancy looked for its Irish roots and tried to come to terms with Gaelic Ireland. Too late. While they played a large part in the affairs of the League, its membership remained small. But after the turn of the century that membership suddenly increased by leaps and bounds, as the learning of Irish became a popular means of asserting a new communal identity. The League became 'politicized'. Like the GAA it became a vehicle for the expression both of popular culture and of popular political aspirations.

While the widespread, demotic, assertion of nationality increasingly took the form of learning Irish, often a halting and stumbling Irish, a parallel movement, of a much smaller number of writers and intellectuals made use of Irish in a much more indirect way. To labour through a conversation with a friend in broken Irish might be good for the soul of a nationalist, but it was not good for the soul of an artist, particularly a literary artist. 'The Irish Renaissance', as one commentator put it, 'is unique among nineteenth-century nationalist literary movements in that its writers mostly chose to use something other than the traditional language of their country. It is impossible to imagine a Tolstoy or a Dostoevsky choosing to write in the French of the Russian aristocracy rather than in Russian, but the Irish writers were faced with a more complex linguistic problem. The traditional language of Ireland, Gaelic, was virtually dead by 1880; millions of people had spoken it before the famine, but, by the time Yeats began to write, only about one person in 100 in Ireland was exclusively Gaelic-speaking'.[7] Yeats himself did not know the language, and he rightly observed that 'Gaelic is my national tongue, but it is not my mother tongue'.[8]

One of the founder members of the Gaelic League was Douglas Hyde, a protestant member of the Anglo-Irish gentry from Co. Roscommon. He learned Irish and published texts and translations of Irish poetry and the songs of the Irish-speaking people of Connacht. He was one of those who strove to keep the League 'non-political', and he was to resign from its presidency when politics seemed to take over. Another founder-member was John MacNeill, an Ulster catholic, who in time began to sign himself 'Eoin MacNeill'. For a feature of the revival movement was the re-Gaelicization (often inaccurately) of anglicized Irish names: this was to leave its mark on Irish society in the twentieth century.

The 'Anglo-Irish' literary revival was contemporary with the attempted revival of Irish, and interacted with it. Many of the writers who worked in English drew on the spoken English of the western country people, a language that was only one or two generations removed from Irish and was consequently deeply affected by the syntax, idiom and imagery of the Irish language. In the early work of Yeats the rhythms and assonances of Irish are attempted. John Synge, like Yeats a middle-class protestant, learned Irish, and spent some time on the wholly Irish-speaking Aran Islands. His plays use a language which draws on the rhythms and sounds of Irish. They also recreate, although somewhat as a pastiche, the value-systems of the rapidly vanishing Gaelic world. To many of the 'Irish Irelanders', particularly those in the towns, to whom the Gaelic League was catering after the beginning of the century, these values were shocking. Their own were (although they fondly believed otherwise) largely those of the lower middle class of late Victorian England.

The foundation of the Abbey Theatre in Dublin was an important event in the development of the literary movement in English; but the Abbey, and those who ran it (notably Yeats and Lady Gregory) existed on very uneasy terms with the demotic movement which embraced the devolved

Gaelic League and the Gaelic Athletic Association. When Synge's great play, 'The Playboy of the Western World', a statement of universal significance set in the west of Ireland, opened at the Abbey, it was greeted by riots. People who had been schooled in nationalist–revivalist ideas felt that it reflected on the pure morals of the Irish peasantry.

But the hostility between two groups of people with different attitudes to Irish culture was blunted and modified by many truces, and even alliances. Yeats, the dominant figure in the literary movement – in so far as it was a movement – was in love with an English lady of remote Irish descent, Maud Gonne, whose interests were not literary at all, but revolutionary. Like Parnell's sister Fanny, or Oscar Wilde's mother, she burned with patriotic ardour (in her case on behalf of an adopted country) which was directed against the crown and the whole British connection. She found in the Paris of the turn of the century an atmosphere free from that Anglo-Saxon dullness that was increasingly being resented. Yeats resisted her powerful influence, which would direct his art into nationalist politics. But he too was a nationalist of a sort and was busying his powerfully creative mind in the fashioning of a myth that would raise the holy island of Ireland out of what he called 'this filthy modern tide'. He wrote, among much else, at the beginning of the century (1902) a little play in which the old theme of the goddess of sovereignty is given new life. The setting is Killala at the time of the French landing of 1798. A poor old woman who comes in from the road to a peasant's cottage, singing snatches of old songs, influences the peasant's son to leave the arms of his bride-to-be and go to join the French. At the end of the play the peasant turns to his younger son, still a boy, and asks him: 'Did you see an old woman going down the path?' To which the boy replies: 'I did not, but I saw a young girl, and she had the walk of a queen.'[9] Towards the end of his life (he died in 1939) Yeats was to say:

> . . .I lie awake night after night
> And never get the answers right
> Did that play of mine send out
> Certain men the English shot?[10]

One of the men he had in mind was, like so many in these movements, a poet, in a mode close to that of the English 'Georgians'. Patrick Pearse, born in Dublin, was the son of a stonemason (engaged largely in the manufacture of tombstones) who had migrated to Dublin from England. His mother was Irish. Shy, withdrawn, romantic, a hero to his younger brother and his sisters, Pearse spent most of his comparatively short life trying to assimilate the true, non-English, old Gaelic culture to which he longed to have belonged, and which he romanticized. He was active in the Gaelic League, became editor of its paper, *An Claidheamh Solais*, and liked to spend time in a cottage at Rosmuck in the Connemara Gaeltacht (Irish-speaking area). A cultural nationalist most of his life, he was drawn towards radical politics, and attracted the attention of the reviving Irish Republican Brotherhood, who recruited him. He was deeply interested in education as a means of national renewal, and he founded a school, St Enda's, on the outskirts of Dublin, where he hoped to free young spirits and to place before them high ideals of chivalry and of commitment to the service of an ancient nation and a suffering people. But he was in part what he would least have wished to be, a product of the somewhat stuffy urban cultures of the early twentieth century, with all their illusions about war and glory. In his verse and in his prose, there are muffled echoes of Rupert Brooke and G.K. Chesterton.

There were many others, good writers, bad and indifferent, in a remarkable period in which an unusually high proportion of the population was actively interested in political ideas, some of which were shopworn, some new-minted.

Not all the writers and propagandists of this time were concerned with art or romantic ideals. There were some who saw Ireland's salvation in economic change. T. P. Moran, editor of a journal called *The Leader*, and Arthur Griffith, a journalist who had worked in South Africa and who edited in Ireland *The United Irishman*, were two who, in different ways, preached doctrines of economic self-sufficiency. They were far from radical in their views, advocating the fostering of Irish industry behind barriers of protective tariffs and envisaging an economy of small farmers and small capitalists. Griffith elaborated political ideas too, advocating that Ireland and Britain should form a dual monarchy, on the model of the Austro-Hungarian empire. He founded, in 1905, a political party which tried to provide an alternative to the policies of the Irish parliamentary party (reunited since 1900 under the leadership of the Wexford Parnellite, John Redmond) and which achieved some very limited success in local government elections. Griffith's organization, under the presidency of the writer Edward Martyn, emphasizing ideas of self-help and self-sufficiency, was called '*Sinn Féin*' ('Ourselves').

The economy of the country continued, outside the north-east, to be backwardly rural. A railway system, begun in the 1830s (with, significantly, two separate growth-points in Dublin and Belfast) had been developed throughout the nineteenth century, with government backing and encouragement. If the Irish railways never gave their investors the returns hoped for, they supplied a transport network that had a stimulating effect on the economy of many parts of the country (even though, partly for security reasons, some of the stations were located outside the towns they served).

Successive, and growing, British bureaucracies tried to tease out Ireland's problems. There were numerous Blue Papers and commissions of inquiry, reporting on poor laws, famine, transport, fisheries, education, art and many other topics. Ireland, for British administrations, was a lesser India, opaque, burdensome and a source of employment for the middle classes. Under the conservative governments that continued with little interval after the defeat of Gladstone's first home rule bill, many institutional reforms were attempted. The policy was described as 'killing home rule by kindness'. Among the changes were the setting-up of a more representative system of local government, the establishment by the state of a national library, a national gallery of art, and a national museum, the operation of a 'Congested Districts Board' to provide means of improvement and employment in the impoverished and overcrowded west, and the institution of a department of agriculture. But what was probably the most significant – indeed revolutionary – change was brought about through a series of land acts (the last in 1909). The ownership of a great deal of the arable and grazing land was transferred gradually from the landlords to the tenant farmers – the farmers being subject to payment of annuities to reimburse the state for its purchase of the land. This brought about not only economic but cultural and social revolution. The ascendancy landlords, descendants and heirs of the expropriators of the sixteenth, seventeenth and eighteenth centuries, were cut off at the roots, and the tenants, who often fancied themselves the inheritors of some immemorial 'original' ownership, moved in. But the long economic depression of the late nineteenth century affected Ireland badly; there had been near-famine again in the 1870s, and in the opening decade of the new century the country was still very poor and backward. Emigration continued on a large scale, mainly to America.

There was one movement of people at the end of the century which was not on a large scale but which added a significant element to the Irish population. Jews who had fled from the Czarist Russian pogroms, of 1881 and later, found their way to Ireland. Before their arrival there were only a few hundred Jews in Ireland, mostly in Dublin. The number now went up to about 4000, in small communities in Dublin, Belfast, Cork, Lurgan, Limerick and elsewhere. They dealt in clothing and general trade, and many in the first generation earned their living as pedlars. In that time of image- and myth-making they were to engage the attention of James

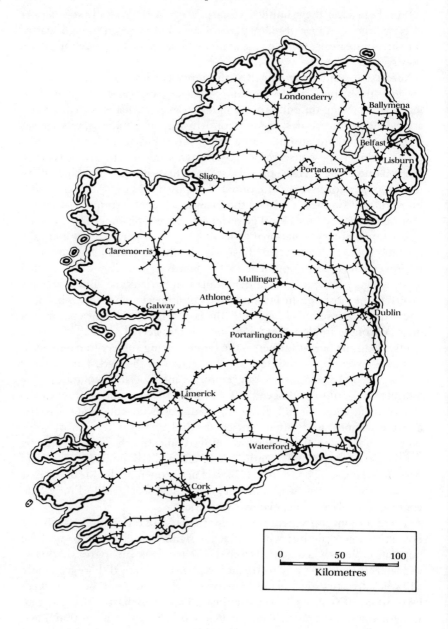

Map 19   Railway system in the early twentieth century (1906)

Joyce, the young catholic graduate of the new university in Dublin, who was to seek freedom through art, through a centrifugal odyssey from Dublin (the 'centre of paralysis'), through detachment from the surface accidents of Irish life, through avoiding the 'nets' of language, nationality and religion, and through a cosmopolitanism which would be deeply rooted in a particular culture. The Dublin *homme moyen sensuel* whom he made his Everyman was Leopold Bloom, a fictitious baptized second-generation Jew of that migration.

Politics overtook the social, literary, cultural and economic developments in the country early in the second decade of the twentieth century. But it should be borne in mind that the socio-cultural manifestations of Ireland at the beginning of the century were not wholly of local origin. While still including, as it were, many enclaves of remoteness, the country by 1900 occupied a geographically central position in the world of developing technology. In the new century, the outside world impinged directly on out-of-the-way places in the form of German bands, troupes of travelling players (including the circus) and, increasingly, commercial travellers. But the trans-Atlantic cable, with a terminal at Valentia, Co. Kerry, had been functioning since 1865, and within the first decade of the century the bicycle, the motor car, the aeroplane and wireless telegraphy were beginning to bring about a transformation in communications. Electric tramways were moving a commuting population in Dublin and Belfast. By 1910, when Edward VII died, to be succeeded by his son George V, one of those turning points which are visible only by hindsight had been reached and passed.

Dublin and Belfast, in their different ways, contrasted with most of the country. Dublin, seedily monumental, commercial, with a reach-me-down court and a large military garrison, housing a third of its people in foetid slums, was the stage for the enactment of a midsummer night's dream as a remarkable number of active minds applied themselves to the creation of imagined worlds. Belfast, harshly business-like, combining puritanical fanaticism with the worship of the golden calf, made crude distinctions: catholic barmen and mill-girls; protestant capitalists, engineering hands and shipworkers. Its illusions were as great as Dublin's, its glory more recent and more 'modern' – but the first industrial revolution, which had made it, was in fact already over. The shipyards reached their high point in 1912: Belfast launched the 'Titanic', one of the largest ships afloat for the brief days of her maiden voyage, which ended, incomplete, when she struck an iceberg in the north Atlantic and sank with the loss of 1513 lives.

In 1906 the long period of conservative rule in Britain came to an end with the great electoral victory of the liberals, under Henry Campbell-Bannerman. Their majority was so large that they had no need to make promises or concessions to the fretful Irish. But when they attempted what was, by European standards, a belated reform of the British social system, they brought upon themselves a constitutional crisis that was soon not merely to involve, but to be dominated by Irish issues. Campbell-Bannerman resigned because of ill-health in 1908 and was succeeded by Herbert Asquith. David Lloyd George became chancellor of the exchequer. In November 1909, Lloyd George's budget, which had been passed by the Commons, was rejected by the Lords. Asquith asked for a dissolution of parliament and fought an election in January 1910 on the issue of the 'unconstitutional' behaviour of the Lords. He won, but with a much reduced majority (liberals 275, conservative–unionists 273, Irish nationalists 82, labour 40). John Redmond, leading the re-united party of Parnell, was in a position of some power, and home rule was back on the parliamentary agenda. In a second general election in 1910, the liberals lost three more seats and were exactly equal in numbers to the conservative–unionists; but the Irish nationalists, with eighty-four, and the labour party, with forty-two, provided a solid majority for constitutional change: clipping the wings of the House of Lords and introducing home rule for Ireland.

The Lords were humbled first. Their power of veto was reduced to a two-year delay. The government then turned to Irish home rule, which now had only to pass the Commons. The Lords' absolute veto of 1893 could not be re-enacted.

Ulster unionism was much better organized to meet this emergency than it had been thirty years before. But it now had to meet, as well as the danger from politically organized Irish nationalism, the comparatively new force of organized labour, which sought to redraw the lines of political division in Ireland on the model of economic class rather than religion or nationality. Socialism and anarchism were great bogeys for the comfortable classes of the time, in Europe and America: forces of unknown but threatening potential. The followers of Karl Marx and of other revolutionary thinkers and leaders were cutting across the grain of jingoist, imperialist and nationalist propaganda (not only sponsored but to a large extent believed by the ruling groups of the age) and attempting to appeal to a universal common interest of urban workers and rural peasants against the mighty of the earth. The shrewder manipulative politicians, like Joseph Chamberlain, had been quick to perceive that the working classes of the new mass society were as crass, as callous and as selfish as their social superiors, and had prejudices which could readily be inflamed.

In Ireland, the land revolution by its very nature made for a new conservatism; but there was still a landless or land-poor element in the rural population. Rural radicalism continued to manifest itself, as it had for more than 100 years. The overthrow (from above) of the power of gross landed property, however, opened the way to new forms of rural political agitation and organization. Co-operatives were formed; labourers tried to form combinations in their own interest. Within the two large urban populations of Dublin and Belfast, workers' combinations had long existed in craft unions, but large numbers of workers existed at or below the limit of subsistence and without the capacity to assert a right to the recognition of a common humanity. In 1907 Jim Larkin, Lancashire born of Irish parents, came to Belfast, organized the dockers and brought them out on strike. Sympathetic strikes followed: Larkin succeeded in bringing catholics and protestants out together and in bringing out on strike the police sent to control the agitation. He was, however, only a temporary organizer for the National Union of Dockers. In 1908, when his Belfast employment ceased, he moved to Dublin and began organizing there. In 1911 James Connolly arrived in Belfast as organizer of the Irish Transport and General Workers Union. Connolly, born in Edinburgh, had served in the British army. He was a Marxist and had been a founder of the Irish Socialist Republican Party in 1896. He had spent some years in America where he was active in the trade union movement and had contact with the syndicalists. For him, much more than for Larkin, labour organization was a part of politics.

The social, constitutional and international crises became one in the second decade of the century. Instability appeared to mark British politics. Women were conducting a spirited campaign to demand parliamentary votes and had provoked outraged and violent reaction. The curbing of the powers of the House of Lords convinced many conservatives that the liberals had overstepped the bounds of the constitution. In Ireland the ascendancy families and their connections found that the polity that had subsisted in the country for two centuries was being undone: their lands were being transferred to the tenants and home rule was to be introduced by a government that commanded the necessary votes in the Commons and could no longer be baulked by the Lords. And there was talk, fear – and in many quarters hope – of European war.

The Irish unionists realized that their best hope of preventing home rule lay in the solidarity, on the constitutional question, of protestant Ulster. A very able Dublin unionist barrister, Sir Edward Carson, was chosen to lead Ulster resistance to the measure by all available political means. In September 1911 he spoke to a meeting of 50,000 people on the outskirts of

Belfast, in Craigavon, home of Captain James Craig, a rich Ulster businessman. He promised to resist the passage of the threatened home rule bill but advised secession, should the bill pass: 'We must be prepared . . . ourselves to become responsible for the government of the protestant province of Ulster.'[11] There was immediate response and a commission was established to prepare for a provisional government of Ulster should the occasion arise. This move was supported by the conservatives in Britain. Winston Churchill, first lord of the admiralty in Asquith's liberal government, came to Belfast to support home rule as his father had come more than a quarter of a century before to oppose it. His visit was a fiasco. The crowds that greeted him were hostile; even though heavily guarded by soldiers he was unable to speak in central Belfast and had to slip away through Larne with his mission unaccomplished. In 1912, addressing huge meetings, both in Ulster and in England, the conservative leader Bonar Law committed his party to support the Ulster unionist defiance of the government, which had assumed a menacing character.

The bill was introduced in April 1912. It resembled, with some modifications, the two earlier bills. But within weeks of its introduction the government, in private communications to Redmond and others, had begun to respond to the unionist resistance by discussing the possible exclusion of some Ulster counties from the operation of the bill. Redmond opposed this; but the unionists increased the force and widened the scope of their agitation. They designated 28 September 1912 'Ulster Day' and prepared a form of words for a 'solemn covenant' (on the precedent of the Scottish covenant) to which people would subscribe on that day:

Being convinced in our consciences that Home Rule would be disastrous to the material well-being of Ulster as well as the whole of Ireland, subversive of our civil and religious freedom, destructive of our citizenship, and perilous to the unity of the Empire, we, whose names are underwritten, men of Ulster, loyal subjects of His Gracious Majesty King George V, humbly relying on the God whom our fathers in days of stress and trial confidently trusted, do hereby pledge ourselves in solemn Covenant throughout this our time of threatened calamity to stand by one another in defending for ourselves and our children our cherished position of equal citizenship in the United Kingdom, and in using all means which may be found necessary to defeat the present conspiracy to set up a Home Rule parliament in Ireland. And in the event of such a Parliament being forced upon us we solemnly and mutually pledge ourselves to refuse to recognize its authority. In sure confidence that God will defend the right we hereto subscribe our names. And further, we individually declare that we have not already signed this Covenant. God save the King.[12]

The signing followed religious services throughout the province on 'Ulster

Day', which was a Saturday. 471,414 people (men and women) subscribed, according to the organizers.

The bill, however, passed the Commons, and was rejected by the Lords in January 1913. The Ulster Unionist Council decided to form a body to be known as the Ulster Volunteer Force and to recruit up to 100,000 signatories of the covenant into its ranks. The Lords' veto on the home rule bill would hold up its enactment only until late 1914. The UVF acquired arms as rapidly as it could, and drilled its men, who were commanded by retired British officers. A close associate of the liberal government, Lord Loreburn (lord chancellor until June 1912) wrote to *The Times* suggesting that a private conference on Ulster be held to prevent civil war. Carson indicated to the government that he had many supporters in the army. The king intervened privately to express his concern at the decisions his officers might have to make. The government began negotiating with Redmond on the possibility of a partition of Ireland.

Redmond's party enjoyed the support of a large majority of the Irish electorate, but it is virtually certain that that majority wanted more, not less, than home rule; just as the extreme unionist opposition to the bill was almost certainly founded on a conviction that home rule would be the beginning of a process rather than the solution of a problem. Redmond was in an impossibly difficult position. He appeared to have achieved Parnell's objective; but the prize was turning to dust in his hand. He was no Parnell; he had been much more accommodating to the British parliamentary and political system, and many of his temporary allies regarded his politician's skills with suspicion.

Speaking (in Irish) at a great home rule meeting on 31 March 1912, Patrick Pearse said:

Let us arouse our spirit again. There are enough brave men here to bring the British empire to nothing, if only we were of one mind and set about the matter in the right way. It is not our purpose to bring the British empire to nothing. What do we want? The freedom of the Irish. We aren't always all in agreement. We disagree on small matters. That's of no importance. We are all agreed on this: that it is our duty to free our race, by one means or another. That is enough.

There are some among us who would be satisfied under the English crown so long as we had freedom in our own territory; that is, without interference by foreigners in what concerns only Irish. . . .

There are others of us who never bowed head or bent knee in homage to the king of England, and who never will. As everyone knows, I belong to this latter group. But it seems to me that I would betray my people on the very day that battle is joined, had I not answered the call to today's assembly; since it is clear to me that the bill which has been proposed will be of advantage to the

Irish, and that the Irish will be stronger for the fight under this act than without it. . . .

Let it not be thought that I am accepting the bill in advance. No one is accepting the bill in advance. The one who would do so is a fool. We might have to reject the bill. All we are saying is that the Irish have to be heard from now on; that we must now be served; that our patience is at an end. The Irish are now proclaiming – two hundred thousand of them speaking here and now as one – that they want freedom and that with God's will they intend to achieve it. Let us unite and win a good bill from the foreigners. I think we can extract a good bill from them if we summon up enough courage. And, if we are cheated this time, there are those in Ireland – and I am one of them – who will advise the Irish never again to deal and negotiate with the foreigners, but to answer them henceforth with the strong hand and the sword's edge. Let the foreigners understand that if we are betrayed again there will be bloody war throughout Ireland.[13]

It was not so much this kind of menacing – but, it must have seemed, empty – expression that troubled Redmond as he came under intense governmental pressure to take the two steps backward of partition in exchange for the one step forward of home rule. Rather, it was that his party had an uncertain command in a rapidly changing Ireland: home rule, without compromise, was its *raison d'être*. A compromised bill would leave the future very uncertain. Redmond seems to have persuaded himself that the Ulster unionists were bluffing. But when they began organizing militarily, he was drawn on to dangerous ground.

1913 was a year of growing public excitement. The temporarily blocked home rule bill agitated not only Ireland, but Britain. In Ulster the UVF were drilling and arming. In Dublin, some of the major employers, led by the catholic William Martin Murphy, formed a federation and locked out the workers who joined the Irish Transport and General Workers Union, organized by Larkin and Connolly. Mass meetings organized by the union were attacked by the police, leading to deaths, and a private, Marxist, military force was formed – the Irish Citizen Army – to protect the workers. It was modelled on the UVF. At the end of 1913 another military organization was formed, the Irish Volunteers.

This move was a response to the formation of the UVF. The fenian organization, the Irish Republican Brotherhood, had undergone a rivival since the beginning of the century – in particular since 1898, when committees throughout the country had arranged centenary commemoration of the republican uprisings at the end of the eighteenth century. Statues of '98 pikemen were put up in many towns. More importantly, secret oathbound groups of IRB men became busy recruiting young men and swearing them in to a new conspiracy to establish an Irish republic. Pearse, by 1913, had been recruited into the IRB. In November he wrote in praise of the UVF:

It is foolish of the Orangeman to believe that his personal liberty is threatened by Home Rule; but, granting that he believes that, it is not only in the highest degree common sense but it is his clear duty to arm in defence of his threatened liberty. Personally I think the Orangeman with a rifle a much less ridiculous figure than the Nationalist without a rifle. . . .[14]

Eoin MacNeill, of the Gaelic League wrote at the same time, in *An Claidheamh Solais* an article entitled 'The North Began' in which he too pointed out that the nationalists too should arm. The IRB (to which he did not belong) decided that MacNeill, a university professor, should be the respectable figurehead of the Irish Volunteers. Redmond, who had no part in the initial formation of this force, could not allow himself to be outflanked politically by it. He demanded a majority for his nominees on its executive, and his command of political opinion was such that this could not be refused. But the Volunteers were now responding to one kind of covert (IRB) and two kinds of overt (MacNeill and Redmond) control. The government prohibited the import of arms into Ireland, but in 1914 successful gun-runnings were undertaken on a large scale by the UVF and on a small scale by the Irish Volunteers (all from Germany).

Meanwhile, an attempt by the government to move against the UVF, in advance of the passage of the home rule bill, in March 1914, had been subverted. The British high command leaked information like a sieve to Carson and Craig, and fifty-eight officers in the Irish military headquarters at the Curragh, Co. Kildare, refused to serve against the Ulstermen. The government backed down. An amended bill was sent to the Lords, on 23 June, providing that Belfast, Derry, and counties with an appropriate majority, might opt out of home rule for six years but no longer. Carson refused this outright. The Lords sent the bill back to the Commons with an amendment excluding all Ulster from home rule. The Commons passed the bill without the Lords' amendment and it received the royal assent and became the Government of Ireland Act 1914 on 18 September. England had then been at war for nearly seven weeks. The operation of the bill was suspended for the duration of hostilities, which were expected to last for not more than a few months.

The British army was small, professional, composed of long-service soldiers, and not drawing on conscripts. The government attempted to expand it rapidly by recruiting volunteers. Both Carson and Redmond were prepared initially to offer the UVF and the Irish Volunteers respectively for the defence of Irish shores against German invasion for the duration of the war. But Carson was persuaded to offer 35,000 of the UVF to the regular army for general service. 29,000 of them in fact volunteered, and the greater part were formed into the 36th (Ulster) Division, which was moved to France in October 1915. The government refused to have a similar division, with its own colours, officers and designation, formed from the Irish Volunteers. But, in a speech at Woodenbridge, Co. Wicklow, soon after the outbreak of war, Redmond called on the Irish Volunteers to join the British army. He was persuaded that Irish 'loyalty', shown now, would be rewarded at the end of the hostilities. Most followed him, many going individually to England to join various regiments, to a total of about 80,000 men. But a section of the Volunteers split away, retaining the original title, 'Irish Volunteers'. Those who stayed with Redmond became known as 'National Volunteers'.

The propaganda that propelled many young men into the British army in 1914, and many young women into auxiliary services, was mendacious in the extreme. As the European war dragged on, doubts set in. The botched operation in the Dardanelles in 1915, in which Irish casualties were heavy, increased the doubts. But some had opposed involvement from the start, as the wrong war, against the wrong enemy. For Connolly it was an imperialist war: the workers of Europe should have thrown down their arms, or shot their officers, rather than slaughter one another. For Pearse, the enemy was England, not Germany, Austria or Turkey. The IRB decided that the war created the circumstances for an Irish insurrection. Connolly and the Citizen Army independently decided that it gave a chance to strike against imperialism. Early in 1916 Connolly was persuaded to throw in his lot with the Volunteers, and an uprising, to be supported by an import of arms from Germany, was secretly planned for Easter Sunday. Almost everything possible went wrong. The arms were intercepted on Good Friday. Eoin MacNeill, although nominally commander-in-chief of the Volunteers, had not been informed by the IRB plotters until the last moment. He cancelled the parades and movements ordered for Easter Sunday and sent countermanding orders throughout the country. The British authorities – who also became fully aware of what was afoot only at the last moment – relaxed their alertness in relief and deferred (until after the Easter holiday) following through. Then Pearse, Connolly and their colleagues decided to go ahead with an uprising, however forlorn, summoned such force as they could, and seized buildings in Dublin and a few other places at noon on Easter Monday.

A small column of Irish Volunteers, with a still smaller contingent of the Citizen Army, marched along Sackville Street in the centre of Dublin, halted at the General Post Office, wheeled into the building, expelled the

clerks and customers, and began smashing the windows with rifle-butts
and filling the spaces with sandbags. Pearse, elected by the IRB 'president
of the Irish republic', walked out into the street and read aloud a leaflet,
badly printed in a miscellany of typefaces, which was being pasted up here
and there:

Irishmen and Irishwomen: In the name of God and of the dead generations
from which she receives her old tradition of nationhood, Ireland, through us,
summons her children to her flag and strikes for her freedom.

Having organised and trained her manhood through her secret revolutionary
organisation, the Irish Republican Brotherhood, and through her open military
organisations, the Irish Volunteers and the Irish Citizen Army, having patiently
perfected her discipline, having resolutely waited for the right moment to reveal
itself, she now seizes that moment, and, supported by her exiled children in
America and by gallant allies in Europe, but relying first on her own strength,
she strikes in full confidence of victory.

We declare the right of the people of Ireland to the ownership of Ireland, and
to the unfettered control of Irish destinies, to be sovereign and indefeasible.
The long usurpation of that right by a foreign people and government has not
extinguished the right, nor can it never be extinguished except by the destruction
of the Irish people. In every generation the Irish people have asserted their right
to national freedom and sovereignty: six times during the past three hundred
years they have asserted it in arms. Standing on that fundamental right and
again asserting it in arms in the face of the world, we hereby proclaim the Irish
Republic as a Sovereign Independent State, and we pledge our lives and the
lives of our comrades-in-arms to the cause of its freedom, of its welfare and of
its exaltation among the nations.

The Irish Republic is entitled to, and hereby claims, the allegiance of every
Irishman and Irishwoman. The Republic guarantees religious and civil liberty,
equal rights and equal opportunities to all its citizens and declares its resolve to
pursue the happiness and prosperity of the whole nation and of all its parts,
cherishing all the children of the nation equally, and oblivious of the differences
carefully fostered by an alien government, which have divided a minority from
the majority in the past.

Until our arms have brought the opportune moment for the establishment of
a permanent National Government, representative of the whole people of Ireland
and elected by the suffrages of all her men and women, the Provisional
Government, hereby constituted, will administer the civil and military affairs of
the Republic in trust for the people.

We place the cause of the Irish Republic under the protection of the Most
High God, Whose blessing we invoke upon our arms, and we pray that no one
who serves this cause will dishonour it by cowardice, inhumanity, or rapine. In
this supreme hour the Irish nation must, by its valour and discipline and by the

readiness of its children to sacrifice themselves for the common good, prove
itself worthy of the august destiny to which it is called.

Signed on behalf of the Provisional Government,

Thomas J. Clarke, Sean Mac Diarmada, Thomas MacDonagh, P.H. Pearse,
Eamonn Ceannt, James Connolly, Joseph Plunkett.[15]

The insurgents' plans made little military sense. They occupied, with a
total force of not much more than 2000, buildings in central Dublin and in
a few other places in the country. Then they awaited attack. In fact their
action was a classical example of the 'propaganda of the deed' so widely
proclaimed as a tactic by anarchists at the end of the last century. The
British, taken by surprise, moved steadily but slowly to take the
republican positions. They brought artillery to bear and reduced the centre
of Dublin to fiery ruin. They marched companies of inexperienced troops
through the streets to charge sandbagged buildings occupied by riflemen:
they displayed heroic but foolish courage and suffered many dead and
wounded. The Volunteers held Dublin for almost a week, fought steadily
and bravely, and enacted a drama.

This was, initially, a perplexing event, not only for the British
government, but for most Irish people. The insurgents as they surrendered
(under Pearse's orders) and were marched away at the end of the week,
were reviled by Dublin people, many of whom had sons or husbands
serving in the British army. The writer James Stephens, taken as much by
surprise as most people by the rising, asked himself immediately
afterwards what had happened:

A great many of our men and women and children, Volunteers and civilians
confounded alike, are dead, and some fifty thousand men who have been moved
with military equipment to our land are now being removed therefrom. The
English nation has been disorganised no more than as they were affected by the
transport of these men and material. That is what has happened, and it is all
that has happened.

But when he went on to try to puzzle out why it happened, he came to a
conclusion which showed that what he had described was not *all* that had
happened:

Why it happened is a question that may be answered more particularly. It
happened because the leader of the Irish Party misrepresented his people in the
English House of Parliament. On the day of the declaration of war between
England and Germany he took the Irish case, weighty with eight centuries of

history and tradition, and he threw it out of the window. He pledged Ireland to a particular course of action, and he had no authority to give this pledge and he had no guarantee that it would be met. . . .[16]

General Maxwell, in command of the surrendered ruins, believed in firmness. He had the leaders of the uprising tried by court martial. Within twelve days in May 1916, in twos and threes, fourteen of them were shot in Kilmainham gaol. Many others were to be executed, but the pressure of American opinion mounted on Asquith and he stopped the killing, announcing to the House of Commons on 11 May that: 'The government has come to the conclusion that the system under which Ireland has been governed has completely broken down.'

As other people besides James Stephens tried to grasp what had happened, they came to similar conclusions. George Bernard Shaw, writing in the *New Statesman* on 6 May, referred to the British explanation of the war as one for the 'rights of small nations' (with particular reference to the German violation of Belgian neutrality in 1914), and wrote:

Be very careful what political doctrine you preach. You may be taken at your word in the most unexpected directions.

I wonder how many of those who have made such resounding propaganda of Sinn Fein for small nationalities for twenty months past would have died heroically for their principles in the burning ruins of the General Post Office in Sackville Street. . . .[17]

Yeats was to put it more succinctly:

All changed, changed utterly:
A terrible beauty is born.[18]

Within weeks another terrible beauty was born. The Great War took a new course in 1916, with the Brusilov offensive, the Verdun offensive, and, on 1 July, the Somme offensive, as the generals tried to break the deadlock on the fronts by brute force, employing tremendous artillery bombardments and vast masses of men to break through the too-effective defences that had produced stalemate. On the Somme, tens of thousands of those who, responding to Kitchener's call for volunteers after the outbreak of war, had filled the ranks with ignorant good will, went into action. They were marched, laden down with equipment and supplies, across open ground, rank after rank all day, against German wire and machine-guns. The Ulster Division was decimated. Along the line other divisions, both of 'old sweat' regulars and of the New Army, included tens of thousands of Irishmen, and many of them too fell. About 2500 Irishmen were killed or died of wounds received on the first day of battle. Ulster was numb with grief as the telegrams arrived – protestant Ulster, which had had no quarrel with Germany. Catholic Ireland was slowly coming to the conclusion that the men who had occupied the Post Office had fought for Ireland; the men who died equally bravely on the Somme had fought for Britain. A great shift in public opinion was taking place.

The shift was slow and uneven. The catholic bishops gave no clear response, as a body, to the Easter rising. They had lost faith in Redmond as a leader of the catholic interest. The Jesuit journal, *Studies*, began a series on 'Poets of the Rising' – the first stage in secular canonization. *Sinn Féin*, with which the rising was associated in the public mind, began to attract recruits both from the young and from the supporters of the parliamentary party, and to change its own outlook.

The British government tried to renegotiate an Irish settlement. A coalition government was formed at the end of 1916, under Lloyd George. In 1917 the government tried to pacify Ireland, offering concessions within a home rule framework while also trying to accommodate Ulster (Carson was now in the government). What they offered had become irrelevant. An amnesty returned the Easter week prisoners to Ireland. They had been showered with insults, rotten vegetables and stones as they were marched away as prisoners in 1916. In 1917 they returned to the welcome of rapturous crowds. *Sinn Féin* began to win by-elections. Redmond's party was in disarray. He died in 1918 before it was rejected outright.

In 1917 the British and French armies were in effect defeated on the western front, but they were saved from destruction by the American entry into the war. It took about a year, however, before American force could be effectively deployed in Europe. In early 1918 the British decided to apply military conscription in Ireland. This attempt completed the process of political change. The catholic church through its bishops and priests denounced it – although Lloyd George had linked conscription to an offer of immediate home rule. By now, Britain's war no longer interested Irish nationalists: if they were to fight they would fight Britain. The conscription crisis of 1918 enabled *Sinn Féin*, now reorganizing with considerable help from the 1916 Volunteers, to seize political leadership finally from the old parliamentary party. Conscription was not imposed: to try to do so would have employed more soldiers than would have been gained. And American power saved the collapsing allies in time.

In the general election that was held immediately after the war had ended on 11 November 1918, *Sinn Féin* in Ireland swept the Redmondite nationalists from the political scene, except in Ulster. There, where the unionists had a strong showing, the nationalist population were also less taken by the republicanism of *Sinn Féin* and returned some members of the old party. But, overall, the *Sinn Féin* victory was overwhelming. They elected seventy-three members of parliament. Twenty-three unionists were elected in Ulster, two by Trinity College and one by a Dublin surburban constituency. The *Sinn Féin* members had pledged themselves in advance not to take their seats in Westminster but to assemble in Ireland as the parliament of the republic that had been declared in 1919. The electorate endorsed the republic; but the electorate of east Ulster as clearly endorsed the union, with a clear majority in the Belfast region.

In Dublin the first assembly of *Dáil Éireann* (the parliament of Ireland) was held in the Mansion House in January 1916. A roll-call was taken. Twenty-eight *teachtaí dála* (deputies to parliament) were recorded as present, thirty-seven (mostly unionists) as absent, thirty-six as 'jailed by foreigners' and four as 'pursued by foreigners'. The *Dáil* passed an act defining its own powers, issued a declaration of independence and of a republic, appointed delegates to the peace conference, issued a message 'to the free nations of the world' and published a statement of principle entitled the 'democratic programme'. It appointed, initially, four ministers – for finance, internal affairs, external affairs and defence.

The *Dáil* attempted to set up an administration for the country, ignoring the *de facto* British administration. Its members swore allegiance to the republic. Although there was a minister for defence, the *Dáil* never succeeded in establishing adequate civilian control over the now reorganized Volunteers. These, especially the released 1916 internees, had become politically very active, through the GAA, the Gaelic League and *Sinn Féin*. They had brought out the vote, with ward-heeling efficiency and roughness, in the 1918 election. Many were impatient with the 'talking-shop' of the elected politicians, and they looked in the *Dáil*, not to the minister for defence but to the minister for finance, whom they felt to be one of their own. Michael Collins, from Co. Cork, had worked as a boy clerk in the post office in London. Still young, he came to Dublin for the Easter rising and was in the GPO garrison. Now he began to display a talent for intelligence work and for organizing military supplies.

The British immediately attempted to suppress *Dáil Éireann*, which however became accepted by most of the population as the legitimate parliament and government of the country. Soon violence began, initiated when the Volunteers began raiding for arms. The Volunteers, becoming commonly known as the Irish Republican Army, attacked the Royal Irish Constabulary. This armed police force, recruited in Ireland and stationed in barracks throughout the country (but constables were not placed in their home counties), besides doing regular police duties, methodically gathered political information and forwarded it regularly to Dublin castle. Now, in a campaign of ambushes, bombings and shootings, they were driven from their outlying barracks and forced back into the larger towns. Dublin castle was deprived of its eyes and ears. Troops were drafted into Ireland and auxiliary police forces were formed, one recruited from demobilized army officers, the other, less exclusively selected, soon to be known from its hastily assembled and motley attire as 'the black and tans'. These were to conduct vigorous forays into the rebellious countryside. Guerrilla war began, and the whole civilian population became involved through midnight searches for arms, curfews, proclamations of martial law, internment and, in due course, murder, and official reprisals (including the burning of towns) for IRA ambushes. Elected local authorities found themselves at odds with the central authorities, since they gave allegiance in many cases to the republic, not the crown. Crown forces in mufti murdered one lord mayor of Cork; another died after a seventy-three-day hunger strike in a British jail. Collins's people, particularly a special service unit known as 'the squad' pursued the police relentlessly. When the British sent over a number of military intelligence officers, under cover, to Dublin, to rebuild the Dublin castle intelligence system, Collins had them assassinated in their beds in simultaneous strikes early on the Sunday morning after their arrival.

By 1921 this clumsy deadly conflict had exhausted both sides. The British government understood from both police and military that to restore control in Ireland they would have to draft in tens of thousands more troops. The IRA was short of arms, of training, of places to hide and re-group, of competent leaders still at large. The *Dáil* had endeavoured with little success to have Ireland's case for self-determination heard at the peace conference in Paris and to have the republic internationally recognized. To fund their operations they issued bonds, and the president of the *Dáil*, Éamon de Valéra, a surviving Easter week commandant, spent months touring America, speaking to great and enthusiastic crowds on behalf of the republic.

Meanwhile, Lloyd George's government had come up with yet more constitutional legislation for Ireland. The Government of Ireland Act, 1920, partitioned the island into two parts, 'Northern Ireland', consisting of the six counties of Antrim, Down, Londonderry, Armagh, Tyrone and Fermanagh, and 'Southern Ireland', consisting of the remaining twenty-six counties. The line of division had been reached by tacit agreement with the Ulster unionists, who wanted as big an area as possible consistent with their being able to maintain a secure electoral majority. Three counties of

Ulster, Donegal, Cavan and Monaghan, were omitted because to include them would provide only the slimmest and most precarious unionist majority (several general elections had produced for all-Ulster an *anti-*unionist majority of one in terms of Westminster seats). Although half the area of the new 'Northern Ireland' had a nationalist majority, the great concentration round Belfast secured, overall, a two-to-one plurality for the unionists.

The act provided for two separate parliaments for Ireland, with devolved powers similar to those stipulated in the earlier home rule bills. It also provided for a 'council of Ireland' and for the possibility that Northern Ireland and Southern Ireland might re-unite, by consent. Elections were held for the two parliaments in May 1921. *Sinn Féin* and *Dáil Éireann* ignored the British act: in their view British law had no force in Ireland now. Only four members attended the parliament of 'Southern Ireland', to adjourn *sine die*. But in Belfast, the parliament of Northern Ireland was opened by the king on 22 June. In his speech he appealed for peace, clearly giving a signal for the beginning of negotiations with the *Dáil*. Public opinion in the world, and more importantly in Great Britain itself, had recoiled from what was happening in Ireland.

A truce was arranged and preliminary negotiations were conducted between de Valéra and Lloyd George. Then in December a negotiating team, headed by Griffith (vice-president of the *Dáil*) and Collins, was sent to London. They were offered much less than the republic that had been proclaimed in 1916 and 1919 and in due course they were put under great pressure, including the threat of 'immediate and terrible war' to sign terms that came far short of what their colleagues in Ireland hoped for. When they returned with their terms there was dismay. De Valéra, among others, was not prepared to accept them. But it had been a plenipotentiary delegation, and the articles of agreement had been signed. The British parliament proceeded to debate them straight away, in a special session just before Christmas.

The proposed treaty retained partition, and gave Northern Ireland the option, through the Belfast parliament, to continue the operation of the Government of Ireland Act, 1920, there. Those parts of that act which related to 'Southern Ireland' were to be replaced by a different arrangement. The twenty-six counties, to be known as the Irish Free State, were to have a status 'in relation to the Imperial Parliament and Government and otherwise . . . that of the Dominion of Canada'. The Irish Free State, in other words, was to have its own armed forces, revenues, postal services, laws and external relations. Britain however retained some naval and military bases on Free State territory and was to

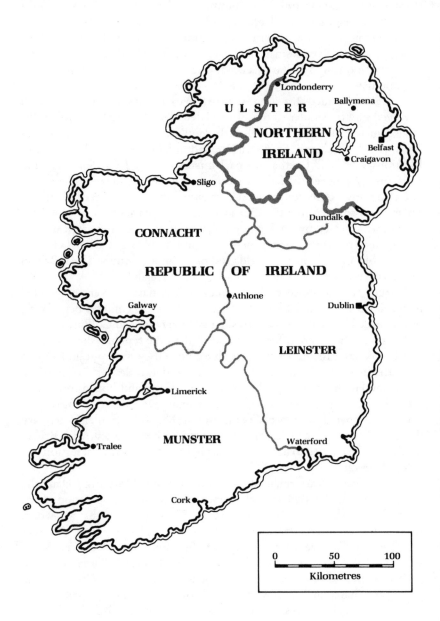

Map 20 Partition

have a supervisory voice in the new Free State constitution, which must embody the treaty itself.

The debate on the agreement in the British House of Commons was almost perfunctory, although with expressions of good will to Ireland. The king, in his very brief speech opening the session, said:

It was with heartfelt joy that I learnt of the Agreement reached after negotiations protracted for many months and affecting the welfare not only of Ireland, but of the British and Irish races throughout the world.

It is my earnest hope that by the Articles of Agreement now submitted to you the strife of centuries may be ended and that Ireland, as a free partner in the Commonwealth of Nations forming the British Empire, will secure the fulfilment of her national ideals. . . .[19]

J. R. Clynes, offering the full support of the labour party to the agreement, said: 'Some time or other the quarrel had to end, not only as between this country and Ireland, but as between the Northern part of Ireland and the South. It is better to end it now than to go on facing the certainty that at some future date, after greater losses and greater embitterment, statesmen will have to try again to serve the cause of peace and produce a settlement. . . .[20]

10 *Among the nations of the earth*

The treaty marked a war-weary pause. In the discussions that preceded it, the British government had been puzzled. The extremes which Irish opinion had revealed, not among tiny groups but apparently among large parts of the population, were unexpected: the widespread conviction that Ireland was and always had been a wholly distinct nation; the commitment to a republic. But for thirty years or more, British government had been growing aware, slowly, that the United Kingdom was overextended by imperial responsibilities. There was an uneasy sense of waning power, given most active expression in the abandonment of 'splendid isolation' at the beginning of the century. The Great War left Great Britain severely hurt in fortune and shocked by the loss of a whole generation of young upper-middle-class men, the faithful agents of its social system. Now, a victor nation in the war, the British found their empire in danger of being dismantled like those of Germany, Austria and Turkey. In the settlement they imposed on the Irish they tried to fashion the new federal empire (such as had been envisaged, for example, by Cecil Rhodes, a supporter of Irish home rule) that would maintain 'the British and Irish races throughout the world'.

The Irish who had voted for *Sinn Féin* were forced to awake from another dream. The Easter rising – a non-inevitable event if ever there was one – had come as a bolt from the blue; but for a while its aftermath had seemed to make possible what nationalist Ireland had been taught, for a century or more, to aspire to.

In the second half of the nineteenth century there were a few books which could be found, throughout Ireland, in nationalist homes. One of them was an anthology called *Speeches from the Dock*, and the best known speech in it was Robert Emmet's, made when he was condemned to death for his 1803 uprising. The most familiar words were: 'When my country takes her place among the nations of the earth, then, and not till then, let my epitaph be written.' Was it now time to write Emmet's epitaph? After all the excited expectations of the years from 1916 to 1921, no nationalist could assert that it was. But to some, a compromise had now been reached that seemed to open the way to it; to others it seemed to close the way.

In Westminster, the speeches made on the Anglo-Irish agreement reveal some mental laziness, stemming perhaps from weariness of what seemed further pointless bloodshed after the huge blood-letting of the Great War. Speakers repeatedly expressed satisfaction at the final solution of an old problem. But the problem was still there.

The Irish debate on the agreement took place, in *Dáil Éireann*, in December 1921 and January 1922. It was very different from the British debate. The division was sharp and harsh: between those who saw the treaty as the way forward to the republic, and those who saw it as a forswearing of the oath of allegiance to the republic which all had taken. The debate was long, bitter, recriminatory, and tragic. Inexorable fate seemed to take the centre of the stage on which the play of the republic had been mounted. It is of the greatest interest that partition was not the central issue – it was touched on only marginally. The question was the oath of allegiance to the crown. The sticking-point, when it came to it, was not 'the nation' (for all were nationalists) but monarchy as against democracy. Finally, on 7 January, the *Dáil* approved the treaty by sixty-four votes to fifty-seven. De Valéra, in the minority, resigned the presidency to Griffith and withdrew.

This led, in a matter of months, to civil war. The Irish Republican Army, still acting semi-autonomously, took its own vote on the treaty and divided off by units. The British army, once the treaty was ratified by both parliaments and the necessary arrangements had been made, began withdrawing from its barracks in the twenty-six counties. The union flag came down from public buildings, and the republican tricolour of green, white and orange went up – not the older green flag, displaying the harp without a crown, that had long been the nationalist banner. The tricolour, an invention of the days of Young Ireland, rarely seen since, had flown beside the green flag over the GPO in Dublin in Easter week and had become the '*Sinn Féin* flag'. It now became the official emblem of the new Irish state.

After some negotiations and an election the division remained between pro-treaty and anti-treaty forces, including armed forces. The government force, now the National Army, finally moved against the republicans. It was urged on, and supplied with some military equipment, by the British, who insisted that, whatever its difficulties, the new Dublin government must fulfil its obligations under the treaty. Fighting lasted for something over a year. The defeat of the republicans was bloodier than the 1916 rising or the guerrilla war against the British had been.

As the civil war went on, the Free State government acted ruthlessly and effectively against its opponents, reacting to terrorist tactics with state terror and executing a number of people without trial. It suffered its own losses. Collins, who had tried to avert war between former comrades-in-arms by organizing a clandestine campaign in Northern Ireland (contrary, of course, to the treaty) was killed in an ambush in Co. Cork, just a few days after Griffith died of a stroke. On the other side, de Valéra, who took over the political leadership of the republicans – but followed rather than led in the fighting – called ultimately for the laying down of their arms.

By and large it was social and political radicals of various shades who took the republican side in the civil war. Afterwards, for some time, the republicans remained outside parliamentary politics. They refused to take the oath of allegiance, which became a requirement for entry to the Free State *Dáil*. But the Labour Party, founded by James Connolly (who had been shot after the Easter rising by a British firing squad) had stood aside in the 1918 election, to give *Sinn Féin* and the national cause a clear field. It subsequently contested elections and formed the main opposition in the *Dáil*.

The government party was initially made up of members of *Sinn Féin* who had voted for the treaty, but, reorganized under the name *Cumann na nGaedheal*, it soon came to include other elements. It was a government of very young men when it first took office after the treaty. After the deaths of Collins and Griffith, its head for a decade was W. T. Cosgrave, who had experience of local government and who had been in the 1916 rising.

The civil war was destructive. In areas that were temporarily out of the government's control, republicans attempted social revolution, burning many homes of the gentry and others, in some places attempting experiments such as the setting-up of soviets. The government, which had begun (especially under Collins) by regarding the treaty as a measure that had been forced on Ireland, to be interpreted expediently and circumvented where possible, soon came to look on the treaty as an end in itself. This took place under the pressure of civil war, when the continued existence of the Free State and its government was in the balance for a while, when ministers and their staffs worked in siege conditions and in many parts of the country, outside their control, land was seized and the landlords' houses went up in flames. In this period, the strongest will to maintain government authority at all costs was displayed by Kevin O'Higgins, minister for home affairs and, later, for justice. In a belated act of violence, after peace had returned, he was assassinated in 1927.

By the mid 1920s the shape of the new Ireland, north and south, was beginning to be discernible. The previous fifteen years of upheaval at home and abroad had brought about sweeping political change. Home rule, on the lines envisaged since the 1880s, had been achieved, ironically, in Ulster, where the idea had been so powerfully resisted. On the rest of the island had been conferred, as it were out of the blue, 'dominion status'. This left two political questions to be answered: what, for the future of the British empire, did 'dominion status' mean?; and, would the people of the twenty-six counties accept dominion status in place of the all-Ireland republic that had, for five short years, appeared on their horizon like a mirage?

The transfer of land from landlords to tenants had accomplished a revolution. Social change now accelerated its completion. The protestant ascendancy had suddenly become a rapidly declining force. A catholic mercantile and professional class was now, precariously, in control, in alliance with the more substantial farmers. It was dependent, because of the instability of the country, on British good will and support. But the disorder and bloodshed had released forces of much more fundamental social change, and these the new government was determined to resist and subdue.

As the new state took shape, it revealed itself to be reactionary, extremely conservative and counter-revolutionary. The church had in effect, after 1914, abandoned its tacit alliance with the nationalist parliamentary party (which had been perceived, rightly, as representing conservative catholic interests in Ireland) but had given no further clear direction until after the treaty was signed. Then the bishops unequivocally supported the Free State government. The government in turn fully supported the bishops and, by privately consulting them on a wide variety of legislative matters in which they felt the church had a legitimate interest, made them in effect partners in government.

The church had all the more influence because of the huge migration that had established catholic communities of Irish origin and settlement in many parts of the world. Emigration had continued until the Great War, as the population of Ireland continued to decline. By 1911 there were little more than half as many inhabitants of the island as there had been in 1841. But in the USA, Great Britain, Canada, Australia and other places there were now many millions of Irish origin and, very often, of Irish sentiment.

Within Ireland, new church building, going on since before emancipation, had supplied the re-invigorated parish system with basic requirements. The national school system had met the demands, not only of the Roman catholic church, but of the other churches, by a compromise which gave the churches considerable control over the subject-matters of the instruction of very young people. Religious orders of nuns, priests and brothers, many of them directly concerned with teaching, had been founded or re-introduced, and their convents and monasteries were becoming increasingly numerous in the towns and countryside. Many of the landlords' houses were to come into the hands of religious orders, so that in certain aspects the Irish social landscape was to come to seem to be disconcertingly intermediate in character between Spanish and English.

The Jesuits, besides offering to the sons of more prosperous catholics a pastiche of the English public-school system, had struggled to maintain a catholic university. In 1908, the university question had reached a conclusion of a sort with the setting-up of the National University of Ireland, with colleges in Dublin, Cork and Galway. The Queen's University of Belfast was independent of this system, as was the University of Dublin (Trinity College). Although the National University was secular by charter, and was declared by the Roman catholic church to be quite unsatisfactory for catholic education, none the less the university structure in practice, then and in the decades that followed, reflected the denominational division.

Missionary activity had become important in the work of the church by the turn of the century. As well as going out in their hundreds of thousands as secular migrants, young Irishmen and women in growing numbers went in the service of the church to a great variety of places, including Africa (especially West Africa), India, China and South America, as well as the cities of Britain and North America. The point was reached, before the middle of the twentieth century, when approximately a third of the Roman catholic bishops of the world bore Irish names. And one lay organization, the 'Legion of Mary', founded by Frank Duff in Dublin in the 1920s, was to come to have much influence in what was later to be known as 'the third world'. This world-wide activity of Irish catholicism followed great protestant activity of a similar character in the eighteenth and nineteenth centuries, exemplified by the part played by Irish methodists in establishing methodism in the United States, and by Irish protestant missionary activity in nineteenth-century China.

Emigration had virtually ceased for a few years after the beginning of the Great War. In the 1920s it began again. Independence had not provided a living for all the people of the new Free State. On the contrary, many people and many areas were worse off than they had been. Agriculture was inefficient, but had enjoyed something of a boom during the war when Great Britain (the principal market) had had the greatest difficulty in importing food from farther afield. But, in spite of the co-operative and other improving movements, Irish producers had not equipped or adjusted themselves to compete in the world market created by developments in transport, refrigeration and communication.

Here and there the British withdrawal had local depressive effects, notably in the garrison towns. The new political border had disruptive effects on nearby towns, both in Northern Ireland and in the Irish Free State. And the uncertainty of the future, the breakdown of order, the neglect of maintenance of services and communications during the troubled years, all had an unfavourable effect on what was already a primitive and impoverished economy.

In the early and middle 1920s there were some significant movements of people. Many unionists, mostly protestants, moved from the new Free State, either across the border into Northern Ireland or to Britain or the colonies. Some catholic nationalists moved from Northern Ireland into the Free State. Committed republicans, harassed by the Free State police, went in some numbers to America, where they found sympathizers to receive and help them, and founded an attitude among sections of Irish-American society which regarded the Free State, as they themselves did, as an illegitimate usurpation of nationalist Ireland.

The new government, in its initial concern to maintain the state, was faced not only with its external republican opponents but with some internal remnants of the revolutionary spirit. The army and the government itself underwent purges which cast out or silenced for a time those who tried to sustain the spirit or the views of the years from 1916 to 1921. In the process the army was brought firmly under civilian control. It was not possible to continue the Royal Irish Constabulary in any form: that force had been too unpopular. A new police force was formed, the *Garda Síochána* ('guard of the peace', or 'civic guard'), which was unarmed, although it was established in circumstances of civil war. To arm a new force, of whatever kind, at that juncture would have been to tempt fate. In fact the new force was able to gain some public confidence just because it did not carry weapons. But, like the old RIC, it was centralized and housed in barracks.

The civil servants in Ireland had the option, under the treaty, to retire on favourable terms. Despite this, large numbers elected to remain. The British-founded administration carried on, through the very difficult years 1922 and 1923, and by the time the civil war came to an end the state machinery was functioning just as it had been before the British left. More significantly, the attempts that had been made in the time of revolutionary fervour to set up an alternative to the British legal system were wholly rejected. There seems to have been no serious attempt, for example, to consider the continental system stemming from the Code Napoleon.

Instead, the archaic but familiar tradition, with all its trappings and rituals, was retained in full, subject only to some administrative modifications, and the injustices and discriminations inherent in it were perpetuated.

There were a few new departures. A written constitution was adopted in 1922, after some difficulties with the British government, which was concerned to see to it that no circumvention of the treaty was involved. A policy directed to the revival of the Irish language was developed. Irish was to be taught in the schools, so that the coming generations would speak the language. But there were difficulties, including a shortage of teachers competent to carry out this task. And placing the onus on the children relieved the adult population of responsibility in the matter. The enthusiasm that had brought tens of thousands to regular language classes not very long before had now dissipated.

The catholic church came to have a say in the formulation of government policy which it had not previously enjoyed. Otherwise, efforts were made to prevent rather than to encourage change. In economic and some political matters British *laissez-faire* liberalism in its nineteenth-century form was taken as a guide. Even the limited social services that the United Kingdom had introduced since the beginning of the twentieth century were plainly regarded as somewhat adventurous. Bourgeois values were so accepted that balancing the books was regarded as high political virtue – to the extent that there were cuts in old-age pensions and, in some cases, in the wages of the poorest paid.

Divorce had been available to the rich who could afford to sponsor a private member's bill in parliament (an interesting vestige of the old aristocratic custom of polygyny, persistent in Christian Europe). The church made it clear that this was not acceptable, and it ended. The state attempted to enforce Roman catholic moral rules in private as well as in public life, with considerable support from the protestant churches, which at this time had not yet been fully converted to nineteenth-century liberalism. In due course the censorship of books, for example, reached absurd lengths.

North of the border, the new arrangements stemmed from a longer-standing counter-revolution. After the passage of the Government of Ireland Act, 1920, which partitioned the country, but before the first parliament of Northern Ireland met in 1921, the British government began the reorganization of the newly defined entity, 'Northern Ireland', to meet the circumstances of the all-Ireland revolt of the time. A new armed reserve police force was locally recruited, some full time, some part time. There were initially 'A', 'B' and 'C' classes of special constables. Class B – part time constables doing duty in their own localities and bringing their weapons home with them – was in practice a protestant force, largely made up of those who had joined the UVF before the war. It was given a fairly free hand. By now the general Irish conflict had acquired an added venom in Ulster. It was there, in part, a continuation of the inter-denominational conflict that had been occurring sporadically for many years.

When the first Northern Ireland parliament met in 1921, it had, of course, an overwhelmingly unionist membership (most nationalists went to *Dáil Éireann*). It elected Sir James Craig as its first prime minister. The tasks facing the new government chiefly concerned the safeguarding of the political territory that had been carved out for it by the Government of Ireland Act. This act was given no recognition by *Dáil Éireann*, and the IRA was as active in the six counties as in the twenty-six. The government had to retain such control as it could in these circumstances (it took over internal security, but was precluded by the terms of the act from directing the military: this was reserved, with other major powers, to London). It had to ensure that in dealing with the republican insurgents the British government did not renege on partition. After the treaty was signed, it had to handle, as best it could, the provision (in the treaty) for a boundary commission to examine and if necessary recommend a re-drawing of the border.

As the government of Northern Ireland had not been a party to the treaty, it felt it could best deal with the boundary commission by ignoring it. Craig refused to appoint a representative of Northern Ireland to sit on the commission, although the appointment had been provided for. The British government therefore made the appointment, choosing a Belfast unionist, J. R. Fisher; but the Belfast government was uncompromised should the commission, consulting the 'wishes of the inhabitants', decide to remove territory from Northern Ireland. The Dublin government nominated Eoin MacNeill as its representative on the commission. A South African, Justice Feetham, was appointed as chairman. The commission eventually was moving towards recommending a revision of the border unfavourable to the Irish Free State. MacNeill resigned; Cosgrave conferred in London with Craig and the British government, and on 3 December 1925 signed an agreement recognizing the existing border.

In Northern Ireland, as in the Irish Free State, a civil war took place. The protestants mounted a ferocious onslaught on the catholics; the IRA retaliated with reprisals, including the assassination of politicians. In this conflict, in 1922, 232 people were killed in Northern Ireland. The Free State, in its early months, attempted in various ways both to protect the northern catholics and to withhold recognition from Northern Ireland. A boycott was attempted against northern goods, products and trade. But by 1924, Northern Ireland, like the Irish Free State, could be seen to have survived. By Christmas of that year curfew was lifted from Belfast, after four and a half years.

The Royal Irish Constabulary was disbanded in 1922 and was replaced by a new force, the Royal Ulster Constabulary. Establishment of the RUC as a single, centralized, force had been recommended by a committee set up by the Belfast minister of home affairs. The committee also recommended that the force should have a strength up to 3000, a third of whom should be catholic. Although catholics were recruited, their numbers never brought them up to this proportion. The special constabulary, previously established by the British government, remained a wholly protestant force. The RUC, like the RIC, was a paramilitary armed body with political intelligence functions.

The police were given extraordinary powers through the Civil Authorities (Special Powers) Act 1922, under which the minister of home affairs had authority to make regulations which could suspend virtually all civil liberties.

The security of the state was the chief initial concern of the Northern Ireland as of the Free State government. But the problem was different. The six-county area was an arbitrary device designed to contain the largest possible territory (about 6000 square miles, or less than 2 million hectares) which would yet provide a safe unionist electoral majority of two to one. But what was electorally safe was not necessarily safe in circumstances of civil war. The IRA's guerrilla war against Britain had been conducted throughout Ireland, and they, of course, gave no recognition to the border. The British army remained in Northern Ireland when it withdrew from the Free State, and its arms were available to sustain the new partition arrangement (although on behalf of the British, not the Northern, government – an important distinction that derived from the provisions of the Government of Ireland Act). But a campaign of terror domestically directed was the main weapon employed to defend the new arrangement. It was wielded, mostly, unofficially. The course of the civil war south of the border soon saw the IRA in the North, as well as in the Free State, in a hopeless position. But these years of conflict left the people of Northern Ireland more bitterly divided and embittered than before.

Northern Ireland had, in truth, an impossibly divided community. Most protestants not only supported the union but, after several generations of political and physical conflict, they supported it vehemently and determinedly. They were not, however, a homogeneous community, either socially or politically. The total number of protestants of all denominations was to the number of catholics as about two to one. About 45 per cent of the protestant population consisted of presbyterians, about 37 per cent of anglicans, and the rest of methodists, Plymouth brethren, baptists, congregationalists and smaller groups.

Among all these there were different interests and different approaches to general political questions. But they did not want catholic government from Dublin. The catholic third of the population of the newly defined area was, by and large, opposed to the union, opposed therefore to the distinct political existence of Northern Ireland. These nationalists refused consent both to the continued British rule of the area and to the home rule of the Belfast parliament. In practice, the withholding of consent was compromised in a thousand ways from the day the border was established: people had to live their day-to-day lives. But under the rule of parliamentary democracy it created a fundamental problem for the state.

The British government, which was supreme (in all matters the parliament of Northern Ireland was subservient to Westminster), dealt with the problem by withdrawing its attention from it as far as possible. It left the matter to the subordinate parliament in Belfast. Some of the Belfast politicians, at the beginning, believing that the future of Northern Ireland must involve accommodation of the nationalists, tried to initiate measures (in educational policy, for example) that would tend to close the denominational divide, or cross it. But they were quite unsuccessful. Neither the catholics nor the greater part of the protestants would co-operate.

Politics became distorted as a result. Elections were plebiscites, fought on the issue of the union. The unionist, or conservative, party always won, drawing votes from people who would in other circumstances vote for labour, liberal or other candidates. The unionists, without British interference but with the ultimate backing of British power, used their own power, derived from this, to operate a system which in practice kept the catholic nationalists under social, political and military control. The Northern Ireland system of government looked like the British system, and in many ways it was like it; but in other ways it was quite different. The Special Powers Act, suspending at government will the whole libertarian operation of British government, was perhaps the most significant legal distinction. But, probably more important was the political and social behaviour of the two cohabiting but bitterly opposed communities. This is what made the most striking difference, leading, for example, to half a century of one-party rule in the Belfast (later Stormont) parliament.

After a decade of operation, partition had created a stark contrast. The

Free State government had very thoroughly and effectively defeated the republicans. In the process it had largely purged its own republican past and had relied heavily on the moral authority and support of the Roman catholic church. It had, practically without cavil, accepted the church's own view of its proper role in the state. It had followed deeply conservative social and economic policies. Cosgrave had made an attempt to conciliate the unionists in the Free State, appointing a number of them to the senate, as was his prerogative under the constitution. But some of these were alarmed by the ways in which the Free State attempted to impose on its citizens the current views of the catholic church about how they should behave and what they should (or, rather, shouldn't) read – including much of current literature. Some protestants shared the same views, but some, not all of them unionists, did not. Yeats in a famous speech to the senate, to which Cosgrave had appointed him, accused the government, in the matter of divorce, of turning meanly on the Anglo-Irish – 'no petty people'. The government party, *Cumann na nGaedheal*, with its depressed and depressing view of its function in the new independent Ireland, began to show some signs of disintegration, as farmers, old parliamentarians and others hived off to form special interest groups supporting the government on most issues but not all.

Meanwhile de Valéra, after a spell in prison at the end of the civil war, showed himself to be politically ambitious and to have gained in the years since 1916 the unquestioning support of a section of the people. In his views on many social, economic and moral matters he had much in common with Cosgrave; but he had come into conflict with the bishops and Cosgrave had not. He now set about freeing himself from what he had called in a moment of stress 'the strait-jacket of the republic'. He did this, first, by separating himself from *Sinn Féin* (which he could not control) while taking pains in the process not to separate himself from the rhetoric of the republic; second, by founding, in 1926, his own party, *Fianna Fáil*; third, by devising a formula by which he could subscribe to the oath of allegiance (required under the constitution) while satisfyiing himself that he was not taking it, and so enter the *Dáil*. In two elections in 1927, *Fianna Fáil* left *Sinn Féin* far behind and showed itself to be a major electoral threat to the Cosgrave government. In 1932 *Fianna Fáil* won more seats than any other party and, with labour support (but not participation), was able to form a government.

By this time the world was in economic depression, and hunger was abroad in the land – as in many others. Northern Ireland had been depressed since partition, rallying only feebly in the general boom of the late 1920s. Its plodding and heavy-handed government had all but exhausted its creative energies in fending off destruction; its finances were precarious; its relations with Britain were difficult (mainly in financial matters) and it too had to cope with some fissiparous tendencies activated by extreme protestant and bluenose groups. By the early 1930s, beating the protestant drum was a large part of the political tactics of Craig and his ministers.

In 1932, the Irish political landscape presented a dreary scene: two restrictive, repressive and generally negative confessional systems aping the procedures of open societies. All the sound and fury of the early part of the century, far from leading to some creative anarchy, had produced this stasis. And the British withdrawal had left behind, like a constipating potion in the wells, the imperial civil service (which changed masters smoothly south and north of the border), the English legal system, and a governmental culture from which several essential elements (such as the 'old-boy network') were for the moment missing.

De Valéra and his party came to office in 1932 partly, perhaps, because they offered some echo of former excitements, something beyond the anti-climax of the 1920s. The change of government happened smoothly. Cosgrave's party had tried to stave off defeat by accusing *Fianna Fáil* of being communistic and anti-catholic. It was less than a decade since the two sides had been opposed in a bloody and savage civil war. *Cumann na nGaedheal* feared that when de Valéra came in he would proceed to dismantle the administration they had built up. Some in *Fianna Fáil* feared that the Free State army they had so recently fought would stage a coup to prevent them from taking office. Neither happened.

Other groups did not think that such orderly and mannerly transfers were either praiseworthy or for the good of the people who found themselves walking a mile to the well to fetch water before independence and a mile to the same well to fetch water after independence. Such groups, radical elements of *Sinn Féin* and splinters from it, were a small minority. None the less, in absolute numbers, the republicans from whom de Valéra had separated himself were still formidable enough. A rump of the IRA survived, and its 'army council' directed political activities (through *Sinn Féin*) as well as planning future uprisings. But in 1934, when some of these dissidents tried to bring the IRA, *Sinn Féin* and the whole 'republican movement' in the direction of radical socialism, they failed. *Fianna Fáil*, with populist programmes, propaganda and attitudes, had captured a significant mass of the people.

De Valéra's new Free State government set out to do two things: to heal the wounds to pride inflicted on a great part of the nation in 1921, especially by those clauses of the treaty which forced the sworn

republicans of three years earlier to return to allegiance to the king; and to
endeavour to make the Free State economically self-sufficient.

De Valéra proceeded to dismantle the treaty piecemeal and by ingenuity,
observing its letter and destroying its spirit. He did not, for example,
abolish the office of governor-general – the king's representative in the
Irish Free State. Instead, he made it absurd, nominating a follower of his
own, who was committed to making a nonsense of the office. He then
produced an involved legalistic argument against continuing to transmit to
Great Britain the land annuities collected from Irish farmers, in repayment
of the purchase price advanced by the British government to buy out the
landlords. The basis of the counter-claim against the British government
was an argument that Ireland had been overtaxed for a prolonged period
under the Union.

The British reacted to this by imposing heavy duties on Irish products,
and the Irish government retaliated with its own duties on British imports.
The ensuing tariff-war, known in Ireland as the 'economic war', brought
hardship to the countryside, since it hit the cattle trade, but it also rallied
support for de Valéra as Ireland's champion against England.

The *Fianna Fáil* government also moved rapidly away from
participation in the devolution and development of the British empire.
Cosgrave's government had shown an interest in this, using the 'Canadian'
status conferred on the Free State to advance hand-in-hand with Canada
to the greater autonomy which the dominions achieved through the treaty
of Westminster. De Valéra's interest was different: he tried to have Ireland
play a part 'among the nations of the earth'; and he took much more
interest in the League of Nations. President of the Council of the League
in the early 1930s, he played a part, modestly strutting his hour. He spoke
more frankly and bluntly than was customary, not merely to denounce
aggression. He stated the case that world peace depended on the League
acting when aggression occurred – not just when the interests of great
powers were directly involved. He seemed to be committing Ireland to
join in collective action on such terms, but to indicate that it was not
prepared to do so when the great powers, wholly in their own interests,
were calling the tune. However, he was diplomatically skilled, and what
he seemed to say was not explicit.

This democratic attitude was not confined to the world stage. In office,
de Valéra became much more of a democrat than he had been in
opposition. An inept pseudo-fascist movement, the Army Comrades
Association, or 'blueshirts', was formed by elements of the former
government party. They were organized initially to defend freedom of
speech at the political meetings which, in the early 1930s, were often

broken up violently. But the defenders of free speech formed themselves into military-style units and, in their uniforms, salutes and march-tunes, emulated the nazis and fascists. De Valéra coped with them, not without some rough assistance from the IRA, still quite active and forcefully opposed to fascism and to 'Free Staters'. But overall, political violence had declined. The blueshirts were soon diverted to Spain where an Irish brigade spent some time supporting (if not actually fighting for) General Franco and Christian civilization. At the same time, another Irish contingent, in the International Brigade, fought for the Spanish republic on the Guadarrama.

Ireland gradually moved away from 'dominion' status. De Valéra took advantage of the British abdication crisis, when Edward VIII resigned the throne, to rush through legislation which reduced the king to a cipher in Irish affairs. In 1937 he placed before the electorate of the Irish Free State a new constitution, which was approved by a fairly narrow margin. This instrument, which has no mention of the king, made the country virtually a republic. To have the constitution passed by referendum, it was necessary not to be opposed by the church. De Valéra, a believing and practising catholic himself, was quite prepared to pay the price exacted for this. He wrote into the document many sections, including an absolute prohibition of divorce, that attempted to express the ethos of a catholic people by embodying in the clauses much of the catholic social teaching fashionable at the time.

For example, Article 41.1 states that:

1^0 The State recognises the Family as the natural primary and fundamental unit group of Society, and as a moral institution possessing inalienable and imprescriptible rights, antecedent and superior to all positive law.

2^0 The State, therefore, guarantees to protect the Family in its constitution and authority, as the necessary basis of social order and as indispensable to the welfare of the Nation and the State.

Article 41.2 states:

1^0 In particular, the State recognises that by her life within the home, woman gives to the State a support without which the common good cannot be achieved.

Article 43 deals with property:

1. 1^0 The State acknowledges that man, in virtue of his rational being, has the natural right, antecedent to positive law, to the private ownership of external goods.

2° The State accordingly guarantees to pass no law attempting to abolish the right of private ownership or the general right to transfer, bequeath, and inherit property.

On religion, Article 44 states:

1. 1° The State acknowledges that the homage of public worship is due to Almighty God. It shall hold His Name in reverence, and shall respect and honour religion.

2° The State recognises the special position of the Holy Catholic Apostolic and Roman Church as the guardian of the Faith professed by the great majority of the citizens. [This section has been repealed by a subsequent referendum.]

3° The State also recognises the Church of Ireland, the Presbyterian Church in Ireland, the Methodist Church in Ireland, the Religious Society of Friends in Ireland, as well as the Jewish Congregations and the other denominations existing in Ireland at the date of the coming into operation of this Constitution.

2. 1° Freedom of conscience and the free profession and practice of religion are, subject to public order and morality, guaranteed to every citizen.[1]

These articles illustrate, among other matters, how the perception of women's place in political society had shifted from the equal comradeship that appears to be envisaged in documents of the revolutionary period to the *Küche, Kirche, Kinder* outlook of 1937.

Protestants had their civil and religious rights guaranteed, but the protestant proportion of the population of the Free State, which had declined sharply in the unionist exodus after partition, was continuing to decline, although more slowly. This was in large part due not to state policy but to the operation of the *Ne Temere* decree promulgated by Pope Pius X to come into effect on 19 April 1908. *Ne Temere* clarified catholic rulings on marriage, and it affected marriages between Roman catholics and other baptized persons. Such marriages must, according to the rulings, be celebrated before a catholic priest with the prior consent of both parties and with a commitment to bring up the children of the marriage as Roman catholics. The effect of *Ne Temere* was that in the many parts of the country where protestants had become very few in number, they must choose from a too-limited range of possible marriage partners of protestant faith, or migrate, or, by marrying catholics who followed their church's ruling, reduce the number of protestants in the next generation. By 1971, protestants of all denominations formed less than 5 per cent of the population of the state.

The 1937 constitution coped less than thoroughly with what had become known as the 'national aspirations' – to reunification and to the revival of the Irish language. Irish became the first official language of the state, although English was also an official language. An implicit claim to jurisdiction over the whole island was embodied in the preliminary Articles 2 and 3, although the succeeding body of the constitution applies to the *de facto* twenty-six-county state. No effort was made to express the ethos of a protestant people.

The state ceased to be the Irish Free State and was named instead 'Ireland'. Since this, of course, was and is the name of the whole island (another implicit claim to jurisdiction), there was now no correct way of referring to the *de facto* state, which immediately began to be called by the Irish word for Ireland – *Éire*.

In the 1930s, the state achieved a modest degree of self-sufficiency. The government had applied a tariff-protected import-substitution policy, something like what Arthur Griffith's *Sinn Féin* had advocated at the beginning of the century. The self-sufficiency was to be put to the test when war broke out in Europe on 1 September 1939. A few years later, during the war, in 1943, de Valéra broadcast an address to mark the fiftieth anniversary of the foundation of the Gaelic League. Looking back and reflecting on the ideals of the turn of the century, he evoked a famous image:

That Ireland which we dreamed of would be the home of a people who valued material wealth only as the basis of right living, of a people who were satisfied with frugal comfort and devoted their leisure to the things of the spirit – a land whose countryside would be bright with cosy homesteads, whose fields and villages would be joyous with the sound of industry, with the romping of sturdy children, the contests of athletic youth and the laughter of comely maidens, whose firesides would be forums for the wisdom of serene old age. It would, in a word, be the home of a people living the life that God desires that man should live.[2]

In 1938 the Irish government reached an agreement with Chamberlain's government in Britain, which ended the 'economic war' and by which the British agreed to vacate the ports and bases they occupied in Irish Free State territory under the terms of the treaty of 1921. The question of Irish re-unification was discussed, producing some anxiety in the government of Northern Ireland, but this discussion made no progress.

De Valéra offered Northern Ireland 'home rule within home rule' – that Stormont could retain its existing degree of autonomy, but under Dublin rather than London. The offer was rejected with contempt by Lord Craigavon (formerly Sir James Craig), the Northern prime minister. De

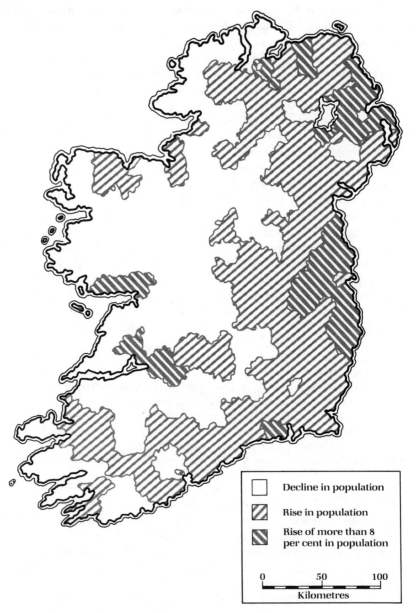

Map 21 Population change 1966–71
Based on the *Atlas of Ireland* (Royal Irish Academy, Dublin, 1979, pp. 52–3
(Department of Geography, Trinity College, Dublin), simplified).

Valéra was by now attempting to suppress the IRA, but that organization, although much reduced both in numbers and in the support it commanded since the 1920s and early 1930s, was reorganized and militant. It 'declared war' on Great Britain and began exploding bombs in that country. De Valéra introduced legislation suspending some of the liberties guaranteed (except in state of emergency) in his new constitution, and proceeded against the IRA, almost as ruthlessly as the first Free State government had proceeded against his own comrades at the time of the civil war.

Northern Ireland, as part of the United Kingdom, was involved in war with Germany from 3 September 1939. De Valéra had the support of all the political parties in the *Dáil* in declaring the Irish state's neutrality. There were not many sympathizers with Nazi Germany in the country (although there were some) but a large part of Irish public opinion regarded Great Britain as the cause of Irish partition and as a power still wrongfully occupying part of Ireland.

As it happened, the state succeeded in remaining neutral throughout the war. Both German and British leaders considered invasion of Ireland, both concluded that the probable disadvantages outweighed the possible advantages. In so far as it was consistent with formal neutrality, however, de Valéra's government (in office throughout the period) collaborated with the Allies and was wholly successful in controlling German attempts to use Ireland as a base for espionage and other operations.

The experience of neutrality in world war both confirmed Irish independence and revealed the great economic and other weaknesses of independent Ireland. Emigration, increasing through the 1930s, reached a very high level in wartime, as thousands of Irish people joined the British labour or fighting forces. The population continued to decline, but the state was unable to support even the greatly reduced numbers (which fell, in the post-war period, to little more than 2.8 million in the twenty-six counties).

De Valéra retired from party politics in 1959, when he was elected president. He had been prime minister from 1932 to 1948, from 1951 to 1954, and again from 1957 to 1959. Ironically, it was John A. Costello, leader of Cosgrave's old party (now called *Fine Gael*), who, as prime minister in the inter-party government of 1948–51, declared a republic and took the Irish state finally out of the British Commonwealth.

By then the deficiencies of the *Fianna Fáil* import-substitution policies were becoming plain. Government policy had helped to provide jobs in small industries but they were balanced by jobs lost on the land. Emigration in the 1950s increased to numbers that began to match the great outflow at the end of the previous century. Most of the migrants, however, now went to Great Britain. And at home the population was ageing, with a very high proportion of unmarried people.

This marked a cultural, social and economic crisis, the nature of which it is too soon to discern clearly. It was taking place around 1950, immediately after the war, and, in different ways, it was to affect all Ireland by the 1960s.

De Valéra's successor as *Fianna Fáil* leader and prime minister, Séan Lemass, presided over a wholly new direction in policy that reflected the crisis. The state turned away from protectionist and self-sufficiency programmes and began to plan vigorously to attract investment from abroad and to open up to world trade. In due course a free-trade agreement was made with Great Britain, and in 1973 Ireland and Great Britain (along with Denmark) joined the European Economic Community.

Ireland had come to independence with a moderately good infrastructure, largely formed under the union: near-universal literacy, fairly good internal and external communications, good information, administrative and cultural resources. In the 1930s, 1940s and 1950s, the state, through an increasing number of 'semi-state companies', had intervened positively in many areas of economic and social life: in energy and power, food processing (as in the beet-sugar industry), transport and communications, industrial development and marketing, the bloodstock business, and many others. The country now had an experienced managerial class, which showed great capacity in the development of such businesses as airlines (Aer Lingus, established in the 1930s), shipping (largely a wartime enterprise) and the imaginative utilization of available resources, such as the peat bogs.

In the 1960s and in the early 1970s the face of Ireland began to be transformed by the signs of a new prosperity. After the country joined the EEC this was very marked on the farms. A rapid and startling demographic change took place. The population of the state rose sharply, to almost 3.5 million people, of whom, in the early 1980s, about half were under 25 years old. Meanwhile, just as suddenly, the world recession which followed the oil crisis of 1973 seemed to undo the new prosperity, or part of it, for a while.

In the North, the experiment in home rule devolution that was initiated by the Government of Ireland Act, 1920, lasted, after a fashion, for just over half a century, until 1972. The fundamental division in the community on the issue of the constitution placed on Northern Ireland a strain which ultimately reached breaking-point. In many ways Northern Ireland functioned like a normal part of the United Kingdom. But in many ways it did not. Its institutions, for example, were centralized in an un-

English way (as, incidentally, were those of the independent state south of the border).

But the serious tensions arose from the need, perceived throughout the period by the unionist local majority in the area, to keep the nationalist minority from taking over. The general tolerance which by the late twentieth century had become one of the happier manifestations of British society (at its peak in the 1960s, since declining) was absent. Hostility and tension led to the practice of kinds of discrimination which were effective enough in the depressed and hungry 1930s. There was one serious outbreak of violence in Belfast in the mid 1930s, mainly directed against catholics. The IRA continued a shadowy existence, and during the war, north as well as south, made some very unsuccessful efforts to become effective allies of Britain's enemy, Germany. After the war, in the late 1950s, the IRA attempted a campaign of sabotage and armed raids along the border which was even less successful, partly, as they admitted, because of lack of public support, partly because of firm action against them by both Irish governments.

However, the British post-war welfare state gave opportunities, most importantly in education, to the more deprived section of the population, which was predominantly, although not wholly, catholic. The higher catholic birth-rate had not led to more than a very slight increase in the catholic proportion of the population because of differential emigration, the result of different economic circumstances. That began to change. And when a post-war generation of catholics, from a background of unemployment and poverty, achieved not only secondary but university education, they rebelled against conditions they found intolerably irksome. The rebellion took the form of a civil rights agitation, which was met by Stormont prohibitions and clumsy police force. Violence became widespread, leading to the deployment of large numbers of British soldiers on the Ulster streets. The IRA revived, in a distinctive Northern form, the 'Provisionals', who drew on the long tradition of denominational conflict in Ulster.

The bloodshed that ensued led to the suspension of the 1920 constitution by the British parliament and government in 1972. Great Britain took over direct rule of Northern Ireland, and, after some experiments, this settled down to a proconsular style. The duration and character of the violence in the North pointed up both the difference in experience between the people of the Republic and the people of Northern Ireland and the difference in outlook that had developed over half a century.

But these events are too close for their meaning to be very clearly discernible. The consequences of the crisis of the post-war decade in

Figure 19   Bogside, Derry, 1957
After a photograph by Paul Kavanagh, published by Glen Photography, Dundalk, Ireland.

Ireland are still working themselves out. In the 1980s the country is undergoing rapid and unpredictable change. Its population is, in the 1980s, about 5 million; of whom perhaps a little over 850,000 are Ulster protestant unionists and loyalists. It has urbanized in ways which in some respects resemble urbanization in the 'third world', and Dublin, with more than a million people, has grown to be twice the size of Belfast. The population, while growing (by more than half a million in about twenty years) has also shifted to the east coast, north and south of the border. The young urban population are in many ways inhabitants of what McLuhan called the 'global village' of the late twentieth century. They are shaping a new history.

Notes

Chapter 1   Before history

1 Sir Cyril Fox, *The Personality of Britain: its influence on inhabitant and invader in prehistoric and early historic times* (Cardiff 1932), pp. 25–35; Sir H. J. Mackinder, *Britain and the British Seas* (Oxford 1906).

2 See the discussion on Estyn Evans, *The Personality of Ireland: Habitat, Heritage and History* (2nd edn) (Belfast 1981), pp. 35–37.

3 G. Eogan, *Excavations at Knowth – 1*, Royal Irish Academy Monographs in Archaeology (1) (Dublin 1984); see also, M. J. O'Kelly, *Newgrange: archaeology, art and legend* (London 1982).

4 Gordon Childe, *The Prehistory of European Society* (Harmondsworth 1958), p. 172.

5 Sean P. Ó Ríordáin, 'A Burial with Faience Beads at Tara', *Proceedings of the Prehistoric Society*, 21 (1955), pp. 163–73.

6 Frank Mitchell, *The Irish Landscape* (London 1976), p. 158.

7 Frank Mitchell, *The Irish Landscape*, p. 163.

Chapter 2   Celtic Ireland

1 David Greene, *The Irish Language* (Cork 1966), pp. 6–7.

2 Heinrich Wagner, 'Near Eastern and African Connections with the Celtic World', in Robert O'Driscoll (ed.), *The Celtic Consciousness* (Toronto, Mountrath and Edinburgh) (Mountrath and Edinburgh edn 1982), pp. 51–67.

3 See J. D. Bateson, 'Roman material from Ireland: A re-consideration', *Proceedings of the Royal Irish Academy*, 73C (1973), pp. 21–97; R. A. G. Carson and Claire O'Kelly, 'A catalogue of the Roman coins from Newgrange, Co. Meath, and notes on the coins and related finds', *Proceedings of the Royal Irish Academy*, 77C (1977), pp. 35–55; Atlas der Urgeschichte Band 1, Hans Jürgen Eggers, *Der Römische Import im freien Germanien* (Hamburg 1951).

4 Alwyn and Brindley Rees, *Celtic Heritage* (London 1961), pp. 146–72.

5 David Sproule has pointed out that: 'It does not seem that the word *Connacht* can originally have meant "the descendants of Conn": it may have meant "headship" or "supremacy" from *cond* or *conn* "head" and later have been

interpreted as meaning "the descendants of Conn", Conn Cétchathach being derived from the word *Connacht* rather than *vice versa*.' The suffix *-acht*, he points out, is not a collective suffix but an abstract suffix, as in *filedhacht*, 'poetry'. D. Sproule, 'Origins of the Éoganachta', *Ériu*, **35** (1984), pp. 31–7; see also F. J. Byrne, *Irish Kings and High-Kings* (London 1973), p. 168: 'The terms Leth Cuinn and Leth Moga are, however, also capable of another interpretation: namely, "the chief's half", and "the slave's half".'

6 D. A. Binchy, 'Secular Institutions', in Myles Dillon (ed.), *Early Irish Society* (Dublin 1954), p. 56.

7 G. Dumézil, *Mythe et Épopée: l'idéologie des trois fonctions dans les Epopées des Peuples Indo Européens* (Paris 1968); see also the discussion by Proinsias MacCana in *Celtic Mythology* (Rushden 1984), pp. 59–61.

8 F. J. Byrne, *Irish Kings and High-Kings* (London 1973), p. 30.

9 See Desmond McCourt, 'The dynamic quality of Irish rural settlement', in Buchanan, Jones and McCourt (eds.), *Man and his Habitat: Essays presented to Emyr Estyn Evans* (London 1971), pp. 126–64.

Chapter 3   Church and state

1 J. P. Migne (ed.), *Patrilogiae Latinae*, vol. 51: Prosper of Aquitaine, *Chronicum integrum*.

2 Charles Thomas, 'Saint Patrick and fifth-century Britain; an historical model explored', in P. J. Casey (ed.), BAR British series 71 (Oxford 1979), *The End of Roman Britain*, pp. 81–101, esp. pp. 86–7.

3 K. Meyer, *Sanas Cormaic: An Old-Irish glossary compiled by Cormac Úa [Macc] Cuilennain* (Halle 1912), p. 1000.

4 J. J. O'Meara (ed and trans.), *Giraldus Cambrensis (Gerald of Wales): The History and Topography of Ireland*, (revised edn) (Mountrath 1982), p. 84.

5 W. Stokes (ed.), *Félire Oengusso Céli Dé* (Henry Bradshaw Society 1905), pp. 23–7; text and translation in David Green and Frank O'Connor, *A Golden Treasury of Irish Poetry A.D. 600 to 1200* (London 1967), pp. 61–6.

6 Máire MacNeill, *The Festival of Lughnasa: a study of the survival of the Celtic festival of the beginning of harvest* (Oxford 1962), *passim*.

7 John Kelleher, 'Early Irish History and Pseudo-History', *Studia Hibernica*, **3** (1963), p. 118.

8 L. Bieler (ed.), *The Irish Penitentials (Scriptores Latini Hiberniae*, vol. 5) (Dublin 1963), pp. 74–95.

9 David Greene and Frank O'Connor, *A Golden Treasury of Irish Poetry A.D. 600 to 1200* (London 1967), pp. 27–32.

10 Greene and O'Connor, *ibid*, pp. 148–50.

11 L. de Paor, 'The Art of the Celtic Peoples', in R. O'Driscoll (ed.), *The Celtic Consciousness* (Mountrath and Edinburgh 1982), p. 126.

12 A. O. and M. O. Anderson (eds.), *Adomnan's Life of Columba* (London 1961), pp. 474–5.

Chapter 4   The sword-land

1   Donncha Ó Corráin, *Ireland before the Normans* (Dublin 1972), p. 127.
2   A. Gwynn, 'The Irish Missal of Corpus Christi College, Oxford', in C. W. Dugmore and C. Duggan (eds.), *Studies in Church History*, vol. 1 (London 1964), pp. 47–68.
3   E. Curtis and R. B. McDowell, *Irish Historical Documents 1172–1922* (London 1943), p. 17.
4   See Frank Mitchell, *The Irish Landscape* (London 1976), pp. 183–4.
5   Frank Mitchell, *The Irish Landscape*, p. 188.

Chapter 5   The English conquest

1   Art Cosgrove, *Late Medieval Ireland, 1350–1541* (Helicon History of Ireland) (Dublin 1981), p. 94.
2   See Brian Ó Cuiv, 'The Irish language in the early modern period', in T. W. Moody, F. X. Martin and F. J. Byrne (eds.), *A New History of Ireland*, vol. 3 (Oxford 1976), p. 510.
3   See D. B. Quinn, *The Elizabethans and the Irish* (Ithaca, NY 1966), pp. 35–6; Huntington Library, Ellesmere MSS, EL 1701 (September 1573).
4   See D. B. Quinn, *The Elizabethans and the Irish*, pp. 138; Fynes Morison, *An Itinerary* (London 1617); see also *Calendar of State Papers relating to Ireland, of the reign of Elizabeth, 1 November 1600–31 July 1601*, ed. E. G. Atkinson (London 1905), pp. 251–5: 'My Lord Mountjoy's discourse concerning Ireland, sent in March 1601'.
5   *Calendar of State Papers relating to Ireland*, 1600–1, p. 305; Lord Deputy Mountjoy to Privy Council, 1 May, 1601, Dublin Castle.

Chapter 6   The protestant settlement

1   J. J. Silke, 'Primate Lombard and James I', *Irish Theological Quarterly*, **22** (1955), pp. 131–3; quoted in A. Clarke, 'Plantation and the catholic question, 1603–23', in Moody, Martin and Byrne (eds.), *A New History of Ireland*, vol. 3, p. 217.
2   A. Clarke, 'The government of Wentworth, 1632–40', in Moody, Martin and Byrne (eds.), *A New History of Ireland*, vol. 3, p. 268.
3   P. J. Corish, 'The Cromwellian conquest, 1649–53', *New History of Ireland*, **3**, p. 345; quotes S. R. Gardiner, *Oliver Cromwell* (London 1901), p. 179.
4   P. J. Corish, 'The Cromwellian conquest, 1649–53', *New History of Ireland*, **3**, p. 342; quotes Abbott (ed.), Cromwell, *Writings* vol. 2, p. 146.
5   Translation by Thomas Kinsella. Séan Ó Tuama and Thomas Kinsella, *An Duanaire 1600–1900: Poems of the Dispossessed* (Mountrath 1981), p. 105.
6   P. J. Corish, *The Catholic Community in the Seventeenth and Eighteenth Centuries* (Helicon History of Ireland) (Dublin 1981), p. 49.

7   F. G. James, *Ireland in the Empire 1688–1770* (Cambridge, Mass. 1973), p. 22.

Chapter 7   Ireland in the British Empire

1   Herbert F. Hoie, 'Irish Bardism in 1561', *Ulster Journal of Archaeology*, **6**, (1858), pp. 165 and 202.
2   Translation by Thomas Kinsella. Séan Ó Tuama and Thomas Kinsella, *An Duanaire 1600–1900*, p. 112.
3   Translation by Thomas Kinsella, *An Duanaire 1600–1900*, p. 164.
4   *Memoirs of the Marquis of Clanricarde* (1722). See D. Greene and F. Kelly (eds.), *Irish Bardic Poetry: texts and translations, together with an introductory lecture by Osborn Bergin* (Dublin 1970), pp. 5–8.
5   L. M. Cullen, 'The Hidden Ireland: Re-Assessment', *Studia Hibernica*, **9**, (1969), pp. 7–47.
6   Edmund Burke, in *The Reformer*, no. 7 (Thursday, 10 March 1748). See A. P. I. Samuels, *The Early Life Correspondence and Writings of the Rt. Hon. Edmund Burke LL.D.* (Cambridge 1923).
7   J. S. Reid, *History of the Presbyterian Church in Ireland*, vol. 3 (Belfast 1867), p. 97, quoting Blair's *Life* (Edinburgh 1754), p. 51.
8   J. S. Reid, *History of the Presbyterian Church in Ireland*, vol. 3 (Belfast 1867), p. 294 n. 22, quoting Stuart's *Armagh*, pp. 488–9.
9   G. L. Lee, *The Huguenot Settlements in Ireland* (London 1936), p. 17; quotes Proclamation cited in T. Gimlette, *The Huguenot Settlers in Ireland* (Waterford 1888).
10   Mrs M. J. O'Connell, *The Last Colonel of the Irish Brigade: Count O'Connell and the old Irish life at home and abroad 1745–1833 (London 1892), p. 207.*
11   *Quoted by Richard Twiss, A Tour in Ireland in 1775* (London 1776), p. 151.
12   Sylvester O'Halloran, *An Introduction to the Study of the History and Antiquities of Ireland* (Dublin 1772), p. i.
13   L. de Paor, 'The rebel mind: republican and loyalist', in R. Kearney (ed.), *The Irish Mind* (Dublin 1985), pp. 162–3.
14   *The Collected Poems of W. B. Yeats* (London 1952), pp. 147.
15   Arthur Young, *A Tour of Ireland*, vol. 1 (Dublin 1780), p. 405.
16   Arthur Young, *Tour of Ireland*, p. 406.
17   William Shaw Mason, *A Statistical Account or Parochial Survey of Ireland drawn up from the communications of the clergy*, vol. 1 (Dublin 1814), 484–5.
18   C. E. Carrington, *The British Overseas* (London 1950), p. 68.
19   J. H. Plumb, *England in the Eighteenth Century* (Pelican History of England, 7) (Harmondsworth 1980, p. 82.
20   See G. Sigerson, *The Last Independent Parliament of Ireland* (Dublin 1918), p. 2.

21   See W. W. Seward, *Collectanea Politica; or the Political Transactions of Ireland*, vol. 1 (Dublin 1801), pp. 294–6.

22   R. Koebner, *Empire* (New York 1965), p. 253, Harlow and Madder, *British Colonial Development*, pp. 179–82.

23   R. Koebner, *Empire*, p. 256; Harlow and Madder, *British Colonial Developments*, p. 178.

24   *Parliamentary History*, **25**, p. 587.

Chapter 8   The United Kingdom

1   Jonah Barrington, *Personal Sketches of his own Times*, 3 vols. (London 1827–32).

2   See George O'Brien, *The Economic History of Ireland in the Eighteenth Century* (Dublin and London 1918), p. 86; Sir James Caldwell, *Proposal for employing . . . children* (Dublin 1771); see also A. Young, *Tour in Ireland*, vol. 2, p. 37.

3   Edward Ledwich, *A Statistical Account of the Parish of Aghaboe in the Queen's County, Ireland* (Dublin 1796), pp. 61–3.

4   P. W. Wilson, *William Pitt the Younger* (Gardan City, NY 1930), p. 286.

5   Henry Inglis, *A Journey throughout Ireland during the Spring, Summer and Autumn of 1834*, vol. 1 (London 1834), pp. 10–11.

6   Maurice R. O'Connell (ed.), *The Correspondence of Daniel O'Connell*, vol. 1, 1792–1814 (Dublin 1973), p. 370.

7   See W. E. Vaughan and A. J. Fitzpatrick (eds.), *Irish Historical Statistics: Population 1821–1971* (Dublin 1978).

8   Lord George Hill, *Facts from Gweedore* (London 1887) (facsimile edition, Belfast 1971), pp. 16–17. The facts given in Paddy M'Kye's memorandum were challenged at a public inquiry in 1858 by witnesses from Gweedore who denied that the poverty was as great as he outlined; but, as the witnesses were members of the families concerned, the testimony must be taken with some reserve. See Sean 'ac Fhionnlaoich, *Scéal Ghaoth Dobhair* (Dublin 1983), pp. 54–82.

9   Hubert Butler, 'The Country House – the Life of the Gentry', in R. B. McDowell (ed.), *Social Life in Ireland 1800–45* (Cork 1957), pp. 36–7. Reprinted in H. Butler, *Escape from the Anthill* (Mullingar 1985) as 'The Country House after the Union',

10   Thomas Moore, *Irish Melodies by Thomas Moore illustrated with engravings from drawings by eminent artists* (London 1856), pp. 25–6.

11   A. Griffith (ed.), *Thomas Davis: the thinker and teacher: the essence of his writings in prose and poetry* (Dublin 1914), p. 60.

12   Griffith, *Thomas Davis*, p. 54.

13   W. Bennett, *Narrative of a recent journey of six weeks in Ireland, in connexion with the subject of supplying small seed to some of the remoter districts* (London and Dublin 1847).

Chapter 9   Revolution

1   Tomás de Bhaldraithe (ed.), *Cín Lae Amhlaoibh* (Dundalk 1970), p. 25. My translation.

2   See S. Ua Casaide, 'An Fíor-Éirionach, a Scarce Tipperary Journal', *Journal of the Waterford and South-East of Ireland Archaeological Society*, **15**, (1912), pp. 107–11.

3   W. M. O'Hanlon, *Walks among the Poor of Belfast* (Belfast and Dublin 1853) (facsimile reprint, Wakefield 1971), pp. 33–4.

4   R. V. Comerford, *The Fenians in context; Irish politics and society 1848–82* (Dublin 1985), p. 114.

5   See A. T. Q. Stewart, *The Ulster Crisis* (London 1967), p. 22.

6   *Collected Works of Pádraic H. Pearse: Political Writings and Speeches* (Dublin, Cork and Belfast 1924), p. 94.

7   Richard Fallis, *The Irish Renaissance: an introduction to Anglo-Irish literature* (Dublin 1978).

8   W. B. Yeats, *Irish Fairy and Folk Tales*, preface.

9   W. B. Yeats, 'Cathleen Ni Houlihan', *The Collected Plays of W. B. Yeats* (new edn.) (New York 1967), p. 57.

10 W. B. Yeats, 'The Man and the Echo', *The Collected Poems of W. B. Yeats* (London 1952), p. 393.

11 R. MacNeill, *Ulster's Stand for Union* (Edinburgh 1922), p. 51.

12 A. T. Q. Stewart, *The Ulster Crisis*, p. 62.

13 *Scríbhinní Phádraig Mhic Phiarais* (Dublin and London 1919), pp. 266–7. My translation.

14 P. H. Pearse, in *Irish Freedom*, (November 1913): *Collected Works of Pádraic H. Pearse: Political Writings and Speeches* (Dublin, Cork and Belfast 1924), p. 185.

15 D. Macardle, *The Irish Republic* (4th edn.) (Dublin 1951), pp. 166–7.

16 James Stephens, *The Insurrection in Dublin* (Dublin and London 1916), pp. 73–5.

17 G. B. Shaw, in the *New Statesman* (6 May 1916).

18 W. B. Yeats, 'Easter 1916), *Collected Poems*, p. 203.

19 Hansard, *The Parliamentary Debates: Official Report*, fifth series, **149**: *Fourth Session of the 31st Parliament of the United Kingdom of Great Britain and Ireland*, 12 George V (special session of 14 December 1921, on Articles of Agreement).

20 loc. cit.

Chapter 10   Among the nations of the earth

1   Bunreacht na hÉireann (Constitution of Ireland): D'achtaigh an Pobal an 1 Iúill, 1937 (Enacted by the People 1st July, 1937) (Dublin 1937).

2   Maurice Moynihan (ed.), *Speeches and Statements by Éamon de Valéra 1917–73* (Dublin 1980), p. 466.

Suggestions for Further Reading

A comprehensive and detailed multi-volume survey has, at the time of writing, been appearing for some years, under the editorship of the late T. W. Moody, F. X. Martin and F. J. Byrne. This is *A New History of Ireland*, published by the Oxford University Press for the Royal Irish Academy. Two of the main volumes and some of the auxiliary and special volumes have so far been published. The reader who requires detailed information, including bibliographical information, is referred to the *New History*.

There are several good one-volume short histories. These include J. C. Beckett, *A Short History of Ireland*; Conor and Maire Cruise O'Brien, *A Concise History of Ireland*; R. D. Edwards, *A New History of Ireland*; and Robert Kee, *Ireland: a History*.

There are two excellent series of short books covering periods and aspects of Irish history. These are the Gill History of Ireland, edited by James Lydon and Margaret MacCurtain (eleven volumes) and the Helicon History of Ireland, edited by Art Cosgrove and Elma Collins (volumes still appearing: a total of ten is planned).

Several surveys with a somewhat different emphasis may be referred to. These include E. Estyn Evans, *The Personality of Ireland*; Frank Mitchell, *The Irish Landscape* and L. de Paor, *A Portrait of Ireland*.

M. Herity and G. Eogan, *Ireland in Prehistory* covers the prehistoric period. For pre-Norman Ireland, besides volumes in the series mentioned above, there are several surveys of aspects of the period available, including M. and L. de Paor, *Early Christian Ireland*; F. J. Byrne, *Irish Kings and High-Kings*; Kathleen Hughes, *The Church in Early Irish Society*; and L. Bieler, *Ireland, Harbinger of the Middle Ages*.

G. H. Orpen, *Ireland under the Normans* (4 vols.) and E. Curtis, *A History of Medieval Ireland*, are older works of wide scope covering the later Middle Ages.

There are many works on modern Irish history. J. C. Beckett, *The Making of Modern Ireland 1603–1923* is a standard text. F. S. L. Lyons, *Ireland Since the Famine*, covers a narrower period in considerable detail. Robert Kee, *The Green Flag*, is a detailed history of Irish nationalism.

The special problem of Ulster is covered in a number of works including some volumes in the series mentioned above. Among them are A. T. Q. Stewart, *The Narrow Ground*; Conor Cruise O'Brien, *States of Ireland*; Michael Farrell,

Northern Ireland: the Orange State, and David Miller, *The Queen's Rebels.*

Facts about Ireland, published by the Department of Foreign Affairs in Dublin provides a useful introduction to the country.

Finally, there is a one-volume outline, based on a series of television lectures by different scholars, which has found a wide readership. This is T. W. Moody, and F. X. Martin (eds.), *The Course of Irish History.*

Index